FINDING HARMONY

A family's journey across Europe and beyond

GEORGE NEWMAN

GEORGE NEWMAN
LONDON

Published by George Newman

London

Copyright © George Newman 2013

The moral right of the author has been asserted

First Published in Great Britain 2013

Typeset by Joanna Chichester-Clark & Priory Graphics

Cover design by Priory Graphics

Printed in Great Britain by Peppermint Press

ISBN 978-0-9926491-0-4

to Patricia

CONTENTS

ACKNOWLEDGEMENTS

I wish to express my warm thanks to the following for their contribution to this work:

My daughter Joanna, who has typed up the manuscript, helped to select the illustrations, designed the maps and family trees and given immense editorial support. My wife Patricia who has listened patiently whilst I have read drafts to her and who has provided invaluable suggestions. My son-in-law Mark Chichester-Clark, who took the colour photographs. My cousin Gerald Braunthal for his thorough research into the Braunthal family tree, including his visit to Brody. The Viennese court records office which responded with useful answers to my enquiries. Mr Schaner for kindly showing me the Jewish cemetery in Trencin, and inviting me to his home, the former family Neumann house.

And I am grateful to my Aunt Lena, for her long-sighted act in collecting together so many irreplaceable family documents and photographs when she was forced to emigrate from Vienna in 1938, and for bringing these papers safely to London. During and after the Second World War, this unique collection was preserved and added to, above all by Lena, but also by other members of the family. Without these actions, this book would not have been possible.

George Newman, London 2013

PREFACE

My father started writing this book when in his eighties, working amidst his archive in his crowded study, overlooking a wild Wimbledon garden. For years, our local postman in Derbyshire has delivered envelopes containing the latest manuscript pages, which I have typed up in instalments. In this way the work has taken shape, set out not chronologically but thematically. The subject matter has broadened out from my father's personal experience of the Anschluss to a sweeping history on both sides of his family, peppered with an extraordinary cast of characters.

The gradual genesis of the book has meant that the narrative shocks have been as great for me as they will surely be for the reader. Figures are introduced against a backdrop of haute bourgeois life in the 19th and early 20th centuries, a world of Strauss and Sachertorte. "Imagine the Neumann girls before the First World War! In 1912 Lena and Trude were 22, Mizzi was 17 and Hedy was 15. They were beautiful, vivacious, musical, romantic, intelligent". As the chapters steadily took shape on my computer screen, I felt I was getting to know these young women, their surprisingly modern education, their theatre and opera outings, their fashionably plump appearance and corseted dresses. Yet by middle age, Mizzi would be sleeping not in a Biedermeier bed in a comfortable Vienna apartment but on the verminous floor of a hut on a collective farm in Kazakhstan. Her only son would be killed on the Russian front.

This is not just the account of one family. The events described by my father illuminate some of the most colourful – and indeed darkest – episodes in European history, from the 19th century right up to the 1940s and beyond. Intriguingly, at times our forebears were not bystanders of history but played a role in shaping inter-war Socialist politics.

Whilst other Jewish family memoirs may cover the same period, this work offers something unique: it draws upon an astonishing preserved archive of hundreds of letters and documents dating back to the 1800s. Cultural diaries from before the First World War; clandestine poems on scraps of tissue paper smuggled from a Viennese prison cell; an account of life at a Russian labour camp received in London in 1941, postcards from the Italian front...

Many items are written in 'Kurrent' or 'Schrift', an old form of German handwriting based on late medieval cursive writing. Others are composed in a pre-war German short-hand, long since extinct. Manuscript documents in English appear indecipherable. As for the content, it is arcane, with individuals referred to by a multitude of nicknames, and a peppering of family jokes and allusions.

Yet, like some party trick, my father Hansi can read it all fluently. Having spent months creating an archive of labelled storage envelopes, with a flourish he extracts a war-time postcard written to fool the censors, or an unmarried girl's shorthand diary, and reads it aloud without hesitation. Who would have thought that a pre-war Austrian education would prove so useful? It goes without saying that the special skills needed to read these documents are being lost. As he is one of the few remaining people who can still make sense of this archive, it is all the more significant that Hansi has sorted, translated and interpreted the material, and turned it into a narrative.

How these papers came to be gathered together at my father's house in London is a story in itself. When my grandfather Paul Neumann's sister Lena left Vienna in the autumn of 1938, she chose to bring with her chests of family documents. I try to imagine Lena in the family's bare apartment, selecting and packing up countless documents as outside the Nazis patrolled the streets of Vienna, and again later in London making carbon copies of outgoing correspondence. All these papers were later passed to my father, who kept them carefully for years until they again saw the light of day, when he worked through them for this book.

But more interesting than how, is why. Running through the generations, I see a moral imperative to preserve the family history, against a backdrop of wars and forced migrations. Most poignant for me are those official documents from across the Austro-Hungarian Empire dating back two or three generations, bestowing family members with professional recognition, legal status or honours, complete with official Habsburg crests and Latin inscriptions. All respectfully preserved and brought to England. All worthless in Vienna in 1938.

This book by my father is the latest manifestation of this same moral imperative to tell a story for the next generation, to bear witness to past events. In doing so he vindicates the actions by his forebears who preserved the family history so well. And he recounts his own memories of a changed world.

As I write this preface I can hear the happy squeals of two of the next generation: my son Sam and daughter Grace. The other four grandchildren will also one day appreciate this book: my sister Helena's son Max and daughter Isabella and my brother Paul's two sons Strabo and Peri.

On a highly personal level, music runs as a theme through this book, just as it has through Hansi's life. From time to time there have been interruptions to work on the book, as he has laid down his pen in favour of the viola: practising for chamber music evenings with family and friends. My pianist mother Patricia, whom he met appropriately at a concert over fifty years ago, still accompanies his repertoire of viola pieces every day.

Indeed my father's love of music, both as a player and enthusiastic opera-goer, sings through these pages. For the reader, music seems to symbolise a joyous life force, a force that triumphs over the darker events described. What a true reflection of my father.

Joanna Chichester-Clark

Braunthal Family Tree

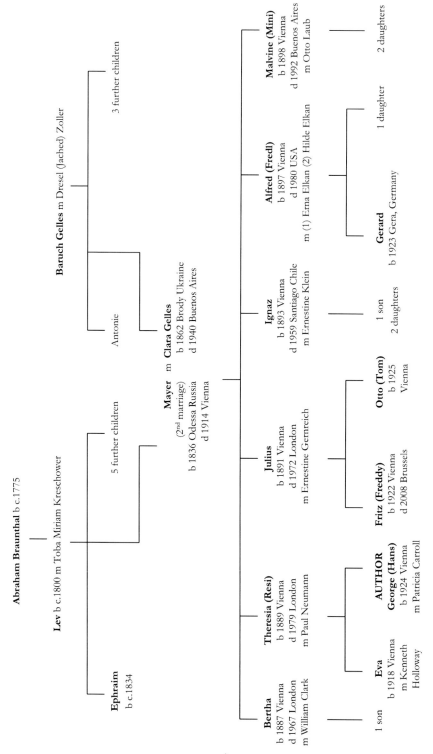

Abraham Braunthal b c.1775

Lev b c.1800 m Toba Miriam Kreschower

Ephraim
b c.1834

5 further children

Baruch Gelles m Dresel (Jached) Zoller

Antonie

3 further children

Mayer m Clara Gelles
(2nd marriage)   b 1862 Brody Ukraine
b 1836 Odessa Russia   d 1940 Buenos Aires
d 1914 Vienna

Bertha
b 1887 Vienna
d 1967 London
m William Clark

Theresia (Resi)
b 1889 Vienna
d 1979 London
m Paul Neumann

Julius
b 1891 Vienna
d 1972 London
m Ernestine Gernreich

Ignaz
b 1893 Vienna
d 1959 Santiago Chile
m Ernestine Klein

Alfred (Fredl)
b 1897 Vienna
d 1980 USA
m (1) Erna Elkan (2) Hilde Elkan

Malvine (Mini)
b 1898 Vienna
d 1992 Buenos Aires
m Otto Laub

1 son

Eva
b 1918 Vienna
m Kenneth
Holloway

AUTHOR
George (Hans)
b 1924 Vienna
m Patricia Carroll

Fritz (Freddy)
b 1922 Vienna
d 2008 Brussels

Otto (Tom)
b 1925
Vienna

1 son
2 daughters

Gerard
b 1923 Gera, Germany

1 daughter

2 daughters

NEUMANN FAMILY TREE

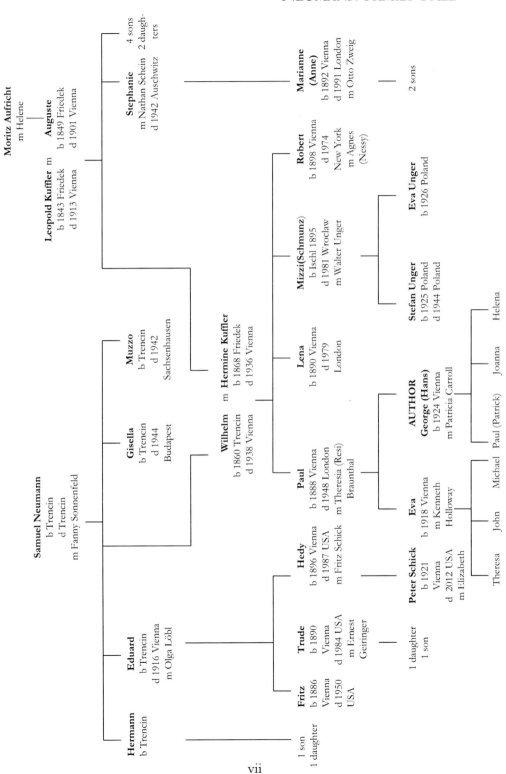

CHAPTER 1

A journey from Brody to Vienna

It now seems so unlikely, but in 1928 I was four years old and lived in Vienna. I was called Hans Neumann. We had just moved to a modern block of flats, built a few years prior to the First World War. It had a marble staircase and stained glass. We lived on the second floor in very large accommodation. Our flat had a northerly aspect, but the view looked over a slope of allotments towards the Vienna Woods. Beethoven and Schubert had walked within a few miles. Gersthof was the name of the suburb, and we lived at Gersthoferstrasse 105, in the 18th District. It was a more elegant and suitable address than the smaller and darker flat nearer to the city centre in Währing at Semperstrasse 58, where we lived till then.

In those days, there were few private cars in Vienna. I remember travelling by car to my new home. I have faint memories of events when we were still living in the Semperstrasse - my grandfather, Wilhelm Neumann, coming through the door with outstretched arms, and my mother saying, "Hier ist der Grossvater" (here is your grandfather). For me, he was an awe-inspiring figure, and remained so until his death in 1938.

The new flat had splendid intercommunicating double doors with horizontal brass handles, aristocratic high ceilings and traditional parquet floors. The rooms were heated with beautiful tile stoves, free standing and reaching to the ceiling in their glory. In this setting my home had a lasting influence. Vestiges of 18th and 19th century Vienna were there with their evocative reminders of Rococo grandeur and Biedermeier solidity.

On the 18th January 1928, for my fourth birthday, our family doctor,

Ernst Sternfeld, gave me an American Indian outfit, feathered headgear, axe, shield, spear. He was an old friend of my parents and had officiated at my birth; hence he remembered my birthdays. I admired these objects from the mysterious outside world. In the pre-television age, cowboys and Indians had not yet invaded the drawing rooms.

Dr. Sternfeld emigrated to British North Borneo (Sarawak) after the Anschluss. It was possible, in 1938, to get a visa to Shanghai or to Borneo, especially if you were a doctor. When the Japanese arrrived in 1943, they interned all Europeans. No distinction was made between Jews and non-Jews. He was the doctor in the camp. After the war he returned to Austria and visited us in London. He explained that he had to see someone who had been with him in Sandakan. "Was he a close friend?" I asked. "Yes" he said, "he let me share his mosquito net for three years".

Ernst Sternfeld was a real family doctor. He was the doctor to my mother Theresia (Resi), to my father Paul, his brother Robert, and his sisters Helene (Lena) and Mizzi. And of course, he was also the doctor to my sister Eva and my doctor.

Mizzi fell madly in love with him, but he was not interested. In 1913, the nature of homosexuality had to be explained to her. Years later, after the Second World War, when I visited her in Poland she told me what a terrible shock that revelation had been to her.

I see my life as a series of kaleidoscopic episodes, as a mosaic of the past. I prefer the caprice of selection to the strait-jacket of chronology. Sometimes I hear the actual German words which were used so long ago. I remember the vocal timbre of my father's beautiful voice. His speech was song, full of resonance with a wonderful range of colour, bass-baritone in quality. His consonants could be soft or crisp, but never harsh, his vowels were sometimes elongated and inflected with melody. His diphthongs had depth. His short sounds were never clipped. It was High-German with a Viennese accent, far removed from the archetypal caricature of Prussian Berlin.

As a district judge and, later, as a lawyer in criminal and commercial cases, he was used to speaking in public. There was something intensely theatrical about his rhetoric and his timing was perfect. He was a great *raconteur*, recalling personalities of his father's generation and the great opera singers and actors he himself had heard before the First World War. His repertoire of jokes seemed endless, all told, of course, in German. But they had the appropriate ethnic accents of the Habsburg Empire: Bohemian, Hungarian, and above all, Jewish. His face was flexible and he could shade his features with vicarious melancholy or illuminate them with a flourish of humour. I have his voice, and my son Paul has mine. As I think of my father I hear him. And I hear my son. Nature has been kind to provide a transcendental genetic double echo.

The only time I remember visiting Dr. Sternfeld's surgery was in 1930. It was situated in the Schwarzspanierstrasse, a fashionable part of the city. Later, I often passed the house as I travelled to town on the E2 tram, and was reminded of him. I see the waiting room on that day, with its delicate black and white pictures on the wall, and hear my mother telling me that they were papercuts. Suddenly the door opened and Dr. Glasberg, Dr. Sternfeld's partner walked through. He greeted us warmly. Shortly afterwards, I heard my father tell my mother that Glasberg had killed himself. Suicide had not yet entered the realm of my consciousness. Many years later, I found out that Dr. Glasberg had performed an abortion, that it had gone wrong, and that the woman had died. The double death became the tragic sensation of Vienna.

After that visit it was discovered that I had a spot on the lung, mild tuberculosis. It was customary in those days to send patients to recuperate at high altitudes. Arosa, in Switzerland, 1800 meters high, was chosen for me. The clear mountain air was considered to be very beneficial. I lived there, on and off, for two years, and did not attend a formal school. It was not until I returned to Vienna in 1932 that I started going to a primary school in the Scheibenbergstrasse.

In 1930 there occurred another memorable family event. On the

6th September my grandfather Wilhelm Neumann celebrated his 70th birthday. Family and friends gathered in Velden on the Wörthersee. The owner of the hotel Bundschuh, a certain Neustadtl, was a great friend of the Neumanns. He put on a celebratory lunch for many guests and set up a large horseshoe-shaped table. I was waiting with my nanny in the salon dining room, which was completely empty. Suddenly the doors opened and the guests marched in, my grandfather leading the procession. I remember my father delivering a congratulatory oration, ending with "Hoch soll er leben, drei mal hoch!", roughly translated as "three cheers".

Wilhelm Neumann was a well-known journalist. Until 1918 he wrote for the *Fremden-Blatt*, the semi-official Imperial Court newspaper, and a mouthpiece of the government. After the fall of the monarchy, he continued to provide articles for a variety of Viennese papers. He died mercifully in his bed on 2nd April 1938, a few weeks after the Anschluss. How often I have been thankful that antibiotics did not yet exist to defeat his pneumonia. Had lived about four years longer and if he had not been able to leave Vienna, he would have perished under terrible circumstances.

Who was he, where did he come from, what did he do? The greatness of his personality makes the task of answering these questions difficult, even disrespectful. But I see him now, ordering me to write about him, to speak for him. He wants to be remembered, he and his wife, Hermine Kuffler.

Wilhelm Neumann was born in Trencin. Today this is in Slovakia, but on the 6th September 1860 it was in Hungary and part of the Austro-Hungarian empire. His birth certificate is in German. A copy of the entry from the original register was made by the Trencin Rabbinate on the 18th April 1884, with a subsequent endorsement in Hungarian in 1895, authenticated by a government ministry stamp.

A historical explanation seems now appropriate. The disastrous war with Prussia in 1866 culminated in the defeat of the Austrian army at Königsgrätz and the loss of Venice and Silesia. Austria was shut out of

Italy and Germany. The government in Vienna was weakened and the various nationalities of the empire increased their demands for regional self-government. Concessions had to be made. The dual monarchy was instituted. Henceforth the Hungarian language was to be used to a greater degree in the legal, political and administrative process. The constitutional change-over from the monolithic structure of Austrian hegemony to a greater degree of power-sharing was symbolised by the new abbreviation for the title of the monarch, and for matters relating to the monarchy. Henceforth the sovereign was no longer Kaiser von Österreich, König von Ungarn etc, etc, but Kaiser von Österreich UND König von Ungarn etc, etc. The modest word "and" emphasized in a very neat Viennese manner the separatism of the Hungarian crown lands. Thus K.K. (Kaiserlich, Königlich) was changed: K.u.K. (Kaiserlich *und* Königlich) became the official appellation.

In 1973 I visited the Neumann house in Trencin, near the medieval city gates. The long low terraced building reminded me of the old houses in Grinzing, outside Vienna. It was a typical example of 17th or 18th century Austrian domestic architecture, immortalised by its association with Haydn, Mozart, Beethoven and Schubert.

The then owner, Mr. Schaner, gave me a copy of the Trencin land registry, and told me that my great-grandparents had occupied the first floor, where we were sitting. Samuel Neumann and his wife Franciska (Fanny), née Sonnenfeld, and their five children had lived there more than a century ago. The house was sold as part of Samuel's estate on the 17th October 1892.

Mr. Schaner then took me to the old Jewish cemetery. The weathered headstones were mostly illegible, and in any case I would not have been able to read the Hebrew inscriptions or identify the single letters that take the place of Arabic numerals. The names and dates were unrecognisable, but I had an overwhelming feeling of territorial imperative when I stood on the earth that covered them.

In the Baedeker guide book of Austria, including Hungary, Transylvania, Dalmatia and Bosnia, published in 1896, Wilhelm's birthplace is described as follows:

"Trencin, Hung. pop. 5200, capital of the county of that name, on the left bank of the Waag, is commanded by the ruins of an old fortress. The castle-well, 473 feet deep, was hewn in the rock by Turkish prisoners. The tower, 108 ft. in height, commands a beautiful view. Interesting Piarist Church. The Gothic Parish Church of the 14th century (altered in 1528), to which a covered flight of 122 steps ascends, contains a fine monument of a Count Illésházy (died 1648; an alabaster statue in a niche of black marble). Opposite the town, on the right bank of the Waag, is a ruined church and further on is the semi-ruined monastery of Skalka."

The Turkish invasions, culminating in the abortive sieges of Vienna in 1529 and 1683, left their mark in Trencin as in so many other places in Hungary and the Balkans. Samuel Neumann, born around 1829, was well aware of the cataclysmic impact of the wars, which finally ended only about a century and a quarter before he was born.

Trencin in the 19th century was truly trilingual. Slovak was spoken by the indigenous population of shop-keepers and artisans and of course by the peasants of the surrounding countryside. The middle classes and the aristocracy were mainly Hungarian. German maintained its presence, supported by the cultural strength of its literature. In any case Vienna was the great social, economic and artistic magnet and for that you had to speak German. In the Neumann household, German was spoken and it was Wilhelm's mother-tongue. He could also speak fluent Hungarian and Slovak.

In Trencin, Wilhelm's school would have been Hungarian, and German was taught as a matter of course. Wilhelm must have quickly acquired a thorough knowledge of the great German writers, dramatists, poets and philosophers.

Wilhelm had a natural gift for telling a good story, a *raconteur*, someone interested in the cultural, social and political events of the day, and especially in the personalities that activated them. It was natural for him to become a journalist.

When we moved to the Gersthoferstrasse in December 1927, I stayed with my maternal grandmother, Clara Braunthal for a few days, so as to be out of the way. At that time, Clara lived in the suburb of Heiligenstadt, a name forever associated with Beethoven's Heiligenstadt Testament, which he wrote there on the 6th October 1802. At the serious onset of his deafness, his physician, a certain Dr. Schmidt, advised him to move to the quiet village, as it then was, of Heiligenstadt, away from the noise and bustle of Vienna. The hearing did not improve and at the end of the summer of 1802, Beethoven was in deepest despair. The Testament is addressed to his brothers, but is really a shout of desperation, a plea for sympathy and understanding meant for the whole world. The greatest composer suffered the worst affliction. The collapse of his hearing was the cruel selection of fate. Ever-growing silence invaded him, but he triumphed: the great creator, sovereign, writing his masterpieces which he was destined not to hear.

Beethoven died in 1827. A mere hundred years later I stayed with my grandmother in Heiligenstadt; the district had remained largely unaltered. Many of the old 17th and 18th century houses were still there but change was on the way. Opposite her flat, Boschstrasse 2, the Socialist municipality of Vienna had built the first of their large subsidised housing complexes, the Karl Marx Hof, consisting of hundreds of flats with low rentals that workers could afford. These so-called "Gemeindehäuser" soon became famous as icons and flagships of the special brand of Austrian radical Social Democracy known as "Austro-Marxismus".

My grandmother, looking out of her window in 1927, could not have foreseen that seven years later, in 1934, the Karl Marx Hof would suffer heavy artillery shelling and that a civil war would end in the defeat of "Red Vienna" and its messianic dream.

Her oldest son, Julius, was imprisoned on the very first day of that conflict and was not released until January 1935, eleven months later.

I have vivid memories of my maternal grandmother. She had a close relationship with my mother and frequently came to visit us in the Gersthoferstrasse. On several occasions she joined us on our holidays in the Austrian mountains and lakes.

I loved her very much. She was kind and warmhearted and always interested in exactly what I was doing. Soon after I started the violin in September 1932, she, of course, had to hear all my pieces, and naturally praised them. She was my ready-made audience from the outside world. Soon I found out that she did not know too much about music, but it did not seem to matter. After I had played, she always said: "und jetzt geh, und üb' weiter" (and now go and practise some more). She wanted her six children and her twelve grandchildren to do well. She shared their successes and was distressed when they faced difficulties. Their lives should be better than her own.

On the 16th July 1932 Clara was seventy. She was staying in Weyregg on the Ossiacher See, less than ten miles from Velden where Wilhelm spent his 70th birthday two years earlier. Both festive days were in the summer when the lakes and mountains offered an attractive alternative to the heat of Vienna. I remember Clara embracing me. I remember standing in the lake, trying to teach my young cousin Jagna to swim. It was a unique occasion with all twelve grandchildren in one place. But the summer of 1932 had a valedictory poignancy. The rise of Nazism cast an ominous shadow over Austria. The South American branch of the family returned to Buenos Aires and Santiago. The others emigrated to New York, London, and to Brussels, followed by London. By 1935, my mother was the last of Clara's six children left in Vienna.

Immediately after the Anschluss, the German annexation of Austria in March 1938, the caretaker of the block of flats where Clara lived wanted her out because he wanted her flat. He was on the ground floor in rather small and dark accommodation, and she lived on the first floor. The compulsory eviction of Jews and their removal to the ghetto of the Leopoldstadt did not start until 1939. However the eagerness of the Nazi caretaker, who did not want an old Jewish lady living above him, made her emigrate in good time. Rather than move round the corner to a new home she would travel all the way to Buenos Aires to be with her daughter Mini and her family, she declared with characteristic determination. She shut the door of Boschstrasse 2 for the last time in July 1938, after more than 30 years' residence. She gave away the contents of her flat but took with her a symbolic memento of the past: the brass nameplate on the front door: *Braunthal*. After travelling half-way across the world and back, it has now come to rest in London, in our *vitrine*.

My grandmother had never been outside Austria. She took the train to Genoa and boarded an Italian transatlantic liner which stopped at Rio de Janeiro and Montevideo, eventually arriving at Buenos Aires on the 6th August 1938. She told Mini that the journey was a voyage through paradise. Stewards kept the cabins clean and tidy, waiters in uniforms served at table, the bands played, people danced. For years Clara had faced financial difficulties and had lived a simple life.

This life started in Brody in 1862, which at that time was in Galicia, part of the Austro-Hungarian empire, very near to the frontier with Tsarist Russia. Today it is in the Ukraine. My mother occasionally spoke about her maternal grandmother. Clara's mother was Dresel (Jached) Gelles, née Zoller. She was apparently very religious, certainly orthodox. Her head was covered at all times, in the house as well as outside, and when she cut her fingernails she burnt the shavings rather than throw them away. She and her husband, Baruch Gelles, had five children, of whom Clara was the second oldest. The oldest, Antonie, eventually became Mini's mother-in-law when Mini married her first cousin, Otto Laub, one of Antonie's sons. There is thus a double link with our South American relatives.

In Chamber's Encyclopedia (1908 edition), Brody has the following entry: "Brody, a town in Galicia, is situated on a swampy plain, surrounded by forests, 89 miles ENE of Lemberg by rail. Leather and flax manufactures, breweries, refineries and fur dressing are carried on. The trade, which has fallen off lately, is almost entirely in the hands of the Jews, who form three-fourths of the inhabitants so that Brody has been called the 'German Jerusalem'. Pop. 17,534."

Brody has an important part to play in my family history. Not only was Clara born there, but Mayer Braunthal, her future husband, my grandfather, arrived there from Odessa in late 1840 or early 1841. My mother told me with a certain amount of wonderment how her father Mayer described his journey from Odessa to Brody as a young boy. He travelled as he put it "auf der Axe", literally "on the axle" of a horse-drawn wagon. In 1840 the journey must have taken several weeks.

In Galicia and the Bukovina there were many small towns with a large, even predominant, Jewish population, the so-called 'Shtettls'. But Brody, so near to the Russian frontier, had the special function of a trade emporium that dealt with Russia, Poland and Turkey. It suffered the typical fate of a border town. It was founded in Russia in 1584 and was granted a charter in 1684 at the time of Tsar Peter the Great. Russian invasions of what had become the kingdom of Poland and the various partitions of Poland were finally followed by Austrian rule in 1772. The advent of the railway age put an end to the horse-drawn wagons from far-away places which had been such a familiar sight in the streets of Brody. The city was bypassed and went into decline, and Mayer and his first family (not yet married to my grandmother Clara, his second wife) arrived in Vienna between 1869 and 1871.

Mayer Braunthal was born in Odessa, in Russia, on the 20th April 1836. He was the second of four children. His parents were Lev Braunthal and Toba Miriam Kreschower. On reflection, genealogy can be transformed by the romance of history. Mayer's older brother Ephraim was probably born two years earlier, in 1834. But even if there had only been a year between the brothers and Lev had only been twenty years old at the birth of his first child, he would have been alive in 1815, the year in which Napoleon was defeated at Waterloo. A great-grandfather far-away in the East and the French Emperor outside Brussels on that fateful day.

The family name Braunthal is extremely rare. In Brody in the 18th and 19th century, it is a reasonable assumption that Braunthals were related. The father of Lev Braunthal was probably an Abraham Braunthal, born about 1775. This Abraham Braunthal had a younger brother Ephraim. In the Brody land tax records of 1844, Ephraim is entered as the owner of building No. 1369. Thirty-five years later, in the 1879 registry, Ephraim and his heirs are deleted and the ownership of No. 1369 is transferred to Mayer. There is thus a very strong case for assuming that Ephraim was Mayer's great-uncle and the brother of Abraham, Mayer's grandfather, my great-great-grandfather.

To my mother, the Braunthals were basically Brody people. She thought that Mayer's father Lev had temporarily moved from Brody to Odessa, the thriving commercial and financial city on the Black Sea, the Russian gateway to the world. They did not stay there very long because Lev's fourth child, Amalie, was the first one born back in Brody in 1845, only the first three including Mayer having been born in Odessa. There is documentary evidence of emigration of Brody Jews in the 1820s, arriving in Odessa in search of a better world. But it may now seem surprising that there was at any time an exodus to the East, back to Russia.

In the absence of the archival certainty of birth or marriage certificates or cemetery records one can also speculate on the radical alternative, namely that Lev was born in Odessa or elsewhere and that he moved to Brody for the first time in 1840 or 1841 to join other Braunthals already resident there.

My mother was proud of the fact that her father Mayer was born in Odessa, even if he left as a young boy. In her eyes Odessa was a great city with a history and the mysterious allure of a cosmopolitan culture. She often told me the story of Uncle Kreschower. One day this Uncle Kreschower appeared in Vienna on a visit from Odessa, in about 1893. My mother would have been about four years old, because she was still living at Obere Donaustrasse 63, the house where she was born. She described him in great detail. "He came through the door. He entered the room. He was tall, with blue eyes, fair hair, and the characteristic high cheekbones of the Slavs. He was "ein richtiger Kosak in hohen Stiefeln" (a real Cossack wearing high boots).

Uncle Kreschower was a relative of Toba Braunthal, my mother's grandmother, whose maiden name was Kreschower. For my mother this visit left a life-long impression, a glimpse into a far-away world of yesterday.

Less than a year before my father's parents married, another wedding was celebrated: Mayer Braunthal married Clara Gelles on the 18th April

1886. They were events of a very personal significance, fixed in the smooth progression of consecutive years. Mayer was forty-nine, actually two days short of his fiftieth birthday, Clara was twenty-three. It was Mayer's second marriage. They were to have six children, Bertha, born in 1887, my mother Theresia (Resi) in 1889, Julius in 1891, Ignaz in 1893, Alfred in 1897, and Mini in 1898. My mother's birthday was on the 18th August, the same day as that of the Emperor Franz Joseph. It was celebrated as a public holiday. Occasionally, on her birthdays, she would remind me of the general festive atmosphere. "Der Geburtstag von Kaiser Franz Joseph war am selben Tag. Es war ein Feiertag" (The birthday of Kaiser Franz Joseph was on the same day. It was a day of celebration).

Mayer's first marriage to Scheindel Lea (Charlotte) Papernik took place in Brody on August 20th 1865. After the birth of their first child, Antonie, on February 9, 1869, they moved to Vienna and had five more children, Moses, Eduard, Isaak, Mina and Ottilie.

My mother thus had six stepbrothers and sisters, but only ever mentioned Eduard and his younger brother, not by name, though. She thought there were just these two stepbrothers, whom she never met. She spoke of Eduard with the natural admiration reserved for artists. He was born on March 24 1873. In 1893, he enrolled at the Academy of Fine Arts in Vienna. In 1899 he received a travel scholarship to Rome, but it probably would not have been the coveted Prix de Rome, won at about that time or earlier by Josef Hoffmann and Otto Wagner. According to the 1928 edition of the German 'Who's Who', he journeyed throughout Italy, Sardinia, Sicily and Crete. During the First World War, he was a war artist for the Austrian army, and afterwards exhibited in Vienna and abroad. My cousin Gerald (Jerry) has one of his paintings, a rather academic landscape. Eduard was there when the Secession first shocked a conservative Viennese public, showing works by Gustav Klimt. What an opportunity to study art in Vienna in the last years of the 19th century! Eduard lived through the valediction of the *fin-de-siècle* and was exposed to the allure of Art Nouveau. I have often wondered what his work was like and where it now might be. After a divorce families often divided. My mother told me of the very sad occasion when Mayer saw Eduard in the street walking towards him. When they drew level, Eduard walked straight past without saying anything. I still hear my mother's words, rising in anguish: "Stell dir vor, da geht der Sohn an dem alten Vater vorbei, ohne ein Wort zu sprechen." (Just think, there goes the son past the old father, without speaking a word.)

There are no descendants of the six children from the first marriage. Antonie was a spinster and died in Vienna, aged sixty-one, on December 29, 1930, Moses died in 1878, aged six. Eduard and his second wife, the actress Emma Margarete Paak, left Vienna on the 27th January 1939. They moved to Hamburg. Eduard died during the war, I do not know how, when or where. His wife, Emma Braunthal, survived, and continued to live in Hamburg. It was there that the wife of my mother's brother Alfred, Hilde Braunthal, visited her. It was in 1952, when Hilde worked for the United States High Commission in Germany, the American administrative body of the occupation. In addition to their zone in the south, the Americans were responsible for a small coastal enclave within the British zone, near Hamburg. Soon afterwards, Hilde and Alfred visited us in London. She told us how strange and exciting it was suddenly to meet another Mrs Braunthal. The best hotels in Germany were reserved for allied military personnel, and members of the Civilian Control Commission were given equivalent army ranks. Hilde explained to us that as Director-in-Chief of Social Services in the American Zone she had the equivalent army rank of an American Major-General. Alfred, on hearing this, sat up in his armchair and quipped: "And what is the husband of a Major-General called?"

I will continue with the remaining three children of Mayer's first marriage. It now seems long ago, and no member of my branch of the family knew them, but they were after all my grandfather's children.

At the end of the nineteenth century there was an increase in the number of Jews who converted to Christianity, or had their children baptised at birth. In Austria, the Protestant Church (die evangelische Kirche) was more tolerant than the official Catholic Church, easily receiving these converts. The official severance from the old faith and the acceptance of a new religion was intended to strengthen the act of assimilation, alas to no avail. Anti-semitism became increasingly racial, eventually ending in the Holocaust. Baptism was no safeguard.

It was also possible to leave the Jewish Community by registering as 'konfessionslos' (without religion). Bureaucracy, at the time, demanded information under the heading of religion. But Austria was becoming more secular, especially in the early years of the young republic, and a new official classification was created. Civil documentation enabled one to substantiate the change, and the Kultusgemeinde (the Jewish Community) issued the necessary certificate.

Isaak, Mayer's fourth child, was born on the 14th June 1874. He married Anna Papernik, probably a cousin, as Isaak's mother was a Papernik. Anna was born on the 24th June 1876. In 1904 Isaak resigned from the Kultusgemeinde, and repeated it more formally in 1928. It made no difference. On the 12th March 1941 he and his wife were deported to Poland and murdered.

For Mina, born on the 15th September 1876, I have no information. Ottilie the last child was born on the 28th October 1878. Fate treated her kindly and she died in Vienna on April 7, 1939. Neither Ottilie nor Antonie married; now they lie in the same grave in the Zentralfriedhof (Central Cemetery) of Vienna, the first and the last of Mayer's and Charlotte's children.

My mother did not know that Mayer's family was so large when he left Charlotte. It was Gerard's research, which uncovered so many details of Braunthal family history. Not only did he discover more children of Mayer's first family, but his painstaking labour revealed the astonishing existence of further Braunthals in the previous generation. Hitherto we knew that Mayer had an older brother, Ephraim, and a younger sister, Amalie (Mali). The complete new list should now read: Ephraim, Mayer, Chaje Freude, Jakob, Mali Golde (Amalie), Chane Rachel and Scheindel Debora. Once again my mother did not know of another uncle and of the additional three aunts, or of the various cousins living in Vienna. But she did speak very kindly of Amalie (Tante Mali). Neat statistics can always round off a welter of information in condensed form. Mayer and his second wife Clara had six children. Mayer and Clara, at the latest count (August 2003) have more than a hundred descendants.

Grandmother Clara would have been thrilled at the sheer size of her progeny. The global distribution of her descendants in Europe, North and South American, even in Hawaii, would have astonished her. It was, after all, a long way from Brody, where she was born. I remember Clara so clearly, fore-shadowing my mother, my mother's mother, a second mother. They had the same figure, the same soft skin and the same energetic temperament to do their best. They were single-minded in their devotion to their families and hoped for (and expected) excellence.

In Brody in the 1870s when Clara started work at the age of about twelve, conditions were grim. My mother told me that Clara had to work all day, often twelve hours or more. She had to cover umbrellas, that is sew the coverings to the frames. It was piecework, virtual slavery. According to my mother, the workshop was in fact one of those primitive covered courtyards with an opening to the street. It was dark and damp.

Uncle Julius thought that Mayer, after his divorce from Charlotte, may have asked a marriage broker in Brody, a 'Schatchen', to find him a nice local girl. In the 19th century, arranged marriages were not unusual, but the degree of selection, consultation, negotiation and persuasion varied considerably. Romance was a feature, but not necessarily the only consideration. In his opera *The Bartered Bride*, once misspelt on the playbill of a touring company as *The Battered Bride*, thus illustrating the importance of a single letter, Smetana created the unforgettable role of the archetypal marriage broker Kecal, one of the great bass roles in the opera repertoire, a comic prototype, tinged with self-importance. In the ethnic mythology of Jewish humour, the marriage broker has an intriguing role of verbalising the infinite variety of unexpected results.

On the 26th December 1937, I went with Lena to *The Bartered Bride* at the Opera. It was her Christmas present. I treasure the memory. We sat in a box. Richard Tauber sang Jeník, Maria Reining was Marenka, and Fritz Krenn sang Kecal. The great Tauber, the wonderful lyrical tenor, there he was standing on stage, singing. It was one of the great moments in the awakening of my musical life. I did not know that a voice could be so beautiful. Ten years later, I heard Tauber again. The Vienna Opera had come to Covent Garden for a three-week season, and on Saturday the 27th September 1947 Tauber made a single guest appearance as Don Ottavio in Mozart's *Don Giovanni*. Unforgettable was his 'Il mio tesoro in tanto'. During the preceding recitative, I longed for the opening of the aria. When it came it had the paradox of miraculous musical experience. Time stood still, seconds became eternal, I glimpsed paradise, and when it was over it seemed as if it had never happened.

After a decade of exile in London, Richard Tauber accepted this invitation from his old opera company to sing with them once more. He was seriously ill with lung cancer but no one in the audience realized it. There was rapturous applause. He died a few weeks later on the 8th January, 1948, at the age of fifty-six.

During the previous twenty-five years, Tauber had formed a musical association with Franz Lehar, the composer of, among many other works, *The Merry Widow* and *The Land of Smiles*. He made the most famous number from this operetta 'Dein ist mein ganzes Herz' his signature tune and, according to *The Times* obituary, sang it ten thousand times.

But he would be equally remembered as a great operatic tenor in *Tosca, Faust, Die Zauberflöte, Der Freischütz, Carmen, Die Fledermaus, Mignon,* and *The Bartered Bride*. Lena told me that his Don José in *Carmen* was so wonderful. She heard him on 25th November, 1934, a day before her 44th birthday.

The Bartered Bride was not the last opera I heard in Vienna before the war. A month later, on 30th January 1938, six weeks before the Anschluss, I went to my first *Don Giovanni*. On that occasion, Anton Dermota sang Don Ottavio, which he repeated at Covent Garden with the Vienna Opera on the 20th September 1947, a week before the Tauber performance. How fortunate I was to hear the Tauber voice, the tenor legend, the wonderful legato, and Dermota's noble eloquence so early in my Mozartian life.

It was on Thursday 25th December 1930, that I went to my first opera, *Hänsel und Gretel* by Humperdinck. The Staatsoper had a special tradition. It presented the work only once a year, on Christmas Day in a double bill. During the long interval evocatively indicated on the programme as "Nach *Hänsel und Gretel* ist eine längere Pause" (after *Hänsel und Gretel* is a longer interval), there was time for seasonal refreshments. What followed was a one-act pantomime, *Die Puppenfee* (*The Fairy Doll*), in which a collection of mechanical figures is brought to life in a toy shop. The programme had been carefully planned to send the children home with a carefree smile.

I found *Hänsel und Gretel* a little slow-moving, and was longing for the moment when the witch is being pushed into the oven. When it came, I was frightened and upset. I can recall the dramatic climax. Memory may be veiled by nearly eight decades, time has shed its diaphanous layers over the image, but I still see the 'Knusperhäuschen' (the gingerbread house) on left of stage. The incineration was presented with unforgettable realism. It was only fairy-tale horror, but so eloquent in the Age of Innocence, not yet destroyed by violent television. The cast list on these festive occasions included great stars. In 1930, Hänsel was sung by Rosette Anday and Gretel by Adele Kern. My Aunt Lena's opera book will help me bring to life their careers and at the same time I can imagine Lena listening to wonderful music.

On the 2nd January 1928, Adele Kern sang Papagena to Lotte Lehmann's Pamina in *The Magic Flute*.

Lena heard them again on the 10th September 1929 in *Rosenkavalier* as Sophie and as the Marschallin. In 1929 on the 27th November, one day after her 39th birthday, Lena heard Adele Kern as Despina in *Cosi Fan Tutte*. And then a year later, on the 20th November 1930, six days prior to her 40th birthday, Lena must have enjoyed her as Olympia in *The Tales of Hoffmann*. What a wonderful Gretel I must have heard! At that time, Adele Kern was at the height of her career. On the 5th

January 1931, less than two weeks after the Humperdinck, Lena went to *Ariadne auf Naxos*. Adele Kern was Zerbinetta, and Lotte Lehmann was Ariadne. Richard Strauss conducted. Rosette Anday was a great Delilah, and on 14th May 1930, Lena was fortunate enough to hear her. On the 13th September 1933 Lena went to *Die Fledermaus*, and Rosette Anday sang Prince Orlofsky. Her darker voice made for an ideal Hänsel.

There I was, not quite seven years old, on my first visit to the Opera, listening to two glorious singers. I still remember entering the auditorium on that 25th December 1930: Its sheer size, the glorious height, the tiered boxes, the festive balconies, curved in gold and plush red beauty, the painted curtain. For the first time, I climbed the Grand Staircase, with its festive wide central section, framed by the outward curl of narrower steps. In the Loggia, on the first floor, overlooking the Ringstrasse in the manner of a Renaissance palace, there were paintings by Moritz von Schwind of scenes from the operas.

On the 12th March 1945, at the end of the Second World War, the Russian bombardment of Vienna set the opera building alight. But the shells, flying over the roof from the south, landed in the auditorium, leaving the façade and the Loggia smouldering, but still standing, and sufficiently undamaged for the frescoes to be saved and restored.

Moritz von Schwind reappeared in my life in 1970. That was the year that the world celebrated the 200th anniversary of Beethoven's birth. I was in the British Museum searching for suitable pictorial material for a festive publication when I came across four engravings of scenes from Beethoven's opera *Fidelio*. I found the Schwind pictures in an old vocal score, and they date from the 1830s. Under the title 'Fidelio Illustrations' I published them, adding music quotations.

I think of Mayer and his many visits to the opera, slowly climbing up to the fourth gallery. I try to visualise my other grandfather Wilhelm on many grand musical occasions, wearing black tie, the winged collar, the stiffly starched shirt front held by a row of seed-pearl mounted gold clips. I have his cufflinks. He threaded them through the button-holes, he adjusted them, he manipulated them and daily he lived with them. They speak to me. They are an intimate link.

CHAPTER 2

Life at the Ferdinandstrasse:
Hermine and Wilhelm Neumann

Only a mile or so from the Braunthals' home at Obere Donaustrasse 63, downstream along the banks of the Donaukanal, in the Leopoldstadt, was the Ferdinandstrasse. There, at No. 14, my father Paul Neumann was born on the 15th March 1888. The Ferdinandstrasse means a lot to me. My grandmother, Hermine Neumann (née Kuffler) arrived in Vienna in about 1870. The Kufflers moved into Ferdinandstrasse 14, and my grandmother lived there for the rest of her life. After her marriage to Wilhelm Neumann she continued to live there, moving from the first floor to her new home on the second floor. Two of their four children, Paul and Lena, were born there. Hermine and Wilhelm died there. Lena lived there until she left Vienna in 1938.

At some point, the Kuffler parents also moved to the second floor, next to the Neumanns. Wilhelm took over their flat when it became vacant and created internal access through Lena's bedroom by breaking through a massive structural wall that separated the apartments. Strangely the large rooms on the other side were never used. They were mysteriously out of bounds. On one memorable occasion, however, my grandmother opened the doors. She led me through a suite of large rooms, darkened by drawn Venetian blinds. They were full of cupboards, beds, tables, chairs. For me, it was frightening but exciting, this furniture depository in the half-light. In a large wooden chest was a huge pile of Uncle Robert's violin music. "Nimm dir was du willst" (take what you want) she said.

I treasure the music which came from him. There are short bravura pieces, a few concertos and some studies. Particularly evocative is the first edition of the revised *Etudes faciles dans tous les tons majeurs et mineurs pour le violon avec accompagnement d'un second violon ad libitum* by Jacques Dont, book 1, op. 17, published by Cranz in Leipzig. The folio-sized cover page is transfigured by the sepia-coloured beauty of traditional typography. In the top right-hand corner the signature of Robert Neumann has been added in fine pencil, the initials R and N drawn with the delicate flourish of thick and thin calligraphy.

When Robert was ten years old in 1908, his parents Wilhelm and Hermine bought him his first full-size violin. In addition to the customary advice from Robert's teacher, Wilhelm would have consulted the highest authority. A little earlier, in November 1907, Willhelm had asked his friend Kommerzialrat Ludwig Bösendorfer to select a special piano from his workshop for Lena's seventeenth birthday. The piano, with its old-fashioned feet, its beautifully restored ivory keys, and above all, its lovely sweet Viennese descant and mellow lower registers, stands in our home. It reminds me of the Ferdinandstrasse, and even more of Lena's room where it stood. When it was Robert's turn to have an instrument, Wilhelm may well have spoken to Arnold Rosé, for many years the leader of the Vienna Philharmonic Orchestra, and Gustav Mahler's brother-in-law. Or he might have gone to Georg Bauer, the famous Geigenmacher in the Neues Konzerthaus. At any rate a substantial violin was bought for Robert.

In due course Robert joined the army and when he returned he did not feel like playing again. The violin case had been placed on top of his cupboard as a silent reminder and remained there for several years. One day, as the result of more than thorough spring cleaning, the case was lifted and immediately opened. It was empty! Robert had sold the violin some years earlier, but did not want to tell his parents. The empty case acted as a decoy, but it was a time-bomb that would erupt with eventual discovery.

Years later, Robert told me that he wanted the money to take a girl (a 'Katzerl' as he called her) on a luxury holiday. This would probably have been prior to his first short-lived marriage to Bessy Schreiber in 1926 or 1927. Imagine the scene. He was in his twenties in the 1920s. He was a young director of the prestigious Creditanstalt, probably aided by the influential position of his father, Regierungsrat Wilhelm Neumann, with the Rothschild bankers. He had the social title of "Herr Bankdirektor".

Soon after the war, Robert bought his first car. He was one of the early motorists in Vienna, at a time when there were no traffic lights or driving tests, and you could park where you wanted. He told me that he had bought several exclusive Italian or French sports cars, ending up with the 1935 Bianci coupé in which I travelled on several occasions.

Robert's girl would have stepped into the low car in a crêpe dress, stopping at the knees, her hair cut short in a total gesture of emancipation. Robert, most likely, would have worn a white linen suit, the jacket with extra wide lapels, the wide-legged trousers, the silk shirt fastened with a characteristic broad tie. More evocative would have been his 'co-respondent' shoes, so-called because of their fanciful association with marital infidelity. These shoes had dual-tone brogue toe caps and were worn with panache.

Throughout his life Robert was always very elegantly dressed and very courteous to ladies. He naturally held all doors open for them and ushered them through with a slight bow, the implied gesture of precedence and the chivalrous smile of old Vienna.

On that occasion, he would have enacted once again the rôle of chauffeur and Don Juan, travelling south at high speed along empty roads. Where might they have gone? After 1918 the fashionable resorts along the Dalmatian and Istrian coast declined. The aristocracy and the *jeunesse dorée* of Vienna no longer visited Abbazia and Ragusa, Fiume or Corfu. This was now a lost world. The Austrian Riviera was no longer. Nice, Monte Carlo, Monaco and especially the exclusive Menton were now the places of high elegance, symbolised by the Ruhl and the Negresco hotels on the Promenade des Anglais in Nice.

Hermine considered the smooth running of the Ferdinandstrasse her life's work. Little did she know as a young girl that one day she would be Frau Regierungsrat Hermine Neumann, a prominent member of Viennese society. She was born Hermine Kuffler on the 3rd January 1868, in Friedek. Until 1918, it was in Austrian Silesia, but it is now in the Czech Republic. On Hermine's birth certificate, made out by the district rabbinate of Teschen on the 2nd October 1874, her father Leopold Kuffler is described as 'merchant' and her mother is entered as Auguste Aufricht. The number of the house in Friedek is 120, with no road name given.

Hermine Neumann presided over the Ferdinandstrasse with undisputed authority. Up to the outbreak of the First World War, her four children lived at home. In 1914 my father Paul was twenty-six, Lena twenty-four, Mizzi nineteen and Robert sixteen. There was Frau Rosa, the wonderful cook, who had been with the Neumanns for more than forty years until that day in the autumn of 1938 when Lena was to shut the door of the Ferdinandstrasse for the last time. And above all, there was Helene Sohr, affectionately called Lala, who started her work as a Kinderfräulein (nanny) when Paul was very small, and continued to live there until her death in 1935. She would have had nowhere to go and my grandparents allowed her to stay in her little room facing the courtyard. Lala had been a member of the family for so many years. The children loved her long after they had grown up. Lala, in Hermine Neumann's eyes, was a faithful family retainer, who had to be provided with a 'grace and favour home'.

Frau Rosa hardly ventured outside the kitchen. Next to her domain was her bedroom, also, of course, overlooking the courtyard. And this small room she had to share with a long succession of much younger maids. I remember Annie, the last Stubenmädchen. Lena told me years later that Annie's day had been long. In addition to making breakfast, cleaning and tidying nine rooms, dealing with laundry and shopping, she had to look after Lena's dog, Billy, a rather aggressive long-haired dachshund given to her in 1936 by Bernhard Altmann, the textile magnate. Frau Rosa also went shopping, usually to the local market, the Karmeliter Markt, about half an hour away. All purchases had to be carried home in stout leather bags and because of the sheer weight of potatoes, flour, sugar, let alone meat and vegetables, several journeys had frequently to be made on the same day. The washing for so many people was a major task. Huge bundles were carried to the nearby laundry but a lot was done at the Ferdinandstrasse. I remember the large bathroom with its tin bath-tub.

In a corner stood the massive mangle in its formidable cast-iron frame. The rollers were adjustable, narrow for sheets, wide for towels. Next to it, the scrubbing board was at the ready. It was an oblong metal tray, framed in pine, the surface undulating with narrow horizontal ribs. This humble household object, bearing the rigours of the brush like a long-suffering beast of burden, this thing of domestic utility, how can it possibly become a vehicle of transcendental imagination?

Not at the time, of course, but after a lifelong love of art, I see the world with eyes that have looked upon thousands of paintings and sculptures. I am reminded of a detail, I savour the mood, I reflect on colour, I see the detail within the detail within the detail. Architecture has made me feel space. Sculpture has added its intimate way with the third dimension. Painting has spoken with the infinite language of beauty. Memories of special works stand like signposts on my journey.

On my last visit to Florence, I once again stood outside the Baptistry and looked at the Andrea Pisano door. The Life of St. John, the Baptist, is cast in twenty bronze plaques which were made seven hundred years ago. One episode I look at with special longing, the baptism of Christ. The Saviour stands in the river Jordan, the water covering the lower part of his naked body. A veil of twenty-six thin waves reaches up to his hips. The flowing water is sensitively moulded into a diaphanous curtain that reveals the legs in the classical posture of the Renaissance. It was the delicately smooth ridges of the flowing river, for me the focal point of interest in this bas-relief, that suddenly made me think of the scrubbing board. In a bizarre act of correlation, the profane regularity of the board's machine-pressed aluminium, and the divine detail of the bronze indentation of the flowing Jordan stirred my memory after seventy years.

My grandmother had a woman who came to do the sewing, a so-called Weissnäherin (a seamstress for whites), and so did my mother. The shirts for my grandfather and father were made at home, or at bespoke shirtmakers, and so were the traditional night shirts. The finest silks or linens were used. Buttonholes were hand sewn, the buttons mother of pearl, the monograms carefully stitched. I still have one or two of my father's carefully preserved linen shirts, mementos of interwar fashion, with their idiosyncratic bespoke extra length, all, of course, to be drawn over the head, and open only to the waist.

My grandmother's cares and duties seem to have been never-ending. The social lives of Lena and Mizzi had to be scrutinised and monitored. Lena's piano teacher, a certain Fräulein Wetter, came to the Ferdinandstrasse for the lessons. Robert was taught the violin at home. The additional domestic help of a "Bedienerin", someone to carry heavy carpets to the courtyard to be beaten with carpet beaters, or to clean the silver and do the ironing for so many, made it possible for my grandmother somehow to underpin the organisation of the Ferdinandstrasse. The girls had English and French lessons, Lena had dancing lessons and later joined a prestigious tennis club in the Prater.

Every day for years, my grandfather Wilhelm Neumann left the Ferdinandstrasse home punctually and walked to the Rothschild office in the Renngasse, where he worked as their press consultant.

Indeed, there were many daily routines. I was only present at the occasional Sunday lunch, which was served precisely at one o'clock. After lunch my grandfather would wind the case clock, tightening the seven-day spring with a brass winding handle. Taussig, the great director of the Creditanstalt, presented it to my grandfather at the end of the 19th century. This clock now stands in our hall. Often when I wind it, I think of him. He held the handle, he touched it, he used it. My grandfather would then go to his study and bring back his cigar. It was a so-called Virginia, a very thin long cigar, with special tobacco from the American South. But what was so special in my eyes was the way it was lit. At the narrow end of the cigar, a yellow piece of straw slightly protruded, looking with hindsight very much like the mouthpiece of an oboe. My grandfather pulled out the straw, which was nearly the same length as the cigar. He cut the mouth end with his cigar cutter, inlaid with mother of pearl. He set light to the straw and with it lit the cigar. It would have been sacrilege to have used a match, completely against the tradition of lighting this kind of cigar. My grandfather told me that the straw, when pulled out, left behind a narrow hollow tunnel which made drawing of air through this long cigar easy.

I invariably asked him to blow smoke rings. I see him now tilting his head back and puffing out three or four perfect rings. Expertise was measured not only by the number of rings one could blow in one exhalation, but also by their perfection. "Schöne Ringe blasen ist besser als kleine Wolken" (it is better to blow beautiful rings than little clouds) my grandfather said. How did he do it? He drew deeply on his cigar, filled his lungs with smoke, shaped his mouth in a ring, and then in little gasps of breath blew out smoke past curved lips.

Wilhelm kept his cigar boxes in the bottom right-hand drawer of his large desk. I have one of the empty boxes, itself a work of art and a poignant reminder of the past. The box (boîte nature) has lettering and image engraved into the wood. The name of the cigar, Figaro, immortalised by Mozart and Rossini, is boldly inscribed on the proscenium arch above a stage on which the valet/barber is facing us with a conspiratorial look of intrigue. As I open the box, the evocative aroma of Cuban tobacco, stored from long ago, envelopes me with nostalgia.

Wilhelm must have come to Vienna in his late teens. On the 18th September 1880, just after his 20th birthday, a signed article of his appeared in the feuilleton section of the *Wiener Allgemeine Zeitung* entitled 'Die Studierwuth' (The Frenzy for Study). Wilhelm laments the craze for further study, irrespective of ability or financial resources. The rich can ultimately become adequate doctors or engineers, the poor succeed only if they are exceptional. False ambition of parents has so often caused misery for children.

This is the earliest article I have by Wilhelm. The fifteen hundred words were not unusually long for the feuilleton, so often a proper short essay. Exceptionally, it is signed Wilhelm Neumann, but normally Wilhelm used a nom de plume, 'spectator', 'quidam', 'memor', or sometimes three stars. The article was reprinted in the *Agramer Zeitung* on the 23rd September 1884. This time the story is called 'For the start of the school year' and does not have Wilhelm's name. It is interesting to speculate how it came about that the principal newspaper in Agram, now Zagreb, the capital of Croatia, gave this article pride of place on its front page four years after its first appearance in Vienna. Wilhelm must have been very amused when he read the first article on the 18th September 1880, as his name is preceded by the title 'professor'. "Not yet twenty-one, and they have made me a professor," he must have thought.

Wilhelm joined the staff of the *Fremden-Blatt*, the prestigious voice of ministries and chancelleries, in 1886. In the same year, on the 3rd November, aged 26, he also became a member of Concordia, the famous confederation of journalists. Exactly fifty years later, on 2nd November 1936, with bureaucratic exactitude, the President and Vice President sent a golden jubilee letter of congratulation to Wilhelm:

… in good and bad times, on happy and sad days, you have held high the banner of the Concordia. Your wise counsel, your enthusiastic devotion to the interests of the organisation hand-in-hand with the putting aside of your personality, has established the ongoing management of the confederation which enabled it to fulfil its sometimes onerous duties. If it became necessary to make difficult decisions, to find the right way out of the turmoil of clashing interests (aus dem Wirsal einander wiederstrebenden Interessen), then everyone of us, quite naturally, is captured by the thought: above all, we must know what Wilhelm Neumann has to say about it (vor allem müssen wir wissen, was Wilhelm Neumann dazu sagt)…

A few weeks later, on the 1st December 1936, at the annual meeting of the association, the minutes record the gratitude and admiration of those present.

A certain Hofrat (privy counsellor) Wilhelm, his name an appropriate coincidence, drew attention to a 'golden wedding anniversary' which the Concordia had the occasion to celebrate. A few days earlier, Regierungsrat Neumann had completed fifty years of membership (thunderous applause).

Hofrat Wilhelm recalled that Regierungsrat Neumann had just started his journalist career in 1881 at the Wilhelm News Agency. Subsequently he fulfilled an important role at the *Fremdenblatt*, a function which secured for him, right into his old age, his political and diplomatic connections, which he still enjoyed.

Hofrat Wilhelm proposed that the joyful demonstration be entered in the minutes.

Regierungsrat Neumann, deeply moved, thanked those present. He recalled that he missed the Annual General Meeting of the Concordia the previous year for the first time, because he had been seriously ill, and how a letter from the Concordia had given him comfort and had raised his spirits during those difficult times.

He also remembered the letter from the Concordia more than six years earlier on the occasion of his seventieth birthday, which included the following sentence: 'there is probably no close colleague whom you have not helped by word and deed'. He regarded this declaration with pride. He concluded with the assurance that he would never forsake his principles of helping others and that he would always remember with gratitude that he owed his career as a journalist to his colleagues, and, not least, to the Concordia.

The President concluded: "We know that you were and are the ideal Concordia-Patriot and, if you say that you will continue in this way, we are certain of it". (Wir wissen, dass Sie das Ideal eines Concordia-Patrioten waren und sind, und wenn Sie sagen, dass Sie es bleiben werden, so sind wir dessen bei Ihnen sicher.)

That congratulatory birthday letter for Wilhelm's 70th birthday on 6th September 1930, from the Concordia, was echoed in a widespread of coverage of the event by the Viennese press. The similarities and variations in the reports, in spite of, or even because of their different lengths and editorial emphases, build up a composite portrait of Wilhelm, the journalist and human being. After half a century, starting in pre-First World War Habsburg Vienna, and still active fifty years later, he had earned the respect and affection of his colleagues and became a true doyen, the byword of integrity, the hallmark of veracity, of real application:

Neues Wiener Tagblatt

...The heartfelt congratulations for the ever-young birthday person which would however be incomplete, if they were not to mention and praise his compassion and tireless willingness to give assistance, especially to his journalistic colleagues. More than great is the number of those who, not in vain, have sought his encouragement and support, which he dispensed unhesitatingly, and who have benefited from his conscientious, well-considered advice.

Wiener Allgemeine Zeitung

...With such an alert mind, which is fully pre-occupied with ongoing journalism, there is no need to cling to the past. Wilhelm Neumann, formerly the Economics Editor of the Fremdenblatt, was known far beyond the frontiers of the old monarchy, and is also, still today, a newspaperman who writes what he wants to say in excellent style and with superb comment.

Die Stunde

...Young and fresh, like a forty year-old, he is still part of public life, with an active mind which lives in the past, but in no ways denies the present. Even today, Wilhelm Neumann is in close contact with Vienna's art and theatre world. His memoirs, should he write them, would contain many interesting chapters of the city's economic development, which for years has been so closely integrated with its society.

Der Wiener Tag

... Famous bankers, such as the Governor of the Bodencreditanstalt, Theodor Ritter von Taussig, and Generaldirektor Palmer of the Länderbank, who occupied a very important position at the time in Vienna, but also eminent industrialists, such as Wilhem Krestanek, Chairman of the Prager Eisenindustriegesellschaft

(Iron Manufacturers of Prague) regarded Regierungsrat Neumann with great respect and frequently sought his advice on matters of importance.

Neue Freie Presse

… His youthful energy, which his many friends wish him to display for many more years, is linked to his completely modern attitude with which he confronts all the problems of the present time, be they economic or political. Regierungsrat Neumann is greatly appreciated by his colleagues, because at all times he effectively offers support for the safeguard of their professional interests, and because he has accomplished much good in the Concordia. Furthermore he has often proved his willingness to help individual cases.

Die Prager Wirtschaft

… Whenever Theodor Ritter von Taussig, the all-powerful Governor of the Bodencreditanstalt and President of the State Railway was on his daily walk from the Teinfaltstrasse (his office) to the Schwarzenberg Platz (Palais Rothschild), he was always accompanied by Neumann. On the occasions of major share issues, when the mighty of the Rothschild group, Gustav Ritter von Mauthner (Credit-Anstalt), Theodor Ritter von Taussig and Baron Siegmund Kornfeld (Ungarische Allgemeine Creditbank) were in conference, Neumann certainly, sooner or later, joined their deliberations … Baron Albert Rothschild did not fail to consult Neumann if he thought that a project concerned the general public. And that is why, in quite changed circumstances, the presidents, chairmen and managing directors of domestic and foreign companies, seek his advice and friendship … Not only does he know and read all newspapers, but also all newly published books including his grand-daughter's latest English school essays.

Pester Lloyd (the premier German daily in Budapest)

… His articles display an extraordinary knowledge of the political and social conditions of the old and new Vienna. With their elegant style, and the distinguished and modest nature of the author – he nearly always chose a pseudonym – they are models for the young generation of journalists who have in him a true support.

The *Pester Lloyd* was the only paper to print his obituary on 14th April 1938:

As has been reported to us from Vienna, the outstanding journalist Regierungsrat Wilhelm Neumann has died there after a long illness. Neumann, a Hungarian, came to Vienna in his early years, where he studied at the University and devoted himself to journalism. He soon rose to a well-respected position in the Viennese press. His profound knowledgable expertise, his far-reaching connections, his honourable and reliable mode of contact gained for him both within and outside his journalistic profession many friends and admirers.

The Viennese press, by then under Nazi control, of course ignored the death of a prominent Jew. How this silence contrasted with the congratulatory articles they had published eight years earlier.

My Aunt Lena brought with her from Vienna family papers, including some of Wilhelm's articles. However, they only date from 1918, after the collapse of the Habsburg empire and the closure of the *Fremden-Blatt*, with the two exceptions mentioned above. In the Nationalbibliothek in Vienna, Wilhelm's thirty-three years' contribution to the *Fremden-Blatt* are preserved for posterity. And so, of course, are further articles in other newspapers.

Wilhelm loved facts and figures. He would have approved of an overview of the articles which I have in front of me. For 1925 I have seven articles, for 1926 there are thirty-two, for 1927 forty-five, for 1928 forty-two, I have fifty-nine articles for 1929 and there are thirty-nine articles in 1930. I have eleven articles dated 1931, and one article each for 1933 and 1934. Altogether there are two hundred and thirty seven articles, from various newspapers, a testimony to his energy and industry.

He had a fine style, which enabled him to present involved subject matter with clarity. His encyclopaedic memory stored a rich treasure trove of personalia. He knew leading figures in banking, politics and industry. As a young man he had joined Rothschild, the bankers, as their press consultant and remained with them until 1938. Wilhelm had the natural curiosity of a great journalist.

The article in the *Neues Wiener Journal* on the 27th October 1925 is typical. It is entitled 'Generalintendant Bezecny' and has the subtitle 'What a friend relates' and is signed Memor. In twelve hundred words Wilhelm describes the career of his friend, who had died some twenty years earlier. Bezecny had started his professional life in the Ministry of Finance and eventually became governor of the prestigious Bodencreditanstalt, the official premier bank of Habsburg Vienna. He was also entrusted with the overall administration of the Court theatres, which included the Opera and the Burgtheater. Dr. Josef Freiherr von Bezecny as Generalintendant (General Administrator) had to negotiate subsidies and control their expenditure. In the official court hierarchy he was responsible to the First Principal Imperial Court Chamberlain (Erster Obersthofmeister), "der oberste Theaterherr" (the supreme theatre gentleman) as Wilhelm calls him. Bezecny had to deal with Prince Konstantin Hohenlohe and later Prince Rudolf Liechtenstein, who themselves reported to the Emperor. Bezecny was a great negotiator. Although his appointment was meant to ensure economy he was very concerned to provide the highest standards. His expertise as a banker enabled him to extract that extra money for great conductors, singers and actors, and furnish his theatres with lavish productions, all of which made the Vienna Opera and the Burgtheater world famous.

What makes Wilhelm's articles so fascinating are the personal reminiscence, anecdotal detail, biographical insight.

In his diaries, Hugo Thimig, the great actor and a former director of the Burgtheater, speaks of Bezecny and Wilhelm. The entry for the 30th January 1898 reads: "Bezecny has consulted Herr Neumann of the *Fremden-Blatt*.". Bezecny faced a crisis caused by a change of directors at the Burgtheater and wanted my grandfather's advice. Wilhelm speaks of Bezecny: "Bezecny war nicht das, was man einen wirklichen und rechten Bureaukraten nennen durfte. Er besass nicht die ausdauernde

Beharrlichkeit eines Solchen, er war nicht blos ein Aktenmensch, aber wenn sich im Finanzministerium die "Restanzen" auf seinem Tische häuften und es sogenannte Postarbeit zu verrichten galt, dann war Bezecny imstande, sich für mehrere Tage und wohl auch Nächte in seinem Bureau einzusperren und in einem Aufwaschen alles zu erledigen" (He was not what one would call a true and real bureaucrat. He did not have the ongoing endurance of such a person. He was not just a man of documents. However if there was a mountain of incoming papers on his table at the Ministry of Finance and he faced a so-called 'rush-job' he was known to lock himself into his office for several days and possibly nights and to finish everything in one clearance.) Bezecny came from humble beginnings and was proud of his successes. Wilhelm writes that he basked in the glamour of the Court and was "stolz auf die Fülle von höchsten in-und ausländischen Orden, die seine Brust schmückten" (proud of the many Austrian and foreign decorations that decorated his chest).

The diversity of Wilhelm's subject matter, politics, finance, industry, art, is nearly always related to the great personages of the 19th century, many of whom he knew. His style is detailed, and not given to superficial generalisation. He can be critical but treats personalities with respect. His approach is narrative and documentary, set mainly against the background of the Habsburg Empire in the decades before the First World War. The length of his articles, often fifteen hundred to two thousand words or more, have their modern equivalent in feature articles for weekly supplements, periodicals and magazines. He often used the special style and format of the feuilleton, which allowed him to construct an imaginative environment in which to house his subjects. All facts were thoroughly researched and substantiated. He graced his prose with *bon mots* and aphorisms and drew on his extraordinary memory to embellish a story-line with biographical treasures. When Wilhelm reached the age of seventy in 1930 he retired, and I have only a few articles after that.

Whenever I went to the Ferdinandstrasse, Wilhelm was sitting at his desk. This was invariably on Sundays. He was reading or writing.

On entering my grandfather's study on these memorable occasions I would go across and kiss him. He was in his beautifully carved chair which was tall-backed and generously upholstered, comfortable as an armchair, but equally suitable for desk use. I see it now as a typical Viennese compromise of lingering Biedermeier domesticity and *fin de siècle* luxury. Over lunch the inevitable question was asked: "How are you getting on at school?" I was an average pupil, very different from my six years older sister Eva, who was an academically brilliant role model.

Hermine perhaps met Wilhelm in 1886. She was then eighteen, he was twenty-six. He was a very handsome, young, energetic journalist. She was sensitive and shy, caring and loving. She was deeply attached to her seven younger brothers and sisters, and deputy motherhood must have matured her.

They probably got engaged in the autumn of 1886. In December 1886 Wilhelm visited his brother Hermann and his wife Marie in Ménes-Gyorok, near Arad in Transylvania, then part of the Austro-Hungarian empire, now in Romania, called Manastur. He was away for only a few days. Hermine wrote every day. It was their first separation. On Friday, the 3rd December 1886, Hermine writes only a few hours after Wilhelm's departure: "… und doch, lieber Wilhelm, ist mir so öde, wenn ich daran denke, daß ich dich heute nicht zur bestimmten Stunde erwarten darf." (I feel so desolate, dear Wilhelm, if I think that today at a certain hour I would not be able to expect you.) In a second letter on the same day, in response to an immediate letter from Wilhelm, Hermine writes: "… so will ich dich (sic) versichern, mein lieber Wilhelm, daß ich ebenso glücklich mit dir sein werde, ob uns nun das Glück hold sein wird oder nicht." (I assure you, my dear Wilhelm that I will be just as happy with you, if fortune now smiles on us or not.) On the fourth of December, Hermine could only write a short letter as she had to go to a cookery school from half past eight to half past twelve. On Sunday the 5th December, Hermine thanks Wilhelm for his (second) letter. She explains that writing her first letter made her feel apprehensive and lost for words, but that subsequently she could freely write about everything. On that Sunday she is about to go to the opera with her mother, to *Preciosa*. And on the 6th December she writes: "Gestern, wie du schon weißt, waren Mama und ich in der Oper and haben uns sehr gut unterhalten. *Preciosa* ist doch ein altes Stück, doch spricht das Ganze auch die Musik so zum Herzen, daß ich gerührt war. Nicht mehr, das war wieder mal die alte kindische Mine, der die hohe Würde, Braut zu sein, noch gar nicht paßt, und doch weiß sie, was ihren Wilhelm glücklich macht, und wird selbst immer glücklich sein, wenn er es ist." (Yesterday, as you already know, Mama and I were at the Opera, and enjoyed it very much. *Preciosa* is indeed an old play, but the whole thing, also the music, so speaks to the heart that I was moved. Enough of that, that was once again the old childish Mine who is not yet used to the great dignity of being a bride, but even so she knows what makes her Wilhelm happy, and will always herself be happy if he is too.)

Preciosa is now completely forgotten, but it enjoyed some popularity in the 19th century. Weber added incidental music to a melodrama in which there is in effect only a single principal singing role. The chorus is used dramatically; the opening *Bolero*, the forest chorus, with its echo, the Gypsy March, the airs de ballet all provide colourful detail of a romantic world. Preciosa's famous aria 'Einsam bin ich, nicht alleine', must have had a profound effect on Hermine. She would have been able to follow the plot, Weber with skilful originality accompanying the spoken dialogue.

The work was written in 1820 but was still in the opera repertoire sixty years later. In her letter to Wilhelm she speaks of *Preciosa* without further explanation, and reminds us of the fate of so many works that have sunk into obscurity.

Hermine did not have to wait too long for her wedding. The marriage took place on Sunday the 6th March 1887. Hermine and her father, Leopold Kuffler, would have travelled the short distance from the Ferdinandstrasse to the Leopoldstädter Temple in the traditional

Viennese 'Fiaker', the elegant Landau, pulled by two shiny black horses, not, of course, the 'Einspänner', a more modest carriage to which only a single horse, frequently a more everyday grey or piebald was harnessed. Inside the synagogue, the ladies were in the gallery: her mother Auguste and her sisters Stephanie, Anna and Olga would have been joined by Hermine's aunts and cousins from the Kuffler side of the family.

The Neumann ladies from Trencin were Wilhelm's mother Fanny (née Sonnenfeld) and his sister Gisella. Wilhelm had two older brothers, Hermann, the wine merchant from Ménes-Gyorok, near Arad, and Eduard, a Doctor of Law and future successful lawyer, living in Vienna. Their wives Marie (Mariska) and Olga (née Löbl) excitedly joined the others. As Wilhelm's young sisters-in-law, they wanted to have a good look at the lady of his choice. Downstairs, Wilhelm's father Samuel and Wilhelm's younger brother Muzzo (Moritz), together with his two older brothers, provided Wilhelm with the full family support of Neumann men. It was one of the very rare occasions that all five were together after they left home.

I have left Hermine's grandmother, Helene Aufricht, to the end. She definitely attended the wedding, but I am not sure if Moritz Aufricht, her husband was still alive in 1886. With Helene Aufricht I feel a personal link. She died on the 25th November 1890, one day before the birth of my father's sister, Helene (Lena), who was born on the 26th November 1890 and appropriately named after her. Helena, our daughter, has inherited the family name. My father was only two and a half years old but he remembered her, sitting at a small table in the Ferdinandstrasse, a table which is now in our house, a treasured memento of my great great grandmother.

A great number of more distant relatives must have attended the wedding, quite apart from the many friends and acquaintances. Wilhelm must have been very popular at the *Fremden-Blatt* which he joined a year or so earlier. As a collective present they printed a special Wedding Issue, a four page newspaper with the official heading Fremden-Blatt Wien, Sonntag, 6 März 1887 Nr.64, 41 Jahrg (Vienna, Sunday 6 March

1887, No. 64, Year 41). The typography and lay-out of the title look exactly like that of a genuine edition. Similarly, the contents are presented in the usual typeface and point size. Telegraphic reports, for instance, are preceded by their provenance printed in the traditional way in slightly larger bold letters. Letter-spacing for emphasis (be it ironic, humorous, stag-night pornographic or complicated puns with a double-entendre) occur very frequently. The idea is to indicate to the reader: please smile or laugh here. In German gothic typography, letter spacing was used much more frequently than the subsequent italics which were possible only with the introduction of modern lettering. Even so some articles have letter spacing on practically every line, to make sure that on no account a joke is missed or an allusion not fully flavoured.

Wilhelm obviously furnished the office with basic details and contributed the family context. He must have written some of the material. But how much? Did he perhaps write nearly all of it? Did Wilhelm have a final editorial input, or indeed exercise some sort of censorship? Was the edition printed early on that Sunday and was it taken straight round to reception, so that Wilhelm would have seen it there for the first time? Or was it printed a few days in advance? At any rate it was carefully proof-read, as there is not a single mistake in the text.

The paper consists of subjects dear to Wilhelm's heart: reports from the Stock Exchange (Börsenberichte), a court piece, foreign press quotations, extracts from the Budget Committee Report of the Ministry of External Affairs, a cable from 'Herminia' an imaginary region in the Balkans, cables from special correspondents in places with family connections, references to Abbazia, the fashionable resort on the Dalmatian coast, the pearl of the Austrian Riviera, chosen for the honeymoon, an imaginary portrait of the bride, weather forecasts, poetic domestic advice including the essential provision of Apfelstrudel – all coloured by the boisterous humour of a best man.

The marriage took place at 2 o'clock and the reception was celebrated at the elegant hotel Oesterreichischer Hof, am Fleischmarkt, a prestigious venue of Old Vienna.

Neumann and Braunthal Family Origins

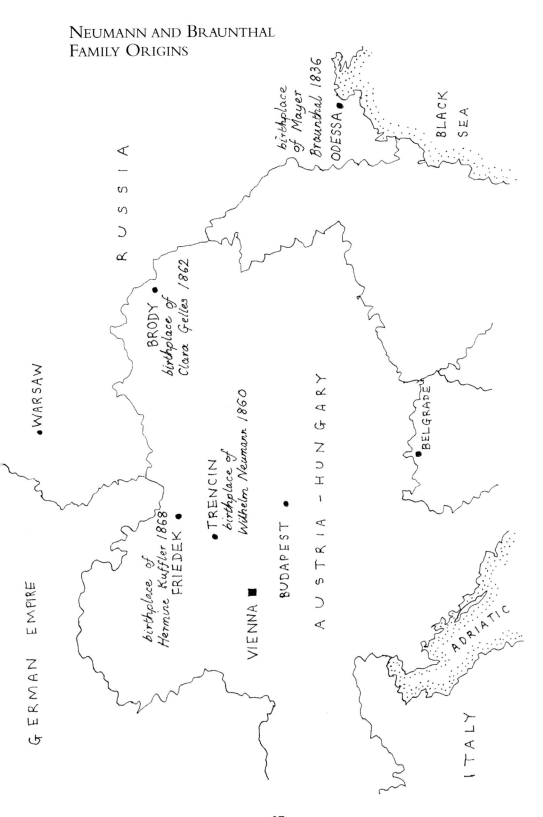

Map labels:

- WARSAW
- GERMAN EMPIRE
- RUSSIA
- BRODY — birthplace of Clara Gelles 1862
- birthplace of Mayer Braunthal 1836
- ODESSA
- BLACK SEA
- TRENCIN — birthplace of Wilhelm Neumann 1860
- birthplace of Hermine Kuffler 1868 — FRIEDEK
- VIENNA
- BUDAPEST
- AUSTRIA-HUNGARY
- BELGRADE
- ADRIATIC
- ITALY

The four grandparents have several things in common. None was born in Vienna. Three were brought up in a multi-lingual environment, Mayer speaking German with some knowledge of Russian and Polish, Clara speaking German and some Polish, Wilhelm with his German, Hungarian and Slovak, only Hermine speaking nothing but German as she arrived in Vienna in about 1870.

In addition the grandparents would have understood some Yiddish, but would not have spoken it. Basically the patois is German, but its authenticity depends on the degree of incorporating Hebrew words, and especially on the idiosyncratic use of grammar and syntax. It is not codified and like many ethnic languages relies on oral tradition, rather than phonetic transcription, let alone structured orthography. Although some isolated words became part of the rich Viennese-German catchment, my grandparents might only occasionally have used them. They were anxious to speak proper High German, culturally and socially so desirable.

Birth certificates and marriage certificates were issued by the relevant Jewish authorities. The denominational registration of births continued in Austria until the Second World War and my sister Eva and I are listed by the Israelitische Kultusgemeinde Wien, the religious administrative body. At school at the Bundesgymnasium in the 19th District, in Döbling, I was taught how to read Hebrew as part of my religious education, without necessarily knowing the meaning of every word. Key passages in Genesis, prayers, and liturgical texts had to be mastered practically by rote.

At my school, the professor teaching religion, a certain Benjamin Murmelstein, was very strict. He had devised an unforgettable system. In the selected passages for reading and translation, the Hebrew words were numbered consecutively, the numerals written above the text in pencil. The numbers were then transferred into a small vocabulary book in long columns, with the German next to them. Of course the syntax of the two languages is very different, making the Old Testament read: "In the beginning created God". No grammar of any kind was taught.

One day an inspector arrived, a kindly man who brought a book full of short sentences in Hebrew. He opened the book with a ceremonial flourish which did not augur well for us. We had never been asked to translate from the Hebrew unaided, and had always been helped along with continuous annotated German. Murmelstein was desperate and picked on Michael Schwind, a great friend of mine, to translate the few words. He had attended some Saturday afternoon Hebrew classes, but only managed the first word: "One", he said after some thought (he had learnt to count). After a lot of prompting the word 'swallow' was arrived at. Schwind knew the word 'makes' and the preceding negative adverb 'not'. The inspector went through three of the four seasons to leave Schwind with the logical conclusion that 'spring' was the missing word. I still see the inspector's triumphant face: "One swallow does not make a spring", he said. "Very good my boy".

After the Anschluss, Rabbi Murmelstein was a leading member of the Israelitsche Kultusgemeinde in Vienna, working with Adolf Eichmann, before himself being deported to Theresienstadt concentration camp in 1943, where he was the last elder of the Jewish Council. After the war, he was accused of collaboration with the Nazi authorities, although in an interview in 1975 he claimed that he tried to use his position to help Austrian Jews. He died in Rome in 1989.

The Neumann household was enlightened. There were no observances of any kind, no Friday prayers, no lighting of candles, no dietary restriction, no prohibition of Saturday travel. There was no hint of orthodoxy. My grandmother Hermine's mother, Auguste Kuffler, may have come from a more religious background. I have the beautiful leather-bound Book of Prayer that belonged to Moritz Aufricht, Auguste Kuffler's father, my great-great-grandfather. On the inside cover he wrote several lines in Hebrew, signed and dated Moritz Aufricht 1848. Hermine's own prayer book, published in 1885, shortly before her wedding, is bound in ivory with silver clasps. On the back page in beautiful handwriting, she listed the date of her marriage, the exact time, date and place of birth of her four children, referred to as our son, our daughter. In addition to the official names in birth registers, Jewish children in the 19th century were often given typical biblical or folk names which however were never used or recorded. Hermine added them in brackets: Paul (Meyer), Helene (Leah), Fanny (Fradel), Robert (Samuel). Fanny was Mizzi's original name.

Wilhelm never went to the synagogue. His wife Hermine certainly went once a year on the Day of Atonement. The Leopoldstädter Tempel at the end of the Ferdinandstrasse was only a few hundred yards away. Hermine and her sisters Stephanie and Olga had the same reserved seats for nearly forty years.

My visits to the local synagogue, in the 18th District, in Währing, were intermittent. Murmelstein, our professor of religion, was supposed to check our attendance at the special Saturday services for the young. As proof that we had been there, we had to produce a weekly calendar card at our next lesson, the so-called 'Kalenderblatt', which was given out during prayers. I remember the cards, passports, so to speak, to piety. None of the boys went regularly. Occasionally Murmelstein would enter the classroom with the single-word command: 'Kalenderblatt', and after the customary lecture on the importance of sustained religiosity, there was an upsurge in attendance, which however soon subsided.

The cards had Hebrew and German side by side, prayers, blessing and the relevant rubric from the Pentateuch. Even as a young boy, I admired the beautiful serifs of liturgical Hebrew, and the delicate Gothic typography of Bible German, twin symbols of a common culture, soon to be destroyed together with the temple and some of the children with whom I was praying.

The only time I went to the synagogue in the Leopoldstadt was in 1935, on the Day of Atonement. It was to be Hermine's last autumn. Lena, my aunt, arranged an even larger 'breakfast' in the Ferdinandstrasse, the evening meal after the twenty-four hour fast. There must have been two dozen or more people at table, the extended family, including some of my grandparents' brothers and sisters. The interconnecting double doors were opened to the next room to make more space. We ate off beautiful Limoges china, which is now in our home. The glass was from Lobmeier, a famous Viennese manufacturer, and a friend of Wilhelm's. The delicate designs were etched on fine glass, considered the height of elegance.

In the afternoon it had been arranged that I should join Hermine and her sisters, Stephanie and Olga in the synagogue, upstairs, on the women's balcony. At a certain juncture, the rabbi blows the ram's horn, the shofar, and I was anxious to see and hear this in its proper setting. On the stairs I met the temple servant, the Shames (a kind of verger) who gave me a stern look, but let me pass. Although I was only eleven, I was quite tall and looked older. "Who is this young man," he rightly thought, "who is joining the women on the holiest day of the year?"

CHAPTER 3

The Anschluss: flight from Vienna and Paul's arrest

When I visualise the past, the 19th century, the early lives of my grandparents, I think of Vienna. The houses where my parents were born were there. So were my grandparents' homes. For the first fourteen years of my life Vienna was home. On Saturday the 12th of March 1938, I lost it forever, and on Monday the 14th March, at about 2 o'clock, I said goodbye to my father on the platform of the Westbahnhof, and travelled with my mother to Zurich in Switzerland. A new life was about to unfold.

It is more than seventy years since then, but many memories have become prophetically ominous in retrospection. When we arrived in Feldkirch, the last station before the border, customs officials boarded the train and shouted: "Deutsche Passkontrolle" (German passport control). The customs officer, in his announcement, verbalised the momentous change which had formally occurred at midnight on Friday, the 11th March, when Austria ceased to exist. Afterwards my mother told me that when she heard the world 'German' it felt "so wie ein Stich ins Herz" (like a stab in the heart).

As they opened the passports, they picked out people with Jewish names. We had to get out and go to the customs hall, where the suitcases were thoroughly searched. Each item of clothing was held up and shaken. I was frisked. A young French woman was led off and came back crying. She had been forced to undress. They were looking for illegal export of cash. We were advised we should only take a light suitcase each, and a few schillings. I opened my violin case. They looked inside the instrument. Were there rolls of banknotes there? They did not look at the label. They probably did not know about them. In any case, it did not have a bogus Stradivarius label, which might have caused a problem.

Feldkirch was now German, and so was Vienna. After what seemed an eternity, the train moved on. Soon we stopped in Buchs, on the other side of the frontier. We were in Switzerland.

The relief was indescribable. My mother was sure that my father would follow shortly. My sister, Eva was already studying at Oxford. But on Saturday, the 19th of March my father was arrested, and was held in custody in Viennese prisons until May 1938, when he was released. It wasn't until the 7th July that he joined us in England.

Every hour of my last day in Vienna seems very real, everlastingly immediate. After breakfast I went to the floor above ours, to visit my friend Georg Pekarek, the son of the owner of the house. The previous two days, the Saturday and Sunday, the first two days of the Greater German Reich, we spent all day playing Monopoly. Our parents were glad we were out of the way.

By lunchtime on the 12th March practically every house had a swastika flag flying outside. Illegal Nazi depots had stored them in readiness. My father was worried because our block of flats had no flag. Pekarek was Jewish and the block of flats could easily be identified. My father went to the flat next door. There, his great friend, Richard Teschner, had his famous Marionette Theatre. Teschner was not Jewish. My father asked him to accompany him to the local police-station, about half-a-mile down the road. It was quickly established that Aryan tenants in blocks of flats owned by Jews were allowed to fly flags. They immediately obtained a flag. It must have seemed very surreal to them: My father organising the provision of a swastika flag with Richard Teschner, a humanist, deeply committed to fight Nazism, acting the role of enthusiastic support of the new order. The flag was very long and narrow, stretching down over several storeys, the infamous format of a Nazi banner, used in organised total political decoration. The house is on a corner. Hanging from the Teschner salon, the flag could be seen in the Gersthoferstrasse and in the Messerschmidtgasse. When my father came home my mother asked me to leave the room. She was terribly upset and frightened. To go to the police on the very first day of the Anschluss for whatever reason seemed to her quite wrong. "Sofort fängst du was an" (immediately you start things), she said.

Events were moving very fast, and had done so for the previous few weeks. On Sunday the 13th March, Adolf and Grete Redlich came to see my father. They were very great friends of my parents. He was a successful lawyer (Rechtsanwalt). What should they do, what advice could my father give them on that terrible day? "Leave at once", he said. He may have also told them that my mother and I would be leaving the following day. At any rate, I was not told until about midday on Monday. Once in New York, Adi Redlich, as he was called, changed his name to Adolphus Redley. He had become a very successful attorney. When I visited Adi and Grete in 1968, he showed me a big painting of a Vienna street scene from the 1910s. On Sunday, the 13th March, they stepped into a train, and left everything behind. When I saw the picture it had only recently been returned to them, an early example of restitution, which now half a century too late, is slowly being enacted.

Immediately on the 12th March, Czechoslovakia, Hungary and Italy either closed their frontiers or made entry capriciously hazardous. My father had found out that Switzerland was still open (without an entry visa). Air travel was still in its infancy. On the back of an opera programme the Dutch airline KLM proudly announce, in 1937, three flights per week to Amsterdam, with connecting flights to London. One had to go by train.

We arrived in Zurich late at night on the 14th March, and on the 15th went to the French consulate to apply for transit visas to travel through France to Belgium, thus avoiding the more direct route through Germany. That Tuesday, the 15th March, was my father's 50th birthday, the first day of my emigration, the first day as refugee. Oh how differently we had envisaged it. We were about to set off for the consulate. My mother stopped and said: "Bist du sicher, dass du mitkommen willst?" (Are you sure that you want to come with me?) The consulate was crowded with a long wait for visa applications, anxious people on the run.

When we returned to the hotel, we saw the newspapers in the lounge. They carried photographs from Vienna. This was the pre-television age, not yet saturated by ongoing news images, not yet softened by colour. The black and white prints are etched in my memory. We saw the Viennese marching along the Ringstrasse, swastikas everywhere, flags, banners, armbands, arms raised. And then there was a picture of Hitler outside St. Stephen's Cathedral being welcomed by Cardinal Innitzer, the Primate of Austria. A big rally had been arranged in the cathedral square, packed with chanting crowds. Church bells were ringing and a swastika banner had been hoisted from the tall spire. Innitzer had left the sanctuary of the episcopal palace and had walked to the centre of the square to greet the waiting Hitler. And then came the moment captured in the picture. Innitzer raised his hand in the Nazi salute. The 'Heil Hitler' of the Cardinal became the icon of Nazi triumph and Catholic submission.

Fateful miniature scenes are fixed in my memory. And now, as I think of my final days and weeks in Austria, they parade themselves, they want to be described, they want to be part of my testimony.

On Saturday February 12th 1938, exactly one month before the Anschluss, I was travelling by train back to Vienna with my school, after a week's skiing holiday in the mountains. Suddenly someone came into the compartment and said that Schuschnigg was in Berchtesgaden to see Hitler. I felt an instant terrible foreboding, framed by the question: what will happen to us?

I did not have to wait long for my answer.

Soon after lunch, on that 11th March, the last day of independent Austria, Vienna fell silent. The city was waiting. The radio played patriotic music and it was announced that Schuschnigg would speak to the nation. No one seemed to be about in the streets. People were gathering round their radios for the broadcast.

Rumours began to circulate that the plebiscite, Schuschnigg's last minute gamble to confirm Austria's future, scheduled for Sunday 13th March, had been cancelled. As the afternoon wore on, I became aware of the tension outside.

Usually the noise from the street was audible right up to our second floor. But nothing moved. The eery stillness was so tangible you could feel it. I listened to the broadcast, sitting in my parents' bedroom. Fanny, our faithful cook was there. My parents were out.

Schuschnigg told the people that he was yielding to superior force and that he did not want bloodshed. At the Nuremberg Trial of Nazi War Criminals, after the war, Goering boasted about his part in the fateful events of the 11th March. He was in Berlin, Hitler in Berchtesgaden. The two spoke to each other several times that day. Goering was in constant touch with the Austrian Nazis and issued an ultimatum, that unless the Federal President nominated a candidate for Chancellor and formed a government according to German government directives, German troops would cross the Austrian frontier at seven-thirty that evening.

After the broadcast they played the national anthem, the Haydn hymn. I felt a deep sadness. I was afraid. I knew that the old world, my childhood world had gone. After the anthem, the silence outside continued for a few minutes. And then we heard, coming down the street, the ominous crescendo of marching feet. We opened our window and looked down. A column of perhaps a hundred people or more, three or four abreast, was passing our house in the Gersthoferstrasse. They were on their way to the Ring, the circular boulevard round the centre of the city, to join tens of thousands in their Nazi jubilation.

In the middle of the front row, a man was carrying a swastika flag on a pole over his shoulder. Men and women were shouting Sieg Heil, Sieg Heil, Sieg Heil, (victory hail) the Nazi slogan, in time with their marching feet. All along they must have seen people waving and cheering and giving the Hitler salute. They had practically passed our house when someone in the last two or three rows must have noticed two silent faces looking down. Word must quickly have spread: Jews are up there. A monumental page of history had only just been turned, but they expected an immediate response, a raised hand of salute that physical gesture, that Heil, that shout. Anyone who did not shout must be a Jew.

And as the tail end of the marchers passed by, several women looked back at us over their shoulders, shouting abuse and waving their fists. One of them screamed five unforgettable prophetic words in her Viennese dialect: "Mir wearns euch schon zeigen" (we'll show you). At that moment, Fanny, a typical gentile country girl from Lower Austria, was tarred with the brush of racial hatred, because of her association with Jews.

Uncle Robert left Vienna immediately after Chancellor Schuschnigg's broadcast. Twelve hours after Robert left, on Saturday morning, on the very first morning of the Anschluss, two Gestapo men rang the bell at his flat. Agnes (Nessy), Robert's wife, opened the door. "Wo ist der Jude Neumann?" (Where is the Jew Neumann?), they demanded. After the war, she told me the story several times. She always emphasized "der Jude". In the singular, preceded by the definite article, the collective noun was used in the pejorative vocabulary of anti-semitism. Nessy was confronted by evil on her doorstep. "Sie hätten ihn erschlagen," she said (they would have killed him). Nessy was convinced that he had been high up on their hit list. He was a prominent member of the Board of Directors of the Creditanstalt. According to Nessy, his outspoken manner had made him enemies. In any case the Nazis targeted leading bankers, doctors, dentists, professors and lawyers. They were too late for Robert.

My last weeks in Austria were, of course, only the final scenes of a tragedy. It started about five years earlier with Hitler's rise to power. I became increasingly aware that for Jews across the border in Germany, life was terrible. I was only nine years old when the reality of Nazi Germany insidiously cast a growing shadow over our lives. Friends of my parents started to arrive from Germany, Gustav and Toni Stolper from Berlin and Irma Simon from Frankfurt. A year later, in February 1934, there was the civil war, lasting about a week, in which the clerico-fascist government of Dollfuss crushed the military uprising of the Social Democrats, and a few months later on the 25th July Dollfuss was murdered in a Nazi Putsch. Both events are deeply engraved in my memory. On the morning of the 12th February, the army raided the weapons depository of the 'Republikanischer Schutzbund' in Linz, the capital city of the province of Upper Austria. A year earlier, Dollfuss had suspended parliamentary government on a technical issue. He had no intention of recalling it, but instead was busy laying the foundations of a totalitarian corporate state. Austria had a small standing army, but it also had active paramilitary organisations: the Heimwehr, built on the model of Mussolini's black-shirts, on the right, and the Schutzbund, the armed wing of the Social Democracy, fighting for the ideals of socialism.

Dollfuss closed down the Socialist daily newspaper *Die Arbeiter Zeitung* on the staff of which Julius Braunthal had been a prominent journalist. Julius had also founded and edited the popular *Das Kleine Blatt*, a complementary weapon in the fight against fascism, to support the more doctrinaire erudite *Arbeiter Zeitung*. *Das Kleine Blatt* (the small paper) appealed to the ordinary worker. I remember the great novelty of the daily cartoon. It was called 'Wamperl und Stamperl'. The two men discussed serious issues in satirical dialogue. Wamperl ('fatso' in Viennese slang) and Stamperl (the argumentative foot-stamping one) must have reminded readers of Laurel and Hardy whose comic films so often had a deeper message.

Julius was arrested immediately in the morning of the 12th February. Not only was he a prominent Socialist journalist, but he was on the executive committee of the party and of the Schutzbund. His political conviction was reflected in his family life. He married Tini appropriately on the first of May 1917, Labour Day, and he called his older son Fritz after Friedrich Adler, a leading Socialist, a great friend of Julius and the son of Viktor Adler, the founder of Austrian Social Democracy.

Julius thought that he might be executed for High Treason. Three days before the coup, on the 9th February, he had been asked by Otto Bauer, the Socialist leader, to draft a 'Manifesto to the People of the Austrian Republic'. Three type-written copies had been prepared, and Julius added a few sentences in his handwriting as a result of suggestions made by Otto Bauer. Force should be met by force should Dollfuss attempt to destroy the parliamentary constitution. One copy Julius managed to destroy, one was with the printers, but the third was in his office. In the event, after thirteen months in prison, Julius was released on condition that he immediately leave the country.

One can imagine Tini's anxiety. Her husband was imprisoned by his mortal enemies. Her mother-in-law, Julius' mother, my grandmother Clara, was watching the point blank bombardment of the Karl Marx Hof from her window in Heiligenstadt. She could see the terrible gashes in the long chain of huge apartment blocks, which housed thousands of workers. Tini immediately packed some clothes for her sons Fritz and Otto, similarly aptly named after the Socialist leader, Otto Bauer, and sent the boys to us in the Gersthoferssstrasse. She wanted them out of her house, away from Vienna, out of Austria. She did not want them to watch at close quarters the terrible fate that might overtake their father. And that is how my cousins came to stay with us from the 12th to about the 15th February, after which they travelled to Brussels and lived with their aunt Hilde, a staging post on their eventual emigration to England. I cannot forget the two days they spent with us. Their father was imprisoned. They had lost their world. They were about to say farewell to Vienna. Little did I know then, that exactly four years and one month later I would also be leaving, and that my father would be imprisoned a few days later.

On the first morning of their stay, my mother asked me to take Fritz and Otto, later called Freddy and Tom, to the Türkenschanzpark, the park of the Turkish fortifications, only about half a mile from our home.

In 1683, the Turkish army brought its victorious march through the Balkans right up to the gates of Vienna. Kara Mustafa, the Grand Vizir at the head of a 100,000 strong army, calculated that the city would fall after a short siege. But Christendom came to the rescue in the form of King Sobieski of Poland. After a series of forced marches, his twelve thousand men were positioned on high ground, overlooking the city, on the Kahlenberg, one of the last foothills of the Alps. Kara Mustafa, to guard his rear, built a stockade, a redoubt and dug ditches and trenches. Archaeological remains of the earthworks still exist. But it was of no avail. On the 12th September 1683 a bloody battle was fought there, the Turkish army was defeated and the siege was lifted.

Two and a half centuries later, on that 12th February in 1934, a second siege was enacted near the site of that memorable battle. As I walked with my cousins to the Türkenschanzpark we passed an improvised army machine-gun post. One soldier was lying on his stomach in the traditional posture, his belt of ammunition neatly spread at his side. The gun was pointing at the Gemeindehaus (the large municipal complex of workers' flats) in the Gersthoferstrasse. Standing behind the soldier on the ground were two men drawn up in support. Another soldier was patrolling the courtyard, his rifle at the ready, directed at the windows. Large white sheets were hanging from them, in the traditional gesture of surrender. After it was all over, the government announced that large quantities of illegal weapons had been discovered in the various Gemeindehäuser, but people were sceptical and thought a lot had been planted for propaganda purposes. The strange thing was the eerie silence of the scene. As we drew near we stopped speaking. There were no cars, but then in 1934 cars in the Gersthoferstrasse were few and far between. The tram, the number 41, was not running, at any rate none passed us. We were the only pedestrians. When we came back about an hour later, the soldiers were still there. The tension was great. Vienna was waiting. My mother was upset that she had sent us out at such dangerous times. Word had got round that the Gemeindehäuser were under siege and that one might get caught up in cross-fire.

It was all over in about three to four days. Nine members of the Schutzbund were hanged. Only the intervention of England and France prevented further executions. There were hundreds of casualties on both sides. I remember photographs in the newspapers, of a long line of draped coffins being driven along the Ringstrasse, past the Imperial Palace to the cathedral of St. Stefan for the state funeral. That was for the army and the police. The Socialists buried their dead with the bitterness of defeat.

But in the event, there were no victors, no winners, only losers. The Austrian Nazis watched from the sidelines as the government destroyed Socialism, their real enemy. Dollfuss was doing their work for them. As the conflict drew to a close, Vienna was covered with political propaganda posters. Hoardings and billboards proclaimed that the government had saved Austria from Bolshevism, and that the workers had carefully prepared for the armed struggle. "Here are the photos to prove it, look at them," they shouted. There were pictures of arsenals of weapons in the cellars of the Karl Marx Hof. On my walk to school, I passed a poster. I vividly remember it after seventy years. It must have stayed up for many weeks, and twice daily visual repetition left its mark. Four cut-out figures of policemen in uniform were standing in a straight line, each chest covered with a rifle-range target. The bulls-eye was near the heart, concentric circles marking the degree of accuracy of the aim. Above it, in extra-bold capital letters, it read: "Das waren ihre Zielscheiben" (These were their targets!). Underneath it said: "Die Schießstätte war im Keller" (The shooting-range was in the cellar).

A few months later, further bloodshed was to follow. As usual we were in Altaussee for our summer holidays. On Wednesday the 25th July 1934 I was in the kitchen of our rented house (Annerl, Wimmer, Salzbergstrasse). I was speaking to our cook, our faithful Fanny Lechner, and I suddenly said, out of the blue: "Vielleicht wird der Dollfuss ermordet" (Perhaps Dollfuss will be murdered). I may have overhead conversations about the ever-increasing pressure which Germany applied to Austria in the preceding months: the supply of weapons from across the border, the transfer of funds to finance subversive activities, the provision of dynamite for bomb attacks, the support for numerous assassinations of political enemies, closure of the frontier, so painful to the Austrian economy. But even so my remark to Fanny was inexplicable. A few hours later, at 1 o'clock, Dollfuss was shot. Early in the afternoon, the news reached us in Altaussee. I turned to Fanny and said: "Ich hab's dir doch gesagt" (I did tell you about it). I still see her face, her finely chiselled, delicate features frozen in the frightening grip of telepathy. Of course, I should have asked her for written confirmation, at any rate after the war, when I wrote to her on two occasions. In my life, coincidences have occurred which defy explanation. How then should one approach events which imply incredibly remote correlation or none at all?

In the confusion of civil disorder, in the first two days before the army could take full control, there were skirmishes throughout Austria. Fighting broke out between Nazi and government supporters. In the Alps men took their shotguns, roamed the forests and patrolled the villages. They looked for enemies with daredevil amateur bravado. They wanted to avenge the assassination of Dollfuss. They faced those who rejoiced in it, those who saw it as the first step on the way to make Austria a province of Hitler's Germany.

On Thursday 25th July, the day after the assassination, the entry in my aunt Lena's diary reads: "Vormittag und Nachmittag im Ort, abends bei Resi mit Dr. Arnstein, dann noch bei Fritters Radio hören. In Mitterndorf wird gekämpft". (In the morning and in the afternoon in the village. In the evening at Resi's [my mother] with Dr. Arnstein, and then also to Fritters to listen to the radio. In Mitterndorf there is fighting.)

Mitterndorf is a neighbouring village. On that Thursday morning the cry was raised that a group of Nazis had taken up their position there. Some hot-heads in Altaussee got together to drive them out. To give their venture the maximum authority they recruited the most prominent people in the village. And that is how the family Frischmut, the owners of the Seehotel, the premier hotel in Altaussee, lost their son.

The funeral was a few days later in the beautiful village cemetery, by the lake. It was the first time in my life that I had been to a funeral. With other villagers I walked past the open grave, looked down at the coffin and scattered some earth. I knew so many of them. After all, we Neumanns had been coming for so many years. Eduard, a brother of my grandfather, first came to Altaussee in about 1897. He had two daughters, Trude and Hedy and a son Fritz. My father, his two sisters, Lena and Mizzi, and Robert, his brother, joined them most of the time. Imagine the Neumann girls before the First World War! In 1912 Lena and Trude were 22, Mizzi was 17 and Hedy was 15! They were beautiful, vivacious, musical, romantic, intelligent. The connection with Altaussee continued right up to the summer of 1937, the last summer before the Anschluss.

Throughout all these upheavals life just continued. On the 3rd April 1934, Lena went to *Ballo in Maschera* conducted by Bruno Walter. On the 18th April she heard *The Song of the Earth*, again conducted by Bruno Walter. On the 23rd April she saw a play *Alt-Heidelberg* by Meyer-Förster with Paula Wessely as Käthie; *Das kleine Kaffee* by Benatzky followed on the 4th May. On the 30th May Lena went to *Eugene Onegin*, on the 8th June, Huberman and Schnabel gave a violin and piano recital, on the 16th June followed *The Merry Wives of Windsor* and Lena went to *Fidelio* on the 19th June conducted by Clemens Krauss. The cast must have been memorable. Lotte Lehmann sang Leonore, Völker was Florestan, Rocco was sung by Manowarda, Jerger sang Pizarro and Helletsgruber was Marzelline.

Salzburg carried on as usual. On the 23rd August Lena went to the Salzburg Festival and heard Toscanini conduct Mozart's *Haffner Symphony*, the Brahms-Haydn Variations and Beethoven's Seventh Symphony. Two days later, again in Salzburg, Lena saw *Don Giovanni*, conducted by Bruno Walter. On that occasion Ezio Pinza sang Don Giovanni, Dino Borgioli was Don Ottavio and Donna Elvira was sung by Luise Helletsgruber.

In the Autumn of 1937, the Rotunde, the large circular Imperial pavilion, caught fire and burnt to the ground. I could watch the conflagration from the high position of my home, right across the city. And then, a little later, it was the sky's turn to light up with the Northern Lights of the aurora borealis. That hardly ever happens so far south. It was as if the heavens predicted disaster, which was not slow in coming.

On Monday the 14th March 1938, my last day in Vienna, I had just settled down to a game of Monopoly with my friend Georg Pekarek in his flat, above ours. It must have been about mid-morning. My mother came upstairs. Her face was white and drawn. She told me to stop playing and to come home. As we entered our flat, my father's long-time secretary, a Mrs. Sternbach, was just leaving. My mother asked me to say good-bye to Mrs Sternbach. I escorted her from our hall along a corridor to our front door. As I opened the door she burst into tears. I did not then know that Mrs. Sternbach had been summoned from my father's office to come to the Gersthoferstrasse to say good-bye to my mother. I did not bid her a farewell with fateful finality. For me it would mean immediate departure, but Mrs Sternbach did not manage to escape. She was deported and murdered in a concentration camp. As I came back into the hall my mother said we were going to Brussels and that I could take one suitcase, and only a few of my special things. We would be leaving in under two hours. I started crying and she tried to comfort me by saying that we would be staying with Aunt Tini and my cousin Otto (Tom).

I got some music together, the Mozart Sonatas, the Schubert Sonatinas and the Vivaldi *Concerto in A minor*, and of course my Enzensberger violin, circa 1890. It must have been about lunch time. Through the intercommunicating doors from my room into my parents' bedroom I could see my grandmother Clara standing by the window. She had come from Heiligenstadt to say good-bye. She turned to her daughter and said: "Fahr nicht weg. Lass den Mann nicht allein!" (Don't leave, don't leave your husband alone!) For a split-second my mother hesitated and said: "Du meinst, ich soll ihn nicht allein lassen?" (You mean, I should not leave him alone?) And then she quietly said: "Ich muss den Hansi wegbringen" (I must get Hansi away). Soon we had packed and were ready to go. It was time to part. My father had gone through the hall, along the very long corridor to the front door and was waiting. In the hall, by the door that led to the corridor, stood my grandmother and Fanny. They were strangely drawn up side by side. They stood there in silence, grandmother nearer to the door. First my mother kissed Fanny and then my grandmother, and walked on, and then I kissed Fanny. As I bent down to kiss my grandmother I knew I would never see her again. No one spoke. We all felt that words could no longer say what we felt. As I started to walk along the corridor my dog Cherie, my lovely fox-terrier, a gift from Aunt Nessy, started to follow.

Something that could only have taken a few seconds has become deeply engraved in my memory. A flashback can grow into a timeless enormity.

There she was, this seventy-five year old lady saying farewell so quietly, so bravely, subdued by the urgency of parting, oppressed by the fear that all Jews felt immediately, a dread that settled on everything.

I said farewell to Vienna a long time ago. It was in a different century, in a different millennium, before a world war.

But that day, the 14th March 1938, on the railway platform of the Westbahnhof, seems like yesterday. My father took me by the arm and drew me aside. "Benimm dich ritterlich" (behave chivalrously) he said. It was part of the private vocabulary of family language, of family speak, used when I might be going out with my mother to a concert or out to meet some of her friends at a fashionable café in town, presumably to be displayed.

In the awakening world of father and son, of man to man, my father drew upon the medieval image of chivalry. I was supposed to assume the role of knight-protector in attendance, a symbolic escort. It was, of course, an indirect way of saying that I should behave properly. The smile, with which my father invariably accompanied this admonition transfigured its inner meaning, and I was proud to be given the make-believe responsibility of looking after and protecting my mother.

But on that day my father did not smile. His big brown eyes looked at me with infinite sadness. He placed my mother into my ultimate care, afraid of the future. In that second, when he spoke to me like that, I felt old, I felt grown up, and the fairy-tale imagery turned into the harsh world of the refugee. How many times have I thanked providence that our separation was not final, that my father's waving goodbye was not his last gesture to me.

Ten months later, in a letter of congratulation for my 15th birthday, my father reminded me of that departure. It is a declaration of love and a certificate of praise, set within the framework of reflection so dear to him. The letter is still in German, but once war broke out, my father wrote in English. He did not want me to have possible difficulties, receiving mail in enemy language.

6 Acol Road
London NW6
17 January 1939

Mein lieber Hans, auch Giovanni!

Erinnerst Du Dich, was ich Dir bei Deiner Abreise von Wien im März vorigen Jahres sagte, als Du Miene machtest, ein wenig traurig zu sein, und ich Dich bitten mußte, der Muloni tapfer zur Seite zu stehen? Ich sagte Dir, Du seiest doch schon vierzehn Jahre alt und dieses Alter bedeute bei allen Völkern von altersher einen Einschnitt. Man werde von da ab in die Gesellschaft der jungen <u>Männer</u> aufgenommen.

Nun vollendest Du morgen das erste Lebensjahr als junger <u>Mann</u>, wirst fünfzehn. Ich freue mich so sehr, Dir sagen zu können, daß Du Dich <u>sehr gut</u> gehalten hast. Ich weiß genau, daß es mitunter gar nicht leicht war für Dich, Dich in eine so völlig veränderte Umgebung einzugewöhnen. Aber Du hast das sehr schön gemacht, warst fast immer guter Laune und hast der Muloni diese sehr schwere Zeit tragen helfen wie ein 'Ritter'. Daß Du bei all dem in der Schule so ausgezeichnet abgeschnitten hast, ist eine Leistung, mit der ich ganz besonders glücklick bin und so kann ich Dir zu Deinem Geburtstag im doppelten Sinne des Wortes gratulieren...

(My dear Hans, my dear Giovanni,

Do you remember what I said to you in March last year as you were leaving Vienna and were sad, and when I had to ask you courageously to support Muloni (your mother)? I told you that you were now already fourteen years old, an age which traditionally signified a turning point in all societies. From then on one joined the company of young <u>men</u>.

And now tomorrow you have lived through the first year as a young <u>man</u> and will be fifteen. I am so very happy to be able to tell you that you fulfilled your role <u>very well.</u> I am fully aware that from time to time it was not at all easy for you to get used to such changing surroundings. But you coped very well, nearly always cheerful and really helped Muloni bear the burden of these very difficult times like a 'knight'. The fact that you performed so excellently at school is an achievement with which I am particularly happy, and I can thus congratulate you on your birthday in two senses of the word.)

So many were less fortunate. My friend, Walter Jellinek, saw his parents for the last time as he left the station on a 'Kindertransport' (a rescue train for Jewish children) some months later.

As our train drew out, a symbol of German Vienna came into view. Outside, in the square, German police were lined up. I had seen photographs of German policemen, but to see them in real life, in their dreaded uniforms, wearing their frightening tall helmets, confirmed fateful history.

Friends of my parents, a Mr and Mrs Kohn, shared our compartment. After a short while, the doors were opened and two men in Nazi uniform, in their brown shirts and swastika armbands, demanded to see the contents of the suitcases. It was a prelude to the luggage inspection at the frontier. The younger man, hardly more than an overgrown school-boy, asked my mother and Mrs Kohn to empty the cases. Mr Kohn and I were ordered to stand in the corridor on each side of the older man who was watching the proceedings. His face wore a mask of complete indifference. No interaction here at the sight of Jews in exodus. In a terrifying way we had become less than human, things that had to be got rid of. I remember the blankness in his eyes, the impassivity in his expression, all hiding ultimate cruelties.

The other man was looking through my mother's things. And then he asked: "Wohin fahren Sie?" (where are you going?) She replied: "Ich besuche meine Schwester in England" (I am visiting my sister in England). "Eine schöne Zeit haben Sie sich ausgesucht für Vergnügungsreisen" (you have picked a nice time for a pleasure trip), he replied sarcastically. He looked at her and then asked: "Sind Sie eine Jüdin?" (are you a Jewess?) "Ja" my mother answered. After they had gone, my mother was in a great state of shock and had forgotten the conversation. "Hat er mich das gefragt?" (did he ask me that?) she said.

The scene in the railway compartment was a cameo of the age-old Jewish history of persecution and expulsion. The racist question and the terrified answer form the epilogue to my mother's half-century residence in Vienna. She had to affirm her Judaism, soon to be superseded by her conversion to Roman Catholicism.

The change in my father's life was instantaneous. Overnight his world collapsed. No longer was he a successful lawyer, a Rechtsanwalt with a prestigious flourishing practice, a well-respected member of the Vienna Chamber of Advocates. The social respect accorded to him was gone. Irrelevant now that he was the son of Regierungsrat Wilhelm Neumann, or that some of his clients, also his friends, like Bernhard Altmann, Paul Khuner, or Paul Zsolnay, were house-hold names as industrialists or publishers.

My father, who had a deep respect for the sanctity of law, who had worked all his life to uphold it, was soon to experience how it was cruelly broken. Tuesday, the 15th March, was my father's 50th birthday. It was a sad day for him. His intention was to wind up his affairs, to close his office properly and then to follow us as quickly as possible. On Thursday, 17th March, two policeman came for my father, but he was out. They told Fanny that they would come back soon. Very early on Saturday, the 19th, they returned. Fanny offered them some coffee. They declined. My father quickly got ready and they left. He was taken in the first week of arrests.

The factual outline of my father's imprisonment conceals something unimaginable and indescribable. He was first of all taken to the Central Police Jail in the Rossauerlände, taken over by the Gestapo. He told me afterwards that there were eleven men in one cell. On the 15th April he was transferred to the jail of the Landesgericht (the Central Criminal Court). There he was in cell No. 188. He was released on the 18th May.

From the first jail in the Rossauerlände, he wrote five postcards to his sister Lena in the Ferdinandstrasse, and from the Landesgericht he wrote three more times. On the 19th May on his first morning as a free man, he wrote to my mother in England. He arrived in England a few weeks later.

The cards were censored. In his first card on the 21st March, two days after his arrest, he asks Lena to send a toothbrush, toothpaste, a face flannel, a towel, soap (a small piece), hair brush, a pair of socks, handkerchiefs, a paper cup. He writes: "Sollte ich, was ich nicht weiss, länger hier bleiben, so wirst Du's hier oder durch Mezio erfahren. Frage auch ob Bücher, Zeitungen, Schokolade, Äpfel gestattet sind und dann schicke das eine oder andere…" (Should I have to stay here for a longer period, which I do not know, you will be notified either here or through Mezio [a code name for Muzzo, my grandfather's younger brother]. Also ask if books, newspapers, chocolate, apples are permitted and then send me one or the other thing…)

My father must have left just as he was, without taking anything. He concludes the card by asking how everyone is and how his office is coping. On the 29th March he thanks Lena for her card of the 21st March, and for some laundry. He wants to know how everyone is (everyone is underlined). He asks for a towel, a flannel, two handkerchiefs, and adds the words: "Mir geht es gut" (I am well). On the 8th April he thanks Lena for her card of the 3rd April. After dealing with the collection and provision of his laundry he asks after everyone, and sends greetings. He writes: "Grüsse Vater, Resi, Kinder. Wie geht es ihnen und Dir?" (Send greetings to father, Resi, the children. How are they and how are you?) His father Wilhelm had died on the 2nd April. The following day, on the 3rd April, Lena did not want to mention it in her card. She did not want to tell, to add to his sadness. From then on Lena did not specifically mention Wilhelm in her cards.

My father told me only a few things about his imprisonment but he described his homecoming. On the 18th May, on the day of his release he went straight to the Ferdinandstrasse. As he climbed the stairs to the second-floor flat he knew that his father had died. ("Wie ich die Treppen hinaufgestiegen bin hab' ich gewusst dass der Vater gestorben ist.") My father must have felt the significance in Lena's avoidance of Wilhelm's name, of any reference to 'father'. Immediately after the funeral Lena was unable to write at all. On the 12th April my father writes that since Lena's card of the 3rd April he had not heard from her, but hopes that everyone is well and they would soon see each other again. Hitherto Lena had written every third day, as in my father's postcard to her of the 4th April he acknowledges the cards of the 21st, 24th and 27th March.

My father's first communication from the Landesgericht is written on the 16th April. On the 28th April, he thanks Lena for her cards of the 14th, 20th and 24th. He explains that henceforth he would be allowed to write only about once every two weeks. They were also told that they could only receive mail at longer intervals. He asks after his father, and writes: "I received money on two occasions, once 20 Marks, and once 3 Marks. On the second counterfoil I seem to recognise father's handwriting." (Ich erhielt zweimal Geld, einmal 20 Mark und einmal 3 Mark. Auf dem letteren Abschnitt glaube ich Vaters Schrifft zu erkennen.) He thanks Lena for organising the filling in of a form from the Vienna Chamber of Advocates. After instructions to the office, which include tax liabilities, insurance premiums, applications of tax deferment for some of his clients, my father concludes: "Ich bin körperlich gut beisammen. Nur habe ich den lebhaften Wunsch, bald vernommen zu werden. Aber ich kann mir vorstellen welcher Berg von Akten zu bewältigen ist". (I am physically all right. But I have the ardent desire to be interrogated soon. But I can imagine what a mountain of paperwork has to be processed…) It is touching how my father clung to the vestiges of legal procedure. Very soon direct deportation to the camps became routine, the first and only administrative act being the allocation of a camp number, tattooed on the prisoner's arm.

On my father's postcard of the 5th May, there is a request for material for a spring suit or rather autumn suit, obviously wanted for a bribe. He had been arrested soon after his 50th birthday and it gave him the opportunity to ask for something obviously not intended for him! "Ihr wolltet mir zum Gerburtstag einen Kleiderstoff und Selfix Socken kaufen. Ich nehme dankbar an und bitt um Stoff für einen Frühjahrs bezw. Herbstanzug und verschiedenfarbige Strümpfe (Wolle)". (For my birthday, you wanted to buy me fabric for a suit and Selfix socks. I accept gratefully, and ask for fabric for a spring, or rather autumn suit, and stockings of various colours [wool].)

But the card also contains one of my father's poems.

Und wenn Du nachts dem Rauschen Deines Blutes
Nachlauschest in die grosse Dunkelheit
Und wach liegst im Verfluten ohne Schwere,
Dann bist Du Anbeginn und Ewigkeit,
Bist leidbereit und neuen Wegemutes
Und nur noch Fracht auf Gottes Zukunftsfähre.

(And when at night you listen to your bloodstream
Rushing to great darkness
And lie awake, weightless in the flood
You are then beginning and eternity,
Prepared for sorrow, with new courage for the journey
And now just freight upon God's future ferry.)

Later, in his hand-written book of poems, my father added the title 'Trost im Dunkel' (Solace in the Dark) and underneath the poem he wrote 'Geschrieben im Mai 1938, in der Zelle 188 des Landesgerichtes Wien' (Written in May 1938 in cell 188 at the Central Criminal Court, Vienna).

My father told me that in the Landesgericht he was locked up with another man, different from the crowded cage of the Gestapo prison in the Rossauerlände. I tried to imagine how he wrote that poem in cell 188. Would the other prisoner have asked to see it, would he have understood it? What sort of person was he?

They lived side by side, one belovedly familiar, the other a shadow without detail, united by their fearful fate. They must have talked, there must have been interaction, but my father was unwilling to verbalise, to formalise the chain of episodes that made up his time in prison. He came to terms with it by shutting it out, by exorcising evil, and I respected his silence.

I realised no answers would ever be forthcoming, until the day, more than sixty years later, when I made the most exciting discovery. I was looking, once again, through my father's book of manuscript poems, when I saw a thin piece of yellow tissue, tucked into the folds of the back cover. Suddenly it was in my hand, emerging from the camouflage of years, where it had been pressed as a transparency against the back of the book, its colour merging with the ochre of the manila binding.

It was a poem.

Paul Neumann, dem Freund
und Leidgenossen
zu eigen

Und wenn des Tags die Seeligkeit der Ferne
Dich lockt aus enger, steinbedrängter Haft,
Blick <u>in</u> Dich: Sieh dort Sonnenpracht und Sterne,
In Dir Gott täglich neuen Himmel schafft.
Und Vogel Leid auf schwarzen Adlerschwingen
Wird zum Zenith mit Deiner Seele dringen.

28. April   *Franz Kobler*

(For Paul Neumann, the friend
and companion in sorrow
for him alone

And when a day of blissful distance
Lures you from the narrow stone-tight prison
Look within: see the glorious sun and stars,

62

For you, each day, God newly forms a heaven,
And bird of sorrow on black eagle wings
Will thrust your soul to Zenith's firmament.)

Two poems from cell 188! Franz Kobler had taken care to make his dedication look elegant. It was, after all, a presentation. In happier times he would have inscribed a leather autograph album or the title page of a book. But in April 1938, in the Landesgericht, he addressed my father on a small scrap of tissue paper used to interleave laundry. Prisoners were allowed to receive washing.

With a soft pencil he emphasised the thick and the thin, the bold and the hair-line of old-fashioned writing. He must have written very carefully on the delicate paper, decorating it with his personal calligraphy. How was the poem brought out? It does not bear the censor's stamp. My father probably folded it into one of his books. For the two men, there was no second opportunity.

A few days later, my father responded to Franz Kobler's poem with his own poem "Trost im Dunkel". The reply is beautifully balanced, the same length, the same classical feeling of pentameter scansion. My father repeated Kobler's opening words. He forged a link. Both verses rhyme, but my father changed the close pattern of the rhymed couplets. He spread the poetic sound.

My father was deeply poetic by nature. He decorated his diction with adjectival embellishment and with old-fashioned classically-based subordinate clauses, so beloved by the German language. He spoke with the rhythmic cadence of the dramatic actor, and in his poems he could mould the language into the discipline of the sonnet, the explosive density of the epigram, the elegy of valediction, the ballad of transfigured narrative, the eulogy of love. And as my eyes caress the text, as they linger over the beloved script, I am intensely aware of his presence. I hear my father's voice. On several occasions, I asked him to recite the poem to me. His onomatopoeic "Rauschen" was deep and round, so musical, lingering on the vowels. In "nachlauschest" he brought out the poetic beauty of the repeated sound. For "Dunkelheit" he shaded his voice. He released the "d" slowly to make way for a profound "u", evocative of endless darkness. I remember the word "Fracht", the only monosyllabic noun. The opening consonants were resonant, not bright and hard, not clipped, the rolled "r" a trill or ornament, the dramatic gracing of acceptance.

I discovered that pre-war Landesgericht documentation had been preserved. In due course, I received copies of my father's prison registration and court records. He had been brought in by the Gestapo from the prison in the Rossauerlände. His details are also recorded in a Gestapo file, the Namens-Index Kartei, K4 (Index of names file, K4) under the heading Gestapo.

And my urgent question was answered. It confirmed the poem's provenance. Yes, in cell 188 there was a fellow prisoner, Franz Kobler. He was there when my father arrived.

Dr. Franz Kobler was a lawyer, a Rechtsanwalt like my father. He was the author of several books on Zionism, pacifism and Jewish history. Prior to the Anschluss, the Nazis had prepared lists of prominent Jews in banking, industry and commerce. Within the professions, lawyers and doctors were singled out. Journalists and authors were easy targets. Franz Kobler and Paul Neumann were taken in the very first wave of arrests, Kobler the Zionist Rechtsanwalt and activist and Paul Neumann a member of a group of Monarchist lawyers. They would have welcomed the restoration of the Habsburg monarchy and the creation of a Central European and Balkan federation, with Vienna, the Pearl of the Danube, as the capital.

Both men were released without charges being brought, first my father on the 18th May and then Franz Kobler on the 18th June. They were the fortunate ones. In the five weeks that they were together, they must have talked for many hours about their respective circumstances, their families and especially their hopes and their fears. Time was not on their side. The threat of deportation, of instant separation, must have alternated with hopes of release.

They got to know each other immediately. They discovered a mutual love of literature, especially poetry. My father had written many poems as a way of life. He had a mastery over the language, a delicate authority, a sovereignty. With a few syllables he could conjure up a universe. He used his personal palette of words to paint his poetry.

Perhaps Franz Kobler suggested to my father that he would write a poem, a few lines to transfigure his thoughts, to universalise his feelings. And he would expect a reply. It had to be short, paper was at a premium. They would call upon their preconceptual capacity, do without interim versions and directly transcribe their fully-fashioned poems. Kobler was to use a piece of tissue, my father sent out his poem on a postcard. Franz Kobler was a professional author, my father a romantic amateur. But they both felt they could converse in the language beyond words.

And so it came about that the two men wrote to each other. Kobler's poem is dated the 28th April and my father's reply is on a postcard dated the 5th May. In those seven days my father may well have thought that the few lines were his last poetic utterance, his legacy, his solace.

Franz Kobler was fortunate. He managed to travel with his wife safely to England via Switzerland, and after the war continued his emigration to the United States.

Immediately after my father's arrest my sister Eva received a telegram from Adi Redlich, the old family friend who, on my father's advice on that 13th March had already left Vienna. It read something like: "Your father arrested. In great danger". Eva was halfway through her first year at Oxford. She arranged to see the Vice-Chancellor of the University, and she also approached Sir Michael Palairet, the last British Ambassador in Vienna, who had been recalled after the annexation. Sir Michael's daughter, Anne, was a fellow student at the Society of Home Students, which later became St. Hillary's and now St. Anne's. Sir Michael's letter to Eva, dated the 6th May, indicates traditional diplomatic caution.

It reads:

Dear Miss Neumann,

I am leaving for Vienna on Monday. Can I do anything there about your father? I shall of course have not official status, and am only going there to pack up, but can I make enquiries? I got your letter of April 28th, but do not know what to suggest except (what I suggested to Mr. Miles) an enquiry by the Vice-Chancellor of the University of Oxford to the Rector of the University of Vienna. But I do not know whether you and your mother will think this wise. One has to be so careful not to compromise your father by foreign intervention.

Yours sincerely
Michael Palairet

There is a second letter to Eva dated the 6th June 1938. By then, my father had been released, and Eva must have asked Sir Michael for further help, should there be any difficulties with immigration officials on his arrival at Dover.

The address at the top reads, 'Young's Family and Commercial Hotel, 24 High Petergate, York'.

Dear Miss Neumann,

Your letter has been forwarded to me here. Unfortunately, I do not expect to be in London until later on in June, but I have written to Sir Orme Sargent at the Foreign Office and asked him to put you in touch with the Home Office, who I hope will be able to arrange things quickly. I do trust that your father will be in England before long.

Yours sincerely,
Michael Palairet
The Cottesmore Gardens address will always find me.

Michael Palairet seems to have been on holiday, but he nevertheless wrote to his old friend, Sir Orme Sargent. They had both made distinguished careers in the Diplomatic Service. In 1918 they were attached to the Peace Delegation in Paris. In the Great Hall of Mirrors in the Palace of Versailles, the Treaty to end all wars was signed with great ceremony. But it was not to be. My father was acutely aware of the brevity of the inter-war period. In 1918, at the end of the First World War, he was thirty, in 1939, when the Second World War began, he was fifty-one, grown up at the beginning and not really old at the end.

Officially, Michael Palairet had to present the foreign policy of Baldwin and Chamberlain, weakness in the face of aggression, appeasement, not confrontation. But now that my father was no longer detained, and assistance was requested to ease formalities in England, Michael Palairet felt free to act. He would do as much as he could to help Anne's friend at Oxford.

We arrived in England with our Austrian passports. Although Austria had ceased to exist, they were accepted as valid travel documents. At the port of entry, immigration officials stamped the passports. Permission was granted initially for a stay of three months, provided no paid employment was undertaken. Officials often asked to see letters of invitation, or evidence of the means of support.

My mother must have felt relieved, now that the two great Departments of State, the Foreign Office and the Home Office, had been made aware of my father's impending arrival. If there were any questions, any uncertainties, they would be resolved.

The terrible weeks during which my father was in prison, when his fate hung in the balance, were a torment for my mother. She received many letters of sympathy and support.

Eva had a friend at Oxford, Adam Curle, whose mother epitomized the generous way in which so many refugees were received. Mrs Cornelia Curle, affectionately known as 'Cork', was deeply aware of my mother's anguish and offered her London 'pied-a-terre' in Glebe Place, Chelsea, her 'little London cottage' as she called it. My parents could stay there until they found somewhere to live.

On the 9th May 1938, Mrs Curle wrote from Bay Tree Cottage, her country home: '…I wish I could think there would be good news from Austria for you to give me.'

My mother must have told her immediately about my father's poem, because on the 18th May, Mrs Curle's letter reads:

Dear Frau Neumann,

Your letter consoled me such a lot because I longed to be able to help but in the face of all you are going through, I just felt powerless - only full of admiration for your fortitude and so very touched at your talking openly to me. I was very miserable at your having that long walk back without any tea.

It was very good to think you have had the comfort of a poem from your wonderful husband - such a proof of his inviolability.

I am so deeply grateful to you for telling me about him and about your own brave life in the past. It is so hard that you should be called upon to be so brave again.

I hope to read the poem soon and also to see you again and have another walk. Will you please let me know if you hear anything from Mr (sic) Palairet.

My love to you all,
    C C.

As soon as my father was released, my mother received a telegram. She informed Mrs Curle, who replied on the 21st May:

My dear Frau Neumann,

Just a line to say, how I rejoiced to hear of that telegram. It must have been like heaven opening to get it. Adam enjoyed your party so much. I hope you all could feel festive and that very soon you will have a letter, but perhaps letters are not allowed. I shall get your news from Adam. T'is all right about our little London cottage.

Love to you all
    C C.

Three days later Mrs Curle wrote again:

My dear Frau Neumann,

It is so very blessed to think of your happiness. I am sure no one could be stronger to do everything that will be necessary than you. I should think there will be no difficulty about the permit. Probably Mr Pelairet would arrange that for you. And I expect work for your husband could only be found after his arrival - or has he to say he has a job to get the permit? There must be so many things he can teach and perhaps he could start like that till suitable work can be found. I wonder if you can fit him into your little flat. I'm afraid not.

I suppose he will be allowed enough money to get out of the country with. I shall move to London on June 1ˢᵗ. Do please let me know if I can be of any use to you, then. Otherwise you mustn't bother to write. You must have such a lot to do and think about.

Love to you all,

C C.

The Nazis acted immediately to confiscate Jewish property. The first official step in the process that so often led to complete dispossession, including that of life itself, was the compilation of a register of assets owned by Jews, a documentation of wealth, a total list of possessions. The document has the title "Verzeichnis über das Vermögen von Juden nach dem Stand vom 27 April 1938". The applicable date was the 27th April 1938, and the questionnaire had to be returned by the 20th June. The asset list defines who is a Jew, according to the Nuremberg racial laws of 1935. The personal details are given in the first person, making them sound even more racist. It starts with: "Ich bin Jude" (I am a Jew) and continues to spell out the enormity of change, "Da ich Jude deutscher Staatsangehörigkeit bin", (as I am a Jew of German nationality).

In prison, my father had to complete his asset list. He provided financial details for his legal practice, bank accounts and insurance policies. He had to submit a valuation of the contents of his home and office, and list items above a certain value. Among other things, he entered his gold watch and his gold cigarette case. The fear of making an insufficiently detailed entry, or trying to withhold information, was very real. Late, or incomplete returns would result in severe punishment, fine, prison, penal servitude, confiscation of assets, (Geldstrafe, Gefängnis, Zuchthaus, Einziehung des Vermögens).

This asset list formed the basis of official robbery on an unprecedented scale. Jewish bank accounts were frozen and re-named *Sperrkonto* (locked accounts), with very restricted cash withdrawals. Money transfers from these accounts to places abroad were forbidden, and on emigration there would only be a travel allowance of a few Deutschmarks. Businesses and factories were aryanised (arisiert), Germans replacing Jews by means of enforced sales or confiscations. Real estate was appropriated under duress, by new owners or transferred to the custody of the Reich. Jews were held to ransom, their exit permits granted only after they had been forced to relinquish their possessions.

The Nazis were particularly keen to lay their hands on the great art collections of prominent Jewish families. For their owners, the pictures were objects of pride, pleasure and prestige, symbols of patronage, connoisseurship and wealth. The mixture of racial hatred, envy and greed, the despised provenance of the collections and the concomitant destruction of a cultural tradition was characterized by German thoroughness, Austrian zeal and merciless bureaucracy.

Restitution took a long time. In 1995, to mark the 50th anniversary of the foundation of the Second Republic, the parliament in Vienna voted unanimously to establish a fund for victims of Nazi persecution.

In November 2006, I received notification of a provisional payment, together with a letter in German from the Federal Chancellor Austria, Werner Faymann.

Dear Mr. Neumann,

You are one of about 20,700 claimants for compensation from the General Settlement Fund. The amounts which you are receiving cannot of course ever make good the injustice which you, your family, and those close to you suffered.

In no way can that immeasurable sorrow and that terrible injustice be undone. What was taken from you then cannot be reinstated… We are aware that these payments are taking place very late, that many victims could no longer make any claims, and that previous compensation and restitution payments were altogether insufficient…

In December 2006, I had a similar letter from the New York-based International Commission on Holocaust Era Insurance Claims, the separate organisation dealing with insurance policies. Fortunately my father had taken out an insurance policy in dollars and Reichsmark, as well as in Austrian Schillings.

It announces a small interim payment signed by the Senior Counselor for Humanitarian Claims, ICHEIC Humanitarian Fund. It ends: "I fully recognize that no amount of money could compensate for the painful suffering and historic injustices of the Holocaust. Nonetheless, I sincerely hope that you will regard this as a small acknowledgement of those injustices".

I received my final payment in November 2009, seventy-one years after the Anschluss. On the 25th July 2002, I wrote to my case officer. Over several telephone conversations, I had established informality. It reads:

Liebe Fiorentina Azizi:

Unsagbar traurig ist es sich an schreckliche Begegenheiten zu erinnern. 60 Jahre ist eine sehr lange Zeit, aber die schmerzvollen Einzelheiten sind noch immer lebendig. Die damals als Erwachsene entkommen konnten, die also am meisten eine Entschädigung verdient hätten, sind schon lange nicht mehr da.

Mit sehr gemischten Gefühlen suche ich an. Das Unbezahlbare kann nicht rückerstattet werden. Andererseits ist das Geld die einzig objektive Geste einer Wiedergutmachung, die ja nie vollkommen sein kann. Für mich ist die Auszahlung nicht nur quantitativ sondern auch symbolisch.

Mit sehr freundlichen Grüssen aus London und recht vielen Dank für Ihre Hilfe.

George Newman
25th July 2002

(Dear Fiorentina Azizi,

It is incredibly sad to recall terrible events. Sixty years is a very long time, but the painful details are still vivid. The people who most of all deserved restitution, the adults who at the time managed to escape, have long ago gone.

It is with mixed feelings that I apply. One cannot pay back for things for which there is no compensation. On the other hand, money is the only objective gesture of a recompense which in fact can never be complete. For me, the payment is not only quantitative, but also symbolic.

With very friendly greetings from London and with very many thanks for your help.

George Newman)

My father was released from prison on the 18th May. Five days later, on the 23rd May, my father reported to the Gestapo at his local police station. He was issued with an expulsion order. It was a small piece of paper, typewritten, with a corrected spelling mistake, and authenticated by a stamp of the police station in Währing, the command of Exodus. It is headed:

Bezirks-Polizei-Kommissariat, Währing and is dated 23.May 1938

Für … wird bestätigt,
dass Rechtsanwalt Dr. Paul Neumann am 13.Juli 1938 das deutsche Reichsgebiet zu verlassen hat.

(For the attention of … it is confirmed,
that Rechtsanwalt Dr. Paul Neumann has to leave the territory of the German Reich on the 13th July 1938.)

The document was life-saving and as my father folded it and put it in his briefcase, he must have hoped that he would soon be reunited with his family. The text was not yet officially formalized and does not state the obvious, that my father was free to leave earlier.

In less than a week, the Gestapo action would be centralised. At the end of May, the notorious "Zentralstelle für jüdische Auswanderung in Wien" (Central Office for Jewish Emigration in Vienna), was set up in the Palais Rothschild in the Prinz Eugenstrasse. With sarcastic irony, and diabolic symbolism, the elegant aristocratic residence of the most famous Jewish family in Vienna would now house the offices of Adolf Eichmann, the architect of the Holocaust.

My father never spoke about his interrogation or the circumstances of his release. On the 19th May, on his first full day of freedom he wrote to my mother:

> *Wien, der 19. Mai 1938*
> *7h morgens*
>
> *Mein sehr Geliebtes!*
>
> *Alle Worte haben eine andere tiefere Bedeutung gewonnen, wie erst diese Anrede. Ich sende Dir diese Umarmung, als erste Gabe des ersten Morgens. Es ist abermals ein grosses Wunder der Wandlung geschehen. Ich bin noch nicht gesammelt und andererseits noch nicht aufgelockert genug, um Dir mehr zu schreiben. Ich bin tief glücklich darüber, dass es Dir, Eva und Hansi gut und tapfer geht. Küsse die Kinder und sei auf beide liebe Augen geküsst.*
>
> *Von Deinem P.*
> *Ino, der Treue, hat bei mir übernachtet*

> *(Vienna 19th May 1938*
> *7 o'clock in the morning*
>
> *My very beloved!*
>
> *All words have acquired a different deeper meaning, especially this address. I send you this embrace as the first gift of the first morning. Once again, a great miracle of transformation has happened. I am not yet collected and not, on the*

other hand, sufficiently unwound to write more. I am deeply happy that you, Eva and Hansi are well and in good spirits. Kiss the children, and be kissed on both dear eyes.

by your P.

Ino, the faithful one, stayed the night with me)

Innocenz Grafe was a friend of my sister and my parents.

Nearly two months elapsed between my father's release and his departure. He felt a moral and legal obligation to wind up his office in an orderly fashion.

He helped countless people with personal advice and comfort against the background of the disintegration and destruction of Viennese Jewry. A letter in German, dated the 4th June from a certain Lilli Zimmand is a very moving testimony:

Vienna 4. VI. 38

To Dr. Paul Neumann
Advocate for Human Rights and Defence Counsel
Wien 1 Petersplatz 3

The customary form of address at this point is omitted, as none is good enough!

It is impossible, Herr Doktor, for me to leave without at least wishing you farewell with a blessing. You have seriously forbidden me to say "thank you", and I want to keep my promise as far as "saying it" is concerned. But I just can't prevent myself feeling boundless gratitude. I have not prayed for many years, and no longer believe in God – life has robbed me of the possibility to believe. But when I left you today, I knew: God is, and one would have to correct the story of the Creation and write: "and God created man in His own image, and the first man is called Paul Neumann!" All others just happen to be human beings. And with a heart full of conviction I prayed a prayer of gratitude.

I am certain, Herr Doktor, that none of the incredibly many people to whom you are extending a helping hand will ever forget you. It is not only the practical help which you quickly provide as rescue, in every misfortune, but you do it with such a sincere concern for the fate of each individual, and in such a friendly, sensitive manner, that one has only the single wish: may one become like you.

I know I speak from the heart on behalf of countless people, who today are perhaps scattered all over the world, for whom you have done so much, and who themselves, shamefully, could do so little for you, when I beseech God to grant our fervent wishes the strength to protect your life!

Lilli Zimmand

Eventually, after what must have seemed an eternity to my mother, he arrived in Oxford on the 7th July to join us. It was a Thursday and I did not go to school that day. My father was expected in the early afternoon, and my mother and I went to the station to meet him. My mother asked me to wait outside. She did not want me to come in, to be with her on the platform when the train drew in. She wanted to be alone with her husband for the most poignant reunion. I heard the train come in and saw passengers hurry out. My eyes were fixed on the entrance. The old Great Western Railway Station, with its steep approach and narrow doors had the architectural charm of the railway age. The edges of the platform shelters and the various roofs were protected by the traditional weather-boarding of long planks of fretwork, painted dark brown. The walls were covered with the ubiquitous cream-coloured oil paint. Lamp posts stood at various intervals. I do not, of course, remember the details, but the impression was consolidated by the many occasions of my travel to Oxford as a student.

And suddenly my father stood in the entrance. A few feet separated us. I was right outside. My mother had stayed in the hall. It could only have lasted a second, but there he was, motionless, no rush forward with outstretched arms, no welcoming smile. He had the sad eyes, the pallid skin, the expressionless face of prison. I rushed forward to embrace him. And as we separated his face changed. I had held him, I was his son. He looked at me with tenderness and love. He must have felt in me his future, his continuity. We were both so overcome, we were silent.

75

And then he opened his mouth with a new sound. He spoke English for the first time. I hear his two words so clearly after seventy years. The beautiful timbre of his voice coped with the new language. "We go" he said, referring to the immediate but in a sense uttering a clarion call for our future journey.

My parents soon moved to London, but I stayed at school in Oxford. In our school library we had several daily newspapers, and I enjoyed reading them. Then, one day in November 1938, I saw the headlines and the photograph of the principal synagogue in Vienna in the Seitenstettengasse, set alight, in flames. I still remember when I read the reports, the feeling of helplessness in the face of evil. The town, which I had left with my refugee luggage of secular Judaism and Austrian cultural heritage, was still very much part of me.

The reports of these terrible events, of the *Reichskristallnacht* that swept across Germany and Austria, drew special attention to the violence in Vienna, which I had left only a few months previously.

Half a century later, I asked the letters editor of the *Guardian* if the paper would welcome a contribution to mark the anniversary. I was told to be brief, space was at a premium. I had to condense the enormity. My letter to the editor appeared on November 8th 1988 under the editorial heading 'Crystal Clear':

November 9 50 years ago was a prophetic signpost for the final journey of so many German and Austrian Jews. The full might of Nazi revenge for the murder of one of their diplomats in Paris by a Jew resulted in the infamous Reichskristallnacht, during which Jews were beaten and killed, Jewish shops looted, Jewish homes smashed. But of terrifying symbolic significance was the desecration and the burning down of synagogues. It was the first time that the Nazis openly attacked houses of worship which hitherto even they had considered sacrosanct. Once they had crossed that threshold the inconceivable became possible and the road to genocide lay open.

George Newman London SW20

CHAPTER 4

Curtains up

The early years of my father's and Lena's visits to the Opera were under Gustav Mahler's directorship. Those were golden years, those nineteen hundreds prior to the First World War. They were often invited by Trude, their cousin. Her father, Eduard Neumann, a brother of Wilhelm, had a permanent debenture box at the Opera. It was higher up, in the fourth gallery, that another cousin, Anne Zweig, used to sit, spending all her small earnings. Anne's mother, Stephanie Schein (née Kuffler) was one of Hermine's sisters.

Lena and Anne both kept careful opera and theatre diaries.

Prior to the First World War, opera singers were under contract to be part of the ensemble, of the repertoire system, of an opera house. Gradually with the advent of global mobility, cast lists started to include international artists. But even in Mahler's time and earlier, in Vienna, great artists made their appearance, distinguished, in apposition, by the letters 'a.G.' (als Gast, as visitor) printed in bold type after their names.

Anne Zweig (in German 'Zweig' means branch, by which she was affectionately known) died in her 99th year, in January 1991, her memory unimpaired.

One of her favourite stories concerns such a guest artist, Enrico Caruso. It also illustrates the taxing demands on singers to perform several large roles in close succession, frequently required by the varied programme, the in-house casting policy, and the expectations of flexible excellence set by opera houses.

Caruso came to Vienna and sang three times in one week. Anne's diary records the details and underlines the name, the only singer so singled out. On the 20th September 1911 he was Canio in *Pagliacci*, on the 23rd September he sang the Duke of Mantua in *Rigoletto*, and two days later, on the 25th September 1911, he sang Don José in *Carmen*.

Anne was 18 years old at the time, but for her the experience remained vivid for eighty years. She was always very interested to hear about my latest visit to the opera. When it came to tenors, she showed her good judgement by discovering Placido Domingo very early on when he was hardly known. As an aside, in these discussions, she would say: "No ja, ich hab' den Caruso gehört" (Ah well, I've heard Caruso).

Caruso in three operas in one week! What a tremendous occasion. The audiences of those days looked forward to hearing their stars in different roles. They could admire the versatility, the artistry, the style applied to each work, preferably over a short period of time. Leo Slezak's schedule at that time is revelatory. Anne, in her diary, tells the story. On the 7th of September 1911 she heard Slezak as Radames in *Aida*, nine days later, on the 16th September he sang Lohengrin. Then immediately after the Caruso days, Slezak returned to the stage, on the 30th September in Goldmark's *The Queen of Sheba*, on the 4th October in Meyerbeer's *Prophète*, and on the 7th October in *The Huguenots* by Meyerbeer.

Leo Slezak was the darling of the Viennese and is famous for the many anecdotes that decorate his life both on and off the stage. Some were true, some were apocryphal. Anne told me she was there on that night of *Lohengrin*, when the mechanism failed that is supposed to bring on the swan pulling the empty boat. The Chorus had already sung: "Der Schwan! Weh, er naht." (The swan! See it comes.) Elsa had added her: "Entsetzlich! Ha! Der Schwan!" (O horror! Look! The swan!) Still no swan. With growing concern, looking desperately into the wings, Slezak then sang: "Schon sendet nach dem Säumigen der Gral!" (Too long I stay, the Grail for me hath sent!) Swan and boat were nowhere in evidence. The eight-bar slow introduction to the famous "Mein lieber Schwan" (Beloved swan!) had started. Slezak turned to the audience. The vehicle that was supposed to convey him off the stage had failed to appear. Leo Slezak mobilised his sense of humour. Make them laugh it off, he must have thought. And he said "Wann kommt der nächste Schwan?" (When is the next swan?)

Anne's diary for 1911 shows that she went to the opera 45 times and to the theatre 19 times, a remarkable total when one considers that the opera house was closed in July and August. Lena, in her diaries, left a blank page at the start of each season which she filled in with attendance details. For the season 7th September 1910 to the 1st August 1911, the summary reveals the incredible tapestry of music and drama which decorated her life:

Burgtheater	10 times
Opera	20 times
Volkstheater	9 times
Theater an der Wien	4 times
Raimund Theater	3 times
Bürgertheater	twice
Karltheater	twice
Volksoper	once
Neue Wiener Bühne	once
Zirkus Busch	once
Concerts	19 times
Bayreuter Festspielhaus	once

But the total of 73 visits was even higher for the following season: Burgtheater (7), Opera (20), Volkstheater (4), Theater an der Wien (1), Raimundtheater (2), Bürgertheater (2), Karltheater (5), Johann Strausstheater (3), Neue Wiener Bühne (4), Volkstheater (5), Zirkus Busch (1), Tänze (1), lectures (2), concerts (38).

Ninety-one occasions for the period from 14 September 1911 to the 20th July 1912, meant that Lena went out several times a week to theatre and opera.

My father did not keep an opera book, but he told me that when they were in their teens, he frequently went to the opera with Lena. They joined their cousin Trude in her box or accompanied Wilhelm. A few years later, Lena who was so beautiful and in her early twenties, must have stepped into a waiting horse and carriage to be driven to the house in the Ringstrasse, sitting by the side of her latest admirer.

My father was very interested in the theatre. Like Lena and Anne he saw Josef Kainz in all his roles. Many of the great actors and actresses of the time are now, alas, only figures of historical interest. But perhaps Josef Kainz is an exception. He was a superstar, revered by the general public, many of whom had never seen him. He had the transcendental magic, the compelling power of illusion to create his roles. He totally inhabited his diverse characters.

From time to time, my father spoke to me about the Burgtheater prior to the First World War, especially during the time when I was studying Goethe as part of my degree course in English History. In their Final Examination, ex-servicemen were allowed to substitute two three-hour papers from another Honours School in place of the special subject papers, chosen from a list. I had finished a term of lectures and tutorials on St. Augustine and his times, my choice of special subject, when I discovered I could instead offer a German language paper and a paper on Goethe from the German Honours School. I was very fortunate. Professor Stahl at Christ Church guided me through *Faust*, the poems, *Tasso, Werther, Iphigenie*. I had left Vienna at the age of fourteen and had missed proper schooling in German literature.

Although I did not use the church history material, I had the opportunity to listen to Canon Jenkins and have tutorials with Professor Edwards, the great medievalist at All Souls. How privileged I was to have had those eight audiences and to have discussed the Early Fathers, the world of the Eastern Empire, the Byzantine Emperors, the *Codex Theodosius* with its difficult Latin.

My father followed my progress through the centuries, my voyage through time. He was especially curious about all aspects of constitutional history and political science. He had studied Law, and now seemed to relive his student days.

I remember the last time. It was Christmas 1947, my father's last Christmas. We were in the kitchen at Heath Court in Hampstead. As usual, speaking in German, we were talking about my Final Examinations due in June 1948. We were discussing the obligatory booklist, such as *The Republic, The Leviathan, The Social Contract*. And then I described my work on Plato and Aristotle, on Hobbes and Rousseau, on Locke, Hume and Bentham. Suddenly my father stopped me. He looked at me with the conspiratorial expression of hoped-for shared knowledge, of fellow scholarship, that can bridge the gap of years, that can unite father and son. He wanted to hear from me an echo of his youth, of his own studies some forty years earlier. The four syllables he was about to utter seemed to release in him a flood of memories. His face became mellow with retrospection. And he must have known that my answer would be in the affirmative. It was a rhetorical question that would cement the past and the present and would illuminate our communion.

"Auch Grotius?" (Also Grotius?) he asked.

"Ja" I replied. For a split second we were no longer father and son but strangely equal, looking at a great figure of European legal history, a 17th Dutch jurist, who in his writings laid the foundations of the concept of International Law. As I spoke, I felt a deep feeling of belonging, of joint experience, of heritage.

Of course, I remember my father's voice. The pointillist cameo of sound could have lasted for only about two seconds. His beautiful dark vowel sound of "Auch" had the deep-toned sonority of diphthong, rounded off, like a musical phrase, with the two consonants, focused into soft resonance. "Grotius" was invested with theatrical intensity, surely the first time that my father had uttered the name since the First World War. The "o" was elongated for declamatory emphasis, the vowel open, straight, but full of colour.

Sometime in 1947, I started to prepare myself for the special Goethe paper. From time to time, my father would ask: "How is Faust? What is Mephisto doing? What is the latest news on Iphigenie?" He told me that he had seen Kainz in many roles, especially as Hamlet and Mephisto.

Very memorable for him was the 20th November 1906. It was six days prior to Lena's 16th birthday, and as a special celebration the family went to the Burgtheater and saw Goethe's *Faust*. He also recalled that they attended a performance of *Faust* Part 2, which according to Lena's opera and theatre book, took place on the 4th June 1907. The cast list is headed by Gregori as Faust, and Kainz as Mephisto, followed by an astonishingly long list of names. Altogether forty-four actors and actresses took part in a completely uncut version.

My mother was very used to my father telling the same old stories, and I soon came to know certain trigger words which would set off for my father a chain of thoughts, a critical observation, a private theory, which we had heard before. And so it was with Faust. If somehow the conversation had turned to the subject of Faust's timeless message, his originality, his universality, then my father would say that Goethe was far in advance of his time, that he was existentialist in his manipulation and imagery of language, and that for the first time ever an event is described simultaneously in the present and the future, within and without the factual scenario.

The quotation is only short, but the few words had assumed for my father special significance, and I heard them several times. My father, first of all, elaborated the context. And then he spoke the words, melodious, with theatrical significance: "Ein grosser Kahn ist im Begriffe, auf dem Kanale hier zu sein" (A large boat is in the process of being here on the canal). 'Im Begriffe', in the process, for him was imbued with duality, time and motion, nascent modernity.

If one were late for a meeting with him, he might greet one with Schiller's opening lines from *Die Piccolomini*, the central drama of the Wallenstein trilogy: "Spät kommt Ihr – doch Ihr kommt!" (You come late, but you come.) A line from Goethe's poem *Hochzeitslied* might be used: "Bedienet euch immer des Raumes" (Make yourself at home).

In 1941, for a few weeks, I had to share a bedroom with my father. My mother slept with my sister, and the other rooms were used by friends who had just been bombed out. Sometimes, before we went to sleep, I asked my father to recite a poem. And then, more than once I heard *Wanderers Nachtlied*, Goethe's lyrical edifice, eight lines, twenty-four words which encompass a whole universe of calm resignation.

Über allen Gipfeln
Ist Ruh,
In allen Wipfeln
Spürest du
Kaum einen Hauch;
Die Vögelein schweigen im Walde.
Warte nur! Balde
Ruhest du auch.

This is my translation:

WANDERER'S NIGHTSONG
Over all mountain tops
Is calm
In all treetops
You feel barely a breath;
The birds are silent in the forest.
Just wait, soon
You also rest

I still hear his beautiful 'Ruh', with the echoing 'du'. It opened up a world. Then came the poetically repeated diphthongs in 'Kaum' and 'Hauch'. My father seemed to linger on 'Walde' and 'balde', investing the 'l' and 'd' with separate identity, without breaking the sound, speaking with the true legato of an actor, articulation monitored by the beautiful timbre of his voice.

Memorising poetry and living with it was an important part of my parents' education, and continued as an integral feature of my schooldays in Vienna. I remember one particular day at school. It was at the end of my first year at the Primary School in the Scheibenbergstrasse, in the Summer of 1933. Herr Nürnberger, our teacher, came into the classroom and said: "Heute is ein schöner Sommertag. Wir werden ein Gedicht von Goethe auswendig lernen … von einer Rose" (Today is a nice Summer's day. We will memorise a poem by Goethe … about a rose). He wrote out the poem *Heidenröslein* on the blackboard, three verses of seven lines each, immortalised by Schubert. He told us we would have to learn the first verse by the following week. The blackboard would remain up. We would see it all the time. Then came the day. He took the board down and we had to write out the first verse. Over the next week or so, we learnt the whole poem. It was to be the prelude to more difficult tasks awaiting me in my Secondary School, the Gymnasium. There, we had to learn long epic poems by Schiller, famous monologues from Grillparzer and Lessing, just to mention a few.

The great Kainz filled the Burgtheater with his rare and eagerly awaited poetry readings. The appellation is misleading: they were Evenings of Recitation (Vortragsabende). Kainz spoke his words to a packed house of 1,500 people who treasured each syllable of his utterance.

My father told me that he went with Lena to an unforgettable evening on the 27th February 1908 in which Kainz recited Rilke, then only a young poet aged 32. The programme also contained Act 1, Scene 1 of Byron's *Manfred*, Schnitzler's *Die Frau des Weisen,* passages from Homer's *Odyssey*, Schiller's *Die Götter Griechenlands*, Mark Twain's Das *Gewitter.*

Kainz's 'Vortragsabende' came up in our conversation in an unexpected way. In 1947, when I was attending lectures on Goethe's poems in the Taylorian Institute, Professor Stahl usually read out the poems, prior to speaking about them. But sometimes he asked a student to read the text. And so it came about, that on that unforgettable occasion, he looked straight at me, sitting right at the back of the long hall. "We'll have someone from the back today," he said. I pointed to myself, my face with the unspoken expression of "Do you mean me?" "Yes, you at the back," he repeated. We were concerning ourselves with a group of poems entitled *Gott und Welt*, and we had reached the third one *Eins und Alles.*

I thought, I would give them all a surprise. Instead of the customary apologetic mumble of timid undergraduates, speaking difficult lines without fully understanding them, I would present them with a dramatic sound portrait of the text. The first verse illustrates what is to follow; German full of its characteristic z and w sounds, of *Umlaute*, of sustained double s.

Im Grenzenlosen sich zu finden,
Wird gern der Einzelne verschwinden,
Da löst sich aller Überdruß;
Statt heißem Wünschen, wildem Wollen
Statt läst'gem Fordern, strengem Sollen,
Sich aufzugeben ist Genuß.

My father spoke about Kainz once more, later that year. On the 13th November 1947, I went with my parents to a concert in the Royal Albert Hall. Bruno Walter was conducting Beethoven's Ninth Symphony with the London Philharmonic Orchestra. It was the last autumn of my father's life, the last time he would hear the Choral Symphony. The soloists included Kathleen Ferrier, who herself was not destined to sing very much longer.

As we left the Hall, and faced the reality of the world outside, my father must have had many memories of the work over a lifetime. We were discussing the wonderful singing. And then my father said: "Ich hab auch vor 40 Jahren den Kainz gehört" (Forty years ago, I also heard Kainz). *An die Freude* (The Ode to Joy) was part of Josef Kainz's programme on the 16th October 1908, as recorded in Lena's diary, one of the Schiller poems.

I sometimes asked my father about various singers he might have heard prior to the First World War at the Opera. Apart from Slezak, I knew about Schmedes. I asked him if he had heard him in Wagner. My father replied that he had heard his Lohengrin and Tristan.

I looked up the Schmedes performances for the period from the 29th May 1910 to the 19th June, as recorded in Anne Zweig (Branch)'s opera book. Like Slezak, Schmedes, then aged 44, was able to produce an astonishing simultaneous repertoire: On the 29th May, Anne heard Schmedes in *Rienzi*, on the 4th June he sang Lohengrin, on the 8th June, he sang Walter von Stolzing in *Meistersinger*, on the 11th June he was Tristan, on he 14th June he sang Siegmund in *Walküre* and on the 19th June he sang Siegfried. What an achievement to sing six heavy Wagnerian roles in three weeks.

CHAPTER 5

My father from schoolboy to judge

My father started his career as a Rechtsanwalt with a prestigious visiting card. He was the son of Regierungsrat Wilhelm Neumann, the trusted adviser over many years to the Viennese Rothschilds, a well-respected journalist, whose articles are characterised by encyclopaedic memory, attention to detail and factual accuracy. Wilhelm had the essential curiosity to bring to life the great actors on the financial, industrial and commercial stage during the final decades of the Habsburg empire, and he continued to follow closely the careers and fortunes of the leading men and institutions of the new republic.

For my father, lunch at the Ferdinandstrasse was not only a place where you could expect a wonderful meal and great cigars, but where a patriarchal figure would dispense his great experience and knowledge. My father would consult Wilhelm on the background of companies and the competence and reliability of their directors. Although balance sheets could speak for themselves, my grandfather had built up an excellent critical assessment of the fabric of Viennese society, and his connection with the Rothschilds opened many doors, and led to influential contacts.

It was in 1923 that my father was admitted to the Chamber of Advocates. He was 34. There would be just fifteen short years to fulfil his professional potential. In 1938 he came to England, to join his wife and children, to start again. But the arithmetic of time can be cruel, because ten years later he died.

What sort of life did my father have before he became a Rechtsanwalt? It was, after all, more than half of it.

He was an excellent pupil. From 1898 to 1906 he attended the Franz Joseph Gymnasium, achieving the highest grades and passing his final examination, his "Matura", with distinction in all his subjects: Religion, Latin, Greek, German, Geography, History, Physics, Philosophy.

My father's knowledge and love of Homer and Virgil, of Plato and Aristotle, of Spinoza, of Schiller's history dramas and above all of Goethe's *Faust* and Goethe's poems all had their origins at school.

The school was situated in a very elegant part of Vienna, and it must have been Wilhelm Neumann's influence which secured Paul's admission. It was near the Opera House, the Karlsplatz, the Kärntnerstrasse and not far from St. Stephen's Cathedral at the very centre. On his daily journey to school my father travelled through the architectural landscape of contrast. He started in the rather gloomy Ferdinandstrasse, narrow with high 17th and 18th century tenement blocks, stretching into the centre of the old ghetto of the Leopoldstadt. And then he had to cross an arm of the Danube. There, on the other side was a city with its Baroque palaces, splendid Biedermeier town houses, imperial palaces, with mid 19th century Ringstrasse architecture, with Gothic and Baroque churches, and beyond, the green semi-circle of the Wienerwald.

At school, my father made many lifelong friends, one of whom I got to know well. Egon Wellesz was three years older than my father, but that did not seem to matter. He became a respected composer, and in 1932 was given an honorary doctorate in music at Oxford, only the second Austrian to be granted such an honour. The first one was Haydn. It was in the field of deciphering Byzantine music notation that Wellesz became an international authority. My father admired Egon. Egon for him had the mystery of someone preoccupied with Eastern Orthodox Church music written a thousand years ago, making sense of the dots, dashes and scribbles, the hieroglyphs of medieval notation. In his autobiographical memoirs, Egon Wellesz wrote: "Ich verbrachte meine Schulzeit am Franz Joseph Gymnasium in der

Hegelgasse. Dies war eine Mittelschule, an der Latein, Griechisch, Geschichte und Literatur ausserordentlich gut gelehrt wurden ... (I attended school at the Franz Joseph Gymnasium in the Hegelgasse. This was a Secondary School at which Latin, Greek, history and literature were taught extremely well.)

After the Anschluss, in 1938, Egon Wellesz emigrated to England and settled in Oxford. That was the time when I saw him frequently. We were all there. Eva was studying, I was at Magdalen College School, a day boy, and my parents lived there for a few months, prior to their move to London.

Egon and Emmy Wellesz lived in Woodstock Road, in a beautiful Georgian terraced house. His beloved Bösendorfer grand piano stood in his study in the front room on the first floor. It was lined with books and music. In a place of honour hung the framed programme of the première of his opera *Die Bakchantinnen*, performed at the Vienna Opera on the 20th June 1931, printed on silk, in a unique edition.

Egon Wellesz's compositions belong to the Second Viennese School. He was a pupil of Schoenberg, a friend of Berg, Webern and Zemlinksy. Gustav Mahler took an interest in him, and he was allowed to attend many of Mahler's rehearsals at the Vienna Opera. He left nine symphonies, several operas, chamber music, songs and church music.

At Oxford he taught composition and lectured on musical history. He greeted his students with a radiant smile, looking upon them as his 'children' and speaking to them with the charming lilt of old Vienna.

But I also remember the day when Egon's face was desperately sad. My mother had come to Oxford to see me. It was the 1st June 1941, a Sunday, the usual visiting day at the boarding school. We met Egon walking from his home to Lincoln College. He looked at us, no welcoming gesture, and quietly said: "Kreta ist gefallen" (Crete has fallen). The twelve day airborne assault on the Mediterranean island, so strategically important, had ended in a German victory. Three weeks later, on June 21st 1941, Hitler invaded Russia. The three words which Egon uttered on that Sunday ushered in the darkest period of the war.

And then again, there was a wonderful afternoon in the autumn of

1943, during my second term at St. Catherine's to read History. I had been invited to a gramophone recital at Christ Church of Schoenberg's *Gurre-Lieder*, an event arranged in honour of Egon Wellesz, in one of the beautiful large rooms overlooking Peckwater Quad, with a view of the library and its Corinthian pillars. To us Egon was a living legend. He had been a pupil of Schoenberg and had attended the first performance in 1913, in Vienna. When I arrived, Egon was seated in an armchair surrounded by about a dozen students, with the pocket score of the music on his lap. There, at Christ Church, one of the great fortresses of humanism, a storehouse of civilisation in a war that tried to destroy it, I could listen to Schoenberg's music, the German text adding painful solace.

No one spoke, no one stirred during the many changes of the old 78 rpm records. There was total silence. Egon continued to look down at the music. And at the end, when the pile of discs had been put back into the album, Egon asked if they belonged to the music faculty. "They are mine," said my friend Denys Potts. He had bought them in a local music shop for £5, then a very considerable sum of money, which demonstrated his early enthusiasm for Schoenberg. He was to become an eminent French scholar, a distinguished professor and Vice Master of Keble College. But in that timeless moment, Egon looked at him with warmth and affection, with admiration and gratitude for this unique opportunity. And then he spoke the word I remember so clearly. "Bravo" he said, not at all diphthongally English, but with the straight open vowel sounds of Vienna. It was an echo of his bravo, spoken or unspoken, at the first performance of the work, but also at so many other memorable occasions. He told me that he was present at the rehearsal of the premiere of Mahler's *Second Symphony* on the 21st November 1907, which Mahler conducted. It was his farewell concert to Vienna. A few weeks earlier, on the 15th October, he conducted at the Vienna Opera for the last time. It was *Fidelio*. Thus ended his ten year directorship.

During the summer months, when the Opera was closed, Mahler would move to his house on the edge of the Wörthersee, near Velden, where my grandfather spent his 70th birthday. There at Maiernigg, in the grounds of the house, was his small garden hut, where he composed symphonies four to eight and many songs.

Dr. Richter, my Viennese dentist, who managed to escape just in time, told me that as a child, he and his family spent their summers in a house in Maiernigg, very near to the Mahlers. A footpath which they often used, ran along the side of the composer's garden. And as they drew level with the garden hut, Dr. Richter's mother used to say to him: "Und jetzt sei ganz still, mach keinen Lärm, da drinnen sitzt der Mahler und komponiert" (And now be very quiet, don't make a noise. Mahler is sitting in there, composing). And then she raised her index finger to her lips in a sign of silence and they tiptoed past.

It is very strange, but the first time I heard the name Mahler was in the context of walking. I must have been about eight years old and was walking from the Gersthoferstrasse, where we lived, to the nearby Türkenschantzpark. A certain Maria Walter, affectionately known as 'Walli', was taking me out. Walli was originally asked to look after me after my return from Switzerland. She did not live in, but I saw her frequently, especially when she started to wait for me after school, and accompany me for part of the way home. She became a family institution, a family retainer, right up to the day on which I left Vienna.

At any rate, on that day we were walking along. I may have dragged my feet, perhaps my shoes scraped the pavement. Quite apart from not clearing the ground properly with my feet, I probably swayed from side to side as I ambled along. Walli suddenly stopped. I remember it so clearly after almost eighty years: the bend in the road, the trees, the background of the old houses. Of course I have been back on several occasions. Walli stopped and said: "Heb' die Füsse, so wie der Mahler, der Mahler hat die Füsse immer hoch gehoben" (Lift your feet, like Mahler. Mahler always raised his feet high). Mahler was so very famous. People knew him as he walked from his house to the nearby Opera for rehearsals. His eccentric gait had become folklore. I don't think Walli actually ever saw him. Mahler deliberately stamped down with each step, finishing the movement by kicking his legs backwards, or, when in a great hurry, taking very short strides that started with the toes and kept the legs straight. Walli then demonstrated by marking time like a guardsman. And I said: "Wer ist der Mahler?" (Who is Mahler?) and Walli replied: "Er ist ein berühmter Komponist" (He is a famous composer).

And I remember another occasion, perhaps a little earlier, in 1931. We were out on our usual walk, but this time not going into the park. Instead we carried on down the hill. As we turned into the Gymnasiumstrasse, near my future school, I asked Walli where we were going. "Wir besuchen den Hugo Thimig" (We are going to visit Hugo Thimig), she said. "Wer ist der Thimig?" (Who is Thimig?) I asked. And she said "Er ist ein Komiker" (He is a comedian). To apply such a label to a great comedy and character actor, who had successfully directed the Burgtheater through turbulent times and had starred in so many roles was inappropriate. I suppose Walli tried to simplify her answer. She knew that Wilhelm was a great friend of Hugo Thimig and used me as a pretext to come face to face with such a famous stage personality in his own home.

When we arrived unexpectedly at No. 47 we were ushered into Thimig's study. "Das ist der Hansi, der Enkel vom Regierungsrat Wilhelm Neumann" (This is Hansi, the grandson of Regierungsrat Wilhelm Neumann), Walli said. Hugo Thimig gave me a welcoming smile and I repeated what I had just been told: "Sie sind ein Komiker" (You are a comedian). The story soon made the rounds and Wilhelm must have been told immediately.

Hugo Thimig retired two years later in 1933 at the age of almost 80 and died in Vienna in September 1944.

In 1911, my father was twenty-three years old. He had graduated from Vienna University as a Doctor of Law. He was now Dr. Paul Neumann, preparing himself for the professional examinations and the probationary training for an appointment as a judge in a District Court. Europe was only three years away from the Great War, but there were no serious clouds on the horizon. There had been trouble in the

Balkans ever since he could remember. It was nothing new. He was saddened by the rise of nationalism and the ever-growing demand by Czechs, Poles and Hungarians for self-determination and ultimate independence. But he hoped that a compromise would be reached, a federal system, where the ethnic components would co-exist within the larger framework of a constitutional monarchy. Nearly a century would have to pass before the enlarged European Union became a reality.

On that 7th July 1911, the scroll of the Doctorate was placed in his hand. The ceremonial Latin of the time-honoured document is redolent of old scholastic traditions. My father's name is latinised, and is in the accusative case, 'Paulum', with the adjective 'vindobonensem' in agreement: Paulum Neumann vindobonensem (Paul Neumann from Vienna). The parchment symbolised an enrichment, an intellectual achievement, a preparation for life.

He bid farewell to his 'Alma Mater', as the University affectionately was called, where he had spent so many formative years. And as he travelled home to the Ferdinandstrasse along the Ring, he passed the Burgtheater, the Opera House, and the Musikvereinssaal where he had listened to so many memorable concerts. He would have seen the Secession, the exhibition building which was opened with great ceremony in 1898 and in which early works by Klimt, Schiele and Kokoschka had been exhibited. And earlier, he would have admired the ceremonial grandeur of the Imperial Palace, the Hofburg, the residence of Kaiser Franz Joseph. The Habsburg dynasty would soon come to an end. But life seemed to go on as usual.

On his homeward journey, my father, the new Herr Doktor, might have looked right just before crossing the Donaukanal for his home in the Leopoldstadt. For the previous two years, there had been construction on an enormous scale, for the new Ministry of War. It would eventually be finished, just in time, in 1913.

After his doctorate, my father chose to become a judge. He knew that the financial rewards were far smaller than the earnings of a Rechtsanwalt (a lawyer), but he was attracted by the ethical function of the judge, the dispensation of justice, rather than the preparation, the collation, so to speak, of relevant material in an adversarial situation.

His story, 'from schoolboy to judge' is illustrated by documents that reflect the bureaucracy of a bygone age. The University kept a careful register, the so-called Absolutorium, which was presented to each student at the end. It is a record of the lectures which my father had to attend, the number of hours per week of each course, the subject and the name of the professor. Issued on the 31st July 1910 after four years of study, it charts a voyage into the vast realm of law. But there were also lectures on the History of Art, on 19th century Austrian history, on the history of the Papacy, on philosophy, on economics.

The University was anxious to provide its law students with the advantage of relevant, more general education. Professor Max Dvořák introduced his audience to the History of Art in the Middle Ages. He had become an expert on Peter Bruegel the Elder and would certainly have mentioned the *Bauernhochzeit* and the *Bauerntanz* both in Vienna. The two paintings, together with other works by Bruegel and the portrait of Emperor Maximillian by Dürer, gave the Kunsthistorische Museum the imprimatur of eminence.

My father must have bought a print, a colour reproduction of the Bauernhochzeit soon after his wedding. At any rate, I remember it was always there in the dining room in the Gersthoferstrasse, to which we moved in 1927. For ten years, I looked at the picture. I grew up with it. I came to know the man playing the bagpipes, and the man next to him holding the tankard. The couple dancing across the picture made their simultaneous impact. Now, when I see it, the memory of childhood intimacy, of a decade of familiarity is activated. I look for all the private details, the peacock feather in the young man's hair, the spoon stuck into the hat of the dancing man, and strangely, the four stones and mysterious curved object in the foreground. Whenever I look at it, the Vienna provenance is inescapable. It represents a specific room, in which I see my father, my mother and my sister, the picture hanging above the sideboard, the light oak broad frame edging the picture without a mount, the wood chosen to match the dining room furniture.

Professor Dr. Eugen von Philippovich lectured on Economics and their legal framework. His course of lectures in the winter semester of 1909/1910 are entered as five hours per week. In front of me I have my father's copy of Philippovich's work: *Grundriss der Politischen Oekonomie*. It is the fourth edition, 1909, which he must have bought to go with his lectures.

But the name that means more than any other to me is that of Professor Dr Josef Schey, Baron Schey. He was Dean of the Law Faculty and a Fellow of the University Governing Body. The time honoured Latin on my father's doctorate is evocative:

JOSEPHUS LIBER BARO DE SCHEY
Juris Doctor Juris Civilis Austriaci Profesor Publicus Ordinarius
Imperatoris Austriae A Consiliis Aulae
Senatus Austriaci Socius

In my father's third year, his series of lectures dealt with Civil Law and Family Law. It was 1908, six years before my father first met my mother. Little did he then know that Irma Schey, a daughter of the eminent Professor standing in front of him, was a friend of his future wife, a close friendship formed when they were still at school together.

In 1938, one of Josef Schey's sons, Witold, came to London with his wife Gretl, and their daughters Carola and Alix. For several generations, the family Schey had been part of the elegant, social, musical and artistic world of Vienna. Baron Josef Schey had been a father figure to countless lawyers, famous for his Commentaries on Statute Law. Witold was an eminent surgeon.

As a child he had learnt the violin, and brought his instrument with him to England. I knew from my mother that Witold played but she did not know how good he was.

During the war, for a time, Carola and Alix were evacuated to Oxford and it was there, in February 1941, that Carola celebrated her 17th birthday. I was invited. Carola also played the violin, as sometimes happens with fathers and daughters. When I arrived her violin was lying on the table. Suddenly Witold picked it up, sat down with it and put it between his knees like a cello. With the unforgettable downward glance of a real cellist, his head serenely poised over the small instrument, he played the majestic, slow, opening theme from the Dvořák *Cello Concerto*. The eight bars were perfectly in tune, and the tone carefully modulated. Carola told me that it was Witold's party piece, and for some time afterwards I tried to play it myself.

After the war in London, I became a close friend of the Schey family. It was at that time, that Witold showed me his precious instrument. It was made in Cremona, in Italy, by a pupil of Stradivarius, Lorenzo Guadagnini. He allowed me to try it. I played a few random passages, the first time I had ever held anything so wonderful. And then I played a movement from a Bach Solo Sonata. As Witold put the instrument back into its case, he told me that it had a distinguished provenance, and that it is possible that Paganini had played on it during his visit to Vienna.

There are countless legends surrounding Paganini. He came to Vienna in March 1828. His first concert on the 29th March took place in the Redouten Saal. The programme included his *Concerto in B minor*, his *Sonata Militaire* (Napoleon) for G string alone, and his *Larghetto* and *Variation for Violin* on a Rondo from Rossini's *Cenerentola*.

He gave further concerts on the 13th, 16th and 18th April, and altogether appeared fourteen times during his four month stay. He played his own compositions from memory, which was very unusual at the time.

The virtuoso swept aside the technical challenges to his genius. His violin seemed to speak a new language. Several pieces included his left-hand pizzicato, when notes were plucked in mandolin-like accompaniment at the same time as available fingers played a melody with the bow. His revolutionary harmonics gave the instrument the ethereal sound of a dulcet flute. In prestissimo spiccato passages, his bow bounced with breath-taking speed, and the up and down movement of the stick imbued his playing with the excitement of unsurpassed achievement.

His repertoire at the time included the incredible bravura of the Witches' Dance Variations, *Le Streghe*, and the formidable difficulties of his three Violin Concertos.

Pieces which were played only on the G string, with orchestral accompaniment, such as the Variations on *La Preghiera* (The Prayer) from Rossini's *Mosé in Egitto*, and Variations on Haydn's *Gott erhalte* (the Emperor theme) were enthusiastically received. Soon after Paganini's arrival in Vienna, rumours began to circulate that he had stabbed to death an unfaithful lover, and that he had taught himself, whilst in prison, how to play whole pieces on the single G string. He issued a public denial, which, even so, must have added to his aura of daemonic mystery.

The greatest musicians from all parts flocked to hear him. The town went wild. There were articles in the newspapers. Poems were written in praise of him. Numerous portraits were produced. Fashionable cooks called new dishes by his name. Gloves, hats, shoes coats were now 'à la Paganini'. Ladies had their coiffure 'à la Paganini'. His image appeared on ladies' fans, on snuff boxes, on walking stick handles. Ivory violin bow frogs were engraved with his likeness and, as would be expected Paganini appeared on violins. The backs of instruments were decorated with carved images of the virtuoso standing and holding his violin and bow, framed by garlands of laurel leaves. Waltzes were written based on his themes and loaves were baked in the shape of violins.

This was personality cult and popular following, in the age of enthusiasm. What a relief it must have been to forget for a short time the autocracy of Kaiser Ferdinand and the paternalism of Prince Metternich.

A few years earlier, at the end of Kaiser Franz's reign, Vienna was gripped with excitement of a very unusual kind. It was a prelude to the Paganini craze, but for a very different reason. The Pasha of Egypt had presented Kaiser Franz with a giraffe which was duly exhibited in the Zoological Gardens of the Schönbrunn Palace. People rushed to see it. And what happened then was only a mild foretaste of the Paganini visit. There were patisseries made in the shape of giraffes, textiles had giraffe images, or were decorated with giraffe spots; there was wallpaper and furniture, and crockery that incorporated the spotty theme. Women wore their hair 'à la giraffe'.

I asked Witold to tell me something about Paganini and Vienna. At the time, I was studying the *24 Caprices* and playing Tartini's *Devil's Trill Sonata*. Witold was famous for his stories about the great singers and instrumentalists of the past, starting with personal recollection and going back to anecdotal tradition. He told me the story of Paganini in Vienna, buying a pair of gloves. When asked if he wanted them "à la giraffe?" Paganini thought that this referred to the skin of which the gloves were made and explained that he preferred to have them made from the skin of some other animal. "A la Paganini?" asked the salesman innocently.

Witold looked at me with inner intensity when he spoke about his violin and Paganini. His big brown eyes in his handsome face fixed mine with imperative shafts of credibility. He lowered his voice to match the reverence of his utterance, as if he himself stood in awe at the enormity of what he was saying.

How can one describe the love for a glorious instrument? As one picks it up, and places it under one's chin, and caresses it with the bow, it responds. Often I have wondered who might have played on my William Forster II viola, made in London in 1784. How many owners might there have been? How many thousands of times did left hands move up and down the neck? How well did they play? What did they play and where? Of course, old instruments have their history, and one is proud to be part of it. Now, after more than half a century, I still feel the sense of wonder, of reverence on hearing Witold's words: "wie der Paganini in Wien war, hat er vielleicht auf der Geige gespielt" (when Paganini was in Vienna, he may perhaps have played on the violin).

There was also a sad episode in the musical past of the Schey family. Melanie Koechert, a great aunt of Carola and Alix, committed suicide by jumping out of a window. This was shortly after Hugo Wolf's death in an asylum at the age of forty-two in 1903. Theodor Koechert, the brother of Melanie's husband Heinrich, was a leading Court Jeweller (Hofjuwelier) and a great patron of music. He supported the young composer on his arrival in Vienna. Hugo Wolf was penniless, eking out an existence by giving lessons, copying music, scoring and working as a music critic. The Koecherts were rich and famous and their salon was the venue of the most advanced musical circles and the finest literary society. With the Koecherts' help Hugo Wolf quickly made valuable acquaintances. He fell in love with Melanie and she reciprocated, tragically to end in early deaths.

To become a fully qualified lawyer, my father had first to pass various exams and then complete periods of probationary appointments. First of all, there were the Staatsprüfungen (State Examinations), the Final University Examinations. He took three of these, in July 1908, November 1910 and June 1911, all with excellent grades, and obtaining distinctions in Commercial, Financial and Public Law.

Then followed three preliminary postings. On the 14th May 1912 a document was issued by the High Court of Vienna, admission to the Service for Preparatory Judicial Training (Richterlicher Vorbereitungsdienst) at the Bezirksgericht Innere Stadt (Inner City District Court). On the 7th August, my father was directed to the Bezirksgericht Josefstadt, another Viennese district, and on the 4th November to the Vienna District Court. The certificate had the handwritten endorsement: "sehr lobenswert" (very praiseworthy).

This period of initial training came to an end on the 4th February 1913 when my father was accepted by the High Court with a yearly salary of 1,000 Kronen. He had to swear the judicial oath and his official title was Auskultant (literally 'a Listener'). He had to start at the District Court of St. Pölten, to serve what could best be described as his stipendiary pupillage.

St Pölten is about 40 miles from Vienna and my father had to live away from home. In my treasured Baedeker's Guidebook of Austria (1896) there is a money table. 300 Austrian Kronen is the equivalent of 25 pounds sterling, which would make 1,000 Kronen about £80 at that reckoning. It was at any rate a modest renumeration.

Life in the small provincial town must have been rather like an exile, and my father came to Vienna as often as he could. After nearly a year, in January 1914, he was posted back to the Landesgericht in Vienna.

He had successfully completed his tour of duty. The official document, dated 10th January 1914, ends with praise and is signed by the President of the District Court of St Pölten, K.K. Hofrat (Imperial Royal Privy Counsellor) Müllner: "Bei diesem Anlasse spreche ich Ihnen für Ihre hierämtliche sehr eiferige und vorzügliche Dienstleistung und für Ihr tadelloses Verhalten die wohl verdiente Anerkennung aus. (I take this opportunity to express well deserved recognition for the dedicated and excellent performance of your official duties here, and for your impeccable conduct".)

Back in Vienna he was posted to the State Prosecution Service in the District Court of Margarethen, where after seven months, on the 21st August 1914, he was directed to continue his Preparatory Judicial Training.

But against what backcloth of history! On Sunday 28th June, Crown Prince Franz Ferdinand and his wife were assassinated in Sarajevo. It lit the Balkan powderkeg which exploded on the 4th August 1914. For my father, as for millions of others, the old world had come to an end. He continued with his legal training for a few more months, and then, early in 1915, he joined up.

And there was another event which changed his life forever. In the autumn of 1914, he met his future wife.

From time to time, the Neumanns gave a soirée, 'eine grosse Gesellschaft', as my mother described it, and it was to one of these in the autumn of 1914 that Lena invited her. She remembered the moment she arrived at the apartment, how Hermine and Wilhelm looked at her with critical glances of appraisal. "Sie haben mich von oben bis unten angeschaut" (They looked me up and down), she recalled. She was on view in her simple dress, so different from the expensive silk brocade and tulle finery which was fashionable. But for my father it was love at first sight. Afterwards, he said to his sister Lena: "Warum habt ihr mir diesen Engel verschwiegen?" (Why did you keep this angel a secret?) They announced their engagement at the end of 1914, but decided to wait until the war was over. Peace, however, was too slow in coming, and the marriage took place on the 21st January 1917.

CHAPTER 6

The challenge of a century

My parents came from very different worlds. My grandfather Wilhelm's work for the Rothschild bankers had enabled him to establish a wealthy lifestyle, although he preferred to continue to live in the Ferdinandstrasse. My mother told me that the Neumanns could so easily have moved to an elegant part of the city, but Wilhelm and especially Hermine felt that the Ferdinandstrasse was where they belonged. Her parents had died there. She had lived there since she was three. As a journalist of the *Fremden-Blatt*, the official court newspaper, Wilhelm was well respected and the bestowal of the title Regierungsrat at an early age was an official recognition for his profound articles on social, political and financial issues, covering Austro-Hungary and beyond. In 1894 he was made Commander of the Imperial Order of Franz Joseph (Ritterkreuz des Franz-Joseph-Ordens), and later that year he received the Order of the Iron Crown (Eiserne Krone). In the following year, in 1895, King Alexander I of Serbia bestowed on him the Order of St. Sawa. In 1897, Shah Nasir of Persia invested him with the Order of the Lion and the Sun. King Haakon VI of Norway made him a Knight of the Order of St. Olav, in 1907. He received the Commander Cross of the Civil Order of Merit from King Ferdinand of Bulgaria in 1911. And then, in December 1911, King George I of the Hellenes bestowed on him the Order of Our Redeemer.

My father enjoyed a privileged childhood in pre-1914 Habsburg Vienna. As the son of Regierungsrat Wilhelm Neumann he would have a social *entrée*, a niche, an introduction. He was handsome, charming, romantic. In his manuscript book of poems there are several love poems. My mother told me that he had been seriously romantically involved on several occasions before she met him.

By comparison, my mother's home was very modest. In 1906, at the age of 70, Mayer's employment was reduced, and in 1909 he finally retired on a very small pension. The testimonial from the private bank J. & A. Brecher is dated 31st December 1909. There were at that time many small banks, registered on the Vienna Stock Exchange, often agents or correspondents of large financial institutions. The letter heading is a reminder of the great entrepreneurial decades of the second half of the 19th century:

J. & A. Brecher WIEN Telegramme: BRECHER WIEN BÖRSE GIRO-KONTO: "OESTERREICHISCH-UNGARISCHE BANK".

The text reads: "Womit bestätigt wird, dass Herr Mayer Braunthal bei uns seit dem 17. April 1878 bis 31. Dezember 1909 als Buchhalter in unseren Diensten stand und dass er durch seine ausserordentliche Pflichttreue den ihm obgelegen Agenden zu unserer vollsten Zufriedenheit entsprach.

Herr Braunthal verliess den Posten, den er bei uns seit so vielen Jahren inne hatte, lediglich wegen seines hohen Alters". (It is herewith confirmed that Mr. Mayer Braunthal was in our employment from the 17th April 1878 to the 31st December 1909 as a bookkeeper, and that he fulfilled his tasks with an exceptional sense of duty to our complete satisfaction. Mr. Braunthal relinquished the post which he had occupied for so many years, solely because of his great age.)

In 1909 Mayer and Clara's six children were all in their way at critical stages: Bertha, the oldest then aged twenty-three, had started to work in an office a few years earlier and helped financially. My mother was about to take her final school examination, which she did externally in July 1910, at the Mädchenlyzeum run by the famous Dr. Eugenie Schwarzwald. In October 1913 she passed her Reifezeugnis, her matriculation examination to study French at the University.

Julius left school at fourteen to undergo a three-year apprenticeship as a bookbinder. He also collected and delivered heavy washing for my grandmother which she took in to make the small pension go further. His socialist political leanings took root in Berlin in 1912 where he met Karl Kautzky and Rudolf Hilferding, the charismatic leaders of the movement. Shortly afterwards, in December 1912, Julius joined the staff of the *Volksstimme*, a Socialist newspaper in Warnsdorf, in Bohemia. It was the first step in an illustrious career as a socialist journalist. He was called up in 1914.

Wilhelm must have regarded Julius with a certain amount of suspicion, a fervent socialist, the future brother-in-law of his son Paul.

Bertha's story had also become widely known, and was of course reported to my father by my mother. In 1913 Bertha happened to be on a visit in England. She went to Germany in 1914 when war broke out. And there in Berlin she was sent to jail for her communist anti-war activities, but the Austrian government managed to negotiate her release.

The two sisters could not have been more different. Bertha, the life-long communist, a founder member of the German Communist party, and my mother, whose search for salvation made her a Catholic and a Dominican Tertiary. Bertha was a dedicated activist. In 1920 she was appointed party secretary of the women's propaganda section of the Central Committee of the Unabhängige Sozialdemokratische Partei Deutschlands (the Independent Social Democratic Party of Germany). In October 1920, she became a member of the Central Committee. In 1921, she was a delegate of the Second International Women's Conference in Moscow. Family legend maintains that Bertha "sat at Lenin's feet". And then in August 1921, she was elected a member of the Central Committee of the German Communist Party.

In 1917, at the time when my mother married my father, Bertha was a founder member of the Spartakus movement, led by Karl Liebknecht and Rosa Luxemburg, a radical forerunner of the German Communist Party. They were both shot in January 1919 by government militia, and became iconic matyrs. The old order had come to an end in November 1918, and this was the time for revolution and counter-revolution.

For Bertha, the assassination of her personal friends and comrades made her even more resolute. From time to time my mother spoke about her sister and used to say: "Die Bertha hat Scheuklappen" (Bertha has blinkers), referring to her complete political intolerance and absolute single-mindedness in the pursuit of her ideals.

My mother regarded her older sister with a certain amount of awe. In her eyes, Bertha was serious, fully absorbed by a social conscience, and by the messianic dream of world revolution. Bertha was full of personal principles, a vegetarian at a time when it was unusual, and a prominent member of the Vienna Temperance Society (die Wiener Antialkoholiker). In the poor working-class districts of Vienna, cheap alcohol, wine from the vineyards, was an ongoing problem.

There is one story about her and her sister which I treasure. It is a dramatic cameo, the climax of which would only have lasted about two seconds. My mother told me that she was deeply moved by the famous dramatic actor Adolf von Sonnenthal. He was another idol of the Viennese, in memorable roles, which became bywords of theatre history. It was near the end of his life, he died in 1909 at the age of 75, that he appeared in a reprise of greatness, in a series of appearances of unspoken valediction.

My mother never mentioned any theatre or opera diaries similar to those of Lena and Anne. She left Vienna two days after the Anschluss with minimum of luggage and in the subsequent packing many personal documents and letters were destroyed as they might be deemed incriminatory in random censorship.

However, Lena certainly saw Sonnenthal in all his roles during his final years, and my mother on her own, or with Bertha, must have seen some of them. On the 12th and 14th of January 1905, Lena went to *Don Karlos* by Schiller. Sonnenthal was Phillipp II, and Don Karlos was Kainz! It was altogether a distinguished cast. I think of Lena, on that 14th January, aged fourteen, going to something so wonderful a second time. On the 13th May she saw Sonnenthal as Wallenstein in *Wallensteins Tod*, and on the 20th October his Wallenstein in *Die Piccolomini*. She went to *Egmont* on the 24th March 1906 when he appeared as Wilhelm von Oranien. And then, on the 12th June he was King Lear. At the start of the autumn season, on the 22nd September, he was Nathan, in Lessing's *Nathan der Weise*, one of his greatest roles.

Sonnenthal is entered twice more in Lena's theatre book, in 1908, but it was in 1905 or 1906, during which time Lena saw him seven times, that the story of my mother and Bertha is set.

My mother saw Sonnenthal as Lear and as Nathan. So it was probably some time in 1906, that she persuaded Bertha, who had similarly become a Sonnenthal fan, to go to his house and catch a glimpse of him. They found out where he lived, and possibly the times when he was likely to leave his home. Adolf von Sonnenthal lived in Währing, in the 18th District, in the elegant tree-lined Anastasius-Grün-Gasse. It was the 'Cottage', the residential area of the rich and famous who preferred to live in splendid villas in their large gardens, rather than in the centre of Vienna. On a late 19th century photograph, I see the five-storey mansion, beautifully detached, on the corner of the road. The avenue is straight and long and the trees merge at the end, in the far distance. My mother takes up the story: "We arrived and waited. Suddenly he came out, and as he passed us he said 'Guten Abend' ". She invested the four syllables with the dark sonority of a bass voice and the episode became very real, two stage-struck girls greeted by the great Sonnenthal.

School can be the agent of romance. Families are introduced to each other, sometimes with far-reaching results!

When my mother first attended the school of 'Frau Doktor' Schwarzwald, her future sister-in-law Lena had already been a pupil for several years. Eugenie Schwarzwald was a very remarkable woman. She was a pioneer, an educationalist with a deep social conscience, in a world where girls faced serious discrimination. She took over an existing girls school in 1901 at the age of 29, and transferred it to a large house on the Kohlmarkt, in the centre of Vienna. Her progressive school was the first in Austria, where girls could take the 'Matura', the matriculation exam, which was a prerequisite for University admission.

Her friend, Adolf Loos, redesigned the interior and gave the classrooms and the assembly hall a modernist character. The building was crowned with a large roof garden, very innovative for Vienna in the early nineteen hundreds.

Eugenie Schwarzwald persuaded her friends to take some of the classes. She had met Oskar Kokoschka through Adolf Loos, and in 1911 Kokoschka started to teach drawing for three hours per week to senior girls. At different times Arnold Schoenberg and Egon Wellesz taught music. Adolf Loos introduced architecture. She admired Schoenberg and offered him her school in the afternoons, when it was closed for normal teaching. The intention was to establish a free conservatory of music. The courses started in 1904. Schoenberg lectured on harmony and counterpoint, Zemlinsky spoke about instrumentation and musical form. The project did not last long, but it illustrated Eugenie Schwarzwald's enthusiasm for modernity and progress.

My mother left school in July 1903. She was nearly fourteen years old, the standard school leaving age. The school was the 'Öffentliche Bürgerschule (Municipal Secondary School) in the 9th District at Glasergasse 8. At that time, the family lived next door at Glasergasse 21. My mother may not have had far to walk, but she told me how unhappy she was when they moved to that address. It was her third home so far. She was born at Obere Donaustrasse 63 in the Leopoldstadt. When she was about four or five years old, the family moved to a larger flat in the Untere Donaustrasse, in a better area, downstream, along the Donaukanal, that regular loop of the river, which flows through the city.

More room was needed with the arrival of Julius in 1891 and Ignaz in 1893. But a few years later, Clara had to find a cheaper, smaller flat, as a result of Mayer's semi-retirement. Soon she would have two more children, Alfred born in 1897, and Mini born in 1898. My mother described the time in the Glasergasse as very stressful. She was left with a composite sombre memory of the place, of which having to share a bed with Bertha was only a small part. After all that, the final move to to Boschstrasse 2 in Heiligenstadt was an entry into a different world, so near to Grinzing, so near to the Wienerwald and Beethoven country.

When my mother talked about her past, she often mentioned where she was living at the time, and the Obere Donaustrasse inevitably came up with her earliest memories. On one of my visits to Vienna in the 1980s, I looked at the building where she was born, about 100 years earlier, on that 18th August 1889.

The late 18th century, early 19th century tenement block still stood, unchanged, on the embankment. My mother remembered the small dark rooms, facing onto the long, narrow courtyard, where she took her first steps on the cobblestones.

The name of the house, which I heard so often in my mother's stories, the Produktenhof, was cast in elegant capital letters, set in the original wrought-iron arch across the gateway. Suddenly, as I drew level, I was confronted by the familiar word, which I had not expected to see. It was very moving, that personal connotation of the locality. Years earlier, I visited the cemetery in Trencin, where my great grandparents Neumann lie buried. There, I experienced a feeling of ancestral reverence and mystery, which was so strangely similar to that moment in Vienna. Both echoed the poignant topography of family history, with their polarity of birth and death spread out over the Austro-Hungarian Empire.

In the recent redevelopment of the Leopoldstadt, the Neumann house in the Ferdinandstrasse and both Braunthal houses along the Donaukanal were pulled down. Similarly, Boschstrasse 2 no longer stands.

There was one day during her time in the Glasergasse which she especially remembered. It was Monday the 4th December 1898. Vienna was celebrating the Golden Jubilee of Kaiser Franz Joseph. He had ascended the throne at the age of eighteen, the nephew of Kaiser Ferdinand, who had abdicated in his favour, driven from the throne by the revolution of 1848. Now, fifty years later, there were processions along the Ringstrasse, the ideal circular route for ceremonial occasions. My mother was anxious to watch, but Clara, usually so keen to join in, said she was too tired. Eventually my mother was allowed to go with a friend. She just could not understand why her mother wanted to stay at home on such a unique day for Imperial Vienna.

When she returned home she saw and heard the reason. Mini, Clara's sixth child, was born whilst she was out. My mother told me repeatedly that she had absolutely no idea that another baby was on the way. I asked her several times: "Aber wie war das möglich? Hast Du nichts bemerkt?" (But how was that possible? Did you not notice anything?) Clara apparently was always rather stout and wore long loose-fitting dresses.

There was no intention of preparing girls for further education, but rather of helping them with possible future secretarial work or book-keeping. One of the subjects in my mother's 'Entlassungszeugnis' (final school report) was 'Rechnen in Verbindung mit einfacher Buchführung' (arithmetic with simple book-keeping), and another one was similarly descriptive: 'Unterrichtssprache in Verbindung mit Geschäftsaufsätzen' (the language used in teaching, applied to essays on business matters).

The language used for teaching is 'Hochdeutsch', the High German, which is the official German in Germany, Austria and Switzerland. Many regional dialects flourish underneath this umbrella of linguistic unity, a hundred years ago even more so. German is an inflected language and the declension of nouns and the conjugation of verbs, can be subject to endless modification. The syntax and grammar are full of pitfalls, even for a native speaker, and very soon reveal educational status. This then is the Unterrichtssprache in which children learn how to read and write. Mass tourism, social mobility and television have eroded the dialects, but even today I cannot understand the full Styrian dialect (the Steirisch) which is still spoken by the older villagers in Altaussee.

My mother's school report covers the usual subjects but also includes French, which was optional. Her choice would have a profound influence on her future. She was determined to study it at University, and this led her to seek the help of Eugenie Schwarzwald.

She told the 'Frau Doktor' how anxious she was to obtain her Matura in order to study French, and how her parents could not possibly afford the school fees. That was probably about two years after she left school. She was earning some money as a tutor, helping children with their homework. It was quite usual for well-to-do families to engage a 'Hauslehrer'. She gave these 'Nachhilfestunden', tutorial coaching to slow learners. She was briefly a governess, speaking French to two daughters of a rich Bulgarian family in Sofia. Prior to the First World War, French was the cultural lingua franca, especially in Russia, Eastern Europe and the Balkans.

I knew one of my mother's former pupils, Teddy Kremenetzky, because his family owned a house in Altaussee, where the Neumanns spent their summer holidays. I liked Teddy who must have been in his thirties in the 1930s. I admired his grand Packard coupé sports car which had two courtesy seats at the back, outside the car body. A boot-like lid, hinged at the lower edge, had to be opened to reveal the bench and provide the back rest.

It was in this car, in about 1936, that I joined Peter Schick and his mother Hedy (née Neumann), a cousin of my father, for a visit to Salzburg. It is difficult to imagine this now, but at that time a journey in a car was very exciting. In Vienna I had been in a taxi on very few occasions with my parents. This time, I would travel for about two hours over a steep mountain pass, the so-called Pötschen, past the famous Lake of St. Wolfgang (the Wolfgangsee) to the beautiful city, Mozart's birthplace.

Teddy had promised Peter that in Salzburg he would buy him the latest edition of the standard professional stamp catalogue, the 'Michel Briefmarken Katalog'. Peter had a beautiful collection, mine was small, and I was just beginning. When we arrived we went to a large bookshop in the Getreidegasse, near the actual house in which Mozart was born some 180 years earlier. The owner was anxious to make a sale, and realising that the 'Michel Katalog' was very expensive, also produced a cheaper publication, the so-called 'Senf Briefmarken Katalog'. Peter was given his Michel catalogue, very thick, bound in blue.

And then Teddy realised that I also collected stamps. "Du sammelst ja auch" (You also collect). I was too shy to ask for something so substantial and chose the more modest Senf.

From time to time, I opened the beloved red book, and looked once more at the black and white illustrations, the carefully notated alternative watermarks, the prices of used and unused stamps, the size, the evocative details of complete sets, in the alphabetical order of their countries and chronologically listed. It was a catalogue in the fullest sense. The information for the sets was laid out in columns, starting with stamps of the lowest denomination face value and adding the exact date of issue. I could see what I had, and what I would like to have. Stamps for me had mystique and allure; the second half of the 19th century and the first half of the 20th, roughly those hundred years, were the great age of the posted letter. The most famous stamp was there, the Queen Victoria Penny Black, the first stamp ever issued, with the recent auction results of the early Thirties. I looked at the little picture with veneration, the Mona Lisa of the philatelic world

When it came to listing mistakes, the catalogue seemed to be gleefully schoolmasterly. In spite of careful proofreading, errors did occur, admittedly very rarely. The issues were withdrawn, but the stamps which had entered the public domain became real collectors' items and very valuable. Often the faulty part of the stamp was enlarged, showing perhaps irregular perforation or a minute floral imperfection in the decorative border.

After the war, I sold my stamps. Together with my wife, Patricia, I started to collect Antiquarian prints, first editions of music, original lithographs, etchings and engravings. As many a collector before me, I compiled my own catalogue. And sometimes I thought of Teddy's red book, the Senf Briefmarkenkatalog, which had given me so much pleasure.

In my mother's recollection, Teddy had been a very lazy boy and would not do his homework properly. How different from his father, she said, who had arrived in Vienna from Odessa as a young man and built up a factory manufacturing light bulbs. According to her, this was not an ordinary factory, but a truly modern, model factory which anticipated the domestic demand for electricity after the years of gloomy gas.

The Kremenetskys lived in a very grand residence, on the second floor of an 18th century building in the centre of Vienna, and below them was the apartment of Rosa Papier, the famous mezzo-soprano. Occasionally my mother could hear her singing and teaching. The parents of Rosa must have chosen her Christian name with humorous intention, and when my mother first started speaking about her, I asked her rather incredulously: "Hat sie wirklich Rosa Papier geheissen?" (Was she really called Rosa Papier?)

My mother told me that Rosa Papier used her considerable influence at the Opera to secure Gustav Mahler's appointment as Director in 1897, and that one of her pupils, Anna von Mildenburg, would soon dominate the stage singing Brünnhilde, Isolde, Elsa, Leonore, Kundry.

In November 1908, four years after leaving the school in the Glasergasse, my mother received her 'Lehrbefähigungs-Zeugnis' (teaching certificate), when she passed (with distinction) the qualifying examination to teach French. The type of institution in which she was allowed to teach is carefully listed: Bürgerschulen, spezielle Lehrkurse, Fortbildungskurse, Sprachschulen und Lehbildungsanstalten (Secondary Schools, special teaching courses, further education courses, language schools and teacher training institutes). Under the heading of 'Zurückgelegte Studien und abgelegte Prüfungen' (previous studies and examinations passed) the entry reads: Privatstudien (private studies). The private studies referred to the help and encouragement which she received from Eugenie Schwarzwald. Now she could join the staff and help with French. There would be two more hurdles to negotiate. Firstly, the 'Reifezeugnis' (Matriculation) which my mother passed with distinction in July 1910. She was then registered at the Mädchenlyzeum Schwarzwald; she was nearly twenty-one years old. According to the report, she had joined the school the previous autumn. Three years later, in October 1913, she passed her second Reifezeugnis, which made her eligible to attend a university.

Paul's sister Lena joined the school in October 1904, and left in July 1907, at the age of sixteen. She was always an outstanding pupil and passed her Reifezeugnis with distinction in July 1907.

Although my mother and Lena did not overlap as pupils, my mother was frequently on the premises for special studies. On one occasion she had asked to see the Frau Doktor. She was just about to knock on the door when it opened and out came a very beautiful girl, crying bitterly. "Wer ist das?" (Who is that?) she asked. "Das ist die Lena Neumann" (That is Lena Neumann).

Mizzi Neumann, five years younger than Lena, started at Schwarzwald's probably in 1905. There was thus plenty of Neumann connection for friendships to flourish.

Ultimately there would be even more family links. Hilde Braunthal (née Elkan) Alfred's future wife, spent some years at the school. She had a vivid memory of Rudolf Serkin, Rudi as she called him, coming to school to play to the girls.

Hilde was born in 1903 and was a pupil from about 1913 to 1919. Rudi was a few months older, she recalled, and first played at the school when she was in her first year. He became an international pianist of great renown, specialising in the Viennese classics, such as Mozart and Schubert. She remembered him so well, walking to the piano in his short trousers, and Frau Doktor, full of admiration for her young protégé. Hilde could not recall what he played on that occasion but Lena heard him for the first time on the 18th May 1921. Serkin was eighteen, taking part in the Beethoven *Triple Concerto*, joining his future father-in-law, Adolf Busch, who completed the Beethoven concert with the *Violin Concerto* and the *Romance in F.*

My mother was admitted to the University in the autumn of 1913, to read French. Ten years had elapsed since she had left the Secondary School in the Glasergasse, a decade in which her determination to study was sustained by her strength of character. She entered the spirit of her new life with enthusiasm. Professor Kretschmer, her professor, recognised her industry and application, and encouraged her to join a large group of students on a university tour to Egypt and Crete, scheduled for the spring of 1914. They would visit Cairo, the Sphinx, the Pyramids at Giza, and travel up the Nile to Karnak, in what turned out to be the twilight of the Ottoman Empire.

In Crete they would marvel at the palace at Knossos where Sir Arthur Evans had begun his monumental work of excavation and restoration some twenty years earlier. Documentation of the exact itinerary and timetable are lost, but the Rector's speech at the end of the university year refers to about three hundred and fifty students and academic staff who undertook the journey. The University published a booklet which was issued to those taking part. *Wissenschaftlicher Führer zur fünften Wiener Universitätsreise nach Egypten und Kreta, 8. bis 28. April 1914* (Academic guide for the fifth Vienna University journey to Egypt and Crete, 8th to 28th April 1914) had chapters written by various professors on the history, geology, population, climate, flora and fauna.

About sixty years later, my mother showed me the long group photograph, taken in front of a hotel on the banks of the Nile. Unfortunately the right-hand edge had got torn off. She was a little uncertain about a tiny speck in the sea of faces and wondered whether she was on the missing portion. Thirty girls stand among the men, the women in their white blouses and long skirts, and all the men wearing jackets, collars and ties. Topees and cloche hats cover the scene of nostalgic exploration.

The journey would have started by special train from Vienna to the port of Trieste, then part of Austro-Hungary. The University must have chartered a steamship to sail along the Dalmatian coast, cross the Mediterranean and dock at Alexandria in Egypt. It would have been necessary to change to a special Nile boat, a paddle steamer, to continue up the river to Thebes, the ancient capital. She sometimes talked about the three and a half thousand year-old temples at nearby Karnak and Luxor. The Sphinx and the Great Pyramid at Memphis embodied for her the monumental legacy of the Ancient World. But it was Thebes which left the deepest impression. Several days were allocated to tour the large archaeological sites on both sides of the river and to wander round the many temples.

At Karnak in the temple of Ramses III my mother had an unforgettable experience. She told me how thrilling it was to enter the Great Courtyard, flanked by a row of giant pillar statues of the God Osiris. Later that day she decided to go back and look again at the mystery of an ancient civilisation. She slipped out of the hotel and walked the short distance. Let my mother continue the story, which I have heard many times.

"Ich wollt mir noch einmal die Osiris Statuen anschauen. Ich war ganz allein. Es hat schon angefangen dunkel zu werden. Ich steh' vor einer Statue und schau' sie an. Und auf einmal bewegen sich die Augen. Ich schrei auf und renn so rasch ich kann zurück ins Hotel" (I wanted to look at the Osiris statues once more. I was all alone. It had started to get dark. I stand in front of a statue and look at it. And all of a sudden the eyes start to move. I scream and run back to the hotel as fast as I can).

When my mother kissed her father goodbye on that 8th April 1914 it would be their last embrace. He died on the 15th April. Two weeks later, on her return, she was greeted with the terrible news.

Right: My grandfather Mayer Braunthal. As a boy, he travelled from Odessa to Brody sitting on the axle of a wagon, a journey that must have taken several weeks.

Below: Grandfather Mayer Braunthal's phylacteries, which were entrusted by his widow Clara to their daughter, my mother. One leather box is strapped around the left arm, the other is tied over the forehead. Each box contains tiny parchments with Hebrew scripture. Mayer probably wore them only on rare occasions.

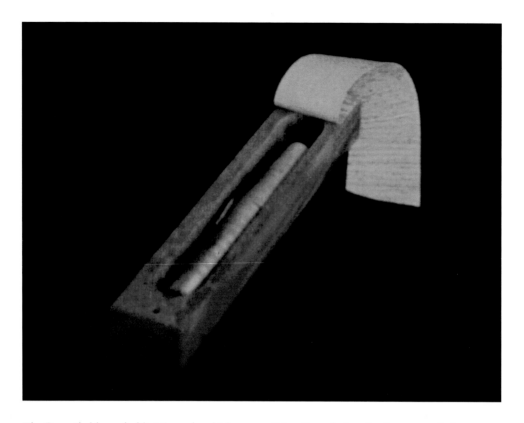

The Braunthal household's Mezuzah, which was traditionally nailed to the door post of a house. On the scroll, the opening words of the Hebrew prayer the Shema are inscribed.

When in 1938 Mayer's wife Clara shut the door for the last time on her Vienna flat, where she had lived for 30 years, she gave away all her possessions but kept the brass name-plate from the door as a memento. It travelled halfway round the world to Buenos Aires and back again, to come to rest in our vitrine in Wimbledon.

Above: My grandmother Clara, as a young woman in Vienna.

Above Right: In Buenos Aires in 1939 aged 77. Her voyage to South America on a transatlantic liner was "paradise".

Right: On the balcony of the Gersthoferstrasse in about 1935 aged c.73, a few years before she emigrated.

Left: Wilhelm Neumann's parents Samuel and Fanny in Trencin, in what is today Slovakia.

Below: Wilhelm's mother Fanny née Sonnenfeld, my great-grandmother.

Below Left: Hermine's father Leopold Kuffler, in a photograph probably taken within a few years of his death in Vienna in 1913.

Above: Wilhelm as a young boy in his birthplace of Trencin, in the 1860s.

Right: On their wedding day in 1886: Wilhelm aged 26 and his bride Hermine aged 20.

Wilhelm's Figaro cigar box still smells of his Virginia tobacco.

When I was invited as a little boy to my grandparents on Sundays, I used to watch closely as grandfather Wilhelm prepared his Virginia cigar after lunch, using this mother-of-pearl cigar cutter. I tell the story on page 24.

Above: Standing outside the gates of actor Hugo Thimig's house in Vienna: my grandfather Wilhelm...
... and myself on the same spot many years later.

Right: The man himself: Hugo Thimig in April 1897. The great comedy and character actor was a friend of Wilhelm and later went on to direct the Burgtheater.

Left: Hermine, who presided over the Ferdinandstrasse with undisputed authority. Her four children were all still living at home at the outbreak of the First World War. The cook Frau Rosa was with the family for forty years until 1938; the nanny Lala stayed on as a family retainer until her death in 1935.

Below: Wilhelm, at the wheel, and Hermine with an aunt of Hermine in 1909.

Wilhelm's younger brother Muzzo, a bank
director who lived in a large elegant apartment
in the Liechtenstrasse in Vienna.
He was deported in 1942 and murdered in a
concentration camp.

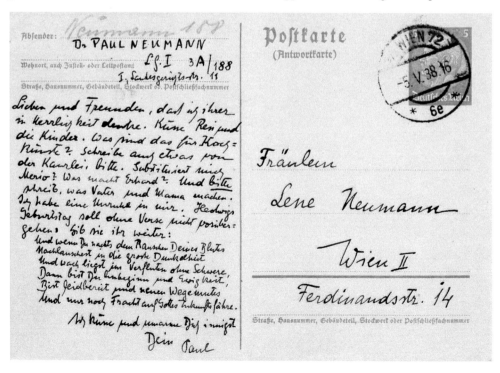

Above: The poem from Paul's cell-mate Franz Kobler, written in pencil on a scrap of laundry tissue-paper, which I discovered by chance decades later placed inside my father's book of manuscript poems.

Below: The postcard sent by my father from his prison cell to his sister Lena in May 1938, bearing his poem. The sender's name Neumann and cell number 188 appear in faint writing at the top.

Above: Franz Kobler, Paul's cell-mate in prison and an eminent writer and historian.

Top Right: From left to right: Hermine, her husband Wilhelm and a younger sister of Hermine Stephanie (Steffi).

Above: Steffi, the mother of Anne, was murdered in 1942.

Left: Eduard, Wilhelm's brother, a successful lawyer who had a permanent debenture box at the Vienna Opera. He took his family regularly to Altaussee in the summers.

Above Left: Lena as a baby.

Above: Lena the beautiful society girl.

Left: Lena.

Below: The immensely popular and successful actor Josef Kainz. My father Paul, his sister Lena and their cousin Anne watched Kainz in all his roles. The actor wrote a personal dedication to Lena on this 1905 photograph. She would have been a stage-struck 14 year-old at the time.

Above: These two sisters, smiling here beside their mother Hermine, were to face very different destinies, as related in Chapter 15. Mizzi, on the right, was exiled from Poland to Russia and Kazakhstan during the Second World War and was to lose both her husband and son.

Josef Kainz as Tartuffe...

...in Arthur Schnitzler's The Green Kakadu...

...as Hamlet...

...as the Fool in King Lear.

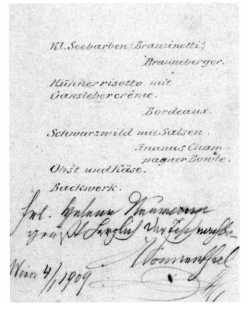

Above: The great actor Adolf von Sonnenthal, as King Lear. My aunt Lena recorded in her theatre diaries how she saw him seven times on stage in 1905 and 1906 alone. My mother often related how she and her sister Bertha once waited outside Sonnenthal's house to catch a glimpse of him. They were rewarded when he walked past the two girls, aged about 16 and 18, and greeted them with the words "Guten Abend".

Above: A menu bearing Adolf von Sonnenthal's autograph and dedication to his 18 year-old table neighbour Lena.

Below: Going down a salt mine, lamps in hand. A studio portrait in Berchtesgaden, near Salzburg, 5th August 1908. From left to right: Robert, Hermine, Trude, Lena, Hedi and Paul.

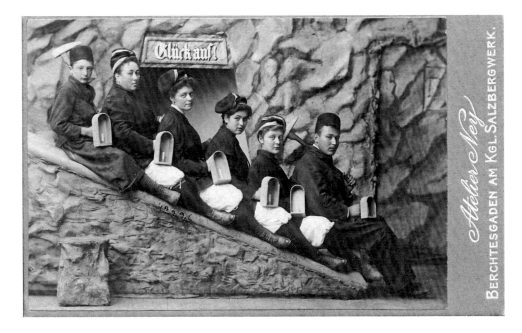

Paul aged 5 with his younger sister Lena aged 3 in 1893...

...a year later...

...and aged 16 and 14 in 1904.

The four siblings Paul, Robert, Mizzi and Lena...

...in 1901...

...and in 1906, the year when 18 year-old Paul graduated from the Franz Joseph Gymnasium, where he was an ouststanding pupil.

Front row left to right: Mizzi with her first cousin Fritz Neumann (the brother of Trude and Hedy). Back row left to right: Robert, Trude, Muzzo, Lena, Hedy. This group portrait was taken in front of a painted backdrop in a studio in Igls, near Innsbruck in Austria, on 8th August 1908.

Below: Author Oskar Jellinek, a close friend of my father, to whom he dedicated his 1926 novella *Die Mutter der Neun*. The story behind this horseback portrait is told on page 201.

Textile magnate Bernard Altmann, the subject of Chapter 14.

Lena's cousin Trude Geiringer, who took the photograph on the back cover of this book.

Bernard Altmann fourth from left, with Lena standing second from right, in Vienna.

Left: Bronze statuette of Kaiser Franz Joseph bearing the inscription 'offizielle Kriegsfürsorge' (official war welfare). It was purchased to support charitable work during the First World War. See page 118.

Above Right: Wilhelm wearing his medals. His standing as a respected journalist was reflected in the widespread congratulatory press coverage on the occasion of his seventieth birthday in 1930.

Wilhelm's medals

Paul (seated left) with his officers and men on the Italian front. Behind are the gun crew.

Paul (seated right), during the First World War.

Top Left: Paul home on leave in 1915.

Top Right: Paul

Bottom: My mother and her sister-in-law Mizzi, seated on a cannon during a visit to Paul (second left) at the Front.

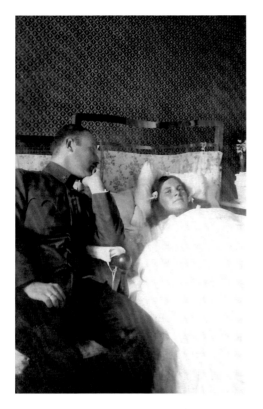

Top Left: Paul on leave in March 1918, with his wife Resi, around the time of my sister Eva's birth.

Above: With my mother Resi and my older sister Eva.

Left: Nessy, who moved with her husband Robert to New York after the Anschluss, but later separated and returned to live in her hometown of Kassel, Germany. I used to visit her in Kassel when I worked for Baerenreiter music publishers.

Dancing in Altaussee: my parents (left–hand couple) with family, in the 1930s.

A rare glimpse of everyday life enjoyed in Altaussee during those interwar summers, a "snapshot" quite in contrast to the posed studio portraits of the era. Facing the camera is my father's cousin Trude Geiringer, née Neumann. In the background, my parents.

Above: My mother's sister Bertha. She was a member of the Central Committee of the German Communist Party and according to family legend once "sat at Lenin's feet".

Below: My mother's fine kid wallet, produced by the Wiener Werkstätte, the association of design studios established in Secession Vienna in 1903. The wallet is described on page 177.

We still have these bookcases and books in London: my mother Resi in Vienna.

The salon in the Gersthoferstrasse, where I grew up. The bust on the tall plinth, seen here on the left, used to stand outside my bedroom. It was too heavy to be brought with us to London. I have often wondered what became of it.

CHAPTER 7

Call to arms

The courtship of my parents was overshadowed by the War. They announced their engagement just before my father reported to his heavy artillery regiment, on the 5th January 1915.

My mother mentioned on several occasions how sad she was that my father's wartime letters to her were not brought out from Vienna. She said they were so beautifully written with poetic love. She had kept them in a wooden box, tied together with a red ribbon. I therefore treasure a small book which my father gave to my mother in the winter of 1914. It is a miniature publication, very typical of the period, 13cm x 9cm, entitled "Rheinsberg, ein Bilderbuch für Verliebte" (Rheinsberg, a picture book for those in love), by Kurt Tucholsky. The board cover has a picture of an elegantly-dressed lady standing in a garden, accepting a rose from an admiring gentleman. The story, illustrated with charming pictures, describes the adventures of two lovers who spend two days in the country. On the fly-leaf my father wrote: "Dies kleine Sommerbüchlein nimms zur Freude manchen Winterabends von einem, der Deines Frühlings tief inne ward an einem Herbsttag. 1914" (Take this small book of Summer for the joy of some Winter evenings, from one who was deeply aware of your Spring on an Autumn day).

Throughout the war, my father served on the Italian front. There was much fighting in South Tyrol and in the foothills of the Alps, but it was on the banks of the river Isonzo, now in Slovenia, that a series of terrible battles took place. On the Western Front, the river Somme became a symbol of massive slaughter. For the Austrians and Italians, the Isonzo meant death for tens of thousands. The struggle was ongoing. There were in fact twelve battles, starting with the first one on the 23rd June 1915, only four weeks after Italy joined the war on the Allied side, and ending with the last one on the 7th November 1917. The Italians suffered enormous casualties, about 300,000, which was half their entire war loss. The Austro-Hungarian losses were about 200,000, perhaps one-sixth of their total casualties.

During the first ten months of the war, prior to Italy's entry, the Austrians fortified the Alps and adapted the impenetrable nature of the terrain, ready for the expected conflict. The valley of the Isonzo was therefore of great strategic importance to the Italians. It was their gateway to the North. It edged the great chain of mountains. It bypassed the impassable.

My father fought along the Isonzo. He was decorated with the Silberne Tapferkeitsmedaille 1. Klasse (Silver Medal for Bravery, 1st class) for his part in the evacuation of heavy artillery pieces out of Gorizia. This must have been during the sixth battle (6th to 12th August 1916), in which the Italians captured the town and established at last a bridgehead across the Isonzo. The Italians lost about 50,000 men, the Austro-Hungarian casualties killed, wounded or taken prisoner, came to 40,000.

Mercifully, my father was not one of them. In a photograph of my father's artillery battery, he is seated with his fellow officers, all wearing their medals. Standing behind is the gun crew of some twenty men. My father never spoke seriously about the war, nor was he full of anecdotes, so-called war stories that might have had a bizarre element. There was, though, the occasion when a Tyrolese peasant was asked how long it would take to march over a mountain pass. He replied in dialect: "Joah, zwa' Stund'. Aber wann a schiaßt!" (Well, two hours… but if they're shooting!) The Austrian army had special sections of mountain artillery (Gebirgsartillerie) with soldiers drawn from the Alps. The daredevil bravado of these country boys is well illustrated by another of my father's stories. "In den Bergen waren die Italiener oft sehr nah. Und die Tiroler haben manchmal mit der Hand in der Luft herumgefuchtelt so als Zielscheiben. Und wenn dann eine Kugel getroffen hat, war das a Pratzenschuß". (In the mountains, the Italians were often very near. And sometimes the Tyrolese waved their hands around in the air, like targets. And when a bullet hit its aim, it was 'a Pratzenschuß' [a shot in the paw].)

The last 18 days of my father's war service were epoch making. On the 3rd November 1918, the Austro-Hungarian army laid down its arms. On the 11th November, fighting ceased in the West, and a general armistice was declared. Kaiser Karl, the last Habsburg, abdicated, and on the following day, on the 12th November 1918, the Austrian parliament proclaimed the new republic. Revolutions broke up the empire into ethnic compounds which demanded the self-determination of statehood. They were days of tremendous upheaval and turmoil. The map of Europe would be redrawn with the creation of the successor states of Poland, Hungary, Czechoslovakia and Yugoslavia.

My father was demobilised on the 21st November and discharged with the rank of 'Oberleutnant in der Reserve, Schweres Artillerieregiment Nr. 1' (first lieutenant in the Reserve, Heavy Artillery Regiment No. 1). He brought home an empty cannon shell case, which stood in the corner of his father Wilhelm's study. It was Paul's war trophy, defused and emptied of gunpowder, very likely a private decommissioning of artillery ammunition, ahead of the organised disarmament demanded by the victors. He certainly arranged the transport on the train from Trieste to Vienna and then transfer to the Ferdinandstrasse in a freight cart, pulled by two dray horses. And at the foot of the stairs, it must have been strapped up with grip handles for two men to pull and two men to lift the heavy weight over each step of the winding staircase to the second floor.

It was probably an eight-inch shell, standing several feet high and weighing about 80 pounds or more, even without its charge. My father called it a Howitzer. The Howitzer cannon was designed to fire its projectile with high elevation and to drop its shells onto places that could not be reached by long-range guns. What an ideal weapon for the mountain landscapes of the Alps, their narrow gorges, deep ravines, their sharp ridges and rock faces.

There it stood for twenty years, and Wilhelm could see it from his desk. But his wife Hermine looked upon it with misgivings. "Und das hat dein Vater vom Krieg nach Haus gebracht" (and this is what your father brought home from the war) she used to say to me. For my father, it was a souvenir, a war trophy. But on a deeper metaphysical level, so dear to his heart, he may have regarded it as a symbol of gratitude that he survived, and as a memorial to his fallen comrades.

Jews had fought for Austria. Many had made the ultimate sacrifice. But that was all forgotten twenty years later, when thousands of Viennese marched along the Ring in the mass hysteria of the Anschluss, on that Friday, the 11th March 1938. With the cruel irony of history my father then faced the threat of death once more, not from Italian snipers along the foothills of the Dolomites or from artillery shells across the Isonzo river, but at the hands of camp guards, the infamous SS Kapos, at the Dachau concentration camp. As each day passed in cell 188, he must have realised that space would be needed for new arrivals, and that deportation would follow.

In the autumn of 1938, Lena left Vienna. She had to empty the apartment in the Ferdinandstrasse, and she telephoned the War Ministry and asked them to collect the shell. When she arrived in England in December 1938, she told us that a few steps down on the stairs, on the first bend, the shell was dropped and rolled down to the half landing. She had to pay for the repair: carved stone inserts that filled four or five damaged treads.

Years later, when Patricia and I visited the Ferdinandstrasse, we saw the steps and remarked on the way the shell had, after all, left its lasting legacy.

Some more portable mementos from the First World War were brought to England, such as my father's medals and a statuette of Kaiser Franz Joseph. The bronze effigy shows the elderly monarch in full dress uniform, standing on a plinth, which bears the inscription 'offizielle Kriegsführsorge' (official war welfare), and was sold to support charitable work.

The following year, this time under Kaiser Karl's reign, on the 11th December 1917, Hermine was decorated with the Kriegskreuz für Zivildienste, zweiter Klasse (War Cross for Civilian Service, 2nd Class). She told me that the welfare work included the distribution of food and warm clothing during the cold winter months.

And now, after nearly a century, I think of Hermine and Paul, mother and son, with their decorations which recognise their service.

As I enter our house, I see Kaiser Franz Joseph, and have walked past him thousands of times. The heavy weight of history, the trilogy of tragedy, seems to rest on the ageing emperor's drooping shoulders. In 1889 his son, the Crown Prince Rudolf and his mistress Mary Vetsera, committed a double suicide at the hunting lodge of Mayerling, near Vienna. In 1898 his wife, the Empress Elisabeth, was assassinated by an anarchist in Geneva, and in 1914, the Heir Apparent, the Archduke Franz Ferdinand and his wife, were shot in Sarajevo by a Bosnian revolutionary.

Crown Prince Rudolf could not hope to emulate another contemporary Crown Prince, Edward Prince of Wales, and parade his mistresses in public. Queen Victoria may have imposed strict royal etiquette with puritanical moral rectitude, but when it came to her son, she turned a blind eye. However, Vienna was not London, a cosmopolitan metropolis with a wide catchment of social tolerance. The Habsburg court was run on Spanish Catholic ceremonial, inherited over the centuries from the Emperor Philip II of Spain, even from his father Charles V. And therefore Crown Prince Rudolf was keenly aware that Franz Joseph would never condone the open infidelity of his son. Thus the lovers chose to end their lives.

On that 28th June 1914, the day of the fatal shots at Sarajevo, Europe was at peace, enjoying a Sunday in early summer. The city of Vienna would have been empty, the Viennese out and about in the Wienerwald, along the banks of the Danube, drinking a glass of wine in the vineyards of Grinzing, or visiting the Prater with its amusements. Some families were enjoying their holiday in the country. My grandparents Wilhelm and Hermine were staying in Bad Gastein, the famous spa with the thundering waterfall. There, at the Hotel Moser, they had been honoured guests for many years. Wilhelm's brother Eduard and his wife Olga, together with their three children Fritz, Trude and Hedy, were as usual in nearby Altaussee, their regular holiday destination.

The news of the assassinations raced across Europe and shattered peace. Everywhere the same haunting question was being asked. Will there be war? There had not been a European conflict for many decades. A generation or more of men had grown up without a call to arms, without general mobilisation. It was in 1870 that France and Germany had last gone to war, and in 1866 Austria and Prussia fought each other. For England, one would have to go back even further, a hundred years to the time of Napoleon.

Immediately, on the very first day after the assassinations, on Monday 29th June 1914, Olga Neumann wrote a letter from Altaussee to her sister-in-law Hermine. It describes how the news was received in the village, but it also expresses something more universal, the worry of a mother for her soldier son:

… Jetzt herrscht hier natürlich entsetzliche Aufregung, die Leute verlassen fluchtartig den Ort, der Seewirth, der bis September alle Zimmer besetzt hatte, ist vollständig leer, ebenso die anderen Gasthöfe. Du kannst dir vorstellen wie beunruhigt wir selbst sind, da Fritz doch militärpflichtig. Im Falle seiner Einberufung würde ich selbstverständlich auch nach Wien fahren. Ein großer Teil seiner Freunde sind bereits bei ihren Regimentern…

(Here, right now, there is of course terrible excitement. People are leaving the place in a rush, the Seewirth, which was fully booked until September, is completely empty, as are the other hotels. You can imagine how worried we are ourselves, as Fritz is liable for military service. In the case of his call-up, I would of course, also travel to Vienna. A large number of his friends have already joined their regiments…)

Right on that first day, men rushed to the colours, ignorant of Flanders mud or Russian frost, in which so many of them would die.

Soon after the Second World War in London, I had actual personal contact with a revolutionary episode that occured during the Great War eight years before I was born. This was not the metaphysical touch of history but the actual grip of the hand of another political assassin. My mother, Lena and I had attended one of Uncle Julius' parties at his home in Chelsea. As we were leaving, Friedrich Adler, who was a fellow guest, came out into the hall to say goodbye. He ceremoniously bowed and vigorously shook our hands.

As soon as the front door was closed, Lena said: "Jetzt hab ich einem Mörder die Hand geschüttelt" (now I have shaken the hand of a murderer). I remember it so clearly, the sheer enormity, and now, as I look at my right hand, I know that it has clasped the hand which held the revolver which fired three fatal shots. On that 21st October 1916, Friedrich Adler entered the restaurant Meißl und Schadn and at point blank range killed the Minister-President of Austria, Count Karl von Stürgkh. He was condemned to death, the sentence was commuted to 18 years imprisonment, but after the fall of the monarchy in 1918, he was released.

Friedrich Adler was a life-long friend of Julius, a fellow Socialist and a prominent political figure in pre First World War Vienna. He edited the magazine *Der Kampf* (The Struggle) and in 1911 he became Secretary-General of the Social Democratic Party.

At first he was following in his father's political footsteps. In 1889, Victor Adler had been the principal agent in forming the Social Democratic Party of Austria and launching *Die Arbeiter-Zeitung* (the Workers' Paper). When war came in 1914, Victor Adler reluctantly supported it but Friedrich Adler became increasingly radical and revolutionary. The workers should unite across national frontiers as a protest against military nationalism and imperial capitalism, a political creed which he advocated, for which he was willing to kill and be killed.

Victor Adler died on the 11th November 1918, the eve of the proclamation of the Austrian republic, his Promised Land. A few years later, in the 1920s, Friedrich Adler was appointed General Secretary of the Socialist International, a post he was to hold for fifteen years.

But it was during the early years of the century, at a time when father and son were dominating left-wing politics, that the Viennese were quick to exploit the latent humour of their surname. With their satirical wit and apposite bon mots, they fashioned the collective appellation for these people called Adler (eagle). 'Der Doppeladler' (the Double Eagle), the heraldic bird of the House of Habsburg, now became the popular emblem of a political dynasty.

Friedrich Adler, in his climactic moment of premeditated political certitude, became a man of instant action and shot the head of a government at war. By contrast, Julius intervened in a revolutionary demonstration not with violence but to save lives. The episode entered family history. Early on in World War II, Julius came to visit us fairly frequently. And it was then, possibly prompted by events, that he told me the story of his involvement in 1918 in the mutiny of a squadron of the Austrian navy. He also described it in greater detail in his autobiography, published in 1945, 'In Search of the Millennium', the title so eloquently epitomising his life-long quest for a socialist utopia.

Julius and the fleet! It seemed so improbable to me, especially as Austria after 1918 no longer had access to the open seas, with the loss of Istria, Dalmatia and the Balkan coastline.

As a schoolboy in Vienna, I had been taught all about the two naval victories in Austrian history. There was the battle of Lepanto in 1571, in which Don John of Austria with his fleet of Venetian, Spanish and Papal galleys defeated the Turks at the entrance to the Gulf of Corinth. Three hundred years later, in 1866, Austria won her great victory at sea, further north, along the Dalmatian coast, off the island of Lissa. It was there that Admiral Tegetthoff sank most of the Italian fleet. He soon became a heroic icon, the Nelson of Trafalgar in Austrian folklore.

Strangely similar to Nelson, Tegetthoff stands on a very high column in the centre of a large square in Vienna at the entrance to the Prater. I passed it whenever I visited the Wurstelprater, that glorious funfair, the giant ferris wheel of the Riesenrad, the old scenic railway, the circus, all so near to my grandparents' home in the Ferdinandstrasse.

But for me there was not that emphasis on maritime history, on the voyages of discovery, on colonisation, on naval exploits in war and peace which are the natural concomitants of the island history of Britain.

In Vienna, the sea was far away. The first memory I have of it was in 1929 when we were on holiday near Ostend in Belgium. I still remember the great experience of seeing the ocean touch the horizon. I was briefed beforehand. "Du siehst nicht, wo das Wasser aufhört (You can't see where the water ends).

And with my landlocked background, Julius' story became even more dramatic.

It was early 1918. Julius, an artillery officer, was serving with a coastal battery overlooking the bay of Cattaro in Southern Dalmatia. On the 1st February 1918 about forty Austrian warships at anchor there hoisted red flags and their commanding officers were seized. But the mutiny was quickly put down. The fleet from Pola, the principal station of the Austrian marine, further up the coast, blocked the bay. German U-boats, based at Cattaro, operating in the Mediterranean, patrolled off-shore, ready to strike. It was all over in a few days. Four ringleaders were shot and further executions would probably follow. Julius describes the march of about eight hundred sailors under guard to their imprisonment in the old fortress overlooking the harbour and the preparation of court martials.

Revolution was in the air. A few months earlier, the Czar was toppled from his throne and his country taken out of the war. Russia had led the way: peace bought with revolutionary victory and military defeat.

Austro-Hungary had its special problems. It was a multi-national state suffering terrible losses, now in its fourth year of war. The Poles, Czechs, Hungarians and Balkan Slavs increasingly aspired to separate statehood in an ever-growing undercurrent of ethnic political discontent.

Hindering the monarchy's war effort was that debilitating centrifugal force, the demands of the various nationalities for their self-determination and independence and the rejection of federal compromise. And men began to ask ever more frequently why they should lay down their lives for the Habsburg empire for which they felt no loyalty.

Time was of the essence if Julius was to save the lives of his comrades. He compiled a report, addressed to his wife Tini, and managed to include it in the official mail bag sent daily from Cattaro to the commanding general of Bosnia, Herzogovina and Dalmatia, stationed at Sarajevo, to be forwarded to Vienna.

Victor Adler was informed and persuaded the Minister of War, General Stöger-Steiner to halt further executions. Workers in the munitions factories might well come out on strike in a gesture of solidarity. And after that, no further death sentences were imposed, only long terms of imprisonment, lifted, of course, at the proclamation of the new republic.

How so very different was the popular mood at the outbreak of World War One. Europe rushed to the colours with universal enthusiasm. All political parties supported the war, including the various European Labour movements and any notion of pacifism which might have had a calming influence was swept aside in a frenzy of enthusiastic nationalism. Both sides soon produced humorous or hostile invective, which often camouflaged the reality of war.

For Germany and Austro-Hungary, for the Central Powers, the war started on three fronts, with Great Britain and France in the west, Russia in the east and Serbia in the Balkans.

My mother told me that at the time of general mobilisation in 1914, the defiant Austrian popular response to this geographic encirclement was well expressed by three rhymed slogans, aimed at the three national enemies:

Jeder Schuss	*Every shot*
ein Russ	*A Russky*
Jeder Stoss	*Every shove*
ein Franzos	*A Frenchie*
Jeder Tritt	*Every kick*
ein Brit.	*A Brit.*

With the arrival of the twentieth century, the long periods of peace were a thing of the past. The generation of my parents faced two world wars within twenty-one years. Not that the intervening period was one of unbroken peace. Japan and China in Asia, Italy and Abyssinia in Africa, those were far away wars for a small schoolboy. But then came a European war, Spaniard fighting Spaniard, the augmented hatred of civil war.

I was twelve years old in 1936 when it started. That summer I was spending a few weeks on the Belgian coast near Ostend. My aunt, Hilde Braunthal, had organised a holiday for her children, their cousins and friends. On the wall in the dining room was a large map of Spain. Hilde had marked up the government controlled areas with little red flags. Black flags indicated the parts held by General Franco's rebel troops. She moved the flags to keep up to date with the latest shift on the front line. We, of course, all supported republican Spain in its struggle against the growing forces of fascism. And I was reminded of February 1934, and the few days of civil war in Vienna, which ended with the defeat of the workers' uprising. When I looked at the ongoing daily map, I could not envisage a war, something in which I was to fight a mere seven years later, and Spain seemed very far away from the peaceful, sandy Belgian beach. The map metamorphorsed into a board for a wargame, and the flags, with the opposing colours, stood in for the counters used in battle.

CHAPTER 8

Another war

Three generations of my family provided its men for war. In the First World War my grandfather Wilhelm's youngest brother Muzzo, my father and his brother Robert, and my mother's brother Julius all served in the Austrian army.

During the Second World War, Julius' sons Freddy and Tom Braunthal, Ralph Clark, the son of my mother's sister Bertha, and myself were on active service with the British forces. Gerald (Jerry) Braunthal, the son of my mother's brother Alfred, was in the American army. Stefan Unger, the son of my father's sister Mizzi, a member of the Polish army in Russia, was killed in action, in 1944, crossing the river Vistula, in the battle to liberate Warsaw.

My great-uncle Muzzo failed to leave Vienna in time and in 1942 was deported and murdered.

Muzzo was killed, not on the battlefield, but in a concentration camp. I remember when my father told me. It was August 1945, and I had come home on leave from Germany. He said that he had heard from Vienna, that Stephanie and Ernst, a sister and a brother of his mother, had perished. And as I heard this, I cried out: "Auch Muzzo?" (Also Muzzo?). My father nodded. It happened nearly seventy years ago, but I still recall the terrible anguish as I uttered the two words to which I knew the answer.

Hauntingly, over the decades, I sometimes see Muzzo exactly as I saw him for the very last time. He was a bank director, and lived in large elegant apartment, in the Liechtensteinstrasse, a premier address, opposite the Palais Liechtenstein, famous for its art gallery.

Frequently I happened to be right next door to him in a large basement hall, where my boy scout troop used to meet. We discovered the coincidence a few weeks before the Anschluss. And as soon as he knew, some time in the middle of February 1938, there he was, standing outside, looking through the basement window and waving to me.

I felt awkward in front of the boys and at first pretended not to see him. And then came the last time, a week later. He was again waiting outside. I managed to slip by, unnoticed, and take my seat on the back of a motorbike. My scoutmaster had offered me a lift. I was excited. I had never been a pillion rider before, and I felt embarrassed in case Muzzo disapproved. And as we drove off, he was standing there, looking along the pavement, looking out for a pedestrian. His face was stamped with searching disappointment.

Immediately after the Anschluss the scout movement was abolished. Instead, the Hitler Youth hired the hall for their meetings, much to the satisfaction of the Nazi caretaker.

At the outbreak of of the war in 1939, Germans and Austrians in England, so-called 'enemy aliens', had to appear in front of immigration tribunals. Some were real Nazi German citizens, others were Germans and Austrians who had arrived in England prior to 1933, and did not wish to return. But the vast majority were genuine refugees. The Nazis were interned and there were partial restrictions of liberty on a further small group. The refugees were given the official status of 'refugees from Nazi oppression', and were left in complete freedom.

But in May 1940, things radically changed. The 'phoney war' of seeming inactivity came to an end. The Germans, having earlier conquered Norway, quickly overran Denmark, Holland, Luxemburg and Belgium. The British Expeditionary Force was evacuated at Dunkirk. On 10th June, Italy joined Germany and declared war. On 14th June, the German army entered Paris. And then, a week later, on 26th June, Marshal Pétain signed the armistice of surrender, the last act in the fall of France, the final scene in this *Blitzkrieg*, this lightning war in which German tanks had rolled to swift victory. As the overall German occupations progressed, stories began to circulate of treachery and betrayal by pro-Nazi collaborators and sympathisers in areas overrun by the German army. The popular press in England whipped up a panic scare about the thousands of enemy aliens in the country, and the government took military advice in case of invasion.

The first step in this new policy of internment was taken on Sunday May 12th 1940, the third day in the battle for Holland and Belgium. A wide coastal belt, stretching from Inverness to the eastern edge of Dorset was declared a 'protected area'. German and Austrian men aged 16 to 60 were rounded up for temporary internment. At the time, my cousin Freddy was studying at the London School of Economics, which had been evacuated to Cambridge. That was within the coastal belt. He was interned and sent to Canada, facing the dangers of German submarines. After about a year, he was repatriated and released. In 1943, he joined the army, as by then refugees were allowed to enlist in the armed forces. Prior to that, they had been accepted only in the non-combatant Pioneer Corps and not allowed to carry arms.

After the war he stayed on and with his language skills of English, German, French and Russian achieved a successful service career, retiring with the rank of Lieutenant-Colonel. He acted out the paradox of his family history, as high-ranking army officer, his perfect English without the slightest trace of a foreign accent to disturb the officers' mess. Little did they know that he, Frederic Bonnart, was the son of a prominent Viennese Socialist, who himself had suffered imprisonment for his support of revolution, of armed insurrection, of the stand on the barricades. On retirement, Freddy settled down in Brussels and combined his military expertise with his inherent flair for journalism, contributing articles on NATO strategy and the Cold War for the international press.

Fortunately, in May 1940, I was at boarding school in Oxford, outside the restricted zone. But widespread internment of men and women all over England soon followed. A curfew was imposed on all foreigners from 10.30pm (midnight in London) to 6am, and all enemy aliens had to report to their local police stations. Changes of address, even for one night, had to be notified to the police prior to departure and on arrival.

My father was not interned. They came for Uncle Julius, but he persuaded them to return the following day, by which time he provided them with documentary evidence of his eleven-month imprisonment by the fascist government of Austria, and with political character references from the British Labour leadership. His wife Tini, however, was sent to the large internment camp on the Isle of Man for a short period, possibly because she had arrived in England from Belgium only after the outbreak of the war.

Many friends of my parents were interned during that summer of 1940, but by the autumn the policy was halted and refugees were starting to be released. Naturally, my father and mother were worried about me. I was sixteen, just old enough for internment, and Freddy's fate had increased their anxiety.

Three letters from my father recall the darkest year of the war. By now of course he would write in English to me. I am quoting them in full, because they conceal so much love and anxiety.

The first one, on 8th July 1940, deals with my registration at the Oxford Police Station. My father wondered whether I should take with me a letter from my headmaster, Mr. Davies, to confirm that I was a pupil at Magdalen College School, even ask him to ring up the Chief Constable. Mr. Leach, a senior professor of chemistry at Brasenose College and a close family friend had written and offered to help.

The P.S. at the top mentions my aunt Lena, affectionately known as 'Wülfi'. Very occasionally, having saved some precious ration coupons over a long period of time, she baked delicious Viennese pastries in the shape of diamonds, known in family tradition as parallelograms.

Many, many kisses from Wülfi.

(Parallelogramme to follow.)

My dear boy,

You will certainly have been informed that every alien has to call on his nearest Police-Station and to bring along with him his registration book and his identity card. The latter will be endorsed. The endorsement will show the number of the registration certificate.

Please consult Mr Davies wether (sic) it would not be advisable to take a line from his hand with you as a confirmation that you are staying at Magdalen College School. I am sure that he will be kind enough to give you an advise (sic) or even ring up the Chief Constable in order to make some inquiries as to what you have to do.

I had a letter from Mr Leach, who wrote me that he is always prepared to assist you and if you think it necessary or useful to communicate with him regarding the matter mentioned above, please do it.

Love (heaps of)

Pipsch

Please, write a line, what you have done.

On the 19th July, my father wrote to me about the new regulations whereby boys under eighteen resident with British families or in educational establishments would be exempt from internment. He was writing to Mr. Davies, asking him to confirm in writing with the police that I would be returning to school in the autumn.

My father was worried about the interruption of the holidays and wanted to avoid my return to the parental home, to the home of refugees, where there was a much higher risk of arrest than at the house of a British family.

My dear boy,

Just a line to tell you that I saw the new regulations, according to which 'boys under eighteen resident with British families or in educational establishments' will be exempted from internment. I am writing to Mr Davies, asking him to be kind enough to give a written statement to the Police that you will attend the school next year. But, alas, there seems to be a gap regarding the holidays. I therefore asked Mr Davies to include you, if possible, in a team of farm helpers and Eva [my sister] wrote to Mr Leach, wether [sic] he would be able to keep you during the holidays. I don't need to tell you, how greatly we – Mummy and I – are disappointed that we will be deprived of the joy to have you here. But I know that you are my boy and that you will do with good humour, what is a measure for your own safety. It goes without saying that we shall come to see you as often as faisible (sic) and moreover you will have the opportunity of practising music with your friend as often as you like. Should the whole position become clearer, I shall let you know immediately.

Heaps of love
  Yours, Pipsch

Boys from Magdalen College School were 'volunteering' for agricultural work to help a farmer in Oxfordshire, now that farm labourers were being called up. I did not fancy going, living under canvas, even if it hopefully meant playing sonatas with my school friend Walter Jellinek, who had promised to come as well. Walter, the eternal optimist, was sure that we would miraculously find a cottage piano within easy cycling distance of the farm!

A week later, on the 26th July, my father wrote again with good news. I had been invited to stay with a British family, very near our own home. Dorothy Pam, who later became a real family friend, supplied a guarantee which enabled me to live at home, but register her as fully responsible for my loyalty.

About twenty years later, in the early 1960s, on giving up her beautiful home in Hampstead, she presented Patricia and me with her lovely Steinway grand piano (1884), the piano which she had used all her long life. There it stands, and I remember her in 1940 accompanying herself in a Schubert song and singing the Bach-Gounod *Ave Maria* with me providing the violin obligato.

My father's letter is once again anxious about the details of my police notifications. Any uanauthorised travel, any breaking of the curfew, any absence from home overnight or longer, any change of address, however short, was strictly forbidden.

6 Kidderpore Gardens
NW3
July 26, 1940

My dear boy,

I am deeply glad to inform you that we were able to arrange for your stay in London during the holidays. A friend of friends of ours, Mrs Hugo Pam, 171 West Heath Road, NW3 is prepared to grant you hospitality. She is the mother of a boy in [sic] your age and her house is quite near from ours. So it can be hoped that all things will be all right.

I wrote a letter to Mr Davis asking him to be kind enough

(1) to let you have a statement that you will attend school again in the autumn

(2) to lend you his help, if necessary, in the required steps with Oxford Police.

You have, as you probably know, to apply to Oxford Police for being allowed to come to London and to stay here for a while. Please, tell them, that Mrs Pam is prepared to keep you and to take over responsibility. She, of course, is British.

Let us know immediately, when you will arrive in London and take and early train or bus, so that your report to the Police Station can be done on the afternoon of your arrival.

I understand that your tutor has invited you over weekend. Please let me have his address and <u>write at once</u> after having obtained the necessary permission from Oxford Police for your stay in London. The statement from the headmaster that you will return to school and Mrs Pam's hospitality for your temporary stay in London will, I think, suffice.

Love Pipsch

When war broke out, many keen young police constables were called up and joined the Military Police. And so it came about that constables dealing with front desk routine tasks were frequently middle-aged, sometimes paternal, frequently laid back.

It was to such a benevolent constable that I handed in my application for a ninety-minute lifting of the curfew. On the 31st December 1941 I went to the Hampstead police station and asked for special leave to be allowed to stay out until half past one in the morning. I had been invited to a New Year's Eve party, which also meant walking home from Bayswater to Hampstead. The duty sergeant looked up and smiled: "Have a nice time," he said.

As soon as Austrian refugees started to arrive in England in 1938, they set up their exile organisations. It was self-help, to cope with the trauma of emigration. A whole range of associations were formed at the time, such as social clubs, youth centres, legal advice and welfare clinics, employment agencies, music societies, theatre clubs. Austrian artists, musicians, composers and authors became collectively involved. Newspapers and newsletters provided an ongoing background.

But the refugees had also brought with them their differing political luggage ranging from monarchist, conservative and liberal, to social democratic and communist. And it was a group of conservatives and monarchists, this bourgeois Viennese society, mostly Jewish, with its literary, musical and artistic connections which now was keen to use culture as a propaganda weapon.

With the support of eminent English and Austrian academics and scientists, the Austrian Academy was launched on the 2nd May 1940, at the Royal Institution in London. The agenda was clear: the restoration of a postwar independent Austria! The Academy would present Austria's separate cultural identity in a series of lectures and concerts.

The list of patrons included Gilbert Murray, Regius Professor of Greek at Oxford and Sir Edwin Lutyens, the distinguished architect.

The Honorary President was Sir George Frankenstein, G.C.V.O., D.C.L. (Oxon). He had been the last Austrian Ambassador to the Court of St. James and immediately after the Anschluss was granted British nationality and the honour of the Grand Commander of the Victorian Order.

And there were two Honorary Secretaries, Christina Foyle, then only 29 years old, but already presiding over the famous London bookshop, and Dr Paul Neumann, my father.

On several occasions, my mother spoke about this inaugural ceremony. It was the last time, she said, that she and my father went out in grand style, as they had done so often in Vienna. My father wore black tie and my mother was in a silk brocade gown, and over it her long white ermine evening coat. Men wore decorations, royal British honours mingling with medals from Imperial Austria, not long ago an enemy at war. But my father regarded the decorations as symbols of Austria's ongoing existence, as tokens of her continuity. That evening he proudly wore his beautiful gold and enamel miniatures, suspended elegantly from a delicate gold chain. And when I look at them now I am reminded of that last occasion when he wore them.

For my mother, too, there was valediction. Shortly afterwards she sold her evening coat, so luxuriously fashionable in the 1920s and 30s, adorned as it was along the hem with forty white ermine tail tips. Years later, I came across a small brush-like object in a little box. She told me what it was, and that she had taken it off her coat and kept it as a memento of many festive occasions.

With Austria, there had to be music. How I wish I had been there that evening! The highlight of the programme was a group of three Schubert songs sung by Richard Tauber, *Du bist die Ruh', Wohin* and *Ständchen*. But I am happy and grateful that my parents had the opportunity to hear once more a musical legend. Even with the obligatory encores, it must have been, oh so brief, stretched to the timeless scale by a great artist.

It was at that time, that my father first met Archduke Robert, the nephew of Kaiser Karl, the last Habsburg emperor. Robert of Austria had escaped to London, his older brother Otto, the Pretender, had emigrated to the United States.

The Monarchists rallied round the young Archduke, then only in his mid-twenties, with avuncular concern, and the deference accorded to a scion of a nearly seven hundred year-old dynasty. For them, the unfulfilled dream of a double restoration, Habsburg and Austria.

During the war, the Allies were, of course, united in their determination to secure victory as soon as possible. Any weakening of Germany, by appealing to latent Austrian separatism, any propaganda weapon to damage Nazi resolve was used in the armoury of psychological warfare.

And finally, in November 1943, at the Moscow Conference, Stalin, Churchill and Roosevelt declared the restoration of Austrian independence as one of their war aims.

All Austrian refugee organisations had lobbied for this overriding political goal. The Archdukes, with their inherited status, had established access to the top, Archduke Otto with Roosevelt, and Archduke Robert with Churchill. In the corporate bid of persuasion, the Archdukes, as figureheads, certainly played their part.

My father started to see Archduke Robert in 1940, at the time of the opening of the Austrian Academy. They must have discussed the war and the future of Europe and of Austria. I often wonder what my father must have felt, sitting opposite a descendent of the Emperor Maximilian, the Emperor Charles V, or the Empress Maria Theresia. He had, after all, risked his life, fighting for Kaiser Franz Joseph, and his father had been honoured with the title of Regierungsrat. They must have developed some sort of understanding, more than a purely formal relationship.

I remember Archduke Robert's visit to our house in Hampstead. It was in 1941. My father had invited a group of people all specifically interested in the future of Germany and of Austria. Archduke Robert arrived rather late and apologised, saying that he did not realize that the journey from Knightsbridge would take so long. My sister Eva was instructed to open the door when he rang the bell, and for some time beforehand had practised how to curtsey.

A very elderly friend of my parents who was living with us at the time, had been asked to keep out of the way, but of course wanted to know all the circumstantial details as soon as all the guests had departed. In Vienna, she had witnessed the panoply of Imperial ceremonial. On hearing that Archduke Robert had come by public transport she exclaimed: "Ein Habsburg kommt im Autobus?" (A Habsburg comes by bus?)

Among those present was Wilfrid Israel, who was working in various organisations to rescue Jews from Continental Europe. Soon he would move to Oxford. Chatham House, the Institute for Foreign Affairs, had been taken over by the Foreign Offiice and evacuated to Balliol College. He joined them there as a consultant in their German section. We met again in 1943, when I taught in Oxford at the Dragon School, a preparatory school, prior to starting my studies at St Catherine's.

We usually talked about the war, my plans to join the RAF and about life when peace came. Wilfrid did not talk much about his work, but I knew that he had been to Portugal to organise the emigration of Jewish children from Vichy France over the Pyrenees to neutral Spain and then to Palestine, and that he was planning to go again.

And then came the 1st June 1943. Wilfrid Israel was flying back from Lisbon and was shot down. A fellow passenger on that flight was Leslie Howard, the film actor, giving the tragedy wide publicity.

Churchill was a great supporter of Austria, and he took a special public opportunity to voice his thoughts. His eloquence allows no paraphrase, amd makes *The Times* report of the 19th February 1942 so very memorable:

Outside Number 10 Downing Street, yesterday afternoon, the Prime Minister who was accompanied by Mrs Churchill, received a trailer canteen presented by Austrians in Britain to the W.V.S. (The Women's Voluntary Service). The presentation was made by Sir George Frankenstein, formerly Austrian Minister in London.

Mr Churchill said:

"It is not without deep emotion that I attend this simple ceremony. Here we

see the heart of Austria, although trampled down under the Nazi and Prussian yoke. We can never forget here in this island that Austria was the first victim of Nazi aggression. We know that happy life which might have been led by scores of millions in central Europe. We remember the charm, beauty, and the historic splendour of Vienna, the grace of life; the dignity of the individual; all the links of past generations are associated in our minds with Austria and with Vienna."

Turning to Sir George Frankenstein, Mr. Churchill said: "You are here to link us between the dark past, the haggard present, and what I still believe will be the glorious future. We shall struggle on and fight on. The people of Britain will never desert the cause of the freedom of Austria from the Prussian yoke. We shall go forward…"

Archduke Robert of Austria is listed as one of those who attended the ceremony.

A few weeks later, on the 16th April 1942, a letter from the Archduke to my father charts the progress of their relationship. Written in German, it says:

Dear Dr Neumann,

Many thanks for your letter of the 15th April, and the friendly words, concerning my lecture. I am looking forward soon to seeing you here at my home. In the meantime, my best wishes for the new flat.

> *Kindest regards*
> *Archduke Robert*

(On the 1st April 1942 we moved from our rented house near Hampstead Heath to a flat much nearer to a London Underground station.)

Robert's lectures were on "The Future of Austria" and I remember his visit to Oxford sometime later that year when he addressed a large audience in the Oxford Union Debating Chamber, modelled on the House of Commons, with its dispatch boxes and the Speaker's high chair.

The last letter from Archduke Robert to my father is dated 18th July 1942, this time written in English.

Dear Dr. Neumann,

I enclose herewith a letter which I received from The Foreign Office. Would you perhaps approach Mr Nigel Law in that matter and let me know the result of that conversation.

I should be pleased if you could undertake the perusal of the Monitor reports yourself.

Yours sincerely,
Robert of Austria

Archduke Robert and my father were in touch with various public figures who had pre-war Austrian connections and who would further Austria's post-war independence.

Nigel Law was at that time working for the Ministry of Economic Warfare, but, like Michael Pelairet, had been stationed in Vienna in the Diplomatic Service. Both men were recalled, Michael Pelairet after the Anschluss, and Nigel Law in 1914, at the outbreak of World War 1. Archduke Robert was of course fully aware of my father's monitoring work for the *Daily Mail*, and was anxious for my father to see the documents, presumably transcripts of German broadcasts with Austrian relevance.

At the end of 1942, Archduke Robert included my parents on his Christmas card list. The seasonal text is indented on quality thick card, and embossed in an appropriately red ornate Gothic typeface. The impression of red on white, the Austrian national colours, is echoed in the corner by the red, white, red of the Austrian flag. For my father, the card must have been so very evocative. He must have been reminded of his youth, the old Imperial days of Vienna, as he looked at the evidence of a changed world, an English Christmas card from an Austrian Archduke!

After my father's death, my mother often talked about my father's professional life. She explained how his profound classical education, his historical, cultural and moral concept of justice, his reverence for the sanctity of law, and above all, his humanism all somehow blended to provide a broader setting for his adversarial role. He was deeply aware of the frailty of human nature, its fallibility. He was kind, and she suspected that he achieved his successes without gratuitous vengeance. Not for him, she thought, was the head-on, inflexible approach of remorseless confrontation.

In England, Dr. Paul Neumann could not continue with his career as a lawyer. Many of his friends were dentists and doctors. When they arrived they were gratefully received and as soon as war broke out, urgently needed. But the English legal system is very different. In Vienna, a Rechtsanwalt is both barrister and solicitor. There is no separation of professional functions. The Austrian laws are written down, codified, according to the method established at the time of Napoleon. In England, on the other hand, common law, the law of precedent, case law, is substantially applied. Past judgements are elucidated, interpreted and monitored by judges in court to provide organic growth of justice in a changing world. My fifty year-old father had to turn elsewhere, to find immediate work.

Some refugees were able to apply their business, industrial or financial expertise to build up a second career. My father used his German. He joined the *Daily Mail* newspaper. At the outbreak of the war, they set up a department to listen in on German news broadcasts and use the material for their paper. My father joined a group of refugees who were in fact radio monitors, able to provide quick translations and summaries for use, if necessary, in the morning edition.

The war in the air was not only one of fighters and bombers, bombs and rockets. It was also a stream of words, spread all over the world. My father had to report the latest twist of German propaganda to the political editor for the ongoing counter-attack, for the informed response. He felt that he was part of the war effort. On the 3rd September 1939, party politics were suspended, and newspapers united in their aim to strengthen the resolve of the public to defeat the enemy.

The *Daily Mail*, a newspaper with a very large circulation, conservative, middle-brow, identified the contributions from its monitoring office with the by-line: 'The Daily Mail Radio Station'. This was journalistic enthusiasm. They did not broadcast, they only listened.

Of course, the Press was briefed daily by the official channels, but the Radio Station picked up distinctive items of news which could be used to disparage the Germans and boost the morale on the Home Front.

In 1940, France fell and Italy joined the war. More languages were needed. My father told me that the office developed a truly European flavour and developed a cohesion and camaraderie. Alec Rutherford, the manager, an old Fleet Street veteran, looked upon his staff with benevolent puzzlement. "Who are these men?" he must have thought, "such a bizarre cultural assortment". But he knew that they were united by the single aim: Victory!

My father was very popular, and in the long hours that they were together, the men got to know each other well. And so it came about on the occasion of the Silver Wedding of my parents, January 21, 1942, set in the darkest period of the war, that the office conveyed their congratulations and best wishes, typed on an official postcard. The printed details, the heading above the message, are evocative of a bygone age:

Associated Newspapers, Ltd.
Telegraphic Address: "DAILY MAIL, LONDON"
Tel: Central 6000.
DAILY MAIL, NORTHCLIFFE HOUSE, LONDON, E.C.4.

The card was pre-war. On the date line, the first three digits of the year are printed out as 193, with the 41 typed over. It reads:

The Staff of The DAILY MAIL RADIO STATION
Join in Wishing Their Colleague
Mr PAUL NEUMANN and HIS WIFE
MANY YEARS OF HAPPINESS
SILVER WEDDING – JANUARY 21 1942

Stuck down in the bottom left-hand corner is an old silver threepenny piece.

With the coming of peace, the paper started to reduce the size of its Radio Station. The axe of redundancy for my father fell in August 1946. At the time, he was on holiday with my mother in Cornwall, in Tintagel, along the romantic coastline of the Tristan legend.

The notice was sent to him in a letter to his department. Alec Rutherford knew what it was, and opened it for necessary details. He sent it on to me and explained the circumstances and suggested that I should not forward it to my father and so spoil his holiday. I of course agreed.

And then he spoke at length about my father's loyal service for five years, and how he joined the Daily Mail in 1941 at a desperate period of the war. He liked and admired him. And as he talked, I became aware of the bond of familiarity, of which vicariously I had become a part. At any rate, at the top of his letter, he addressed me as Mr Neumann, Jr., two Neumanns now, father and son.

Daily Mail
Editorial Department
Northcliffe House
London E.C.4
5.8.46

Mr Neumann, Jr.

Dear Mr Neumann,

Herewith the letter for your father. I want to assure you that it was not my wish to open it but in the circumstances I had to. Now it is up to you to act and you know what I should do — of course I am speaking only from the point of view of his friend.

I am grieved at this breaking up of our happy family which has stuck together throughout all the hard times. Your father I have always looked on as the gentleman of gentlemen — a loyal and trusty colleague liked by all, in fact a pal we shall never forget. I am sorry.

As one who speaks with heartfelt gratitude,

I am, sincerely,

Alec Rutherford

CHAPTER 9

Letters from the Front

When the Second World War broke out, German and Austrian refugees were anxious to take part in the fight against Hitler, but at first were only allowed to join the Pioneer Corps, the non-combatant auxiliary army battalion used mainly to paint Nissen huts and dig camp drains. It was to be a long road from initially 'enemy alien' to 'refugee from Nazi oppression' and from the internment camp to the officers' mess.

My father, with his legal background, was actively involved in the campaign for official differentiation as is shown by a letter to him from Bertha Bracey. She was a prominent Quaker, who worked tirelessly during the war to assist Jews fleeing Nazi persecution.

> *Society of Friends (Quakers)*
> *German Emergency Committee*
> *Bloomsbury House, Bloomsbury Street, London W.C.1*
> *29.3.1941*

Dear Dr. Neumann,

Thank you so much for letting me see your paper on the Status of Aliens. I like it very much because it is simple, it is a great art in a very complicated matter, bristling with controversial points to be able to draw up a simple scheme, which is not just facile.

I did not feel at liberty to make any use of it, particularly as you had drawn it up for the F.A.P. [Friendly Aliens Parliamentary] Group. I did however follow much the same line in the Chr. Council group which met with Dr. Kullmann [Deputy High Commissioner for Refugees] to explore the question.

We want to raise as few questions as possible, possibly may have to be content with certain ameliorations of nomenclature, e.g. that genuine refugees should no longer be referred to as '<u>*enemy aliens*</u>*' because they are G. and A. [Germans and Austrians]. Also I believe we shall have to avoid any claims based on 'citizenship'. What we actually want is something which may possibly apply to any future groups of refugees – i.e. as status which can apply to those who seek to be granted asylum.*

I am going to be horribly busy when I get back to London, but I would appreciate it very much if we could have a further talk, sometime before the matter is raised in the special meeting of the Joint Consultative Committee.

Kindest regards to Resi and Eva.
> *Yours very sincerely*
>> *Bertha L. Bracey*

By 1943, however, it became possible to join all three branches of the armed forces. The army took the vast majority of volunteers. The recruitment policy for the Royal Air Force and the Royal Navy seemed more discretionary: at any rate, far fewer refugees were accepted.

My father thought it advisable for me to have a letter of recommendation, a character reference, to facilitate my enlistment for service in the RAF, although as it turned out, I was ineligible for flying duties because of my national status. The letter, dated 9th September 1943, is from the Parliamentary Committee on Refugees, from Vera Craig, the Secretary. She met my father in 1940, at the time of the internments. Eleanor Rathbone had set up the Committee in 1938, after the Anschluss. In Parliament, she attacked the policy of appeasement and urged the government to grant entry visas for the refugees. A group of Members of Parliament of all parties watched over refugee problems and raised issues in the House of Commons. It was her advocacy there which halted the policy of wholesale internment and speeded up the eventual release of refugees.

I quote the letter in full, because it now seems so very improbable, this confirmation of political integrity!

Parliamentary Committee on Refugees
ABBey 2249
7, Cowley Street,
WESTMINSTER, S.W.1.
September 9th, 1943

Air Ministry,
Recruiting Centre, London.

Dear Sirs,   *Hans G. Neumann*

I have much pleasure in stating that I have known Hans Neumann for rather more than three years and he is, in my opinion, well qualified by reason of his political and personal integrity, and keenness, to serve as a member of the R.A.F.

I might add that I know his family very well and have agreed to sponsor their naturalisation for which they are about to apply. I should be pleased to answer at any time any questions regarding my knowledge of the boy. He has my best wishes and I hope very much that his application for the R.A.F. may be successful.

Yours faithfully
Vera Craig

I remember going with my letter to the Air Ministry. When the officer behind the desk heard that I was at Oxford, he smiled, but I was too shy to ask if it had the conspiratorial tinge of an alumnus. He told me to register at the local Oxford recruitment centre and join up straight from there, which I did on 10th December 1943. I walked to the railway station with another volunteer recruit. He had been in the Spanish Civil War on the Republican side, he said, and was at least twenty years older than me. By 1943, they took volunteers up to fifty-nine years of age.

The previous day, Spain had been very much on my own mind. I finished my interrupted studies with an interim three hour history examination. Dressed in the obligatory *sub fusc*, the examination costume of white shirt, white tie, dark suit, gown and mortarboard, I struggled to answer questions on 16th and 17th European history. All round me, the free world was fighting for survival, and the detailed study and explanation of events hundreds of years ago seemed to be very remote: Louis XIV of France, Philip II of Spain, the Habsburgs, the Ottomans, the Popes, the Thirty Years War. Soon I would have to face present reality in Germany, translating commands to a defeated enemy.

A month earlier, I was accepted for service in the RAF, and was given a maximum deferment, so that I could still sit that examination.

As soon as my father knew, that I had been officially enrolled, and would soon join up, he wrote to me.

His letter is dated the 12th November 1943, exactly a quarter of a century after the proclamation of the new republic on the steps of parliament in Vienna. The defeated armies of Imperial Austro-Hungary were disintegrating. "Get home" was the watch-word.

My father addressed me as Cox. He was Box, fun names, at the time, which we borrowed from the eponymous Gilbert & Sullivan operetta. But there is so much more in this letter than in-joke appellation. There is love of a father and his reflection on the history of repeated war:

To-day twenty-five years ago- you were still ἐν γούνασιν θεῶν [in the lap of the gods] – I was demobilised (or shall I say in view of the rather more active part we soldiers took in this process at that time: I was demobilising?)

To-day you are about to join.

This all is probably and naturally of greater significance to me than to you. And that is good so…

Sometimes, as if to verbalise the deep feeling of belonging to each other, my father would quote a winged phrase from our shared worlds of Hellas and Rome. Here the words are from the Iliad, written in my father's delicate Greek script.

How I treasure this letter, so symbolic of a bygone age. A father quotes Homer to his son as he goes off to war.

145

I wrote regularly to my mother, in English of course, addressing her affectionately as Blotscherl or Blosoi, and my father by his pet-name 'Pipsch'. The following letter, still on St Catherine's Society Oxford notepaper (later correspondence bore the RAF symbol), was probably my first after joining up, composed in very early January 1944.

Thursday night

Dear Blotscherl,

At last I find a little time to write. It is difficult to know where to start in my account of my daily doings. Well we get up early and go to breakfast (6.15am). I nearly always stay in bed and get up about 7 in order to be ready for parade at 8. You see there is always a very long queue for all meals (about 10 minutes to ¼ hr wait) and I and my room-mates don't think it worthwhile to go. We have a break at 10 and then we have hot drinks and sandwiches.

My fellow-recruits found it very funny that they had signed up to fight the Hun, only to discover in their ranks a man with a suspiciously German name, a foreign accent, and a Viennese nightshirt packed with interleaved red tissue paper from the laundry, instead of the customary English pyjamas. Quite the caricature of the Enemy Spy. At night after lights out, one of them shouted out cheekily in the darkness "Goodnight Hans!" and all round the barrack the men echoed from their beds: "Goodnight Hans!"

The day is divided into periods of about 50 minutes and we never drill more than 3 hours − 4 hours and never more than 1 hour at the time. Then there is gymnastics every day, which is rather enjoyable. We do it in the open air with only a vest and shorts and pullover but one gets used to the cold and now I am never cold doing it.

The rest of the day is filled up with lectures on chemical warfare which I find very interesting and devilishly fascinating. There are many types of gases and even my retentive memory finds it difficult to memorise all the symptoms, smells, counter measures etc.

The other day we went through another gas chamber and my mask is alright. Then we were told to take our masks off and leave the room, which was rather exciting because you had to hold your breath and run to the door as quickly as possible whilst tears streamed down (tear gas).

Then there are first aid lectures which are singularly boring. There seems to be little first aid instruction, because the M.O. (= Medical Officer) nearly always says: "get the patient to hospital as quickly as possible". The boys at the back cough a lot to annoy him so it is difficult to hear this elderly man and the whole business is rather funny.

But the most difficult and by far the most intriguing thing is "air-craft recognition". This specialised and often secret knowledge is taught to us by a series of lectures, by silhouettes, 'laterna magica', and films. I think there must be altogether about 500 different first class fighting planes in the world. In our 7th week we must know 25 different types and it is very difficult at first, because they all look so alike. But soon one sees subtle differences – I quite like it. Some of the boys are real experts, knowing wing-span, bomb-load, fighting-ceiling (i.e. highest level of fighting) top-speed etc etc.

Air craft recognition is a science and we will have an exam soon. I hope I will do alright.

The cleaning of rifle and uniform is a very lengthy business and "should" be done every day. Every day there is an inspection either by the senior NCO (non-commissioned officer) or the officer commanding our Flight. On one or two occasions I was told to shave. They are terribly strict about shaving and even if you shave the night before (because the water is sometimes warm at night) they reprimand you for it. I have had already 3 haircuts since I left Oxford and one just before in London! A record don't you think. It has to be very short, especially on the neck and if it is a bit long one is "detailed" for haircut on such and such a day at a certain time.

I am sorry my laundry is so dirty but as you can imagine it is extremely difficult to get clean and one is lucky to get a bath once every seven days. Most of the dirt on my clothes, however, comes not from me but from various floors. You see when we change for gym or anything else such as "organised games" we put all our clothes on the floor, because there is nowhere else to put them. The floor is naturally very dirty and then in the general scramble somebody usually treads on them. But I will change my clothes more often.

Yes, my playing in the hotel was big fun. It turned out to be a dance and I managed it alright. After that (Dec 31st) I went and played at an NCO's party from our Wing, but soon deserted the band and danced myself. This went on till 1am and the New Year was hailed with tremendous optimism and plenty of alcoholic bevrige (sic). At first I felt a bit out of it because all the men and women were NCO's but that was soon overcome and I enjoyed myself tremendously. This Saturday I am going to one of the many dances which are always being held and the shoes will be very useful.

The boys in my billet are all very nice, especially one who sleeps in my room and is also called Ken!

I have also made the acquaintance of a very nice WAAF!! But more of her after Saturday. I hardly know her. Anyway she is 3 ranks higher and takes an interest in a mere recruit! There is a great social difference between the ranks which, if you consider those who hold the non commissioned ranks, is rather amusing. It is more often the recruits who should look down on the NCO's!! All the NCO's in charge of us are quite decent chaps except the senior NCO (Flight Sergeant) who is unnecessarily strict and inbred with sadistic tendencies.

I got a letter from Walter the other day and he sent me my watch! Did he *pay for it. If so it is rather awkward (don't spell it!!). Do answer this point. Does Yfrah work all day now?* [good friend Yfrah Neaman, the violinist and, later, eminent pedagogue, who taught my two daughters the violin thirty years later]. *How did it come about? Or was it only that day? I have not heard* one *bar of classical music and miss it very much. But I did not realise the extent of my longing until the other day when we were standing outside a house out of which came some Bach. It thrilled me very much and moved me and was sad when we moved on. I find very little time to play the violin and am very tired in the evenings.*

I did not enclose a letter in the laundry-parcel because I was in a great hurry. Please pack *your parcels better. They arrive in the true Blotscherl tradition: all tattered and torn.*

Well dear Blotscherl I must stop now. I hope you like this letter. Tell Pipsch to drop me a line or add a funny 'high-falutin' post-script.

Pussi [kisses]
  Love Hansi

Within a couple of weeks, I was well into my training:

Sunday 14/1/44

Dear Blotscherl,

I sent the laundry yesterday but have not as yet got mine. I hope it will come soon. This last week went very quickly. We are now in the last phase of training which consists of more interesting work and less marching about. We run around the dunes firing 'dummy' rounds and throwing ourselves on the ground when someone blows a whistle – it would be fun in summer, but it is so very cold for these 'games'.

We have started to throw grenades. This is most enjoyable provided you let go of the grenade in time and don't drop it. It only takes 4 seconds to explode. We have not actually thrown real ones only 'dummies' for practising – I am one of the best throwers. We will soon fire rifles and machine guns and throw grenades and I hope to get a high score.

It was at that time that we also had training in the firing sten guns, affectionately called Tommy guns. They are heavy automatic weapons, to be fired from the hip, with the additional encumbrance of sticks of amunition.

I was given the gun and told to run up an escarpment of dunes, firing a spray of dummy bullets. The command struck me as faintly absurd and very unreal. I took the weapon and raised it much higher than I should have done, right up against my chest. After ten years of lifting my instrument, my arms automatically pushed up the gun. "You are not playing the violin now," the drill sergeant shouted. He recognised me. I had played at various camp dances.

We are doing also a lot of running in the sand with steel helmet, rifle, gas mask, and full pack. This is very strenuous and many drop out. My legs and heart seem to be very strong because I always finish in good time. The other day I came 88th out of 200 in a 8 km race. But the most difficult thing is still ahead – the assault course, where you have to overcome all sorts of difficulties in a certain time. But of that later.

It is terribly difficult to get leave from here. 'Compassionate' leave is granted only in extreme emergencies. Moreover Feb 11ᵗʰ is one day after we all leave here so I will either ask to prolong my stay for 2 days or let me go to my new station via London. In any case one does not ask for leave of this sort until about 2 weeks before. You can be assured that I have pulled all the preliminary strings.

We are also getting a lot of instruction in bayonet fighting which is rather gruesome at first. Also we are taught "unarmed combat" or tough 'jiu-jitsu'. In all these things one has to be so very quick. It is all a question of seconds. We make 'bayonet charges' on the beaches. This is good fun. Everybody shrieks and screams and runs at an imaginary enemy and then takes cover. There are also sacks in a wooden frame suspended by strings into which you plunge your bayonet. All this would be rather amusing if it were not so desperately serious.

I am going to ring you up on Thursday to congratulate you (Hochzeitstag) [wedding anniversary]. *I will try to ring up about 9pm. Perhaps Pipsch will be there – I hope so. He has not written a single line since I joined up. I was all the time expecting some 'high faluting' and bob-snobbish, Miltonian, Gibbonian advice from an ex-officer!*

On Thursday I may have a big surprise for you !!!!!! (Pleasant!). Not in the sphere of love but of service. I am seeing my Commanding Officer on Wednesday. Perhaps you can guess, if I tell you that I am trying to get into that part of the RAF which participates more directly in the war. My chances are good, but even so it is extremely difficult for an Austrian to be admitted for flighing [sic] *duties. I met one who has been accepted his name is Kössler. It may be a lengthy business before the Air Ministry say 'yes' but 90% of the battle is won if I made a good impression on the Commanding Officer who holds a high rank and is influential. On the other hand they may reply within a week or 2.*

I hope my eyes will be alright. It would be wonderful to be one of the 6 or 10 Austrians to be admitted for flighing [sic] *duties. My mathematics are good enough to exempt me from the entrance test, because I have passed the School Certificate. Everyone who passes out as a qualified pilot, engineer, navigator, bomb-aimer or wireless operator becomes automatically at least a sergeant getting between 8/6 to 12/6 a day. And it is not too difficult to get a commission after a certain amount of operational flying.*

I hope this distresses you not too much – anyway I have not yet been accepted and may never be. There was never any doubt in me that if I ever get into the RAF I would do my utmost to get accepted for flying duties. I may have become hardened – I don't know. But it seems to me to be the natural thing to aim at in the Air Force, although there are about 70 men on the ground to 1 in the air.

I am not embued with a sudden spasm of heroism but I feel that if I were British I would probably risk my life in the air and that I should not take any nationality as an excuse for staying on the ground and not trying <u>every</u> means of getting into the air.

Although there is a wonderful 'esprit de corps' in the Air Force and Mechanics and pilots are absolutely on the same level and realise their interdependence it is terribly difficult to stand and see them go off knowing that one is not one of them, because of some ruling of the Ministry, not because of educational deficiency or ill health.

Love Hansi

To my disappointment, I was not accepted for flying duties, in view of the fact that I was born in Austria and not a British subject, which, as air crew, would have made it more likely for me to fall into enemy hands. After a month I was transferred to Scotland for training in air-sea rescue.

Sunday 13 / 2 /44
1882507LAC Neumann H.
Marine Craft Section
RAF Station
Helensburgh
Dumbartonshire, Scotland

Dear Blotscherl,

I am slowly settling into this new place and am liking it more and more. My work is diverse and varied. I am learning all about the laws of the sea, about buoys, knots, morse, semaphore, engines, general maintenance, lights etc etc. As I told you there is no course here. One just has to learn as much as one can by oneself. The most difficult thing to get hold of is the specialised terminology. There are hundreds of queer words and phrases and sacred conventions in the nautical world of the Anglo Saxons. Every bit of a boat has a name and it is rather confusing.

There are some real old 'seadogs' here – men who have spent many years on the sea. And they all have this characteristic: their great friendliness and good comradeship. This seems to be very much more pronounced among seafaring men because a ship, however small, is a self-contained community and depends on the cooperation of everyone on board.

We have not had any really rough weather but I hear that they sometimes get real gales up here. Anyway I have not been seasick yet…

The living conditions are very good and the food is excellent. You have no idea what difference all this makes, no matter how stoic or philosophical the disposition of the individual. At Skegness we had to queue for hours in order to have a bath or a meal. Here there is no waiting, no plates to wash, no fires to light, no stairs to sweep. This is all done by so-called 'General Duty' men who are in the RAF with no special trade but just do that. Here also the discipline is not so strict and one feels more like a human being. No longer is it necessary to stand rigidly to "attention" when addressing an NCO. On the contrary we all call each other by our Christian names and one corporal calls me 'Jock-Hans' (Jock is a Scottish nickname).

We are allowed out till 11h. If one wishes one can get a late pass till 1h. One can also get 3 sleeping-out passes per week. It is possible to go to Glasgow fairly frequently but Helensburgh is quite nice too. This has a population of about 50,000 and many rich citizens of Glasgow have their country houses there. I was there yesterday and had a haircut and also a shampoo (the first one since I left home). I did a little shopping buying a clotheshook and 3lbs of lemons and 2lbs of oranges. The oranges are sour and are for the manufacture of marmalade. Last week a shipload of lemons came in and Helensburgh is absolutely full of them. This is the first shipload since the war and it is rather surprising that the distribution is so badly organised, because all the greedy Scotsmen will eat all the lemons. I will try and send some more.

The WAAFS are more apart here than at Skegness. Anyway there are thousands of American sailors here. Nearly every house on the Clyde-front is a pub and they drink a lot of rum and gin. Sometimes there are fights between American and Scottish troops. The English are far less temperamental. There are also lots of Poles but they are not highly esteemed. Nearly everyone is somehow connected with the shipbuilding industry, the Clyde being the greatest centre.

Dear Blotscherl, I hope to come on leave very soon but it won't be before another two or three weeks. I am longing to come home. Did you like my poem??

Love Hans

P.S. I can spit overboard like an old sailor (or according to J.S. Mills, the trajectory of my expectorate is in the nautical tradition.)

After my training, I was posted to the South Coast, near Southampton. For a year of my life, I lived at the edge of the sea and saw its many faces and felt its different moods. Coastal command was proud of its squadrons of Catalina seaplanes. In peacetime, they had flown as far as Australia. They landed on water. Instead of wheels, they were fitted with buoys, and the body of the aircraft was hull-shaped to float. The unusual feature gave the flights the allure of luxury. But now they had to fight. They were fitted with guns on wings and bomb hatches to drop depth-charges onto German submarines. They needed a support flotilla to ferry aircrew to the anchored aircraft and to pull planes ashore to be serviced. I was detailed to paint the hulls of motor-launches and dinghies with thick red paint, appropriately called anti-fouling, which is meant to prevent algae and shells clinging to the timber.

The boats rested on cradles. I had to crouch down and apply the paint quickly with long-handled brushes that reached right underneath. The vessels had to be relaunched with the paint still wet. No protective glasses were issued.

And there was 'shingle-bashing'. Twice a day, the incoming tide swept in pebbles, which piled up on the slipway. Airmen were detailed to shovel the shingle onto waiting lorries. It was back-breaking work and after a while the tailboards always seemed to get higher.

As the Allies advanced into Germany, the Royal Air Force formed Air Disarmament Units to deal with captured airfields and and aircraft factories. Interpreters were needed not just for simple commands, but for the more involved process of clearance and salvage.

German and Austrian refugees applied for transfer, especially as there was automatic promotion to the rank of corporal and sergeant.

And so it was, just before Christmas 1944, that I was posted to SHAEF, Supreme Headquarters Allied Expeditionary Force, stationed at Bushey Park outside London. An interpreters' course had been set up. We had dictation, translation, and technical lectures, which included the reconnection of electricity and telephone landlines.

It was envisaged that there would be mass surrender, and that thousands of prisoners would have to be processed. A few basic phrases could facilitate the process.

Our commanding officer, a Russian squadron leader with an attractive Slav accent, had the novel idea of a practical demonstration. Why not make us march with commands in German? Why not show what we could do, and parade in front of an Intelligence Officer from the Air Ministry?

The day came, it was bitterly cold and there was heavy ground frost. We started marching in threes, perhaps thirty or more, along the avenue in the park which led past the saluting base. As we drew near, I saw her. Whitehall had sent a woman. In the understandable double excitement of gender and language, the duty sergeant, originally from Berlin, became confused. We were approaching from his right side, and as we drew level he shouted "rechts schaut!" (eyes right). I looked in front and saw how some men, with the automatic obedience that had been drilled into them, were looking away from her, but others ignored the command with continental pragmatism and did the opposite.

My friend Feniger was in the centre of the row in front of me and had a good look at her. I did the same. And then he slipped on the ice and fell in full view. I had to take evasive action not to tread on him. What she might have said to our commander is not recorded.

A few weeks later, we joined several hundred airmen for the Channel crossing to Ostend. Lorries had delivered us to the port of Tilbury and we had to carry our luggage to the quayside for embarkation. It all weighed a lot: the kitbag, the backpack, the steel helmet, the revolver and ammunition pouch, and the last but not least the very heavy greatcoat. My friend Herzfeld took a sleeping bag just in case. Many carried shoulder-strap bags with additional personal items. This long column of heavily-laden men had to march past our group of officers, who had taken up their position near the foot of the gangway. From time to time, the Wing Commander saluted. But then, as I passed by, the military expression on his face softened into a smile. He saw what I was carrying. Right on top of my luggage I had strapped my violin. I could not go to war without it.

For the previous ten months I did not need to write letters. I could get home for short periods, I was stationed so near. Now I started again, in fact as we crossed the Channel.

1882507 LAC N.
8501 A.D. Wing
R.A.F., BLA
Monday 5th March 1945

Dear Blotscherl,

I am writing this on board ship, somewhere between England and the Continent. After a lot of waiting about we at last moved off. Fortunately the weather is quite mild and I am not sea-sick. The accommodation is good – a little crowded but there is hot water. I played my violin in an enormous hall in the ship and it sounded well. There is very a <u>very good</u> Canadian violinist with us and he may give me some strings.

Tuesday morning. We are still at sea – the crossing is taking about [deleted by censor] because we are going very slowly and also waited for other ships. As I am writing I can see the [deleted by censor] and it is rather thrilling! I slept very well during the night and in the morning mended one of the socks I am wearing – they are rather bad.

Darling Blotscherl, I am feeling so many things, exciting and deep thoughts.

It is just a month off seven years that I left the Continent. One third of my life has been spent in England and on the whole it was a very happy one, because Pipschi and you helped and loved me so much. I am going to have lunch now, with a face that is smelling sweetly of your talkum-powder.

Thursday evening: Yesterday it was quite impossible to write because we were on the move all day. In the evening at last we came to a very nice town. All the people gave us the most tremendous welcome. The town has suffered terribly through the war and the prices are terribly high. For instance a good dinner (without sweet) costs 90 Franks, 1 kilo butter cost 500 Franks (black market because it is unobtainable on the ration card). Bread is severely rationed and a small roll costs about 8d. All the same I am very happy here. It is all so much like a dream − as if the last seven years were only a few days. In this town, where I have never been before I feel so much more at home than in London somehow. I bought a small French dictionary…

2883507 LAC Neumann
08501 AD Wing
RAF, BLA.
12th March 1945

Darling Blotscherl,
I hope you got my first letter which I sent on Thursday. This one is a privileged letter and is not censored!

I am having a very nice time here. First of all I have contacted a very good pianist, a proffesional (sic) teacher, who is a young girl, aged about 23. (Hear! Hear!) We are going to do some piano trios. Secondly my French is improving tremendously. I can understand most things, and am able to make myself understood fairly well, using the familiar 'tu' whenever appropriate.

It is very difficult to sit down to a meal here and enjoy it because all the time one has to think of all the poor people who have nothing to eat. The other day I was invited for supper somewhere and it consisted of a thin soup and potatoes with an egg. No bread or butter.

I fixed my laundry by giving a woman some chocolate and soap in exchange. She was very grateful and she also mended all my holes!! In the town there are some very good hot baths which I frequent! The other day I had some real ice cream.

Blotscherl, it is so wonderful to be on the Continent again, in spite of all the frightful misery. The people here have retained something inspite of all their adversity – some sort of true European spirit. This atmosphere has become much more intense during the war, because all the people on this Continent have endured the same things.

There is little nationalism, real self-sacrifice to help others and an undying wild, furious hatred for the Germans who have really done the most terrible things. This hatred has a unifying effect which would be of lasting value were it not built on such a negative basis.

Tuesday 13th.

This morning I sent you a field post-card. I hope you will get it sooner than the letter. Yesterday I went for the first time to this girl pianist. We played 2 Händel (D major and E major) and the Spring Sonata. Unfortunately she had no more music, but I am going to buy the Mozart Sonatas (50 Franks or about 7/-). This is very cheap compared with a meal costing easily 100 Franks. On Sunday night I went to hear an operetta or rather it was a play with lots of singing and dancing called "the divorce". The theatre is really beautiful inside all guilded wooden panelling from the good old days before the last war.

Dear Blosoï, what is happening in London? Any concerts?

I must stop now. The food is quite good and we are getting American rations of cigarettes and chocolate.

Love Hansi

1882507 LAC Neumann
8501 A.D. Wing
RAF, BLA.
1st April, 1945

Dear Blotscherl,

This is just to tell you than I am very well and that I got your parcel with the soap. I hope you will not go short. To-day is Easter Sunday and the 1st of April and I think of you both in a seriously joyful and also humorous way.

It is very cold just now but we are very well accommodated. Just three of us

157

in one room: Peter Saunders and Herbert [Herbert Spencer, the reknowned graphic designer who remained a life-long friend after the war]. Tietze-Tante is in another room. There is a corporal here who plays the piano fairly well and we are trying to get a piano from somewhere. This is going to be very difficult because there is here the most terrific material destruction I have ever seen.

Our room is very nice. Herbert (the artist) has brought with him some 30 reproductions of Gauguin, Van Gogh, Dürer and Breugel. These decorate the walls. Also I have hung up my violin-case and one bow and some sheets of music. I also nailed up some keys from a demolished piano and the whole thing looks very surrealistic.

I hope you got my parcel by now. Do send me some candles and a cake sometime.

Darling Bloserl, my mind at the moment is in a great turmoil, but when I think of you and when I get your letters or when I play – these things give me a wonderful sense of perspective in surroundings that either strike you as being completely mad or unreal …

Love Hansi

1882507 LAC Neumann
8501 A.D. Wing
RAF, BLA
5/IV/45

Dear Blotscherl,

I am now allowed to tell you that I came to Germany a short time ago. It was a great experience crossing the Dutch border. Nearly all the Germans have been evacuated and only about 10 or 15% preferred to stay. There are no men or women between the ages of 18 to 35 about. But one can see some Russian and Ukrainian workers. We are in a small town which had a population of 5000 before the war. Now there are only 500 left – those who hid rather than be forcible evacuated. Some places have been more or less totally destroyed. Here there is no water or electricity but I think both will be installed shortly. Blotscherl, all this destruction is so terribly depressing and the people are so broken and utterly despondent. There seems to be no real hatred, not here anyway where they are Catholics. Some seem relieved that for the first time in twelve years they are safe from the Gestapo and they all hope that war will be over soon. Who doesn't?

It will take about 20 years before Germany will be anything like she was.

I am very optimistic about the war. I think it will finish in about 4 weeks. Have you seen Churtl? He is in England and will be able to tell you lots of things about Belgium.

My music? Well I have not had any time at all in the last few days as you can imagine. But we have now 3 or 4 pianos and there is quite a good pianist here. Anyway I try to play as much as possible. I hope you got my letter and field-service post-card. Also I sent you a parcel whilst I was still in Belgium. With this letter I am sending you a post-card from one of the places I was in. It is on the Rhine.

Darling Bloserl, don't be worried about me I am very well, cheerful, and absolutely safe. I have not had a letter from you for 6 days — there must be some delay. I hope you get mine quickly.

Whatever wicked things the Germans did they never never deserved what they now have. It is so phantastic that it seems like a nightmare. What was not yet destroyed and smashed by bombing and shell-fire was done by the fury of the Russian and Polish workers who took swift revenge for years of forced labour.

For the first time in my life, time has lost nearly all its value. There is no hurry because there is nothing to hurry for. Can you imagine no dash at 5 o'clock, no exciting planning how to get off at Friday lunchtime. We work every day.

The food is very good (American rations). We get 7 bars of chocolate and 140 cigarettes FREE per week and I exchange my cigarettes for chocolate.

Our room is slowly being filled with all sorts of trophies we have found. A flag of a shooting-club, beer mugs, and most important we have got hold of wire mattresses and I am sleeping like a king.

I just got your letter from the 3rd. Thank you so much.
I must stop now
love Hansi

1882507LAC Neumann

8501 AD Wing

RAF BLA

9/IV/45

Dear Blosoi,

I am terribly busy these days – there is here in Germany a terrific tension in those last weeks of a 6 year struggle.

The destruction in some parts beats even the wildest imagination. Most of the beautiful cities on the Rhine will have to be entirely rebuilt.

As we moved further inland there was an endless stream of Russian, Polish, French, Belgian and Dutch workers WALKING and starving on the road leading to the West. Yesterday a group of British prisoners of war came into our place. They had been in captivity for 5 years and started <u>marching</u> from East Prussia in the middle of January. They marched 1200 km. On the roads French prisoners wear perhaps American uniforms they were given by the Red Cross, Dutch may wear Danish, Poles Italian.

There are hardly any people (both sexes) between 18-35 left. The S.S. took them all. The vast majority of German prisoners are relieved that for them the war is over and that they are in American not Russian captivity.

Now there is Spring here and the woods are lovely but we never stay long in one place. In none of the places is water or electricity and all water has to be carried over long distances. I have not had a bath since I am in Germany but I did manage to wash myself entirely in cold water once or twice.

We don't get any bread at all just now – only biscuits.

I hope you got my parcel by now. Sometimes I find a little time to play the violin. Always I find time to think of you.

Lots of love Hansi

(censor's signature, illegible)

Dear Blotscherl,

I got your letter and parcel. Thank you so much. The candles came just in time and the kugerln [small Viennese chocolate balls] were absolutely wonderful. I hope you got my parcel now. I sent it away on the 28th February.

Darling Blosoi, I am very well and you need not worry about me at all. We get very good food and at the moment I am again fortunate enough to share a room with Peter.

By the time you get this letter the war in Europe will be nearly over. That realisation makes me very happy and I am sure that I am not the only one.

I still play Bach but apart from the music I produce myself I have not heard a bar of Bach, Beethoven or Brahms since I left Belgium. It is very strange: (I had the same feeling in Skegness) a terrifying silence starts growing into the vacuum which used to be filled by musical thought. Somehow it becomes so much more difficult to imagine music if one is not in constant touch with it. And the paradoxy of it all is the fact that one can never get away from noise: men shouting, marching, lorries, machines, guns, tanks, planes. In fact solitude and silence are rare in a soldier's life.

Conditions here very much resemble the middle ages. Bands of Russian and Polish workers or ex-prisoners of war sweep down on isolated houses or even small villages. There is no real law and order. Any soldier has the power to arrest any civilian and has the virtual, even if not the legal power to seize and commandeer private property. The military law in many respects is very harsh mainly because the German law which it is superceeding was frightfully harsh and the military authorities do not wish to be "weak" in the eyes of the Germans.

It is impossible at the moment to assess the historic truth. Were they all Nazis? How many were? Who was really active? All these questions are impossible to answer. One day one sees the most pitiable sights and hears the most appalling stories of Nazi oppression in their own country and on the next one is confronted by concrete evidence (without doubt, because it is nearly always in the human sphere) of the most devilish, systematic destruction which the Germans as a military formation and as a so-called national unit brought on the heads of others.

It is that intrinsic urge for truth and at the same time the realisation that one will never be able to assess the number of those who gave up their life for and against Nazism and those who just died because they had to – it is that conflict that is worrying me because I am too near to one of the greatest upheavals, both military, political and social to get even a reasonable perspective and yet I am near enough to perceive those details (results of spontaneous reactions, which are usually true and not pre-meditated) which are so easily lost in later times and are usually impossible to record scientifically.

Yet whatever the people were in their political views: their suffering is terrible although in many respects they are in a more favourable position than the Dutch or Belgians. They are better clothed, especially shoes. They have had slightly more to eat, but that depended very much on the locality. The rural districts of the Low Countries did not do too badly either. But whilst nearly all the young men are either prisoners or have been killed, the victorious nations can at least look forward to an early reunion, a swift material betterment strengthened by the realisation that all this suffering has not been entirely in vain. Germany on the other hand, has no future and will not even rise to the status of a second-class nation within 50 years. All her heavy industry is smashed. For years millions will have to rebuild Russia. No nation in Europe will have any trade-relationship with her apart from the very essentials. In the domestic artistic and musical sphere the rest of the Continent at any rate will be "taboo" to her. On top of it all many cities are practically destroyed and it seems more practical to build as if there had never been anything there at all.

Blotscherl all this is so immense and terrifying and I feel so small and helpless somehow. But I have faith and I adhere to certain moral principles, although my actual power over other human beings is greater than ever before and I hope will never be as great again. There is a great danger that if one has very great power all of a sudden, one loses ones true relationship to other people and therefore the true relationship to oneself. Slowly the human element in one's dealings with one's fellow men dwindles, one sees only categories, ranks, nationalities.

For that reason I will never be able to be a good leader because my sympathy and understanding are too predominant and any capacity for sternness and immovable strictness - qualities needed whilst dealing with masses, - not sufficient.

Darling Blosoi, I must stop now give my love to all.
Pussi Hansi

P.S. Who wants to be a good leader anyway? Only fools! (Hear, Hear!) Send me lots more envelopes and also some more lavatory-paper. What a gastronomic end to a communicative beginning, philosophic middle and egocentric finish.

1882507 Cpl Neumann
8501 Wing
RAF, BLA
25/V/45

Dear Blotscherl,

Yesterday I came back from a two-day trip to Wansdorf which is about 20km North West of Hannover. On my return I found your sweet parcel with the bathing costume and the chocolate – kugerln, [illegible] and Kamilosan. Thank you very very much! Lately I have been very busy because Peter Saunders has gone to Brussels to see a psychiatrist because he feels he can't stand this life any longer. My painter friend, Herbert [Spencer], tried to commit suicide a few days ago and is also in hospital with stomach poisoning. But he is very much on the road to recovery.

So you see things are pretty grim out here. The nervous strain is great because firstly one is confronted with continual sadness and secondly the non-fraternisation laws are very strictly enforced. It is quite impossible to talk to any German civilian in the street. Civilians of all nationalities fall at the moment under the same regulations and officially one is liable to penalty for talking to a Polish worker. The reason for that is that at the moment none of these people have proper papers of identification and the Germans have many spies among them.

Think of Germany round about the turn of this century — the land of Brahms and Strauss. Within four decades her cultural life has ceased completely. There is not one bookshop, one music shop or a picture-gallery in Hannover, Braunschweig, Hildesheim or Padeborn for instance. And when I say none I mean it. There are just a few houses and people often searching hopelessly among the rubble.

In Hannover there were up till quite recently 100.000 Russians who terrorised the town to a varying degree. Incidentally I hope to find a good violin sooner or later. How nice if I could! …

…Darling Blosoi I hope you are well and also all the rest.

Love Hansi.

I have not contacted Stephan yet [I was unaware when I wrote this that my first cousin had died in action in 1944]. There is also at the moment no chance of going to Vienna for a day or two because short passes are not being granted at all.

I am sending off shortly some Breugel and Velasquez!!

> *1882507 Cpl Neumann*
> *8501 Wing*
> *RAF, BLA*
> *28/V/45*

Dear Blotscherl,

Yesterday I got your letter from the 19th. I just want to tell you that I find some time to play the violin but I don't read much. (I never have read a lot).

I got a letter from Heinzi Fürth and he does not seem very happy in a village near the Dutch border.

I was in Hannover yesterday to buy a violin but all music shops have been destroyed. I will try in Bad Pyrmont or Hameln. Here there is cinema every night. Yesterday I saw "double indemnity" which was good. Nearly always the film brakes (sic) down or one cannot hear the sound track. All very funny.

We had up till quite recently a German-speaking Squadron-leader with us. He was a Jew and he did some splendid work. Many synagogues are being re-built under his orders by the Germans. Jewish grave-stones which all over

Germany were used to plaster the roads are being collected and the owners of those fields which used to be grave-yards have to bear the expense and provide the labour.

You speak of the experiences I have had. Yes I have had many both terrible and amusing. But in most cases the dignity and holiness of MAN had to suffer and that is really the most tragic aspect of this catastrophy (sic).

Pussi, Hansi

Send me a violin A string some time

1882507 Cpl Neumann
8501 Wing
RAF, BLA
3/VI/45

Darling Blotscherl,

I got your letter telling me about the photos yesterday. Thank you so much. I love getting your letters. They help me such a lot. Here there is so little love and so much hatred and apathy. Although I am very self contained (due to my music) your love gives me great strength in this mad, <u>cruel</u> world. I see cruelty, injustice and destruction every day and outwardly I get used and hardened to these things. But only <u>outwardly</u> – that is my protective armour, otherwise I would have gone mad long ago. <u>Inwardly</u> I try not to think too much. There is no need to keep any great check on my imagination because I have seen nearly all the things that are to see.

It is true: public opinion has a very short memory, but that is due mainly to the lack of individual experience in the matter concerned. Therefore I think that everyone should visit Dachau and Belsen and speak and see the people there. Personally, I saw some of the inmates of a concentration camp near Seesen a few days after their liberation. That was about 6 weeks ago. They were too weak to walk and were driven away by horse and cart. When I passed them those that were able to do so stretched their arms out to greet me. The only thing that had any resemblance with other human beings were their eyes which seemed very deep and sad and unused to the light that shone in them.

Their bodies however were living skeletons and I could not sleep properly that night and many nights after that.

Some time ago I also spoke to a girl from Belsen. She had been sent there eight months ago because she refused to go to work on account of a leg injury she had received in a raid on Munich. She must have been in her early twenties but she looked about 45. Nearly all her hair had been cut off and she had just left the typhus hospital and was walking around Hannover. When I heard her intention to walk to Munich (800km) I told her to go to the Military Government and see if they can help her. But her mind is beyond help even if her body can be cured. She had never lost hope in Belsen but now she just could not understand that she was free again. She is by no means an isolated case. People who for years have endured these camps are in the majority of cases <u>completely</u> different human beings spiritually, and should really be sent to a convalescent home with a staff of expert psychiatrists. Never in my life before have I seen such a face (and that only after 7 months). At the slightest allusion to the horrors of the camp she said: Oh don't speak a word! She was a <u>German Aryan</u>.

Nearly seven decades on, I vividly recall the details of this meeting. We had stopped by the roadside in Hanover, and were opening our emergency lunch-boxes. The sergeant first noticed the shaven-headed woman approaching, and joked: "Here comes a woman who needs a haircut". None of us had ever seen a woman with a completely shaven head. After our conversation, I gave her my unopened carton.

Darling Blotscherl, don't be upset that I see all these terrible things. On the contrary you should be grateful that I had the opportunity of <u>visual</u> proof (which is the only one with a lasting effect). Why grateful? Because it is only when one has seen all that this tortured continent can show up, that one is able to understand this age and this generation. When you go back to the Continent you will see under the superficiality of law and order the latent sorrow and hatred of nations. And you will have to take the <u>reasons</u> for these sentiments for granted. In other words you will have to <u>assume</u> a vital factor in the history of the last few years – a factor, which in my opinion is far beyond assumptions, because the suffering of human beings can never be imagined or comprehended.

It is only by being a soldier in this war and thereby experiencing the loss of freedom and by seeing the horrors of the 20ᵗʰ century European continent that one can somewhat appreciate this era. Even then it is still a far cry from the actual experience of all these millions. But that perhaps is not quite so important.

At first I decided not to write any of these things because I did not want you to worry but now I think that it would make our correspondence too artificial if I concealed to you one of the great experiences of my life – speaking and feeling with the people from Belsen and Seesen.

With all my love
Pussi Hansi

P.S. Send me some more eye-drops: COLOSSAL ARGENTUM (at Boots) also an <u>A-String</u>

1882507 Cpl Neumann
8501 Wing
RAF, BLA
11/VI/45

Darling Blotscherl,

I have not had any mail from you for 3 days. There is probably a delay somewhere. Here is nothing new to report. I am still in Eschershausen, but expect to move soon.

I feel full of apprehension about the future. This continent has not matured politically and socially sufficiently to lay the foundations for a permanent peace. You just can't imagine how much the Germans are hated by everyone else, how much the Poles fear the Russians, how much the Austrians suffered at the hands of the Jugoslavs (sic) and so on. It is in this period of transition between hostilities and the final peace-settlement that political mistakes have their greatest effect. Now all the principles for which we have been fighting are being closely watched by the whole world when they are brought to the test. To compromise now would mean another war. Let us hope for the best.

My Händel Sonata was accompanied by amusing incidents. Firstly they turned a 'spot-light' on me and switched off all the other lights. So I had to stop playing because I could not see the music and started again. Then in the last movement I went straight on whilst the pianist repeated so I stopped and we went straight on. Otherwise it did not go too badly.

Today I met for the first time a German Jewish woman who had not been imprisoned in any way at any time. Isn't it amazing? She told me that she never wore the yellow star because she lived in small rural villages. But there are not many Jews left in Germany.

Here in Eschershausen there used to be many Austrian solders of a Deutschmeisterregiment. They were all killed or captured at Stalingrad.

At the moment the weather is not so good and it is too cold to swim. I hope you get my letters quickly.

Lots of love

Pussi Hansi.

1882507 Cpl Neumann

8501 Wing

RAF, BLA

23/VI/45

Darling Blotscherl,

Yesterday morning, on our way to our new place we had a road accident. Our lorry ran into a tree, trying to avoid a woman. I am not really hurt and was brought straight back to the unit, suffering from only minor injuries on the arm, a slight scratch on the skull and a bruise on the left thigh. There were 6 of us in the lorry but nobody was seriously hurt.

I was the only one that was thrown any distance and was very lucky really.

I am being treated very well in the Unit hospital and the German girls who work in the ward bring me flowers and strawberries.

Today I walked a little and will soon be alright again. The violin I was given here and also my wireless were completely smashed but the other violin is still all right. I have not seen it myself. I expect to leave hospital in a day or two. Last night I slept very well and there were lots of visitors! So there is no need for you to worry at all!!

The day before yesterday we were entertained by a Dutch concert party but there were some Austrians and it was really lovely to hear the Tyrolese accent again.

I enclose a poem:

Concentration camp SEESEN

Time can be tortured
and the pulse beat of seconds
drawn to a single hammer-blow
of everlasting.

Unknown wounds
Trickling wells for one stream,
And the throb of so many hearts
ocean thunder.

The measure of life
strapped to the infinite rack,
but men age – with the regular stars
that fade at dawn.

Eschershausen 23/VI/45

1882507 Cpl Neumann
8303 A.D. Wing
RAF, BLA
30/VI/45

Darling Blotscherl,

As you may have guessed through my long silence I was travelling all the time and arrived safely yesterday with all my luggage at Trarbach. We (that is Tune and I) left Eschershausen on Monday and stayed overnight at Osnabrück. We travelled in a big bus and it was quite good fun.

Then we went to Nymwegen (via Arnhem) in order to be picked up by a small car. In Nymwegen we stayed till Thursday morning. It was a very pleasant change to be allowed to smile at girls and to go about without a revolver. I went to various music-shops but all the music has been sold or is out of stock. I did find a violin shop, however, and played on one or two quite good violins. Life in Holland is very expensive. 10 cigarettes cost about 8/- on the Black Market.

On Thursday we started our lovely journey up the Rhine to Koblenz. We stayed overnight at Herne in Westphalia. This is where Heinz Furth is but he was away for a few days. What a pity!

Friday we travelled all the way down the Rhine and then up the Mosel. The country is very beautiful. For miles and miles the grapes grow on the hillside of the winding Mosel. Have you been there??

I am sending Pipschi £8 (crossed). I am going to another place at 3.30h where there are French troops. I am sent there (in preference to the other interpreters) on account of my French. So don't write until you hear from me.

What a pity that Koblenz is so destroyed! On our way down we passed through Düsseldorf and Köln. It was terrible and hideous.

Lots of love Hansi.

P.S. Wine costs only about 1/- per bottle and it is very <u>good</u>.

My father was curious about my service details, such as initial training, pay, discipline, food, accomodation. For him it must have seemed a shared experience for an old soldier.

I was particular reminded of this in the summer of 1945. I had come home on leave from Germany, and I had only just closed the front door when he asked me: "were you ever under fire?" "Yes, but only under friendly fire," I replied. In April 1945, a few weeks before the end, I was standing on the banks of the Rhine somewhere north of Cologne, with a small RAF disarmament unit, specially formed to occupy abandoned airfields and destroyed aircraft factories. Each squadron had an interpreter seconded to it, and I eventually reached the rank of Sergeant. On that day we had arrived at the edge of the river, the natural frontline. A battery of field guns, positioned about two or three hundred metres behind us, was firing a barrage straight over our heads across the water into a large enemy pocket, still holding out on the opposite bank. The salvos seemed to come in regular intervals of perhaps every half-minute, the booming heartbeat of destruction. And with the bangs came the flashes as the shells left the barrels. There was no reply.

On one memorable occasion my father was reminded of his own artillery experience. It was the summer of 1941. We were living at that time in a large house near Hampstead Heath. There, at the top, on the highest point, overlooking London, was one of the many anti-aircraft batteries, protecting the city. Suddenly, one summer afternoon, we heard the most terrifying explosion, followed immediately by further devastating bangs. I thought it was a string of bombs falling terribly near. The house seemed to shake. I was standing in the hall, my father came out of the drawing room, and my mother stood at the top of the stairs. My father looked at us and said: "Als alter Artillerist sag ich euch, das sind die Unsern!" (As an old artillery man, I tell you they are ours.) My mother told me that when I heard the noise, I went quite pale with fright. But my father recognised a sound of old, a battery of guns in full cry.

CHAPTER 10

Cultural ferment

In November 1918, my father came home from the War to a changed world. Revolutions had swept away Kaiser Wilhelm of Germany and Kaiser Karl of Austria. In Russia, the revolution had taken place a year earlier, leading to Tsar Nicholas' assassination in 1918.

Vienna was now the capital of a small republic. The creation of the new Austria of some six million inhabitants followed six hundred and fifty years of Habsburg hegemony. At the point of its dissolution, the Austro-Hungarian monarchy had been a multi-national state with a population of fifty-seven million.

It was the beginning of a new world.

Dr. Karl Renner was elected as the first Chancellor of the Republic. He was a great Socialist leader, a political theorist, and a publicist. The special brand of the political programme, the mixture of Marxist ideology, modified to suit local circumstance, became known as Austro-Marxismus, and soon Vienna was called "Das rote Wien" (Red Vienna).

At the Town Hall, Karl Seitz, the Mayor, initiated a vast ongoing project of municipal building, consisting of flats for workers, hospitals, schools, old people's homes, children's homes and playgrounds. Gas, electricity and transport were nationalised and expanded. The municipality built public baths, libraries and colleges of further education.

The flats in the Gemeindehäuser (the municipal housing complexes) were imbued with the spirit of modernity. Their hallmark was a contemporary design, a signpost to a better life.

Kitchens had external windows to the road, or onto gardens at the back. Where possible, the front doors of the flats, no more than three or four at a time, opened onto separate landings. There would be more privacy that way. Gone were the long corridors and the outlook into dark courtyards and into other people's lives through rear windows, the hallmark of 19th century housing blocks. Gone were those vast sombre structures that had acquired the popular name of 'Zinskasernen' (rent barracks).

Now, a messianic dream would, wherever possible, be made reality. Blocks of flats would have communal laundries, and communal baths. There would be provision for reading rooms, cafeterias, grocery shops, gyms, advice centres for mothers. The social ethos of welfare was now the new slogan.

Vienna was, of course, also chained to the past. The city is proud of its architectural legacy of empire: the Imperial Palaces, the Hofburg and Schönbrunn. The Belvedere Palace was built as a residence for Prince Eugène of Savoy. Noble families wanted to have town residences in the Kaiserstadt Wien to mark their presence near the Imperial Court. The list of elegant 17th and 18th century town houses of the aristocracy, the so-called *palais*, is a roll-call of political influence and artistic patronage: Esterhazy, Pallavacini, Rasumowsky, Lobkovitz, Schwarzenberg, Metternich, Kaunitz, Fürstenberg, Starhemberg, to mention some of the famous names.

Great cities have architectural physiognomies. Florence is Renaissance, Venice is gothic, Vienna is baroque. Fischer von Erlach gave the town its landmark features, especially the Karlskirche, so much like St Paul's Cathedral. He is for Vienna what Christopher Wren is for London. Over the years, in Vienna, on my many visits to my grandparents, I would see the building as I travelled in the tram along the Ringstrasse.

The church became part of my heritage: the magnificent cupola, the Palladian pillared entrance hall, and especially the two columns on each side, modelled on the triumphal columns of Rome.

But no less was the lasting impact of the Gemeindehaus in the Gersthoferstrasse, the building that I passed every day on my way to school, the building that was besieged in 1934. I was deeply aware of the old and the new.

So, of course, were Wilhelm and Hermine. Women's emancipation took a picturesque turn in the Neumann household of the Ferdinandstrasse, when, soon after the war, both daughters Lena and Mizzi decided to have their long hair cut short. Gone would be the universal bun, to be replaced by the gamin look, so aptly called in German 'der Bubikopf'. The girls decided that they could not possibly tell their mother, so they went on holiday and had it done in Salzburg.

When it was my mother's turn to follow her two sisters-in-law, perhaps a year or so later, she wanted to give my father a surprise. She did not tell him what she was about to do. After her visit to the hairdresser, she hurried home and waited for his return from town. As the front door opened, she expected my father's split second speechless wonder immediately to be transformed into admiration for the new appearance. She would gracefully smile at him, and ask the obligatory question: "Do you like it?" But in the event, they both burst out laughing. They looked at their changed faces, and fell into each other's arms. For on that very same day, my father had secretly been to the barber and had his moustache shaved off! My mother told me the story on several occasions and always emphasized the great coincidence of the mutual surprise, planned simultaneously.

Women wanted to look new and modern and liberated, with their short hair, their fringes, their soft permanent waves. And at the same time, men wanted to put behind them their recent military past and cut off their officer moustaches.

I am fortunate to have a pictorial record of my family going back to my great grandparents. Early family photographs, those taken before the First World War, are evocative. The sitter had to keep very still, the features are clearly etched, there is no implied movement or half tone. The image is printed on thick card from glass plates. On the back of the old pictures is the name and address of the photographer often with ateliers in several towns. The lists speak with nostalgia of a bygone age, with the geography of empire.

In 1900, Robert Neumann, aged about two years, was photographed by C. Pietzner, K. u. K. Hof-u. Kammerphotograph in Vienna, with branches in Brünn, Aussig, Olmütz, Carlsbad and Teplitz. The last two were famous spa towns in Bohemia.

For me, Teplitz is forever associated with Goethe and Beethoven. It was there, in July 1812, that the two met for the first and only time over a period of several days. The spa was crowded with nobility and royalty. There is the familiar anecdote which decorates this historic moment. Visitors walked in the Kurgarten or strolled about in Prince Clary's Schlossgarten. Goethe expressed his vexation at the incessant greetings from passers-by. Beethoven is said to have replied, "Don't be annoyed, Excellency. Perhaps they are bowing to me!".

There is another story that characterizes Beethoven the revolutionary and Goethe the courtier. At the time, the Emperor Franz and the Empress of Austria, the Empress Marie-Louise of France, the King of Saxony, together with grand dukes and duchesses and their entourages were all in Teplitz.

Beethoven and Goethe were on their promenade when some of the illustrious personages came into sight, walking towards them. Beethoven wanted to walk on, arm in arm. The aristocrats would have to make way on either side. But Goethe refused, and stood at the side of the road, hat in hand. Beethoven, swinging his arms, charged right through the midst of the princes, merely touching his hat. They politely made room for him and all greeted him in a friendly fashion. Beethoven waited for Goethe, who was still bowing ceremoniously. And then he told him: "I have waited for you because I honour and esteem you, but you have honoured these people far too much."

If only there had been photography in 1812, perhaps an early version of a tripod with a black sack over the photographer's head! Then one might have seen the two Titans, drawn up, side by side, in expectant stillness.

The pre-First World War pictures were usually taken indoors, in studios. They were stylized portraits, often theatrically embellished by stage props, perhaps a pillar, a bench, a tree trunk. There might be a bush, or a palm tree, a child might hold a stick or an umbrella. Frequently hats were worn. Very popular were backdrops, theatrical scenery of mountains or gardens.

There is a picture of the Neumann children in sailor costume, the boys in their sailor suits and the girls in their sailor tops and matching skirts.

In another photo, Paul and Lena are wearing the ethnic costumes of the Alps, Paul in short leather trousers, held up by traditional braces which were joined across the chest with a decorative broad band, and Lena in her 'Dirndl' dress, her silk apron and the silk scarf held in place by a brooch.

But to have your portrait in oils, to have a picture, fixed for the future, was the height of fashion and luxury. In 1922, Rudolf Huber-Wiesenthal painted my sister Eva. She was four years old. The picture is excellent. She looks at us with her large black eyes, full of serenity and trust. The moment of her gaze is captured in its direct immediacy which has remained unchanged for more than ninety years. Her face is transfigured by the spirit of the Secession and her features are covered by that imperceptible veil which transforms reality into art.

Vienna, in the first decades of the 20th century, was a city in cultural ferment. It is hard to imagine the excitement awaiting the premiere of the latest Mahler symphony or the first performance of an orchestral work by Schoenberg. The tensions and expectations surrounding the great exhibitions in the Secession of the works by Gustav Klimt are now legendary. So many artists and composers, all together in one city Vienna, gave it a unique feeling of cultural compactness.

My parents were part of it. We have reminders of those unique years. The lid for a cardboard box and a sheet of corresponding tissue paper from the Wiener Werkstätte may well have been used for a beautiful scarf woven on one of their looms. Miraculously, the fragile mementos have survived several substantial moves prior to my discovery of them at the bottom of a box containing family letters.

In 1903, the architect Josef Hoffmann and his friend, the artist Koloman Moser, established the Wiener Werkstätte as an association of workshops and studios. Earlier, William Morris and Charles Rennie Mackintosh had led the way with the Arts and Crafts Movement. Now Josef Hoffmann felt ready to realize his vision of totality, of what in Wagnerian terms is called 'Gesamtkunstwerk'. As architect, he could design a house and also provide the contents. His preparatory drawings for his furniture, his chairs, tables, bookcases, desks, sideboards and beds are profound visions of *Art Nouveau*. First class materials were used: oak, walnut, beech, pear, alder and pine. The workmanship of the joineries and cabinet makers, the quality of inlay and veneer, soon made the Wiener Werkstätte famous. Distinctive designs for his silverware and cutlery were beautifully crafted by the Wiener Werkstätte workshops. The studios printed fabrics and wall tapestries. Scarves were woven and block printed. Especially evocative is his glassware: champagne, beer, liqueur, water and wine with their distinctive long stems and their geometric bronze decoration on matt glass.

Josef Hoffmann designed a whole array of leather work, book bindings, handbags, purses, briefcases, folders.

My mother's Wiener Werkstätte wallet is displayed in a place of honour. Fortunately it was hardly used and contained an Austrian passport from the 1930s. The black kid leather is decorated with pressed gold block printing in a repeated pattern of flowers and leaves. The very delicate web of lines is stylised with a touch of geometry, and gives the impression of an overlay of gold tracery.

As I enter the house in London, I see the filigree gold mantle on the leather welcoming me to Secessionist Vienna. And next to it is the tissue: repeated rectangular gold boxes, containing the words Wiener Werkstätte, printed in evocatively designed typography. The three dimensional texture of the gold-dust print gives the sheet the semblance of a frieze of decorative wall tiles.

It all reminds me so much of Gustav Klimt. In 1908, at the Kunstschau, Gustav Klimt exhibited important works which have a golden quality, broken up into mosaic decoration. Adele Bloch–Bauer and Fritza von Riedler, two iconic portraits from 1907, echo the spirit of the Ravenna mosaics of San Vitale, where the Empress Theodora surveys the world with still detachment. Also shown for the first time was *The Kiss* (1908), in which oil paint and golden ornament combine in supreme decoration, to express sexual desire. In Klimt's hands, real gold is more than just another colour. It has the aura of splendour, of riches, of royalty, the monarch of the metals. And its reflection is mirrored in the Wiener Werkstätte. That is hardly surprising. Klimt and Hoffmann had become close collaborators. In 1905, Hoffmann had been commissioned by Adolphe Stoclet, the Belgian millionaire, to design a grand palais in Brussels, and to furnish the entire interior, down to the last spoon, with products from the Wiener Werkstätte, of which the magnificent residency is today the most complete, supreme testimony. For the dining room, Hoffmann asked Klimt to design a large mosaic frieze. Influenced by Byzantium, Klimt used gold, silver, semi-precious stones, coral and enamel, set against a white marble background.

In the Kunstschau 1908, a whole room, room 50, was given over to the products of the Wiener Werkstätte. I like to think that a wallet with a familiar design was on display on that art-historic occasion. But what an occasion! The Klimt room, designed and hung by Koloman Moser, was devoted to no fewer than sixteen of Gustav Klimt's paintings.

My grandfather Wilhelm would certainly have visited the Kunstschau. As a journalist he would have felt professional imperative and overriding curiosity. He would have discussed it with his great friend Ludwig Hevesi, sitting in one of the famous coffee houses, perhaps the Herrenhof or the Café Central.

Ludwig Hevesi was a colleague on the *Fremden-Blatt*, and the most important art critic at the time of Emperor Franz Joseph. When Wilhelm started at the paper in 1885, Hevesi, who was seventeen years older, took an avuncular interest in him, giving him valuable advice. Like Wilhelm, Hevesi was born in Hungary, in fact in Heves. On arrival in Vienna, he changed his name from Hirsch to Hevesi, the man from Heves.

At the time when Lena handed over to me Wilhelm's library, some time in the late 1960s, she individually checked the books. She came across a thick volume, privately bound in elegant dark green leather. There is no title or author stamped on the outside. She opened it and read: Altkunst – Neukunst, Wien 1894-1908, von Ludwig Hevesi (Old Art, New Art, Vienna 1894-1908, by Ludwig Hevesi). She turned back a page to the flyleaf and read out aloud the dedication: "Meinem lieben Freunde Wilhelm Neumann zur Erinnerung an alte und neue Zeiten. W 11/5 09 L Hevesi" (For my dear friend Wilhelm Neumann in memory of old and new times). And then she said: "Der Hevesi war so ein guter Freund vom Vater" (Hevesi was such a good friend of my father).

Hevesi was a great supporter of the Secession and his many articles, essays and feuilletons are gathered together in an earlier book, entitled *Acht Jahre Sezession März 1897 – Juni 1905* (Eight Years of the Secession, March 1897 to June 1905). This book helped in making the Secession a success and Hevesi's contributions were invaluable in shaping the climate of public perception and critical opinion.

The newly-founded association of artists, the breakaway *Art Nouveau* group, needed a separate exhibition building and chose the architect Josef Olbrich. Hevesi was there for the laying of the foundation stone on the 28th April 1898. Ten years later, in his memorial article on Josef Olbrich, who had died at the early age of forty one, Hevesi recalled the occasion. After a simple ceremony, a large laurel wreath, which had been presented to the 'Honorary President' Rudolf von Alt, was distributed among those present, each person receiving a few evergreen leaves. "Sie stehen noch in einer kleinen Vase vor mir und sind wirklich noch immer grün" (they still stand in front of me in a small vase, and are, indeed, still green).

German lends itself wonderfully to scornful invective and Hevesi invents and puts together composite nouns, which strike like deadly shafts. When describing the criticism which was heaped on the architect and the new building, Hevesi says, "Und er tat es unter jenem denkwürdigen Unisono von Wiener Tageshohn, von polyphonem Fünfuhrgelächter des maßgebenden ersten Bezirkes, und von dreimalweisem, neunmalweisen Besserwissen fast sämtlicher

Gebildeten" (and he did it, accompanied by that memorable unison of Viennese daily taunts, by polyphonous five o'clock laughter from the authoritative First District, and by the three times wiser, nine times wiser Know-betters, comprising nearly all educated people).

In 1928, for my father's fortieth birthday, my mother commissioned a second portrait from Rudolf Huber-Wiesenthal. I was four years old, the same age as Eva had been, when I sat for the picture. To have paintings of both children at the same age, by such a well-known artist, would give my father great pleasure. Naturally I was told to keep the whole thing a secret.

I still remember going to the Huber-Wiesenthal villa, and I remember the large studio. When I arrived for my sittings, I was welcomed by the artist's wife Elsa Huber-Wiesenthal, and her daughter Nina, who was Eva's age.

Nina usually got out a cardboard game, a pretend fish tank, with small cut-out fish lying inside. Each fish had a magnetised disk and had to be caught with a fishing rod with a magnet hook. One was not supposed to look inside the tank, but catch the fish by trial and error. I suppose the idea was to relax me after the long journey.

I remember entering the large studio. At the end of one of the sittings, Huber-Wiesenthal asked me to come round and look at the canvas. I did not say anything and he said: "Es ist noch nicht fertig" (it is not yet finished).

It was planned that the picture would be included in a public exhibition, that my parents would be invited, and that my father would suddenly see me on the wall, as a complete surprise. But in the event, my father walked right past the picture and my mother said something like: "Schau, da ist der Hansi" (look, there is Hansi).

Rudolf's wife Elsa Wiesenthal and her sisters Grete and Berta were famous expressionist dancers, 'Die Schwestern Wiesenthal', who performed together or solo.

Isadora Duncan had crossed the Atlantic and taken Europe by storm.

Not for her the short tricot skirt, the frou-frou, the ballet shoes, the corset, or the traditional steps. There would be long flowing dresses and bare feet, a reminder of Classical Greece. She liberated the art of the dance, no longer purely acrobatic or rigidly pantomimic.

But the Wiesenthals brought something special: their music. The sisters all played the piano. Their mother was a pianist. The home was always full of music. Grete, Elsa and Berta understood the music to which they were dancing. They could experience it, they could feel it, only as real musicians can. They could give their art that rare musical insight, a fusion of sound and movement, in a new interpretation of modern dance. Music did not just accompany their dance. They did not regard music as a purely supportive vehicle for their performance. They did not dance to music, or with music, but in music.

They were famous for their Strauss waltzes, *Rosen aus dem Süden, Frühlingsstimmen, Donauwellen*, for their polkas. Elsa also danced to serious music, parts of Schumann's *Préambule, Florestan, Valse Noble, Pierrot* and *Harlequin*.

The sisters made a very successful start to their careers. In March 1907, Elsa and Greta, young ballerinas at the Staatsoper, appeared in the Alfred Roller production of Gluck's *Iphigénie en Aulide*, conducted by Gustav Mahler. They were given important roles in the 'Dance of the Priestesses'. Egon Wellesz recalled the occasion on the 26th June 1960, in his Festrede (festive speech) at the Vienna Opera, entitled 'Gustav Mahler und die Wiener Oper'. He said that Elsa and Grete Wiesenthal's presence and talent "expressed the grace of Gluck's music in *visual terms*".

On the 14th January 1908, the three sisters Greta, Elsa and Berta, made their Viennese debut. The venue was the newly opened Kabarett Fledermaus, designed by Josef Hoffmann, a creation of the Wiener Werkstätte. In the small basement area, the theatre had seating for an audience of three hundred, and the famous bar room soon became the meeting place of the Viennese avant garde. Peter Altenberg, Hermann Bahr and other literary figures seemed to have forsaken the Café Central. Hoffmann covered the bar counter and the walls with about seven thousand irregularly sized rectangular tiles which were decorated with a palette of colour, a truly pictorial mosaic. Hevesi in Altkunst - Neukunst describes the tiles in greater detail: About a thousand of these tiles are decorated; with pictures, drawings, vignettes, symbols, caricatures, modernist references, portraits, satirical ideas, quirky images, in fact with every conceivable figurative humour. "Es ist eines der drolligsten Bilderbücher, ewig aufgeschlagen" (it is one of the funniest picture books, forever open).

The Wiesenthals performed to packed audiences. Outside the entrance, in the narrow Johannesgasse, there was, unusually for those days, a long line of carriages waiting for the audience to come out. After only a few performances, so the story goes, a passer-by asked a Fiakerkutscher (a coachman) why they were all waiting there and he replied: "Ja wissen S'denn das net – die Wiesenthals tanzen doch" (well don't you know, the Wiesenthals are dancing).

Shortly afterwards, Elsa and Grete appeared at the Kammerspiele in Berlin, under Max Reinhardt's direction, in Aristophanes' comedy *Lysistrata*. Engelbert Humperdinck had written the incidental music, and the piece ended with a dance, a visual epilogue, performed alternately by the sisters. The first performance was danced by Grete. According to Huber-Wiesenthal, then still Rudolf Huber, not yet married to Elsa, there was a notable absentee at the première. Elsa did not attend. She did not want to be influenced by her sister's dance.

Max Reinhardt was obviously impressed by Elsa and Grete and invited them again to dance in his forthcoming production of *Sumurun*, a pantomime with an oriental flavour.

Soon Grete was to part from her sisters and tour the world with her dance company. Elsa and Berta continued to dance together and later founded a ballet school.

I remember Elsa Wiesenthal smiling at me when I arrived to have my portrait painted. She must have given me a kiss and probably a piece of Sachertorte after I had finished.

But of course, I had no idea who she was, who she had been. She had danced on the stage of the Vienna Opera on that 18th March 1907 in one of the greatest premieres of Gustav Mahler's directorship. The cast surrounding her was memorable. Gutheil–Schoder sang Iphigénie and Achilles was sung by Schmedes. Richard Mayr, then only thirty years old, sang the role of Kalchas, and Leopold Demuth was Agamemnon.

Equally remarkable were the actors that Max Reinhard assembled for *Sumurun*: Alexander Moissi, Rudolf Schildkraut and Leopoldine Konstantin.

I am daily reminded of the Wiesenthals. Hanging on the wall, side by side, are the portraits of Eva and myself, and two portrait drawings of their daughter Nina, one from 1929, one some years later, with dedications to my parents.

My parents led a very active, elegant social life, within the unique setting of inter-war Vienna. Nearly all their friends belonged to the Jewish haute-bourgeoisie, interlocked by the cultural interests of music and art, by professional association, by commerce and industry, and, of course, by marriage.

I remember some of the very big parties in the Gersthoferstrasse. Even when I was 12 or 13, in 1936 or 1937, I was not allowed to see the guests arrive, let alone stay up a little bit. In addition to Fanny, our cook, my mother usually engaged two maids to serve two or three dozen or more guests. Of course I could hear the excited babble of conversation and the laughter in the room at the end of the long corridor, where I slept on those occasions.

For one *grande soirée*, on the 5th December 1935, my father wrote a poem 'Prolog zu einem Puppenspiel' (Prologue to a Puppet Play). He had arranged a private performance at Richard Teschner's Marionette Theatre, which was next door to our apartment. I can see him now, ushering his guests along the landing for the few steps to the artist's *grand salon*, which could seat an audience of about 50 persons. And he would have stood there with his poetic welcome, facing his friends, and pointing to the large round glass disc, 'der Figurenspiegel' (the mirror of marionettes), behind which would be enacted the magic world of make-believe, no spoken words, but dulcet music from a music box.

Gesprochnes Wort, als kleine Ouvertüre,
Ein Klang, der mit dem Augenblick verschwebt,
Ziemt dieser Welt der Stäbe und der Schnüre,
In der von Meisters zarten Gnaden lebt,
Was sonst nur hinter Traumes Gnaden Türe
Als Bild und körperloses Schemen webt
Und nun in diesem Kreis, der annoch dunkelt
Vor Euerm Aug' bald zauberhaft erfunkelt.

Nehmt dieses Spiel, das mehr ist als ein Spielen,
Nehmt es als Gruß aus einer reinern Zeit.
Zurück zu wild und stumpf vertanen Zielen
Führt dieser Stunde zärtliches Geleit.
Als lichte Schwester unter dunkeln vielen
Trägt sie für euch ein festlich weißes Kleid
Und orphisch aus dem Schattenreich beschwhoren
Atmet euch wieder, was ihr längst verloren.
Blickt Euch nicht um, dann rettet Ihr's nach Haus!
Rumoren schon die Puppen innen?
Nun – wenn's beliebt – es kann beginnen!
Und wem's gefiel, der spende uns Applaus.

(The spoken word as a small overture,
The sound that fades away at once,
Is fitting for this world of rods and strings
Where now the Master's gentle genius brings to life
That which is woven only beyond the blessed door of dreams
As images and action without substance
And now within this circle still in darkness
Will light before your eyes with magic sparkle.

Take this play which is much more than play,
Take it as greeting from a purer age.
Back to wild muddled squandered aspirations
This hour is a tender guide.
As shining sister, faced with so much darkness
She weaves for you a festive gown of white
By Orpheus summoned from the land of shadows,
Breathes back to life what long ago you lost.
Do not look round, and you will get it home!
Are puppets at the back impatient?
So, at your pleasure, let's begin
And if you like it, give applause.)

The poem is so characteristic of my father. For him the world of Greece and Rome was a living reality which began at school. And when I in turn started Greek, he told me stories from Homer and Virgil. He made them immediate and memorable. Several thousand years seemed to vanish as gods and goddesses, great heroes and tragic dynasties, acted out their fate.

CHAPTER 11

A story of books

The republic, which was proclaimed on the 12th November 1918, was called Deutsch-Österreich, a name that was born out of revolution, and which signalled the political intent to create a unified state of Germany. But the victorious allies, fearful of a resurgent Germany, vetoed the proposal, and soon Deutsch-Österreich was renamed simply Österreich.

From 1918, public servants including my father Paul had to swear an oath of allegiance to the new state of Deutsch-Österreich. It reads, in inimitable officialese:

Sie haben das Ihnen abverlangte vorgeschriebene Gelöbnis geleistet und werden im Sinne der Beschlüsse des Kabinetterates vom 23. November 1918 in Ihrer gegenwärtigen Diensteseigenschaft vorbehaltlich der endgiltigen Regelung Ihres Dienstverhältnisses in den deutsch-österreichischen Staatsdienst übernommen.

(You have sworn the required oath, demanded of you, and according to the Cabinet ruling of the 23rd November 1918, are accepted for German-Austrian Public Service, with your present professional qualifications, subject to final establishment of your service status).

On the 17th July 1919, the next step in my father's career was formalised. The Praesidium of the Vienna High Court (Praesidium des Oberlandesgerichtes Wien) confirmed my father as a judge for the Vienna district of Leopoldstadt, with a yearly starting salary of 2,800 Kronen, and 1,200 Kronen as a cost of living supplement.

But in the first years after the War, inflation soared and salaries in the public service became virtually worthless. It was then that my father decided to become a Rechtsanwalt. He prepared himself for admission to the Rechtsanwaltkammer (the Chamber of Advocates), the professional body which confirms legal status. He had to gain practical experience in a role reversal in front of magistrates and judges, and familiarise himself with new court procedures. He duly passed his entrance examination and was entered on the legal register on the 8th January 1923.

A year later, in 1924, the old currency, the Heller and Krone, was abolished and instead the Schilling and Groschen introduced. The painful rate of exchange was a bold anti-inflationary move and economic conditions improved.

It was at that time that my father joined the new publishing company of Paul Zsolnay Verlag as legal advisor and general manager, his first major appointment as a Rechtsanwalt. At home, in the Semperstrasse, another memorable event occurred: I had arrived.

Paul Zsolnay, at the age of 29, had just begun to publish books, and was to become the most important Austrian publisher of contemporary literature. He championed the *belles lettres*, the *Belletristik,* of the Wiener Moderne. When he started, he was financially supported by his rich father, a tobacco magnate, and introduced to Viennese society by the social flair of his matriarchal mother, Andy von Zsolnay, in whose salon many notable figures from the world of music and literature were welcomed. Some of them, the Wiesenthal sisters, Arthur Schnitzler and Felix Salten, were friends of my grandfather Wilhelm and my parents. At any rate, when my father accepted the offer to join the publishing house, he must have felt on familiar territory. The commercial product was German literature, which he loved so much and understood so well.

My father was actively involved in the many tasks which face a publisher. Finding authors and drafting publication agreements and royalty schedules is only part of the business. Editorial supervision, printing, publicity and distribution, are all integral features of publishing. And overshadowing all this is the implied question: How many copies will it sell?

In 1929, after four years as a private concern, the enterprise was sufficiently successful to be launched as a Public Limited Company, with my father as its first Managing Director. But what a success! The very first Zsolnay title, Franz Werfel's novel *Verdi*, turned out to be a bestseller, and by 1930 over 200,000 copies had been sold.

Franz Werfel became a friend of my parents. I remember his name coming up in conversation. As a boy, the name Werfel for me was a feature, a concept, 'ein Begriff' as they say in German. Of course at the time I did not know that he had married Alma Mahler-Gropius, the widow of Gustav Mahler, divorced from her second husband Walter Gropius, of Bauhaus fame. And it was in London, after the war, that I realised that Paul Zsolnay was intimately connected with that circle. He could not really have got closer, because for a short time he was married to Anna Mahler, Gustav and Alma's daughter, whose step-father at that time was Franz Werfel.

Although the Vienna part of my library contains very many Zsolnay books, Werfel's *Verdi* is not one of them. I have often wondered whether my father lent the book but never got it back. I therefore treasure another of Franz Werfel's books: *Die vierzig Tage des Musa Dagh*. It was published in 1933, a fateful year for Jewish authors and publishers. The personal dedication reads: 'Doktor Paul Neumann in freundschaftlichst treuer Ergebenheit. Franz Werfel. Wien 1933.' (For Doctor Paul Neumann in friendship and admiration.) The story is set during the First World War. The Musa Dagh, a mountain on the coast of Anatolia, is the scene of a forty-day heroic struggle of a group of Armenian villagers against the forces of the Turkish army. It ends with the evacuation of the survivors by Allied warships.

Two years later, Werfel's collection of new poems *Schlaf und Erwachen* (Sleep and Awakening) was published by Zsolnay in a deluxe edition. It is bound in fine linen, and decorated with the author's signature and autograph title, stamped in gold block on the cover. This time Werfel inscribed the book for my mother: 'Frau Resi Neumann, sehr herzlich Franz Werfel, Wien, 1935' (for Mrs Resi Neumann, very sincerely).

After the Anschluss, the exodus of Franz and Alma Werfel was a long and hazardous journey through Italy, France, Spain and Portugal, where in 1941, they embarked for the United States. In 1940 they passed through Lourdes, in the South of France. Lourdes was full of pilgrims. They came to pray at the Grotto where nearly a hundred years earlier Bernadette Soubirous, a 15 year-old peasant girl, had visions of the Virgin Mary. At the same time as her ecstasies, a spring appeared and healings were soon reported. The faithful began to flock to Lourdes. They drank the water and bathed to clear their illnesses. And over the years, the numbers swelled to millions. The pilgrimage became a highlight in the Catholic calendar, and in 1933 Pope Pius XI conferred upon Bernadette the supreme honour of canonisation.

There at Lourdes, in the middle of a terrible war, Franz Werfel witnessed this collective expression of faith. He vowed that should he ever reach America safely, he would write a book about Bernadette. He kept his promise with *Das Lied von Bernadette* (The Song of Bernadette). It was turned into a successful Hollywood film in 1943 and won three Oscars. Jennifer Jones played Bernadette. Of course we all went to see it. Afterwards, my father was disappointed at the way the film had spelt out the Holy Visions at the Grotto. He had hoped for more artistic, more implied treatment of the divine mystery.

Paul Zsolnay had the commercial acumen and confidence to introduce foreign authors, such as H.G. Wells and John Galsworthy of *The Forsyte Saga* fame. In the early 1920s, reading English literature had a special *cachet,* and in 1925 John Galsworthy came to Vienna to negotiate publication, translation, and royalty agreements. It was at that time that he presented my father with a signed copy of one of his books. It is a volume from his collected works of plays and novels, containing three plays: *A Family Man, Loyalties, Windows.* The dedication reads: 'for Dr. Paul Neumann, very cordially from John Galsworthy, July 18. 1925'. Age and language barriers were swept aside, my father recalled, when occasionally speaking about John Galsworthy and those Vienna days. And he usually then said how pleased he was that Galsworthy had been awarded the Nobel Prize for literature in 1932, just a year before he died at the age of 66.

Signed books to my grandfather further illustrate the story. According to his daughter Lena, the Zsolnay and Neumann families were originally introduced by a mutual friend, Felix Salten. He had become a regular visitor at the elegant salon of Andy von Zsolnay, and met my grandfather frequently at their regular establishment, the Café Griensteidl.

The coffee house culture of Vienna took its seat in countless locations, where of course there was daily gossip. But the conversations were also elevated, transcendental, critical, political, analytical. Over many hours, and perhaps a small cup of coffee, the many aspects of a civilised life were discussed endlessly, a recent performance at the Opera, the latest play at the Burgtheater, a sensational novel, the political crisis, financial or social scandal. Regular customers had their traditional places. The waiters, in their long white aprons tied round the waist and reaching practically to the ground, brought them their usual orders without having to ask.

In a few select coffee houses, very prominent figures in the world of art, science, politics and many other walks of life met their friends and spread their aura over a wider circle of admirers, who were sometimes privileged to share their table.

If only walls had ears! Then the brilliant stream of conversation might have been recorded for posterity. Perhaps Peter Altenberg at the Café Central is exceptional. He wrote down so many of his *obiter dicta* in his famous collections of vignettes and aphorisms. They are pointillist descriptions and epigrammatic, fragmentary observations of Bohemian life, frequently feminine.

Wilhelm was so much part of that coffee house scenario. He was a creature of habit and the coffee house was his regular meeting place with Felix Salten and Arthur Schnitzler. Lena explained to me that that is where an important part of Wilhelm's life took place, away from the elegant home of the Ferdinandstrasse. It was, after all, a predominantly masculine world, she said, in which that interchange of ideas and information flourished in what could be called a club atmosphere.

Felix Salten met my grandfather Wilhelm in the last years of the

19th century, at a time when Salten was starting his career as a journalist, an art and theatre critic. In 1900, he published his first collection of short stories and after that brought out an average of one book a year. Some were animal stories and *Bambi* became world famous when Walt Disney turned it into a film in 1952. Bambi, the baby deer, alone, abandoned, taking the first steps in the forest, captured the hearts of thousands.

Like Wilhelm, Salten was born in Hungary. But there was that further link of coincidence, which annually acts as a reminder. Both men were born on the 6th September, my grandfather in 1860 and Felix Salten in 1869. According to Lena, it became part of family tradition that her father would always mention it on his birthday. 'Heut' hat der Felix Salten Geburtstag' (today is Felix Salten's birthday).

It was hardly surprising that Felix Salten, a close friend of the Zsolnay family, was an obvious early choice for the new venture, with the publication in 1925 of his *Neue Menschen auf alter Erde* (New People on Ancient Soil). The book has the subtitle *Eine Palästinafahrt* (A Journey to Palestine). Salten describes the new Palestine, the messianic enthusiasm of the early settlers, and the realisation of the Zionist dream. His dedication to my grandfather reads: 'Meinem lieben Wilhelm Neumann in alter Freundschaft. Felix Salten. Wien, Chanuka 1925' (For my dear Wilhelm Neumann in long-standing friendship). Chanouka is the Jewish Festival of Lights which coincides with Christmas.

Two further books by Felix Salten are inscribed with personal dedications. They are typical of Salten's masterly manner in which he invests his animals with the power of speech to articulate their frequently cruel fate. *Freunde aus aller Welt. Roman eines Zoologischen Gartens* (Friends from all over the world. A novel about a zoological garden) was published by Zsolnay in 1931. The dedication reads: 'Für meinen Freund Wilhelm Neumann, herzlichst Felix Salten. Wien 10 April 1932'.

That day was a Sunday, then in Vienna an even more traditional day for meeting family and friends. I can so easily imagine my grandfather and Felix Salten getting together that afternoon at the Griensteidl, or perhaps at the Café Herrenhof.

Spring would have been in the air. The famous lilac bushes on the Heldenplatz, the ceremonial square in the Hofburg, the Imperial Palace, would soon be bursting into bloom, the evocative symbol of renewal.

But across the border, the Weimar Republic was facing its mortal crisis, and in less than a year Hitler would seize power. By the time Felix Salten presented Wilhelm with his last signed book on the 1st December 1933, the reality of Nazi Germany had cast its shadow. The story of *Florian, das Pferd des Kaisers*, (Florian the Emperor's Horse), a white Lippizaner Stallion, a breed still famous in Vienna today, in the Spanish Riding School, is mirrored in the glory and the decline of the Habsburg dynasty.

But the two men must have discussed much more than the life and death of Kaiser Franz Joseph. When Felix Salten gave Wilhelm the book it could no longer be sold in Germany. In the spring of 1933, soon after Hitler's rise to power, the Nazis organised the public burning of books by Jewish authors. People came with their books, libraries emptied their shelves, schools and universities withdrew the titles. Jewish thought, Jewish culture, Jewish literature, was a contamination and anathema to the Aryan spirit. The book burnings and the jeering crowds that surrounded them were preludes to official action later that year, when school and university syllabuses were vetted, and library catalogues 'cleaned up'. By official decree bookshops were forbidden to sell books written by Jews and existing wholesale stock had to be pulped. The authorities placed an embargo on the import from Austria of Zsolnay books by Jewish authors, and blocked royalty payments. On the prescribed list were many notable figures, such as Schalom Asch, Max Brod, Heinrich Mann, Franz Werfel, Arthur Schnitzler, Felix Salten, Oskar Jellinek and Emil Ludwig, to mention just a few.

Zsolnay tried to compromise by publishing authors with Nazi sympathies and even by taking a Nazi into management, but all to no avail. The firm was branded a 'Judenverlag' (a Jews' publisher) and Zsolnay's Swiss subsidiary was soon labelled a 'Gettoverlag' (the publishing house of the Ghetto).

After the Anschluss, Zsolnay managed to come to England and at the end of the war, returned to Vienna and reclaimed his firm, which had been confiscated by the Nazis.

He then also opened an office in London and published books by English and American authors in translation. He correctly surmised that the Germans would be only too anxious to have the opportunity to acquaint themselves with the modern Anglo-Saxon literary world which had been denied to them for so many years. The Nazis had labelled books in English as hostile, decadent and written in the language of the enemy.

In 1945, Paul Zsolnay commissioned my mother to translate one of the books. When they first met some twenty years earlier in Vienna, who could then have foreseen that one day in London she would provide a German version of an English novel? The book by Robert Payne, originally published in 1945 by William Heinemann, with the title *Love and Peace*, tells the story of the Chinese revolution of 1911, the fall of the Manchu dynasty and the rise of Sun Yat-Sen. My mother's translation *Liebe und Frieden*, appeared under the Zsolnay imprint in 1948.

She told me that the task took an immeasurably long time and that she had to ask my father to translate passages with detailed descriptions of torture. For me, the eight words on the fly-leaf are symbols of her industry and determination: Berechtigte Übersetzung aus dem Englischen von Therese Neumann. (Authorised translation from the English by Therese Neumann.)

Robert Payne had spent some time in China during the war as a journalist for *The Times* and as Cultural Attaché in Chungking, where in fact he wrote *Love and Peace*. His subsequent achievement as an author was astonishing, his novels and travel books, but especially his biographies, such as Lenin, Chiang Kai-Shek, Dostoyevsky, General Marshall, Gershwin, Chaplin, Greta Garbo, Lawrence of Arabia, Hitler, Ghandi, Trotsky, Mao, Marx, Albert Schweitzer, Sun Yat-Sen, Churchill, Pasternak.

By the time he died at the age of 72 in 1983, he had earned the epitaph 'the man of a hundred books'. He wrote about two books a year. Even at the early stage in his career, Payne must have already had the reputation of a prolific writer, because my mother said to me "er schreibt rasch und viel" (he writes fast and a lot).

During the war, my father kept in close touch with Paul Zsolnay and in 1946 he asked him for a supporting reference for his application for naturalisation:

Heinemann & Zsolnay, Ltd., Publishers
99 Great Russell Street,
London, W.C.1
April 2nd, 1946

Dear Dr. Neumann,

Messrs. Heinemann & Zsolnay Ltd, of which company I am a Director, have taken a comprehensive interest in my publishing firm of Paul Zsolnay Verlag, Vienna (Austria). Founded in 1923 the Vienna firm acquired the translation rights of the works, among others, of Galsworthy, Cronin and other British authors of renown and succeeded in making modern English literature very popular among the German-reading public in Austria, Germany, Switzerland and other European countries. Apart from the ideological value many thousands of pounds of royalties were paid out through my Vienna firm to authors in this country from 1923 to 1939. During this period you were a member of the Board of Directors of Paul Zsolnay Verlag, Vienna, and its legal advisor.

An attempt is now to be made to restore the rights and activities of my Vienna firm as a British interest and we have asked you to assist us in this endeavour. It will be necessary for myself and someone else to go to Vienna, Switzerland and, possibly, Berlin in the near future. Your close acquaintance with the pre-war conditions of my Vienna firm makes you the obvious choice and we hope that you will soon be in a position to travel for the advancement of these important British economic and cultural interests.

Yours sincerely,

(sgd) Paul Zsolnay

A second reference was required. My father approached Bertha Bracey, whom he first met in Vienna soon after World War I. She was there with the Quakers, engaged in relief and rehabilitation in a defeated city.

A quarter of a century later, after another war, she would become a valuable go-between and facilitate postal communication for the Neumann families, separated in London and war-torn Warsaw.

Friends Committee for Refugees and Aliens
Bloomsbury House
Bloomsbury Street
London W.C.1
27th March 1946.

Dr. Paul Neumann,
9 Heath Court,
Frognall, N.W.3.

Dear Dr. Neumann,

I understand that you are about to make application to the Aliens Department, Home Office, for naturalisation. I trust that in support of your application the following may be of some assistance:

1. I first made your acquaintance in Vienna about 1921, and have been glad to renew it during your stay in this country.

2. Shortly after the outbreak of war, in the autumn of 1939, at your request, I was very glad to approach my Committee and get their agreement to undertake to sponsor the establishment of the Georgic Cooperative Society Limited, an industrial productive society registered with the Registrar for Friendly Societies at the suggestion of the Home Office.

3. I know that you have been president of the Georgic Cooperative from its inception to the present time, and that after the work once got going the Society had an average number of members of between 40 and 50 persons.

4. It seems to me that the Georgic has made a contribution towards the social and economic welfare of persons in this country during a difficult period (a) socially through membership in the Cooperative a number of persons were given useful employment and at the same time been trained for economic independence through the excellent training which the Cooperative gave them in dressmaking and belt and flower making, (b) economically by the production during the war of goods in short supply for home consumption, at the same time establishing a position which could make speedy entry into the export trade from this country as rapidly possible when conditions and war restrictions were removed.

I am glad to know that there has already been some response from countries abroad to take the products of the Georgic.

Yours sincerely,

(sgd) Bertha L Bracey

Directing Secretary.

With classical elegance, the name of the Cooperative is derived from its location in George Street in central London. In a quantum leap of correlation and private humour, whenever I thought of it, I added the single letter 's' to transform it into the title of Virgil's poetic masterpiece *Georgics*. Perhaps my father thought along similar lines.

As soon as my father became a British subject at the end of 1947, he used his new passport to travel to Switzerland, to visit former colleagues and friends. He was away for a few weeks in 1948, and returned on the 15th March, on his 50th birthday. Alas, that was the only journey he was to make. Soon afterwards he had a stroke, and died exactly a month later on the 15th April.

The day before he died, I left home early in the morning; he was confined to his bed. I said goodbye to him at his bedside and told him I would not be home till rather late because I was going to the opera, to hear *Meistersinger*. He looked up at me with his wonderful all-embracing smile, raised his right hand and said "schön". This short positive word was his last utterance to me. My mother told me that that evening, while I was out, they were listening to a broadcast of

Beethoven's *Missa Solemnis*. She said that he drifted into a coma, right at the beginning, during the *Kyrie Eleison*. He died the following afternoon without regaining consciousness.

A few days later, on 28th April 1948, Paul Zsolnay wrote a letter of condolence to my mother. The original was in German.

28th April 1948

The news of your irreplaceable loss which you have suffered has moved me deeply. I beg you to accept the expression of my most sincere condolence.

I am losing with your husband one of my very best friends, and an experienced colleague in my publishing firm, who has stood at my side for 25 years with his help and advice.

I have always unreservedly admired his great human qualities, his distinguished bearing and his intellectual commitment.

May it be a small comfort in your sorrow, that there are many who share your grief, and that the memory of your husband lives on in the hearts of his friends.

Yours very sincerely,
Paul Zsolnay

Whenever I open a book with a dedication to my grandfather, my parents or to Lena, I look upon it with veneration. And now, as I touch the same page on which the author's hand had rested to write his declaration of respect and friendship, I feel as if I were reaching out to him, holding the very object that he once gave them. The many books with inscriptions are very much the testimony of their times. The texts are woven in a tapestry of fin-de-siècle, Art Nouveau and Wiener Moderne, the literature of a changing world. How deeply grateful I am that the books were brought out from Vienna, when so many other people who managed to escape lost absolutely everything.

I treasure a slender volume by Robert Musil, a collection of short stories, entitled *Nachlass zu Lebzeiten* (Posthumous papers by a living author). The dedication to my parents reads: 'Paul und Therese

Neumann in aufrichtiger Ergebenheit (with sincere devotion) Robert Musil, Jänner 1936'.

The book was published not in Vienna, but in Zurich by Humanitas Verlag. The date, the locality and the name of the firm, all bear the sad testimony of Nazi persecution.

My mother recalled the presentation. Robert Musil wanted my father to accept the book as a token of gratitude for the financial help and support provided by the Robert Musil Gesellschaft, of which my father was one of the executives. The author was trying to finish his life's work, his masterpiece, *Der Mann ohne Eigenschaften* (The Man Without Qualities), but was facing serious financial difficulties. He had started the book in Berlin in 1920, and the first two volumes were published in 1930. In 1933 he escaped to Vienna, working on the completion. After the Anschluss he emigrated to Switzerland where he died in 1942, with the third volume unfinished. The novel is a *roman à clef*, with some of the characters faintly disguised, as they act out their lives in the Vienna of 1913, the last year of peace prior to the Great War. There is satire in the book, so much a kaleidoscopic review, a detailed portrait of the decaying fin de siècle world.

There is one book with a special dedication. Instead of the usual private, hand-written declaration, four printed and published words confirm a deep friendship. On a blank inside page, bold letters with typographic sovereignty spell out: Paul Neumann dem Freunde (for Paul Neumann the friend).

It was Oskar Jellinek who so uniquely proclaimed his friendship in *Die Mutter der Neun* (the Mother of the Nine), published by Zsolnay in 1926. The novella, longer than a short story, but shorter than a novel, is typical of Oskar Jellinek's work. It is an account of a day and a night during the Counter Reformation and is set in 17th century Upper Austria. The heroine, the village blacksmith, is the mother of nine sons, nine heretic Lutheran leaders condemned to the gallows by a victorious Catholic colonel. He himself had lost two of his own sons in the fighting, and was particularly bigoted, a convert brought up by Jesuits.

The mother is granted the cruel selection of one son, to be reprieved, and thus condemning the other eight to be hanged. Jellinek transfigures many of his stories with the heightened input of psychological drama, in this case the torturous reflections of a mother unable to choose. In vain she offers her own life.

At dawn, at the place of execution, the colonel on horseback, with his youngest, sickly son, his sole heir, at his side, asks the mother which son she has chosen. "Yours" she shouts, bringing down her heavy hammer on the young boy's head. The father falls dead to the ground. The blacksmith is overpowered and tied to the tree from which her nine sons are being hanged. And when the executioner turns to his tenth grisly task, she is found to be hanging lifeless in the ropes. 'Und niemand hätte zu sagen gewußt bei welches Sohnes Todes ihr Herz aufgehört hatte zu schagen' (And no one would have been able to tell at which son's death her heart had ceased to beat).

The Neumann and the Jellinek families first met in 1901 whilst on holiday on the Semmering, a fashionable outpost of the Alps near Vienna. Oksar was fifteen, my father thirteen and Lena was eleven. My father and Oskar became inseparable. Both studied law, both took their doctorates. Both served on the Italian Front along the Isonzo river, and both married in 1917. But after the war, Oskar Jellinek resigned from his office as judge to devote himself to writing.

Oskar admired Lena, her beauty, her artistic enthusiasm, her fine intellect, but his was the brotherly love of an older sibling.

Over the years, my father must have discussed with Oskar in great detail his various short stories, so many set in the villages of his native Bohemia. Oskar decorated his narratives with the vocabulary of a true artist, in a prose fashioned with wide sweeps of pointilliste descriptive detail. His expressionist poetry is so often coloured by the tinge of melancholy. His many letters in German to my father, firstly after the Anschluss from his native Brünn in Czechoslovakia, and later whilst in exile in Los Angeles, are carefully constructed edifices of literary imagination.

Los Angeles, 15 March 1948

My dear Paul,

A sixtieth birthday, as I can assure you from experience, is not a date of pathos. It brings nothing to a close, and reveals nothing new. Every other date in a lifetime can be more important than the calendar completion of a decade, or the start of a new year or of a new century.

Did the 20th century begin with the first of January 1900? It began, as we know, with the end of the First World War – with us it began in July 1901, the birth of our friendship, a date more worthy of commemoration than the anniversary of your or my physical birth. But the jubilee of your life … coincides more or less exactly with two important anniversaries. The first one is the tenth anniversary of the loss of our country, the other, the hundredth anniversary of the revolution in Austria, for liberty and for freedom of the spirit, which laid the foundation for you and for me, of a homeland which can never be lost. You were born forty years after the first stormy Vienna springtime of the spirit (nach dem esrten Aufblühen des Wiener Geistesfrühlings) and you remained, my dear Paul, faithful to it for the entire sixty years of your serious and partly difficult life, a true son of spiritual freedom and inner striving towards the ideals of humanity (which for the time being, admittedly, have themselves remained an unfulfilled ideal), and the child of a fantasy, endowed with deep insight into the perception of beauty and greatness (und das Kind einer mit tiefem Blick für die Erkenntnis des Schönen und Grossen begabter Phantasie).

After congratulation there was to be condolence. My father died only a month later, and Oskar Jellinek's letter to Lena is dated 20th April 1948.

… For you, his death has deprived you of a very intimate relationship, for me, it follows a decade of separation after nearly four decades in the closest company of the most kindred spirit (nach fast vier Jahrzehnten geistesgesinnigster Seelen und Atemnähe). Who would venture to decide which the more bitter fate? For you, the daily sound of a brother (der täglich vernommene Bruderlaut) has been silenced. I have been robbed of the hope ever again to hear the

200

unforgettable differently from the way that I have heard it during the last ten years: through the mouth of memory (durch den Mund der Erinnerung). Always, always I had hoped to hear his voice once more, which spoke with such clarity and calm about profound things. For to speak about them was his mother tongue. The sublime was his domain (Denn von diesen zu sprechen war seine Muttersprache. Das Erhabene war seine Heimat) …

Oskar's two letters are hinged by cruel fate, the hymn of praise for a birthday friend, followed so soon by the lament of obituary valediction. How fortunate I am to have Oskar's words of friendship, love and grief, written in his inimitable prose.

Oskar wrote several letters to Lena, right up to his death in October 1949, and Paul was ever present. On the 6th February 1949, he thanks her for her kind wishes on the occasion of his 63rd birthday, and then continues:

The pain about Paul grips me again and again. I had a wishful dream-vision which refuses to fade. I imagined him and myself as old gentlemen on a bright sunny day in early summer, sitting on a bench high above Vienna, looking down onto the city, glowing with happiness by the radiant river, and - cheerfully aware of a fulfilled life - deeply engaged in one of those conversations which he loved so much about great things. But where is the city glowing with happiness, where the fulfilled life, where am I, and where, where, where is he?!!

(Das Weh um Paul faßt mich immer wieder: ich hatte ein Wunschtraumbild, das nicht verblassen will: ich stellte mir ihn und mich als alte Herren vor, an einem sonnenhellen Frühsommertage auf einer Höhenbank oberhalb Wiens sitzend, hinabschauend auf die glücksatmende Stadt an dem strahlenden Strom, und - heiter im Bewußtsein eines erfüllten Lebens − einem jener Gespräche über hohe Dinge hingegeben, die er so sehr liebte. Doch wo ist die glücksatmende Stadt, wo das erfüllte Leben, wo bin ich − und wo, wo, wo ist er ?!!)

In August 1916 he presented my father with an indifferent photograph of himself on horseback in officer's uniform. Verse often accompanied his gifts, and I quote it as a fitting epilogue.

Ein schlechtes Bild – ein gutes brauchst Du nicht!
Du trägst in Deinem Herzen mein Gesicht.

Dein Oskar

(The picture's bad, you need no work of art
You carry my true portrait in your heart)

Oskar died a year after my father.

A signed book with the added duality of personal significance brings back memories of my own childhood, of my prewar summers in Altaussee. It was there that the author Hermann Broch lived for the last two years prior to the Anschluss, as guest in the summer residence of my father's cousin Trude and her husband Ernest Geiringer. *Die Unbekannte Größe* (The Unknown Greatness), published by S. Fischer Verlag in Berlin in 1933, just in time, prior to the total prohibition of the publication of Jewish authors, is inscribed: Für Regierungsrat Wilhelm Neumann in aufrichtiger und großer Verehrung Hermann Broch, Februar 1937 (for Regierungsrat Wilhelm Neumann with sincere and great devotion). Broch, the philosopher, the sociologist, gave his creative theories narrative clothing. In his book the young hero, the mathematician Dr Richard Hieck, attempts in vain to measure the incalculable, the strength of his inner physical feelings which he cannot assess. He illustrates the process of falling in love by applied geometry, with his sudden discovery of the Kräfteparallelogramm (power parallelogram) for the balance in human relationship.

Broch is best known for his most famous book *Die Schlafwandler* (the Sleepwalkers), also written partly whilst staying with the Geiringers in 1931. The existentialist trilogy is characterised by a multiplicity of parallel narratives, a web by which the author sought to create an absolute novel.

He has been compared to Kafka, Mann, Musil, Joyce and Proust, for his love for detail and his experimental originality.

The Geiringer house was next to ours, overlooking the lake, on the slopes leading to the famous saltmine. And sometimes I saw Hermann

Broch walk down to the village, smoking his pipe. When I asked my father who he was, he replied: "Er schreibt Bücher" (he writes books).

Altaussee was in an idyllic location for early social fame, with its mineral drinking water, the spa status of nearby Bad Aussee and the healing properties of its saline baths.

One of the first of a long string of famous visitors was the young Empress Elizabeth, the wife of Kaiser Franz Joseph. About 150 years ago she was staying as usual at the Imperial summer residence in the Kaiservilla, in nearby Bad Ischl. She expressed the wish to ascend a mountain with a beautiful view. No Empress before her had demanded such an excursion! First of all there was the long very steep journey in the Imperial coach up and down the Pötschen, an unavoidable mountain pass, and then, on arrival, at the foot of the Loser mountain, the change into a sedan chair, which was carried up to the summit by a team of village strongmen. I have myself climbed the steep ascent, taking me several hours to reach the peak 1,000 metres higher.

Many writers spent some time there: Theodor Herzl, Hugo von Hoffmannstahl, Jakob Wassermann, Arthur Schnitzler. Composers also chose to come, such as Johannes Brahms, Richard Strauss, Gustav Mahler and Egon Wellesz. So many walked round the lake for inspiration that the locals called it 'das Tintenfass' (the inkwell).

For most of the first forty years of the twentieth century, right up to the Anschluss, the Neumann families were regular visitors. There are photographs of me as a very small boy, my recollections date from 1931, after my return from Switzerland.

My childhood memories of those last seven halcyon pre-war Altaussee summers are a kaleidoscope of episodes and images. There was fishing and swimming in the lake, picking wild strawberries or raspberries in the forest, and higher up delicious bilberries. I remember going to rock caves with Peter Schick and Hans Angerer, known as Hackl, my special friend from the village, to bake potatoes on stone slabs. As a special treat, I was taken to nearby Bad Aussee, to the Konditorei Levandowski for their gingerbread Lebkuchen or their Indianer Krapfen, which sacrilegiously could be translated as éclairs.

On Sunday afternoons there was Platzmusik, music played by the reed and brass band of the saltmine workers. They were dressed in their gala uniforms, with their braids and epaulettes, playing their overtures, marches, waltzes and polkas. From their bandroom they marched to the centre of the village (the Platz) and took their place in the splendid bandstand with its beautiful circular fretwood balustrade.

Once a year, in August, the annual village fair, the Kirtag (the church day), transformed the main street into an avenue of small wooden booths, selling food, clothes, souvenirs, costume jewellery and much else. Very popular were the wooden hearts with traditional messages of love and admiration. The chosen text was burnt into the soft conifer with a red-hot steel pin in traditional pokerwork.

Half a century later, I would compose little rhymes with music for Patricia and engrave them on specially made blank bespoke hearts, evocative mementos of our several visits at that time of the year.

On the far side of the lake opposite the village stood a solitary inn called the Seewiese (the Lake Meadow). It could be reached either by walking for about an hour along the edge of the lake or by elegantly and more comfortably crossing over by boat. Every Sunday, there was dancing and I always went. I watched the villagers in their Sunday best, the men in their short leather trousers or their elaborately embroidered black leather knickerbockers, the women in their dirndl dresses covered by silk aprons and scarves. There was at that time no need to organise folk dancing societies for the preservation of complicated steps, group dancing, or the intriguing twist of arms that could form an arch, a private bow window, through which couples could flirt as they waltzed.

The music was provided by Sepp the accordion player, no modern keyboard here but a row of buttons on each side. He knew hundreds of tunes, many with texts that tell an epic story in a dozen or more verses, sung in the heavy Styrian dialect. The words are now largely forgotten and preserved in learned folk music anthologies with the inimitable dialect notated phonetically. Sepp was famous for his yodel singing. You have to hear it, it is so difficult to describe. The yodel is an obbligato input, totally improvisatory, a super-imposed cadenza, a vocalese, a wordless declaration of exuberance. Ideally it should be sung by a high tenor voice, capable of sizeable leaps into the falsetto range. Sepp could yodel with the traditional eloquence of true folk music.

After the Anschluss, the Jewish families who came so regularly no longer came. Treasures from their empty Altaussee houses were stolen or impounded. Their properties were confiscated. And in the background, the saltmine, that centuries-old emblem of village fame and pride, would soon be tainted with notoriety. The Nazis used the mine as a giant ready-made repository. Nature provided them with a safe place to store thousands of paintings and sculptures, tapestries and drawings, looted as their armies swept across Europe. This was no random plunder, but systematic robbery on an unprecedented scale. Although Altaussee was not the only hiding place, it was by far the largest, as over 6,000 works of art were rescued there at the end of the war. Hitler was planning a Führer Museum in Linz. Goering and other high Nazi functionaries were keen to add to their ill-gotten collections. Museum directors and curators, art dealers and auctioneers, academics and experts of all kinds collaborated in this monumental theft. The Nazis were very thorough. With the help of catalogues, archival material, auction records, the great collections were scanned for treasures. Nothing in occupied Europe was sacrosanct. Stately homes, museums and churches were plundered. Michelangelo's Bruges *Madonna* and Van Eyk's altarpiece from Ghent were some of the masterpieces recovered from Altaussee at the end of the war.

It was a near thing. In April 1945, as the American army was drawing ever closer, the local SS commander ordered explosives to be laid in the mine. There would be no restitution. Germany had lost the war, but her enemies, especially Jews and Bolsheviks, would lose their works of art. Just in time, however, the bombs were defused by a villager, a member of the local resistance, dedicated to the re-establishment of a post-war independent Austria. He prevented unimaginable cultural destruction and saved the mine.

That road which led up to it went right past our house. In those days it was just earth and gravel, not yet clad with post-war asphalt.

Tractors pulling heavy trailers clawed their way up the steep slopes and in 1944 alone, transported more than a thousand cases.

When I returned to Altaussee after the war, it seemed so improbable that that very same road, which I knew so well and had used so often, had carried such evil traffic.

How fortunate it was that the mine in Altaussee did not share the same fate as Schloss Immendorf in Lower Austria. That was blown up right at the end of the war, in the path of the advancing Russians. It had been used to store paintings from seized Jewish collections in Vienna. The fanatical SS commandant who ordered the destruction ignited a bonfire of hatred causing Austria's greatest cultural wartime loss. Major works from the Wiener Moderne, including more than a dozen paintings by Gustav Klimt, were destroyed. For the Nazis his paintings, especially, bore the double stigma of Jewish provenance and degenerate art.

The most evocative book on my shelf of autographed volumes is *Reigen* by Arthur Schnitzler.

He wrote the play in the winter of 1896/97, and in 1900 had two hundred copies privately printed for friends. My copy is number 113 and bears the inscription: Herrn Regierungsrath Wilhelm Neumann mit verbindlichsten Grüßen (for Regierungsrat Wilhelm Neumann with sincerest greetings). Arthur Schnitzler Wien 5.9.00.

How proud Wilhelm must have been to read his new title Regierungsrat, best described as Honorary Privy Councillor. He had received the honour less than a year earlier, not yet aged 40, on the 4th December 1899, in recognition for, among other things, his editorial service and journalism at the semi-official *Fremden-Blatt*, and was, according to my father, one of the youngest recipients to be awarded that distinction.

The book was a special present for an old friend, because on the following day, on the 6th September 1900, my grandfather celebrated his fortieth birthday. In the Ferdinandstrasse there would have been a large family gathering, and for Wilhelm a day of double significance, a fresh decade of life in a new century.

And now, as I look back in time, more than a hundred years, helped by photographs, I am reminded: all families were young once. Hermine, on that day, was thirty-two, my father twelve, Lena nine, Mizzi four and Robert two.

It was most probably at the Café Griensteidl, in that revelatory interchange of private hopes and public declarations, that the two men must have discussed the difficulties of getting the text of the play published, let alone performed.

Reigen has the subtitle *Zehn Dialoge* (ten dialogues), which eloquently describes the dramatic layout. In ten scenes of seduction, erotic encounter, and the act of love-making, marked in the text by a series of dashes, Schnitzler draws a picture of sexual morality at the end of the 19th century.

The ten actors appear as interchanging pairs, with alternately the man or the woman from the previous scene reappearing in the next scene, until the full circle has been enacted. Schnitzler realised that the work would run into difficulties, as the opening sentence of his introductory note on the fly-leaf shows: Ein Erscheinen der nachfolgenden Szenen ist vorläufig ausgeschlossen. Ich habe sie nun als Manuscript in Druck gegeben. (The publication of the following scenes is out of the question for the time being. I have now printed them as manuscript.)

After pointing out that stupidity and ill will are always nearby (da jedoch Dummheit und böser Wille immer in der Nähe sind), he concludes with the express wish that his friends should regard the book as a modest gift, personally intended for them by the author (ein bescheidenes, ihnen persönlich zugedachtes Geschenk des Verfassers).

How prophetic were these words. Twenty years were to elapse until the first performance, on the 23rd December 1920 in Berlin. After a six-day obscenity trial, an acquittal, and a few further performances, the play opened in Vienna on the 1st February 1921. The scandal surrounding the German performances had fuelled tense expectation.

When Lena gave me the book in the mid 1970s, the previous fifty years seemed to have shrunk. She talked about her father and Arthur Schnitzler and told me how Wilhelm had treasured the gift, and she wondered how many copies there were still in existence.

Wilhelm certainly went to the premiere, which was a success. But after two weeks of demonstrations, further performances were prohibited. A mob of two hundred, fanned by an anti-semitic press campaign, had stormed the theatre, shouted slogans, smashed furnishings and threw chairs from the balconies.

A year later there were again a few stagings in Vienna and Germany, but *Reigen* had to wait until 1950 for its triumph. It rose from the ashes of notoriety and the bonfires of Nazi hatred in phoenix-like transformation: the name was now *La Ronde*, a French film with an evocative title, a Gallic square-dance of changing partners, directed by Max Orphüls, with Anton Walbrook, Daniel Gélin and Simone Signoret.

Lena did not attend any of these early *Reigen* performances. She may well have been frightened off by the presence of police outside the theatre, and by press reports of disturbances in the auditorium, such as anti-semitic catcalls and the vile distribution of stink bombs.

How much the violence must have shocked her! How much Vienna, the city of Schnitzler, had been polluted! Gradually, the play made its comeback in Germany and Austria, and over the last half century there have been various stage revivals.

Lena, like so many others, had total admiration for everything he had written, had read all his books and had been to so many of his plays.

Schnitzler was constantly in the repertoire, a household name, a dramatist set on the pedestal of popularity. When Lena spoke to me about her past theatre-going, she often mentioned the emotional impact, the cultural experience of Expressionist drama, then so very new, not yet a museum piece of dramatic history. Once again, I open Lena's diaries and read her Schnitzler entries with envy. They are a moving testimony of the high esteem in which he was held and the poignantly contrasting prelude to the *Reigen* reception.

In the years leading up to the First World War, she went to no less than six Schnitzler plays. The first of these on the 28th June 1908 was *Liebelei*, that bitter-sweet tale of flirtation, dalliance and reckoning. She was only seventeen, and I can imagine her mother, Hermine, telling her that the play was unsuitable for a young girl.

Two days prior to her twentieth birthday, on the 24th November 1910, as part of the celebrations, as she recalled, she attended the premiere of *Der Junge Medardus*, a tragic drama set in the Vienna of 1809, in Napoleonic times. The first night of a Schnitzler play remained for Lena an unforgettable experience.

The other plays Lena saw at the time were *Der Ruf des Lebens* (15th December 1909), *Anatol* (7th December 1910), *Das weite Land* (25th January 1912) and *Der Puppenspieler* (30th May 1913), with further plays to follow.

How wonderful it must have been for Lena to see all these Schnitzler plays in the final years of Habsburg Vienna.

CHAPTER 12

A story of pictures

I grew up with pictures. In the salon in the Gersthoferstrasse, in pride of place, hung the 17th century icon, *St Nicholas and Devil*, which my father had brought back from Russia. In the dining room stood a screen with six Biedermeier watercolours of the 1840s, showing views of Vienna. The bespoke, specially-designed light oak screen is hinged into three panels, each framing two pictures, and dates from 1917, a splendid wedding present to my parents. And then, in my room, as long as I can remember, was Oskar Laske's lithograph of Constantinople, from the 1920s. The busy, colourful waterfront, the harbour scene with boats, is overshadowed by the pyramidic edifice of a domed mosque, flanked by slender sentinel minarets.

We were fortunate to bring these treasures to England and as I write, I am looking at my past. A selection, however, had to be made, and among other things, two large nineteenth century busts of Julius Caesar and Augustus Caesar, mounted on shoulder-high marble plinths, had to be left behind. I have wondered what might have happened to them. They stood outside my room on each side of the door and when I started Latin at school they looked at me with silent eloquence.

With my father in prison and my mother in England, it was my Aunt Lena who had the sad task of emptying our home, before she herself left in the autumn of 1938. She had to make difficult choices. Each cubic foot of transport was incredibly expensive, as removal firms cashed in on the exodus. People tried to sell their furniture, but nobody wanted it. Works of art went for knock-down prices at auction, or needed an export licence, and, of course, there was large scale confiscation. Lena never spoke about these terrible months and I never asked her.

From my earliest childhood I loved looking at pictures and after the war, the Tate Gallery put on two ground-breaking exhibitions. The first one, Picasso and Matisse, was followed in 1947 by Marc Chagall. It proved to be a turning point. I was captivated by the colourful dreams, by the various violinists, by the etchings, engravings and lithographs.

Nothing very special happened in my life with Marc Chagall until a few years later. At that time Toni Stolper, a life-long friend of my mother, came to visit us from New York, and she told us that an elderly aunt of hers lived in Vence, in the South of France. We would always be welcome.

And so it came about, when on holiday on the Côte d'Azur, that I called on Ada Desmines, only to discover that she was a neighbour of Marc Chagall.

I plucked up courage and went next door. It was 1954, and Chagall's new wife Vava (Valentina) opened the door. She was protective in her recent role as custodian, I was told afterwards that unannounced visitors wishing to see *le Grand Maître* were usually turned away. After all, some people might have come to look at the nearby Matisse chapel and thought that they might just drop in at Chagall's on the way. In any case, Chagall did not want to see a whole stream of artists.

Vava looked me up and down, rather hot as I must have been, in my shorts and possibly scruffy shirt. I was thirty, most likely younger than many of the more official visitors. I smiled and she asked: "Etes-vous peintre?" "Non," I replied, "je suis violoniste". My three words were the foundation of a friendship.

At that time, Marc was 67 and Vava was 43. Early on he asked me if we could converse in French. His English, he said, was poor, and his German could be summoned up in an emergency. We settled for French. One of the first things Chagall talked about was his *faiblesse*, as he called it, for the violin. He told me that he played the violin as a boy, but soon gave it up as he scratched, and then he looked at me with his penetrating eyes and said, "peut-être vous êtes un virtuose?"

From 1954 to 1958, some time in each of those five summers, I visited him and bought a signed and numbered lithograph which he inscribed with an additional dedication to me or to my mother. Into a small Chagall art book, he wrote on the title page: *Pour Madame Resi Neumann, Marc Chagall 1955.*

The owner of the papeterie in the main square in Vence, where I bought all my lithographs, was amazed at the friendly way in which I was being received at the Maison Chagall over the years. He was especially excited when I showed him the pocket size art book published by Fernand Hazan. Normally, Chagall would not sign a picture, he said, let alone a book. And he told me that a few days earlier, two Swedish tourists had bought a lithograph from him and taken it to the house, only to be refused. He said that the double signature on my lithographs would double their value. In time he looked upon me as a regular client, we became friends and on several occasions he stressed the fact that although all the lithographs were out of print (épuisé), he was still only charging the original publication price. "Nous sommes honêtes". And that is why I only paid 12,000 old francs (£12) for each of those five lithographs.

CHAPTER 13

Touched by greatness!

On one occasion, in the 1950s, I stayed with Ada Desmines and her son Tom for a few days. Tom was a keen amateur violinist and viola player, very well known in chamber music circles along the Côte d'Azur. He did not own a car and found it difficult to cycle carrying both instruments for all eventualities. With pride, he showed me his compromise, which a luthier in Nice had constructed for him according to his specifications.

It was a violin with a fifth string added to the bottom, to give it those extra lower notes. Now he could also play viola music on the violin. He was particularly anxious that I should admire all the modifications: the broader fingerboard, the lengthened bridge with its greater curvature, and the extension at the top for the extra peg. The instrument had a good sound. I had my violin with me, a constant companion on holidays, and he immediately invited two ladies to make up a string quartet.

There I was, with Haydn, in the foothills of the Alpes Maritimes. What an improbable location for his universal genius.

But nothing could have prepared me for the improbabilities of the following day.

Ada Desmines, originally Ada Rosenthal from Vienna, talked to me about her past. She was in her mid-eighties, and she wanted to show me some of her family treasures. She knew I would admire them and would fully understand them.

She carefully got out a box, and inside were a few small bones. "They are fragments of Beethoven's skull," she said. I remember standing there, over-awed by the revelation. She allowed me to touch them. And then she told me her story.

Beethoven was exhumed in 1888 and his coffin transferred from the small cemetery in Währing to the Grove of Honour at the Zentralfriedhof (the Central Cemetery) of Vienna.

According to Ada Desmines, her great-uncle Romeo Seligmann, a professor of the history of medicine at the Vienna University, and an enthusiastic phrenologist, was given the bones at that time for examination, concerning Beethoven's deafness.

Although he bequeathed his large skull collection to the University, he could not part with the Beethoven fragments, and that is how they passed down the family and how she eventually inherited them.

She was anxious to substantiate the provenance, and showed me an official printed document, recording the exhumation on which Professor Romeo Seligmann is listed as one of the officials in attendance.

Whenever I said that I had actually touched Beethoven's skull bones, I was met with understandable incredulity. And on the occasion of Ada Desmines' ninetieth birthday, I asked her to put all this in writing. In her letter of July 1st 1961, she repeated the Beethoven account. At the same time she was worried that she might lose the Beethoven reliquaries (Beethoven Reliquien) if the story became known: 'Bitte um Schweigen da man in Wien uns sonst unseren so sehr verehrten Schatz wegnehmen würde' (Plea for silence as otherwise the people in Vienna might take our most revered treasure).

The ninety year-old Ada Desmines had become uncertain in her recollection. There was indeed an exhumation in 1888, but improbable as it may now seem, he was exhumed twice. In 1863, Die Gesellschaft der Musikfreunde (The Society of the Friends of Music) decided to give Beethoven and Schubert a more memorable resting place in the Zentralfriedhof, rather than the more modest cemetery of the suburb of Währing. They took the opportunity to remove the skeletons for autopsies. Beethoven's skull was of special interest and closely examined. It was then, probably with the connivance of officials, that a few fragments from the back of the head were kept back, not reburied, and eventually came into the possession of Romeo Seligmann.

Anyone at the time looking into the open coffin would not have noticed their absence, as in any case the bones would have been hidden by the cranium. Beethoven's old oak coffin was replaced by an iron one, but the transfer of the composers to the Zentralfriedhof was overruled, and had to wait for another quarter of a century, until 1888. No wonder Ada Desmines had become uncertain in her recollection!

The Evening Post on 1st September 1888 published an eyewitness acount of the Vienna correspondent of *The Times*, which conclusively proves that unlike the exhumation of 1863, there was no time to remove any bones on this occasion.

Very few persons witnessed the exhumation, and most of these were officials. All heads were bared as the coffin was lifted and placed in a settle, where the metal lid was at once prised open and removed. The skeleton became exposed to view. The bones were damp and of a brown colour, showing that moisture must have penetrated into the coffin. The cranium had become detached from the face of the skull, and one of the bystanders took it up in his hand. It looked unusually large. The entire lower row of teeth was complete, and very fine, strong teeth they were, but all the front teeth of the upper row had fallen out. The leg-bones were long; the hands had quite crumbled into dust. The skeleton remained exposed for less than ten minutes but already a gentleman who held a portable camera had taken a photograph while another gentleman, who belongs to an anthropological society, entered into an altercation with the officials who refused to let him take some measurements and a plaster cast of the skull. The lid having been replaced, the coffin was transferred to an iron shell, and slowly borne towards the chapel of the cemetery by six undertaker's men in black uniforms, with cock hats. The officials and other persons present followed in a procession two and two.

The remains were re-interred in the Central Cemetery of Vienna.

Every time I travelled to town on the 41 tram, I passed the old cemetery in Währing. As it stopped there, the conductor would shout

out: "Schubert Park". The cemetery had been turned into a small park, named not after Beethoven but after the more local composer Schubert.

Romeo Seligmann's large collection of skulls was added to by his brother Franz, on his return from the 'Novara' expedition.

For Austria, with her modest maritime history, the 'Novara' voyage was a great naval achievement with a scientific purpose. In 1857, the frigate set sail from the port of Trieste to circumnavigate the globe. It took two years. Many of botanical, mineral and ethnographic specimens gathered along the journey became part of the Natural History Museum of Vienna. Franz Seligmann served on this splendid ship as the high-ranking naval medical staff officer. The frigate had three masts, six decks and 42 cannon. It carried 345 officers and crew, and a contingent of scientists.

Romeo Seligmann was a member of a social circle which included poets, artists and musicians. He attended some of the Schubertiades, the musical gatherings where friends of Franz Schubert met to hear him play his compositions, and accompany singers in his songs. One occasion has been captured in a picture by Moritz von Schwind. Schubert, seated at the piano, is playing to an elegant audience. Romeo Seligmann is standing behind the row of ladies, all listening with rapt attention.

Ada Desmines showed me a small Biedermeier table. Along one side, spaced out, were four concave hollows. I looked at them with puzzlement, and Ada explained that the table had once belonged to Franz Schubert and that the hollows were carved out to hold the bowls of tobacco pipes. Pipe smoking was very popular, and over glasses of wine Schubert and his friends would have welcomed a convenient place to put down their pipes. I tried to imagine Franz, sitting round the table with his friends Vogl and Spaun.

I touched the table gently with reverence, like a pilgrim touching a reliquary. I was standing in front of this small piece of furniture from Vienna, which was a tangible legacy of his domestic surroundings. It had the aura of incredible provenance. But it was also witness to the mystery of Schubert, the genius, the composer of *Die Winterreise*. My lifelong love of Schubert and my years of striving to play his music, combined in silent communion.

Furniture from Schubert and Beethoven reliquaries were followed by treasures from the Goethe estate.

Romeo Seligmann, the universal man of culture, was a close family friend of Ottilie von Goethe, the early widowed daughter-in-law of the poet. That was the connection. That is how the precious mementos found themselves far away from Vienna in that old stone farmhouse in the South of France.

Ada Desmines opened a large jewellery display canteen, and neatly arranged in rows were cameos from Goethe's large collection. They were special. They were cut in an intaglio process. The usual method of creating the image by carving away the background was reversed. The bas-reliefs on the gems of multi-coloured shell or dark-grey pumice were now slender sunken reliefs, which did not protrude above the rim.

I gazed at the engraved profiles of beautiful women, with their hair tied back in classical style, and admired the gods and heroes of Greece and Rome. Some of the pieces were small ovals and others were larger roundels. It was truly a miniature 18th century pantheon of mythology, and for Goethe, who had visited the recently discovered Pompeii, of special significance.

Leda was there with her swan and Orpheus with his lyre. Poseidon proudly waved his trident and Cupid brandished his arrow. They had their attributes. Some pieces were idealised heads which looked for style to the Renaissance, which had swept across Europe only a few centuries earlier.

Ada Desmines showed me photographs of her salon in Vienna with the cameos on display in the vitrine. She pointed to an elegant writing desk and took out a small, silver-encased pencil from the drawer. "They were Goethe's", she quietly said, and gave me the pencil to hold. Goethe's pencil! I imagined what he might have written with it at the table, perhaps a poem, perhaps parts of Faust.

She then pulled out a small book from the shelf. It was a biography of Ottilie von Goethe with passages that dealt with Romeo Seligmann's close relationship with the family. Having explained the connection with Beethoven, she continued her letter of the 1ˢᵗ July 1961:

...von den Beethoven Teilen konnte er sich aber nicht trennen und so kamen sie mit vielen Goethe Souvenirs in unseren Besitz. Über Onkel Romeo steht Einiges in einem Buch: *Ottilie von Goethe und ihre Söhne Walter und Wolf* von Jenny von Gerstenbergk. Stuttgart 1901. Cotta.

(...however he [Romeo Seligmann] could not part from the Beethoven fragments and that is how they, together with many Goethe souvenirs, came into our possession. About Uncle Romeo there are several things in a book: *Ottilie von Goethe and her sons Walter and Wolf.*)

Throughout, Ada Desmines was keen to substantiate her story with provenance, even quoting the publisher and date of publication.

I had admired the table at which Schubert had sat. I had touched a Beethoven fragment. I had held a pencil which Goethe had used. What more could possibly follow?

It came - surprisingly - in the British Library. In May 1986, the Stefan Zweig bequest of seventy-five musical and literary autographs were exhibited. The national press gave the event a great deal of advance publicity, and introduced Stefan Zweig as a prominent Austrian author famous for his biographies of Marie Antoinette, Erasmus, Magellan and Maria Stuart and for his masterly short stories of compressed personal dramas. He was a passionate collector of autographs, which in the case of Goethe even extended to a lock of hair taken on his deathbed. The custom was not that unusual in the 19ᵗʰ century, with grieving relatives and anxious souvenir hunters practically cutting off the hair of the famous.

I was thrilled to look at the last pages of Mozart's thematic catalogue of his works, with entries for *Die Zauberflöte, La Clemenza di Tito*, the Clarinet Concerto, and the Masonic Cantata (K623). In his beautiful script, he listed his masterpieces.

Less tidy was Gustav Mahler's full score of *Urlicht*, later included in his Second Symphony. The bold deletions and additions of his thick pen were so different from Mozart's delicate plume. I admired the full score of Alban Berg's Prelude to the opera *Lulu,* a presentation copy written out for the sixtieth birthday of Arnold Schoenberg in September 1934, and the score of Schoenberg's *Five Orchestral Pieces, op. 16.*

Fascinating were the manuscripts which illustrate the creative process, such as preparatory sketches and unfinished orchestrations. In pride of place was one of Igor Stravinsky's sketchbooks for *Pulcinella,* mainly in full score, bearing various dates between 25th September 1919 and 11th April 1920. Paul Hindemith's composition draft of his first and last movements of his *Kammermusik No 2 (Piano Concerto)* provided an interesting insight of what was to come.

The degree of completion of the sketches varied considerably. The autograph of Claude Debussy's *Fantasie* for Piano and Orchestra consisted of the draft of the solo part with an indication of the orchestral part. I looked with envy at the full score of Bartok's *Four Pieces for Orchestra, op. 12.*

How pleased Stefan Zweig must have been when he found Alban Berg's *Six Pieces for Orchestra* in the original 1909 orchestration, and what story, too, lay behind the purchase of Maurice Ravel's *Bolero,* arranged for piano duet? I tried to imagine Stefan Zweig with Ferrucio Busoni in 1911, when the composer presented him with an autograph of *Indianisches Erntelied.*

Chopin was represented with his *Bacarolle in F sharp major, op. 60,* where his narrow thickly-packed script had to squeeze forty-eight demi-semi quavers into one bar. On display was a leaf with the parts of the second, third and fourth movements in short score of Brahms' *Piano Concerto no. 2.* The handwriting was slightly italic and elegantly casual and executed with a narrow nib. Very different was the immediate graphic impression of the full score of the overture *Rule Britannia,* developed by Richard Wagner. He spread out the music with the luxury of horizontal space and wrote it using a characteristic thick pen. And then there was the beloved Schubert, with an autograph of his song, *An die Musik*. The two verses in the German script decorate the music with antiquarian calligraphy.

The literary part of the exhibition was equally astonishing, with autographs which included Hoffmannsthal, Freud, D'Annunzio, Wilde, Rilke, Romain Rolland, Dostoevsky, Duhamel and Claudel.

Especially evocative for me were typewritten poems by Hermann Hesse, *Sommer 1933,* illustrated by his watercolour drawings.

Hesse had similarly presented my father with a set of six poems and watercolours, beautiful vignettes which echo the landscape around Montagnola in southern Switzerland. The autograph title page 'Ein paar Gedichte von Herm. Hesse' is decorated with a water-colour pen and ink oval, and inscribed with a dedication: Herrn Dr. Neumann überreicht mit Grüssen von H. Hesse (for Dr. Neumann, presented with greetings from H. Hesse).

These watercolours, together with letters and poems by Hermann Hesse are now housed at the British Library, entitled The Paul Neumann Collection.

My father never met Hermann Hesse. He never made the pilgrimage. It was Hesse's wife, Ninon, a childhood friend of my father's sister Lena, who was the literary go-between. Ninon visited Vienna from time to time and had also met my father in the early 1930s in Zurich, when he was there on Paul Zsolnay publishing business, establishing Zsolnay's Swiss subsidiary. Ninon knew how much he admired Hermann Hesse's poems and how greatly he would treasure such a gift.

Like Ada Desmines, I wanted confirmation. Both my daughters Joanna and Helena were studying German and French at Magdalen College, Oxford. I wrote to Sir Malcolm Pasley. I had heard a lot about him from Joanna. He was, she said, an expert on Kafka and in true tradition of donnish eccentricity, he occasionally took a pinch of snuff during tutorials. He replied:

Sir Malcolm Pasley, Bt., M.A.
Fellow and Tutor in Modern Languages

MAGDALEN COLLEGE
OXFORD OX1 4AU
6 May 1986

Dear Mr Newman,

I'm ashamed never to have thanked you for the photocopies of your interesting dedicated copies of the Hesse and Schnitzler private printings. I did consult the massive Hesse-Bibliography by Joseph Mileck (Univ. of California Press, 1977; 2 vols), which reveals that Hesse evidently distributed a number of copies of 'Ein paar Gedichte von Hermann Hesse' to his friends (3 copies in different Swiss collections are listed by Mileck) in 1935; the individual poems were apparently written in 1929/1930.

All good wishes in haste – and with apologies for delay!

Yours sincerely, Malcolm Pasley

Over the years, I got to know the poems well and loved the vignettes. And then, as I looked at something so familiar at the exhibition, I thought of my father and Stefan Zweig.

In Vienna they had met socially, especially in literary circles. In London Stefan Zweig was to become the cultural doyen of Austrian refugees. He and my father were involved in the launch of the Austrian Academy. On May 2nd 1940, Stefan Zweig as Honorary President and my father as Honorary Secretary, represented Austrian aspirations at the festive inaugural ceremony.

How different that was from their public appearance in September 1939 at Sigmund Freud's funeral. They both spoke. There is no transcript extant of my father's eulogy. He would have summarised Freud's famous life and may have mentioned the friendship of the two families, linked by his sister Lena and Freud's daughter Mathilde. Even so to find the right words for such an occasion, in front of such an array of mourners, must have been difficult.

The personal connection of Zweig and Freud was the active correspondence of the two men over many years.

The factual but evocative report in *The Times* is a historic document.

27th September 1939

PROFESSOR FREUD BODY CREMATED AT
GOLDERS GREEN

The body of Professor Freud, who died in London on Sunday was cremated yesterday at Golders Green Crematorium. There was no religious ceremony but before the coffin passed from the chapel, tributes were paid by Dr. Ernest Jones, president of the International Psycho-Analytical Association, Herr Stefan Zweig, and Dr. P. Neumann, representing the Committee of Austrians in England.

The family mourners included the widow, three sons, and two daughters. Among nearly 150 people present – many of them Austrian refugees in this country – were Professor F. Hertz (chairman of the Committee of Austrians in England), Baron G. Fuchs, and prominent psycho-analysts, including Dr. Edward Glover, Dr. Rickman, Dr. Kris, Dr. Hitschmann, and Dr. Bienenfeld.

Dr. Ernest Jones said that Professor Freud had died surrounded by every loving care in a land which had shown him more courtesy and honour than his own or any other, and one which he held in the highest esteem. Speaking of the professor's nobility of character and love of truth, Dr. Jones added that fairness was Freud's favourite word in the English language.

Herr Zweig and Dr. Neumann gave their addresses in German.

The Austrians in London sent a large wreath of red and white carnations, tied with red and white ribbon, and the British Psycho-Analytical Society and the International Psycho-Analytical Association also sent wreaths.

A few weeks after the exhibition had closed, I wanted to have a second look at the collection, not just the pages which had been on view. Comfortably seated in the Manuscript Reading Room of the British Library, with a pile of autograph treasures in front of me, I annotated the typographical niceties of musical handwriting which were of special interest to a music copyist. Over the years I had copied out thousands of pages of instrumental music from orchestral full scores.

I had seen so many manuscript compositions, but I was curious to see more, especially famous ones.

For me it was the way the music was written down, in addition to what it was. How legible is the script? Is it generously spaced or overcrowded? Is it clear or full of imprecisions? Are the noteheads accurate and how carefully are the slurs and dynamic markings annotated? The copyist faces many notational problems related to the extraction of the separate instrumental parts. Where does the music stop, however briefly, in time to turn the page? Where should cues be added to make it easier, just in case the musician gets lost and so on?

I looked at the autographs on which famous hands had once rested. And then, at the bottom of one of the boxes, I saw a small envelope marked 'not for public display'. I opened it to see what it was and out fell a lock of hair. Goethe's curl lay in front of me. With it was a note: 'Haare des Vaters, überreicht an Ottilie von Goethe von Karl Vogel Grossherzog. Sächsischer Hofrat und Leibarzt zu Weimar (hair of the father, presented to Ottilie von Goethe by Karl Vogel Grandducal Saxon Hofrat [Privy Counsellor] Court Physician at Weimar).

Goethe's life ended on the 22nd March 1832 with his famous last words: "Mehr Licht" (more light) as he lay dying in a room darkened by blinds.

I was looking at a reliquary which was a hundred and fifty years old. Very carefully I slid the lock of hair and the note into the envelope and put it back into the box. I folded the manuscripts, ready for collection. It was closing time. And after the attendant had taken everything away and as I was packing up my own things, I saw them. Several white thin curly hairs were lying on my papers. Over the years they must have become separated and loose in the envelope. Had they not lost their corporate significance, now that they were single and no longer part of that surprisingly compact, thick, well-shapen capillary curve? No one could possibly miss them. No one had counted them. I yielded to temptation. Goethe's hair is no longer imprisoned in a library vault. It now rests in a beautiful Wiener Werkstätte jewellery cassette. The small rectangular box has the sides and lid made of stained glass. The leading, separating several small multi-coloured panels, is very pronounced, proud and irregular and very much part of the decorative design. Altogether, this miniature treasure chest poses the inevitable question, what is inside? Hair from the greatest German poet! Reality is transfigured by reflection, not in the usual poetic sense but in actual fact. The scattered hair is doubled in a mirror glass base.

Perhaps Stefan Zweig would forgive the minute dimunition of his legacy, perpetrated by someone with a personal connection.

He would at any rate have been pleased with me in June 1939. Then the all pervading web that had bound together the Jewish cultural life of Vienna was being torn apart. And there was a fifteen year old schoolboy in Oxford buying his books!

I was awarded the form prize and the Greek prize at Magdalen College School. They were seven shillings and sixpence (37½ pence) each and the equivalent of many weeks' pocket money. I was told to choose my own books. I felt rich. I remember going to Parker's bookshop, appropriately called English and Foreign booksellers, opposite Balliol College. I felt a slight moral obligation to find something relevant and started to look at various books on Greece and Rome.

And then I saw the Stefan Zweig collected short stories in two volumes, priced at sixteen shillings. The price is still there in pencil. The shop assistant must have been puzzled to see what looked like a typical English public schoolboy with blazer, school tie and the obligatory straw boater with school colours, wanting to buy expensive books in German. How could he possibly have known that Stefan Zweig, like Franz Werfel, had been a name with which I had grown up? I explained. My two prizes were not quite enough money, only fifteen shillings, but with a smile he reduced the price by one shilling. When I expressed surprise that Parker's had them, the assistant said: "They've sent them over". "They" must have been the Swiss subsidiary in Zurich of Herbert Reichner Verlag Vienna, who had published them in 1935. Zweig, like other Jewish authors after the Anschluss had his books pulped and a ban placed on sales, a fate that he had already suffered for the previous six years in Germany. But also pencilled in on the inside is the date when Parker's took the books into stock: 2/39 (February 1939). Six months later, war was declared and there would be more important import cargoes than German literature.

When my mother saw what I had chosen for my prizes she was surprised. She had expected to see books in English. They would have improved my vocabulary and language skills. They would have been agents of assimilation. After seventy years, I remember the moment: "Du hättest Dir doch Bücher auf englisch aussuchen sollen" (You should have chosen books in English).

But for me, the books with their golden school crests and prize label endorsements became passports to the bitter sweet world of Zweig.

CHAPTER 14

Bernhard Altmann, textile magnate

Bernhard Altmann was a few months younger than my father, and their close friendship dates from the first post-war years. Immediately after the First World War, in 1919, Bernhard, then aged 31, opened a knitwear factory. In Vienna, he quickly became a byword for textile excellence. In 1922 a new building was erected and three years later, in 1925, it was enlarged.

Lena, who was for a time Bernhard's private secretary, told me that the factory in the Siebenbrunnengasse was very large and very modern. The office staff and factory workers, she said, had generous facilities. There were tennis courts and a swimming pool, a large garden, a restaurant, and a children's crèche. Bernhard was a pioneer. He was larger than life. His personality was magnetic. He was an autocrat and he ruled over his four brothers, Fritz, Julius, Max and Hans, all of whom worked for the family firm.

He had vision and commercial courage. In 1926, Bernhard Altmann opened a knitwear factory in Kosino, a few miles to the east of Moscow, and he asked my father to act as legal adviser and to represent the firm in negotiations with the Russian authorities. After Lenin's death in 1924, Soviet economic policy changed and foreign capital on a concessionary basis was welcomed to help industrial development. It turned out to be short-lived and by 1929 Stalin nationalised all foreign enterprises.

Bernhard Altmann took a calculated risk, but even in the short term it proved successful. Labour in Russia was cheap and high quality wool was readily available. But Bernhard also looked beyond sheep to cashmere goats. He realised that a wealthy clientele was waiting for luxury garments. His factory was ideally situated for the spinning and weaving of cashmere wool to be made into cardigans, scarves and coats. After all, it was local produce, from the mountainous regions of Eastern Siberia, or imported from neighbouring Tibet.

Bernhard, throughout his career, continued to supply luxury fabrics, and would search the world for the softest fibres.

From sheep to goats, from goats to llamas. From the highest mountains of Peru and Chile, from the Andes, he bought the delicate hair of the alpaca, a llama-like domesticated creature. The wild-life vicuna, living in the Cordillera mountains of South America, provided even more suitable wool for the essential requirements of ultimate luxury, weightless materials with a caressing texture.

When Bernhard Altmann first started, cashmere was a rarity, and very expensive. Later, after the Anschluss, he emigrated to the United States and built a second career. He produced very large quantities of cashmere. He created a new market.

Several times in the late 1920s, my father travelled to Russia to deal with the setting up and the running of the factory. Occasionally he would talk about his time there, especially when as a small boy I might ask: was it very cold? Did you see any wolves? Later, during the Second World War, as the Germans advanced to within about 50km of Moscow, my father told me that he had been there. He said the Altmann factory eventually had about a thousand employees, and that the management was staffed by Austrians. It was large.

A lasting memento of my father's Russian journeys is the 17th century icon of St. Nicholas and the Devil, now hanging in our dining room. When I look at it closely I am reminded of my father, how he loved that small panel of wood and how he sometimes stood in front of it in silence.

Lena was a great diarist and occasionally she recorded some of her brother's and Bernhard Altmann's journeys. On the 5th February 1928, referring to Bernhard Altmann's departure for Russia, her entry reads: "Abschied für Russland" (Farewell for Russia). The three evocative words encapsulate the mystery of the distant unknown: Bernhard

Altmann's visit lasted less than two weeks. For the 17th February, Lena wrote: "Anruf nach Rückkehr aus M." (telephone call after return from M.), referring to Altmann's return. A few weeks later my father travelled. On the 11th June 1928, she wrote: "mit Paul an der Bahn. Abreise nach Moskau" (with Paul at the station. Departure for Moscow). I can imagine my father taking his seat in the first-class Pullman sleeping car, and waving goodbye to his sister.

The luxury of long-distance train travel is now a thing of the past. Gone are the special wagon-lits with their smart uniformed attendants, with the obligatory samovar at the end of the corridor, serving Russian tea at all times, and, of course, with the famous restaurant car and its *cordon bleu* menu and selected wine list.

The train that my father boarded for Russia took the better part of two days and a night and travelled through Cracow and Minsk, towns famous for their history. In Cracow he may well have thought of the Warvel castle along the banks of the Vistula, and in Minsk the dome of the Grand Cathedral might even have come into view.

I grew up in the age of steam, when the locomotive ruled supreme. As a small boy, I was usually allowed to look at the engine, and I saw the driver and the stoker, all ready for departure. The coal tender was full, and soon the evocative whistle would signal our imminent departure.

The windows along the corridors and in the compartments could be lowered. Underneath, on brass plates, was the warning in German, French and Italian, that it was dangerous to lean out. Even so, inevitably, in view of my subsequent history of always 'getting something in my eye', a piece of smut went in, on one of our long journeys to Switzerland in the early 1930s. I may well have wanted to see the locomotive in full cry, perhaps pulling up a gradient and taking a bend in the track. I was probably anxious to catch a glimpse of the engine as it turned into view, as it left its hidden point at the head of a straight line of carriages.

For the next half year, my father travelled to Russia frequently. Lena records his return on the 6th January 1929, a few days before my fifth birthday: "an der Nordbahn Paul holen" (at the Nordbahn to fetch Paul). The administrative task of dealing with Soviet bureaucracy must have been ongoing and formidable. My mother took the opportunity to join my father. In 1928 that was a real adventure. Hardly anyone in Vienna had been to Moscow, certainly very few women. One of these visitors was in fact my mother's own sister Bertha, who had visited Moscow just seven years earlier as a delegate of the Second International Women's Conference. My mother's passport is endorsed with a visitor's visa and a five-rouble duty stamp, bearing the hammer and sickle.

On the way to Russia, she passed through Czechoslovakia and Poland and at each border control her passport was stamped. For Poland my mother needed a special transit visa which takes up an entire page and is decorated with stamped endorsements of her two journeys.

My mother arrived in Russia on the 11th September 1928 and left on the 14th October. About half a century later, she told me about the small wooden churches in Kosino, and how they had been kept in good repair in spite of an atheist society. She never talked about Moscow. How I now wish that I had asked her about the Kremlin, the Bolshoi and the museums.

But by early 1929, it became clear that the Altmann factory in Kosino would soon be nationalised and my father once again departed for Russia. Lena, as usual, noted his departure, on the 29th June 1929. "Paul zur Bahn begleitet (Moskau)" (accompanied Paul to the station – Moscow). He had to negotiate at least a nominal compensation. And then for the final act, Bernhard Altmann joined my father. On the 1st September 1929 Lena wrote: "Herr A. für Moskau Adieu sagen" (saying goodbye to Mr. A. for Moscow).

It did not take too long to wind up great hopes. They both returned on the 13th September, after a detour, perhaps to Germany, as Lena's entry mentions a different railway station, the Westbahn: "Früh an der Westbahn, Paul und Herrn Altmann abgeholt" (early at the Westbahn, to fetch Paul and Mr Altmann). It was my father's last visit.

But the deep friendship of the Neumann and the Altmann families continued during the lifetime of that generation, and included of course the children, Trude, Bernhard's daughter, my sister Eva and myself.

For Bernhard Altmann, marketing strategy meant expansion and diversification. In 1932, he opened a stocking factory in Paris. In Vienna, he launched his brand of men's socks with the clever trademark SELFIX, ready for English and American markets. The socks had the novel feature of an elasticated band of threads, woven around the top. No need now for men's garters with their suspenders, worn below the knee, to hold up slippery cotton.

Bernhard Altmann negotiated a concession with the Austrian State Railways to install advertising posters on their stations. Suddenly, thousands of long oblong posters were fixed halfway up the pillars that support the roofs above the platforms. The word SELFIX, in memorable bold typography, was inscribed like a motto across a crest, the traditional symbol of eminence. The shield was quartered and emblazoned with weaving looms and sheep, in the manner of the old craft guilds. Below, a large pair of socks stretched diagonally downwards to the bottom of the poster.

After the war, in London, I asked Bernhard Altmann how much the advertising cost. He said he paid three (Austrian) shillings a year for each advertisement. I did not then ask him how many pillars there were.

My memories of Bernhard Altmann go back to my early childhood. It was the result of Lena's intimate friendship with Bernhard that he became a very close, lifelong friend of my parents.

Nearly every Sunday, for some years, Lena was a visitor at the palatial villa in the Kopfgasse, in the elegant suburb of Hietzing. Occasionally she took me along. Nelly, his wife, always welcomed me with a big smile and a kiss. Her birthday was the same day as mine, and somehow this formed a private link. I often think of her on my anniversary.

In their park-like garden, the Altmanns had a greenhouse in which there was a large birdcage full of multicoloured budgerigars. One Christmas my wish was fulfilled and I was presented with a pair of birds. At another time, when I was about six or seven years old, I was cautiously led into this garden house to look at a small crocodile which Bernhard Altmann had brought back from Egypt. To me, as a small boy, the creature seemed very long, as it crawled about in its container.

The Altmanns kept a large staff, commensurate with their grand social position: a cook, two maids, a gardener and a chauffeur.

On one of the rare occasions that I travelled in a private car before the war, it was at night, somewhere in the Alps, in Bernhard Altmann's Bentley. I was sitting between my mother and Lena, and Bernhard Altmann was in the front, next to the chauffeur. Bernhard Altmann made some remark about dipped headlights and used the – for me – unfamiliar word 'abblenden' (to dip lights). And then I asked the chauffeur to demonstrate and to dip the headlights several times. I still remember the embarrassed silence at my repeated request.

The Altmann villa was full of pictures. It was like visiting a museum. I had, of course, no idea what the pictures or any of the other beautiful objects were. But a few years later, cruel history would provide a complete record of his home.

On five days in June 1938, 1,890 items from the Kopfgasse were put up for sale. The entire contents were impounded by the Nazis and the machinery of expropriation applied. The Dorotheum auction house catalogue is a testimony of Bernhard Altmann's connoisseurship, and his personal taste. Three paintings of Venice by Canaletto, a portrait by Waldmüller, paintings by Egger-Lienz, works by Klimt, Degas, Tischbein, Franz Eybl and Rudolf Alt, were only part of his wonderful collection.

Looking through the list, I remember the 17th century Flemish tapestry, which hung in the entrance hall. For me it was a carpet with a picture and I wanted to know how it was made; Lena explained. The description in the catalogue conjures up in my mind a group of figures hanging in a long forgotten locality: Los 129, Große Tapisserie mit großfiguriger Darstellung einer alttestamentarischen, biblischen Szene, rot, blau und diverse Schattierungen von grün und gelb, breite Bordüre mit Blumen- und Fruchtgewinden, teilweise das Bildfeld übergreifend, Wolle mit Seide, Brüssel, signiert B.B., 17. Jahrhundert, sehr gute und farbenfrische Erhaltung, 350 x 410cm. Ausrufspreis 1,800 Reichsmark. (Lot 129, Large tapestry, with large figures representing a scene from the Old Testament, red, blue and various shades of green and yellow, wide border with flower and fruit garlands, partly encroaching onto the image, wool and silk, Brussels, signed B.B., 17th century, very good material and fresh colour preservation, 340 x 410cm, call price 1,800 Reichsmark.)

The auction spoke with grim totality. There were, of course, the pictures, books, furniture, pianos, silver tableware and crystal glass. There were objets d'art and carpets. The contents of the wardrobes were itemised, the suits, dresses, coats, hats, shoes, down to Bernhard's shirts and Nelly's blouses. It was a complete clearout: kitchen utensils and garden tools, table cloths and bed linen, walking sticks, shoe trees, lamps and umbrellas.

More personal for me are two other entries. The birdcage that held the budgerigars is listed as lot 457: Großes Vogelhaus aus Lärchenholz mit Drahtgeflecht, allseits freihstehend, innen zwei Blechtassen, Ausrufspreis 15RM (Large birdcage, made of larch wood and wire netting, completely free-standing on all sides, inside two tin trays, call price 15 Reichsmark).

And then there is the poignant footnote at the end of the catalogue: Ferner gelangt eine größere Anzahl ausgewählter Schallplatten, außer Katalog zur Versteigerung (In addition, a large number of selected gramophone records, not in the catalogue, will be offered for sale).

In the 1930s, gramophone parties were popular. Guests sat in rows and listened to an opera or a symphony, played of course on the old 78s. Bernhard Altmann had a large collection of records, many of them with automatic coupling, suitable for the very latest radiogram. One could enjoy a work without the continual interruption of winding the machine and turning the record.

I remember going to the Altmann villa for a special gramophone programme. Arturo Toscanini had come to Vienna to conduct the Verdi Requiem. That was no ordinary concert, but a solemn memorial in music to honour the assassinated Chancellor Dollfuss who had been murdered three months earlier. It took place, appropriately, on the 1ˢᵗ November 1934, on All Saints Day. I went with my mother, and Lena sat with the Altmanns in their box. The Vienna Opera was a fitting venue. And then, according to Lena, Bernhard Altmann invited us shortly afterwards to listen to Toscanini's recording of the work on his new gramophone.

After the war, I heard Toscanini in two further concerts when he came to London and conducted the four Brahms symphonies in the Festival Hall. It was at that time that Lena reminded me of the Verdi Requiem at the Vienna Opera. Toscanini conducting Verdi was always wonderful, she said, and amongst the singers at that concert in 1934, she singled out the baritone soloist Josef Manowarda, for whom she said she had a special affection. She would have travelled a long way just to hear him sing a scale of C major, just to hear the voice, and her opera books record the memorable occasions of his appearances. The first entry is for the 10ᵗʰ October 1919, when Richard Strauss, the new music director, conducted the premiere of his opera *Die Frau ohne Schatten*. Manowarda had the minor role of the Spirit Messenger, but stood on the same stage as Maria Jeritza (the empress), Richard Mayer (Barak) and Lotte Lehmann (his wife). Soon Manowarda established himself as a great Wagnerian. On the 21ˢᵗ November 1920, five days prior to her thirtieth birthday, Lena went to *Die Meistersinger*, in which he sang the role of Veit Pogner. The next time Lena heard him was on the 8ᵗʰ October 1921 as Hans Sachs. It was a remarkable achievement to sing both *Meistersinger* roles within a year! Even more astonishing is Lena's double entry in 1925. On the 9ᵗʰ November he sang Veit Pogner and then three days later, on the 12ᵗʰ November he was Wotan in *Walküre*.

On the 1ˢᵗ January 1930, on New Year's Day, the Vienna Opera put on a festive performance of *Fidelio*. Richard Strauss conducted, and Monowarda sang Rocco. The ladies on that occasion were Lotte

Lehmann as Leonore and Elisabeth Schumann as Marzelline, a glorious pair.

Frequently, Lena referred to her operatic past as if it had happened quite recently, as if those decades had faded to reveal the jubilant timbre of a voice, a top note, a portamento leading back to a theme. And of course, there were further unforgettable dramatic gestures, perhaps the movement of the head or a raised hand, a few steps, a smile.

And that is how she spoke to me in 1952 after I had been to Alban Berg's *Wozzeck* at Covent Garden. She vividly recollected Manowarda's performance in the title role on 7th May 1930. "Er war <u>der</u> Wozzeck" (he was <u>the</u> Wozzeck), she said, emphasising the definite article to give the ultimate authenticity. Manowarda sang Orest with Richard Strauss conducting his *Elektra*, on the 4th February 1931. Lena records her enthusiasm for Verdi's *Don Carlos*. She went to two performances: on the 6th December 1932, and again on Christmas Day on the 25th December. *Don Carlos* followed the once-a-year *Hänsel und Gretel* matinée performance staged for children, to which I went in 1930.

It must have been very memorable for Lena to go a second time on Christmas Day. Manowarda sang King Philip.

I remember sitting in the stalls at the Verdi Requiem memorial concert, near the front, slightly to the right just opposite the tenor and baritone soloists. And there was Lena in her box, with all her memories.

Bernhard Altmann left Vienna immediately after the Anschluss, on the 12th March 1938 and came to England, and then in 1939 before the war, he went to New York.

He travelled to Oxford to say goodbye to Eva and to me, and took us out to lunch at the Clarendon Hotel, alas now no longer in existence, but then the premier hotel.

He must have told us about his escape, and how he managed to get his wife and family to follow him. And then, I remember it so clearly after seventy years, he leant forward and looked at us with his penetrating black eyes: "Ich hab' alles verloren" he said, "aber es tut mir gut. Ich muß nocheinmal von vorne beginnen" (I have lost everything, but it is good for me. I must start over again).

I was only fifteen years old, and could not imagine the magnitude, the totality of his loss, the literal meaning of the word 'alles' (everything) in that context. In fact, his factory and his villa were impounded, his possessions were sold and his fortune was immediately frozen, later to be confiscated by means of the notorious Reichsfluchtsteuer (the flight from the Reich tax).

After the war, on one of his visits to London from New York, he told me a little bit about his new start in the New World.

He lost his Paris factory when France fell, and by 1941 he was left with about 1,000 dollars. With that he started to trade in cloth, and just after the war, in 1946, he once again founded a knitwear factory. By the end of that year, he had 400 employees. That was the time, he said, of a great shortage of cloth manufacturing machinery because of the demand for military uniforms. And with a certain amount of pride he told me how he had adapted looms and weaving machines normally used for the production of much coarser carpet materials for the more delicate cashmere. Bernhard Altmann was exceptional. At an age when many people are thinking of retirement, he built up a second, much more substantial empire.

It was at that time, in about 1949, that he asked me to help him with his forthcoming publication on the cashmere goat.

I enjoyed my research, and in due course sent him a ten-page type-written report which contained the following sections: historical introduction, a description of the goat, geographic distribution, the fleece, colour of hair, yield, annual quantity, number of goats, microscopic characteristics, chemical properties, general observations.

The beautifully illustrated souvenir booklet was printed privately in a limited edition and distributed to friends and colleagues. With his romantic German, Bernhard Altmann transformed my academic prose into a hymn of praise for his beloved material: "Man muß sie durch die Finger gleiten lassen, man muß über sie hinstreicheln, dann fühlt man, bevor noch der prüfende Verstand es begründet: KASCHMIR ist ein königlicher Stoff! Wer einmal Kaschmir getragen hat, ist dieser Faser verfallen. Kaschmir bringt so vieles, wonach man sich sehnt. Es hat einen seidigen Glanz, ist leichter und wärmer als Wollstoffe. Ein Kaschmirmantel in seinem edlen Faltenwurf reiht sich an jene Kleidungsstücke, wie Hermelin, Brokat und Seidensamt, die man sonst als königlich zu bezeichnen pflegt." (You must let it glide through your fingers, you have to stroke it gently, and then you immediately feel: CASHMERE is cloth fit for kings. Once you have worn cashmere you become addicted. Cashmere provides so many things for which you have a longing. It has a silky sheen, and it is lighter and warmer than wool. A cashmere coat with its noble folds evokes royal garments of ermine, brocade and silken satin.)

Once a collector, always a collector. After the war, Bernhard Altmann started to build up his collection of rare books, and asked me to look out for books from the Doves Press, one of the private presses that flourished in the Arts and Crafts years, in the 20th century.

The titles were published in limited editions of about two to three hundred, with a few numbered copies, no more than perhaps twenty, printed on and bound in vellum. Of special interest to Bernhard Altmann were the German books, plays by Goethe, all of which I eventually managed to find. I started to visit antiquarian bookshops, such as Maggs Brothers in Berkeley Square, and Bernhard Quaritch in Grafton Street. I was successful at Sothebys auctions.

The details of the 1916 Doves Press catalogue fill me with nostalgia, with wistful longing. I only have to read the entries to recall the times about half a century ago, when I held these precious volumes. I remember their slim size, their typeface, graced with elegance, full of symmetry, harmony and slender beauty, classical, refined, with touches of Italian Renaissance.

It must have been about 1951 when I bought *Faust* Part One and Part Two, both on vellum, in an edition of 25 and 22 respectively. *Die Leiden des Jungen Werther*, published in 1911 in an edition of 200 copies, followed. I was delighted when I managed to find a copy of *Torquato*

Tasso, one of only 12 on vellum with illuminated initials in gold. Then there was *Iphigenie auf Tauris*, published in 1912, one of twenty copies on vellum, and finally *Auserlesene Lieder* (Selected Poems) one of ten copies on vellum.

Bernhard Altmann bought several other Doves Press books, such as Milton's *Paradise Lost* and *Paradise Regained*, both in an edition of 300, and Shakespeare *Sonnets* on vellum.

For the rest of his life, he turned to me if he wanted something special, sometimes for a particular reason. At the time when *My Fair Lady* was launched on Broadway, I found him an early edition of George Bernard Shaw's complete works in 16 volumes, uncut, bound in linen. After he had been to a memorable Ring cycle, he bought Arthur Rackham's Wagner illustrations.

And then, right at the end, too late, he wanted to purchase the large and very valuable German library which his close friend Herr Morgenstern had brought with him from Vienna. Morgenstern had emigrated to Bradford where he died in 1960, and his sons wanted to sell.

On the 9th August 1960, on holiday in France, Bernhard wrote to me:

Lieber Hans: Ich danke Dir für Deine freundlichen Zeilen vom 7.8 und deine Zustimmung die Katalogisierung der Bücher anzunehmen. Ich muß jetzt noch das Permit der langweiligen Brüder abwarten. Momentan kaufe ich keine Doves Press mehr.

Ich freue mich, dass Deine Frau in Herbst konzertieren wird. Ich wünsche ihr viel Erfolg.

Mit herzlichen Grüssen an Dich und Deiner Frau
   bin ich Dein Bernhard

(I thank you for your letter of the 7th August and your willingness to undertake the cataloguing of the books. I must now still wait for permission from the brothers, who are taking their time. For the time being, I am not buying any more Doves Press.

I am delighted that your wife is giving concerts in the Autumn. I wish her every success.

With kindest regards to you and your wife
    I am your Bernhard)

I spent several days in a Bradford depository where hundreds of rare books were packed into pyramids of tea chests. Bernhard Altmann wanted complete details, authors and titles, publishers and dates, format, special features such as limited edition, uncut pages, type of illustrations (lithograph, etching, steel engraving, woodcut, copperplate), type of binding (leather, vellum, linen board, buckram). For the very special books he wanted my opinion on their condition, such as loose spines, foxed illustrations, or defective stitching. My bibliophile persona was given full play.

The sale of the books never materialised. Bernhard Altmann died in a Zurich clinic on the 2nd December 1960.

As an epilogue, I have chosen one of his letters to my mother from New York, dated 21st December 1948, because it reflects the love and affection of two families.

My mother had sent him a book and a photograph of my father, who had died in April of that year. Bernhard Altmann's birthday was on the 24th December, on Christmas Eve, and presents to him often merged into one:

… Den Ketzer von Soana hast Du mir schon einmal geschenkt. Es war im Jahre 1925. Und das Buch hat mich unerhört beeindruckt, denn ich war selbst ein Ketzer. Jetzt bekomme ich es noch dazu im Prachtband. Ich bin doch ein Glücksritter.

Pauls Bild ist ausgezeichnet. Wie er lebt und lebt. Ich lasse auch Hans für seine lieben Zeilen danken…

(You have already made me a present of Der Ketzer von Soana [the heretic of Soana]. *It was in 1925. And the book made a tremendous impression on me, because I myself was a heretic. And now I am even getting it in a deluxe edition. Am I not fortunate?*

The picture of Paul is excellent. How he lives and lives. I also thank Hans for his kind words …)

Gerhard Hauptmann's novel *Der Ketzer von Soana* was first published by S. Fischer Verlag, Berlin, in 1918. By the time the edition in my collection was published in 1922, 113,000 copies had been printed, testimony to Gerhard Hauptmann, his high standing, fame and popularity as a great expressionist dramatist and novelist.

Bernhard Altmann was known for his generosity and his lavish hospitality. In Lena's pre-war diaries, there are countless entries when perhaps two dozen guests sat down to a banquet and when many more attended a *grande soirée*. She told me that he made donations to Zionist charities, and was always ready to support relatives and friends.

There was one occasion when I witnessed it. In 1948 the Vienna Philharmonic Orchestra came to London and gave several concerts, to which I went. I befriended Hans Tietze, a member of the 1st violins. He told me that soon after the war, Bernhard Altmann had come to Vienna and heard the orchestra. He was saddened by their shabby appearance and promptly donated enough suiting material for two concert suits each. There were about one hundred and twenty players, all men. "Jetzt sam ma elegant. Der Altmann hat uns geholfen" (Now we're elegant. Altmann has helped us), Tietze said in his Viennese dialect. I remember being impressed by the self-explanatory definite article which preceded the name, which needed no introduction, of pre-war textile excellence. Here was a man who had survived the terrible past and had lost everything, making a very generous gesture of reconciliation to the institution which he had loved and admired throughout his life: the Vienna Philharmonic.

But no one could have foreseen that the name would become world news.

The dramatic story begins about a century ago. In 1907, Gustav Klimt painted a portrait of Adele Bloch-Bauer which became one of the most famous paintings of Secessionist Vienna. After the Anschluss, the picture, together with four other works by Klimt, was seized by the

Nazis, and it took many decades and a new Millennium for the enactment of restitution, for the return of the paintings to the family. The successful claimant was Maria Altmann, née Bloch-Bauer, the niece of Adele Bloch-Bauer. Before the war she married Fritz Altmann, one of Bernhard Altmann's brothers.

Maria Altmann had to fight a long legal battle. In 2004, the United States Supreme Court ruled in her favour, and after arbitration the Austrian government awarded her and her family the five paintings.

In 1907, when Gustav Klimt painted Adele, he looked at her with more than artistic interest. The degree of their intimacy is still subject to speculation, but it is certain that neither could have dreamt that the painting would one day be sold privately for $135 million. By comparison, the most expensive work of art sold at auction is Alberto Giacometti's *L'homme qui marche*, which fetched £65 million at Sotheby's London, in 2010.

How Bernhard Altmann, who had lost everything, would have rejoiced at his sister-in-law's success, at this belated gesture of justice!

5902 C. M. A.

ПОЧТОВАЯ КАРТОЧКА
CARTE POSTALE

NEW YORK

Куда _Наименование места, где находится почта, и области или края, а для станций—наименование железной дороги._

50 PINE STREET

Улица, № дома и квартиры.

Кому _Mr. Robert V. Neumann_
Подробное наименование адресата.

ПОЛЬЗУЙТЕСЬ АДРЕСНОЙ ПОЧТОВОЙ КАРТОЧКОЙ ПРИ НАВЕДЕНИИ АДРЕСНЫХ СПРАВОК

Адрес
отправителя
Adresse
de l'expéditeur
Swerdlowskaja Oblast, Aleksytskij Rayon, Afanasiewskij Rozjezd, ...

Above: Mizzi sent this postcard from a forestry camp in the Urals to her brother Robert in New York. It bears a hammer and sickle and censor's initials.

Right: Stefan Unger, who was to die aged 19 crossing the River Vistula in Poland with the Polish army.

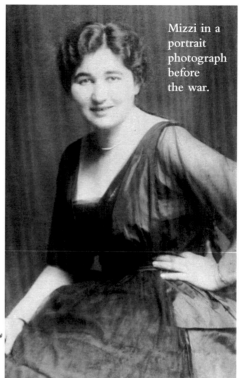

Mizzi in a portrait photograph before the war.

Above Left: Sisters Mizzi and Lena in happier times, probably at the races. Mizzi is holding opera glasses.

Right: Mizzi, standing second from the left, on a school outing.

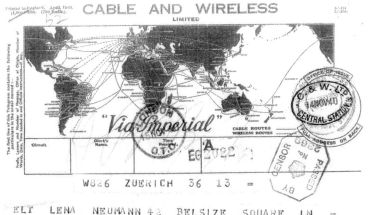

A telegram bearing censors' stamps, announcing the death of Mizzi's
husband Walter.

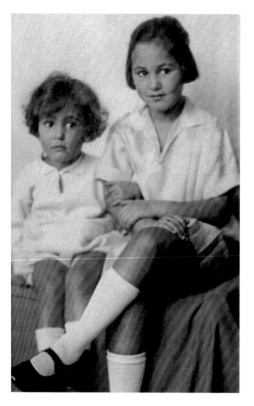

Wilhelm with two of his four grandchildren: myself and my sister Eva, in Gastein south of Salzburg.

Above: With my sister Eva.

Right: My father

Below: My mother

My sister Eva on holiday.

The family in Altaussee in 1932. I am seated second from left.

Playing the viola in front of the two oil portraits by Rudolf Huber-Wiesenthal: my younger self on the left and my sister Eva on the right.

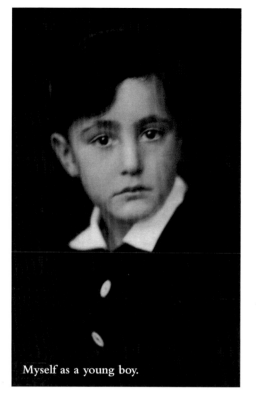

Myself as a young boy.

in Altaussee in 1932, aged 8.

... and aged 11.

Right: Eva in March 1936, aged 18. She
moved abroad alone to study at Oxford
University, unusual for the times.

Left: With my parents and sister. A few years earlier, soon after the First World War, my father had secretly shaved off his moustache and my mother had her hair cut short, as a suprise for each other – by coincidence both on the very same day.

Below: Paul's expulsion order.

Verzeichnis über das Vermögen von Juden

nach dem Stand vom 27. April 1938

des   Dr.Paul Neumann   Rechtsanwalt

der   (Zu- und Vorname)   (Beruf oder Gewerbe)

in   Wien,XVIII.Gersthoferstrasse 105   Straße, Platz Nr.

       (Wohnsitz oder gewöhnlicher Aufenthalt)

Angaben zur Person

Ich bin geboren am   15.März 1888

Ich bin Jude (§ 5 der Ersten Verordnung zum Reichsbürgergesetz vom 14. November 1935, Reichsgesetzbl. I S. 1333

und — deutscher [1]) —   — Staatsangehörigkeit [1]) — ~~fremder~~ —.

    Da ich — Jude deutscher Staatsangehörigkeit [1]) — ~~Staatenloser Jude~~ — bin, habe ich in dem nachstehenden Vermögensverzeichnis mein gesamtes inländisches und ausländisches Vermögen angegeben und bewertet [1]).

    Da ich Jude fremder Staatsangehörigkeit bin, habe ich in dem nachstehenden Vermögensverzeichnis mein inländisches Vermögen angegeben und bewertet [1]).

Ich bin verheiratet mit   Therese   geb.   Braunthal

                                                     (Mädchenname der Ehefrau)

Mein Ehegatte ist der Rasse nach — jüdisch [1]) — ~~nichtjüdisch~~ — und gehört der   jüdischen   Religionsgemeinschaft an.

Angaben über das Vermögen

I. Land= und forstwirtschaftliches Vermögen (vgl. Anleitung Ziff. 9):

Wenn Sie am 27. April 1938 land- und forstwirtschaftliches Vermögen besaßen (gepachtete Ländereien u. dgl. sind nur aufzuführen, wenn das der Bewirtschaftung dienende Inventar Ihnen gehörte):

Lage des eigenen oder gepachteten Betriebs und seine Größe in Hektar? (Gemeinde — Gutsbezirt — und Hofnummer, auch grundbuch- und katastermäßige Bezeichnung)	Art des eigenen oder gepachteten Betriebs? (z. B. landwirtschaftlicher, forstwirtschaftlicher, gärtnerischer Betrieb, Weinbaubetrieb, Fischereibetrieb)	Handelte es sich um einen eigenen Betrieb oder um eine Pachtung	Wert des Betriebs RM	Bei eigenen Betrieben: Wenn der Betrieb noch Anderen gehörte: Wie hoch war Ihr Anteil? (z. B. ¹/₄)
1	2	3	4	5

II. Grundvermögen (Grund und Boden, Gebäude) (vgl. Anleitung Ziff. 10):

Wenn Sie am 27. April 1938 Grundvermögen besaßen (Grundstücke, die nicht zu dem vorstehend unter I und nachstehend unter III bezeichneten Vermögen gehörten):

Lage des Grundstücks? (Gemeinde, Straße und Hausnummer, bei Bauland auch grundbuch- und katastermäßige Bezeichnung)	Art des Grundstücks? (z. B. Einfamilienhaus, Mietwohngrundstück, Bauland)	Wert des Grundstücks RM	Wenn das Grundstück noch Anderen gehörte: Wie hoch war Ihr Anteil? (z. B. ¹/₄)
1	2	3	4

[1]) Nichtzutreffendes ist zu durchstreichen.

Vermögensverzeichnis (VO v. 26. 4. 38)

Paul's official statement of possessions for Jews.

3. P. 9240   Wien, am **6.** Juni   193**8**

Meldungsbestätigung.

Gebühr bezahlt

Die Polizeidirektion in Wien bestätigt zum Vorweise bei
der Konsularabteilung der amerikanischen Gesandtschaft
in W i e n ,

daß über den hiesigen Aufenthalt des Herrn /Frau

Dr. Paul N e u m a n n ,

geboren am 15. März 1888 zu Wien,

zuständig nach Wien,

nebst früheren Meldungen

im Zentralmeldungsamte nachstehende Meldungen erliegen:

Gemeldet vom	bis	Angegebene Vorwohnung	Gemeldete Wohnung	Abgemeldet nach
4.11. 1927	auf weiteres	XVIII.,Semper- str. 58	XVIII.,Gersthoferstr.105, II/9	———
			Gez. M a n h a r t	
		Beglaubigt		
		Kanzleirat		

Swastika stamp on an official document prepared for Paul.

Soon after arriving in England, aged 14 in 1938.

A new life in England, from Lederhosen to English blazer. With my mother Resi and sister Eva, 1938.

19

TESTIMONIUM DE BAPTISMO.

Hisce praesentibus testificor, diligenti facta investigatione,

Theresiam Neumann natam die _18°_ mensis _Augusti_ anni _1889_

filiam _Max_ et _Clara Brunnthal_ (olim _Giller_)

in hac ecclesia _Stae Mariae Assumpt_ apud _Warwick St: London. W1._

baptizatam {fuisse / ~~non fuisse~~} die _21°_ mensis _PN. Novembris_ anni _1938_

Datum die _10°_ mensis _Decembris_ anni _1943_

Petrus Harris Rector.

Min: Cathj:

R.D. Rectori ecclesiae ....

apud ....

My mother Resi's Catholic baptism certificate, her conversion is the subject of Chapter 17.

ROCKLIFF BROS. LTD., LIVERPOOL.

MAGDALEN COLLEGE SCHOOL

Summer Concert

JUNE 14, 1940, AT 8.15, IN BIG SCHOOL

1. Concerto in A major for Pianoforte and Orchestra
   K. 488 (1st Movement) . . . . . *Mozart*
   Solo Piano: W. JELLINEK

2. Violin Concerto in A minor (1st Movement) . *Vivaldi*
   H. G. NEUMANN   arr. *T. Nachez*

3. Songs of the Sea . . . . . *C. V. Stanford*
   (Male Voice Chorus and Bass Solo)
   Soloist: Mr. MAURICE BEVAN

4. Piano Solos:
   (*a*) Prelude and Fugue in D major (Bk. II)   *J. S. Bach*
   (*b*) David's Bündler Tänze, Nos. 4 and 13   *Schumann*
   W. JELLINEK

5. Brandenburg Concerto, No. 2 in F (1st Mov.)   *J. S. Bach*
   (Trumpet, Flute, Oboe, Violin and Strings)

There will be a Collection to meet expenses

Above: Lena (right) and her cousin Anne, newly arrived in London. Lena was to work ceaselessly to try to help her sister Mizzi during the war (Chapter 15).

Above Right & Right: A school concert programme from 1940; I played the first movement of the Vivaldi A minor Violin Concerto...

...and led the school orchestra.

ORCHESTRA

1st Violins	*Violas*
H. G. NEUMANN (Leader)	Mr. STANIER
Mrs. COX	Mr. J. W. B. DOUGLAS
Mr. LLOYD JONES	

2nd Violins	*Cellos*
Mrs. STAINER	Mr. J. SPICER
H. WOHL	D. D. ATTWATER
Mr. D. L. CLARKE	Mr. D. DUPRÉ

Double Bass
Miss P. WOODWARD

Flute	*Oboes*	*Clarinet*
Mr. C. ELLIS	D. MORRIS	Miss K. RICHARDSON
	Miss E. KITSON	
	Mr. K. HUTTON	*Trumpet*
		M. CHANNON

Pianos	*Bassoon*
Miss C. WIBLIN	Mrs. MILFORD
W. JELLINEK	
P. STEPHENS	

CHORUS

The MASTER	T. P. TREES	J. LUNN
Mr. STANIER	D. MORRIS	M. W. BROWNE
Mr. KEMP	A. NELSON	C. FRANCIS
Mr. SAWYER	D. D. ATTWATER	
	P. SKUCE	

Conductor: Mr. JOHN WEBSTER.

We should like to express our thanks to Mr. MAURICE BEVAN, and to those from outside the School who have come in to help the orchestra.

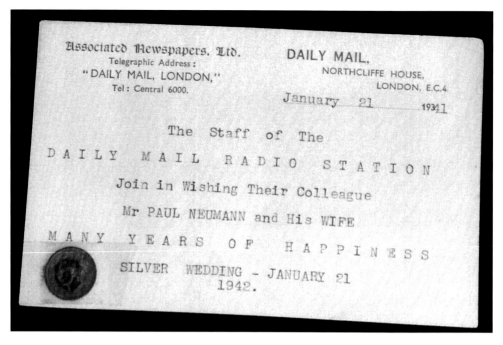

The Daily Mail's silver wedding message to my parents, see page 140.

Here I am with the RAF in Germany, in Spring 1945.

Above & Right: Outside Cologne Cathedral in 1945.

188250 7 Cpl Neumann
8501 Wing
RAF, BLA
17/VI/45.

Darling Blötchen,

Just a short letter. I am still here
but will go very soon to a place somewhere
on the Mosel. I rather dread the journey
with 9 pieces of luggage (do you know what is
what??)

From left to right:
wireless, blankets, hand bag, myself, violin, violin, kitbag
kitbag, rucksack, sleeping bag.

A wartime letter from Germany to my mother, showing my nine pieces of luggage.

At the moment the weather is not so good and it is too cold to swim. I hope you get my letters quickly.

Lots of love

Pussi

Hansi

On parade (if I had to go, but I don't)

shine on boots

Which one is Hansi?

Clues to the answer:
a) one of the airmen has
a.) more hair
b.) no creases in his clothes
c.) no military bearing
d.) no shine on his boots. (The others have little sparks coming from theirs!)

sparkle and glitter of the sergeants boots.

"On parade. Which one is Hansi?" – wartime letter to my mother.

Above Left: In London in 1947, aged 23.

Above Right: My mother with her sister Bertha in London.

Left: My sister Eva and Ken on their wedding day, spring 1944.

Below: With Patricia on our wedding day in 1959.

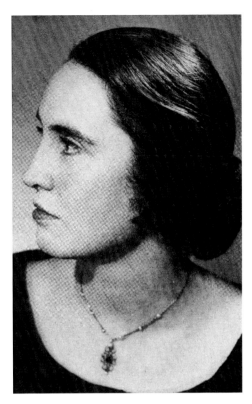

Above Left: A signed and numbered lithograph by Marc Chagall, whom I befriended in Vence, dedicated to me in 1957. My encounters with Chagall are related in Chapter 12.

Above Right: Patricia seen here in her professional portrait as a concert pianist. She performed Grieg's Piano Concerto with the BBC Symphony Orchestra at the opening night of the Promenade Concerts at the Royal Albert Hall in 1962.

With Patricia, Paul (known as Patrick), Joanna and Helena in 1966.

Above: The young father: in our back garden in Wimbledon. The bamboo has grown since then.

Right: How Joanna saw us: a family Christmas card.

Below: A heart for Patricia, described on page 204.

Above: Our three children collecting their MAs from Oxford University in 1992. All three went to Magdalen College, Oxford, which has a family tie as I had been a schoolboy at Magdalen College School. Paul read History, while Joanna and Helena both read Modern Languages. Paul, who uses his middle name Patrick, and Joanna have entered the world of business and banking while Helena has had a career in the art world at Sothebys.

Below: My daughter Joanna in Derbyshire.

My wife Patricia and I share a love of opera. Here we are on a recent visit to Glyndebourne.

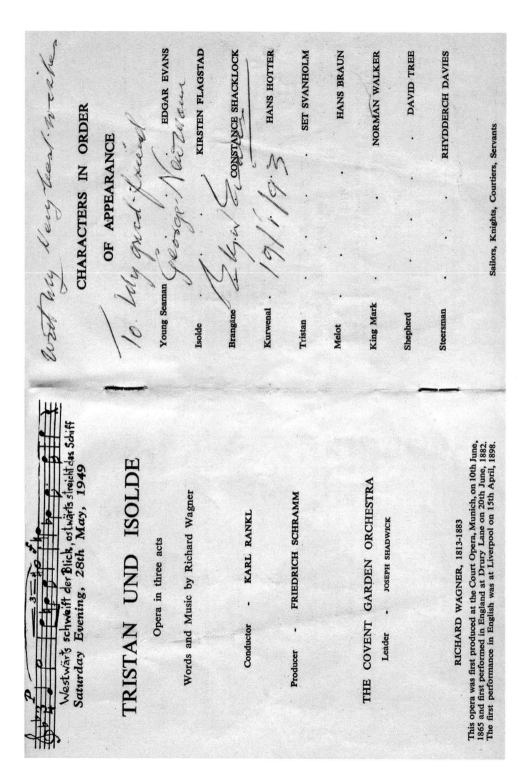

A memorable performance, see page 338. 44 years later, Edgar Evans signed the programme.
I wrote out the music of his opening phrase, with which he starts the opera.

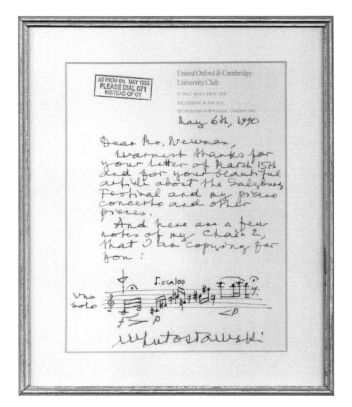

Left: Lutoslawski thanks me for the review of his concert in *Tempo* magazine.

Below: I assisted Stokowski in editing and printing his edition of Mussorgsky's *Night on the Bare Mountain.*

LEOPOLD STOKOWSKI

27 Dec 67

Mr. and Mrs. George Newman
16 Ernle Road
Wimbledon Common
London, S.W.20
England.

Dear Friends

Wishing you well-being in the new year

1067 Fifth Avenue
New York, N.Y. 10028

www.AndreasTischler.com

Meeting the President of Austria Heinz Fischer in March 2013, at the opening of an exhibition at the Austrian National Library to mark the 75th anniversary of the Anschluss.

Photograph © Österreichische Nationalbibliothek/APA-Fotoservice/Hinterramskogler

At the Austrian National Library in March 2013. From left to right: my daughter Helena, son Paul (Patrick), myself, the Director General of the Library Dr. Johanna Rachinger, and the curator of the Library's exhibition to mark the anniversary of the Anschluss, Dr. Bernhard Fetz. The Library now houses the Paul Neumann Collection – some of the books the family brought from Vienna to London in 1938.

CHAPTER 15

Exile to the Urals

My aunt Mizzi's marriage in 1923 to Walter Unger brought about her unusual departure from Vienna to Poland. Who could have foreseen that less than twenty years later, Mizzi and her family would be deported to a Russian forced labour camp in Siberia, in the forests of the Ural mountains, where Walter was to die. With her children, Stefan and Eva, Mizzi would then be sent to a collective farm, a kolkhoz, hundreds of miles further east, to Kazakhstan.

The catalyst that brought my aunt Mizzi and Walter together was his cousin Ninon Ausländer. A few weeks younger than Mizzi, she was born right on the Eastern edge of the Austro-Hungarian Empire, in Czernowitz, now in the Ukraine. Mizzi told me that she first met Ninon in the early 1900s, and that they quickly became close friends. On several occasions, she said, Ninon had joined her and Lena in Altaussee, during those halcyon pre-First World War summers, as shown in a postcard from Hermine in Vienna, in which she added the warmest greetings for Ninon. Soon Ninon was to start her art history studies at the University, and Mizzi would attend some extra-mural lectures. That was the era of Max Dvořák, with his concept of intellectual history, and his detailed work on the Italian Renaissance, together with Hans Tietze, a specialist in art conservation.

Lena went to some lectures by Professor Julius von Schlosser, famous for his special study of art in the Middle Ages. She recorded a series of his public lectures in her diary entries for the 7th May, and the 4th and 18th June 1929.

Schlosser must have left a deep impression. Twenty-five years later she mentioned him, after seeing Benvenuto Cellini's Salt Cellar at the National Gallery in London. With her encyclopaedic memory she related some of the details of Schlosser's description of the creation of the masterpiece: the moulding of the model, the gold casting, the workshop of the goldsmith, the master and his assistants, the polishing of the metal, the delicate repetition of foliage decoration.

The Cellini was the star item in the exhibition 'Art Treasures from Vienna'. Lena was not the only visitor who left the gallery with bitter-sweet memories. For the many art lovers who had fled the city, it was a Wiedersehen with Cranach, Dürer, and with the Baroque glory of the Imperial Collection.

Walter had a distinguished war record, serving on the Russian front. With his engineering skills, he had been attached to motorised, even airborne units. He was taken prisoner by the Russians and after his release and return to Poland, he came to Vienna to visit Ninon. She had told Mizzi all about her Polish cousin. She knew that Walter was hoping to meet one of her nice friends. She knew that he was looking for a wife.

For Mizzi, as she told me herself, the fact that Walter had been a prisoner of war in Russia had added an aura of sympathy and admiration, even before she set eyes upon him. When we talked about it years later, on one of my visits to Poland in the 1960s, she explained and summarised her feelings for Walter. "Es war Liebe auf den ersten Blick" (it was love at first sight).

Soon Ninon and Mizzi were linked by more than just affection, friendship and a bond of culture. They became distant relatives-in-law, following the marriage of Ninon's cousin Walter to Mizzi on the 17th April 1923. Walter was working as an engineer at a chemical plant in Upper Silesia, then in the newly created independent Poland. Krolewska Hutta (Königshütte) was only about two miles from the redrawn frontier and had been part of Germany until 1918.

The hinterland of her new home was the heavy industry of coal mining and iron and steel manufacture, a cultural desert so very different from the splendour of the Vienna Opera or the Burgtheater.

For Mizzi it was a transplant. She had to learn a new language. She would be separated from family and friends.

When war broke out, for Poland two days earlier than for the West, on that Friday 1ˢᵗ September 1939, Mizzi and her family, living so near to the German border, were instantly involved. Her experiences at that time, at the start, and for the next five and a half years, are so eloquently described in her letters and postcards. They reveal her courage and hope which sustained her and her family through unimaginable hardship and sorrow.

Ninon, now living in neutral Switzerland, married to Hermann Hesse, the author and future Nobel Laureate for Literature, provided an additional staging post, as some of the mail from Russia via Switzerland was quicker in spite of the detour. In any case she transcribed and forwarded to Lena letters that Mizzi wrote to Ninon.

With the outbreak of war, postal communications between Britain and the German western part of occupied Poland came to an immediate end. Mail to and from eastern Poland, soon to be overrun and annexed by Russia, three weeks later, was severely disrupted. Russia was still neutral, but even as a Western ally, after the German invasion in June 1941, letters in both directions took several months. Censorship was imposed, people were afraid to describe what was happening. For a period, overseas mail could only be posted from Moscow. But Mizzi found a way to entrust a letter to someone via Italy! It was posted on the 18ᵗʰ January 1940 (in it Mizzi remembers my birthday) and took a long time. Lena, with her secretarial exactitude, endorsed all incoming mail with arrival dates, this one for the 7ᵗʰ June, nearly five months in transit. Lena translated the letter from German in to English.

18 / 1 / 1940

My dear siblings,

At last I have the certain opportunity to send a letter to you, which makes me indescribably happy. I have sent you a telegram several times, and several times I have written via Romania, when that was still possible, but as I did not have any replies from you whatever, I had to assume that you also had not received anything...

...I will try to relate to you chronologically and briefly what we have lived through since 1ˢᵗ September. In detail it would fill volumes – perhaps a kind fate will allow me to tell you everything verbally. I will also leave out my feelings. Everything was terrible, indescribable, I would have to use a whole lot of superlatives.

Well, on the 1ˢᵗ September, at 5.30am, we were woken up by the noise of engines, but it was not until 10.30am, that we learnt from the radio that there was war. All day long we heard air raids on Cracow...

The family immediately went to Walter's relatives in nearby Wieliczka, as their own home in Chorzow was only about two miles from German frontier. However, on Sunday 3ʳᵈ September, the day Britain declared war, rumour swept Wieliczka that it would be evacuated.

...We started our feverish search for a vehicle. On Monday we continued to do so and there were the first terrible air raids on Wieliczka...

...As we could not get a vehicle for love or money, we set off at 8 o'clock in the evening on foot to Biezanow, 14 km, where an evacuation train was supposed to depart. We could only take with us the barest minimum, for each of us two sets of clothes, a suit or a dress, and a woollen jacket. We also packed two blankets, half a loaf of bread, and perhaps 200 grams of sausage. Hugo [Walter Unger's brother in Wieliczka] assured us that the provision of food and drink would be organised at all railway stations, and that we might perhaps travel for 24 hours, instead of the usual six to eight.

That turned out to be ten days, from time to time a loaf of bread, very often without water, in cattle trucks, during the day in sweltering heat, at night very often about nil degrees with numerous air attacks daily, with the dead and wounded all around us. Every day the tracks were destroyed by bombs, there were stops of up to ten hours, and one never really knew if one could go sufficiently far away from the train to relieve oneself, to fetch water or to the nearest village for some food. Countless people with us left behind. I've kept a diary of life on the journey. Four or five times we walked for miles, in order to get to transport which was standing further ahead, by day, by night, panting with our small amount of luggage – do you remember, Lene, I once wrote to you that I see us fleeing along country roads with bundles on our backs. That's how it was, or worse, because we always walked between the rails, stumbling over coarse gravel, over sleepers. How Walter could stand on this remains a mystery to me, even today. Finally, we arrived at 5 o'clock in the morning in Lwow, having covered the last ten kilometres again on foot.

They must have arrived in Lwow on September 13th. They were put up by Walter's relatives.

The backdrop of terrible events now unfolds with the siege of Lwow by the advancing German army, the simultaneous invasion of Russian forces from the East and Hitler's decision to leave the capture of Lwow to the Russians. Walter and Mizzi were right at the cutting edge of history.

The ideological enmity between Nazi Germany and Communist Russia had been papered over by their non-aggression treaty of the 23rd August 1939, which encouraged Hitler to invade Poland a week later. It contained a secret protocol, dividing Northern and Eastern Europe into Russian and German spheres of influence. Russia in due course would annex parts of Finland, and Latvia, Lithuania, Estonia and Bessarabia. But at the heart of the pact was the partition of Poland, not for the first time in her troubled history.

On the 12th September 1939, the day prior to Walter and Mizzi's arrival in Lwow, the German army had entered the outskirts of the city, but had been repelled by the numerically inferior Polish defendants. The family, in fact, managed to enter Lwow after their terrible ten-day journey from Wieliczka just a day before the complete encirclement of the general area by the German army.

The Polish forces fought back heroically, recapturing some of the German positions. And then, on the 17th September, Russia launched her attack on Poland from the east, and by the 19th September had

245

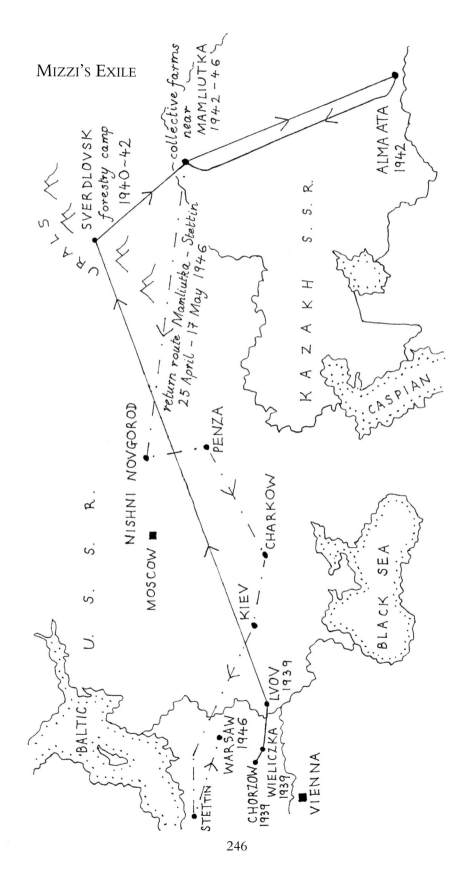

MIZZI'S EXILE

reached the outskirts of the city and joined the siege. On the following day, the 20th September, Hitler ordered General Runstedt to withdraw the German army and redeploy it in central Poland, leaving the Russians the final task of negotiating the surrender of Lwow on the 22nd September.

This then was the family's first week in Lwow, set against the cannonade of German artillery fire from the encircling hills and the rain of bombs dropped by the Luftwaffe on a defenceless city.

On the first afternoon I wanted to buy some essentials, especially shoes as we were practically barefoot − then began, at about half past three, in addition to the day-long air attack, an artillery bombardment − the siege of Lwow by the Germans had begun! I will not even try to describe to you the days that followed, all the other people in the house sat in the cellar. We were so hardened by the journey that we queued for water and bread − we were in fact frequently quite pleased about the shooting because people ran away from the queues and it was our turn sooner. The water pipes had been destroyed by bombardment and one had to queue for hours for a jug of water at the street hydrant.

No farmer came to town with vegetables or milk, no butcher opened his shop − we thought at the time that it was famine, but what it really was we only now know. Twice a day, again and again, sheltering in doorways, I hurried to town in order to pick up something for us to wear. But all shops were shut. Only later did I discover that everything was being sold by the back door. But by then it was too late.

As if by miracle, I obtained for myself a pair of shoes, for Walter, Stefan and Evi I had shoes made by a compassionate cobbler − at that time there were still Lembergers [citizens of Lemberg i.e. Lwow] *who felt sorry for us refugees, later when 1,000,000 were added to the 350,000 inhabitants we were universally cursed. In the course of events, I managed to obtain a winter coat for each of us, a pair of tricot trousers, four pairs of cotton stockings, two pairs of socks, six towels, three pairs of slippers (thin as tissue paper), flannel material for a dressing gown, dress material for Evi and for a skirt for me, and wool for a pullover. I worked it out at the time that this meant over 400 hours of queuing…*

…But imagine the state of our clothes, for instance our stockings. Imagine that since the middle of December we have heavy frost, an average of -15 degrees

centigrade, but for days it was -25 up to -30 degrees, and we are freezing in our summer clothes, absolutely undernourished. In the room, for the last month, it was no warmer than 13 degrees, in the morning, it is usually 8 to 9 degrees, we all have frozen hands and feet. Our staple diet is bread and potatoes, but I have not yet got so far.

On Yom Kippur [23rd September], in the afternoon, after all the streets had been torn up for days in order to build barricades and after victorious sorties against the Germans, the Russians appeared in town. That too, what these hours brought with them, I won't even try to relate.

At first things went reasonably well, that is to say electricity, gas and water, all of which had ceased to work during the last days of the siege, were repaired, there was more bread and the shops were forced to keep open. About 50 percent complied and with a lot of patience and stamina (see above) one could buy something, but in the shortest time all goods were <u>completely</u> sold out, partly because of the Russians, for whom everything here was very cheap, the Rouble was valued at par with the Zloty, in fact five times its normal value, and partly because of speculators, and more and more there were shops with completely empty shelves…

…The children go to the Polish Gymnasium [secondary school] but learn Russian and Ukrainian but no Latin. Walter is working with a group of engineers from Chorzow and Moscice on a project for a nitrogen plant south-east of Lwow, without payment, only the finished project will be paid for. But he has a workers' ticket and because of it he is not in danger, as are other refugees, of deportation to the centre of Russia or of eviction – the two greatest spectres of fear.

We arrived here with more than 6,000 Zloty, that would have been enough for a year for us. But first came the enormous price increase, and on 21st December the Zloty was declared invalid within two hours. At first one waited for days for this directive to be rescinded, it looked dangerously like a rebellion, but man is a more patient animal than one would like to believe, and somehow people managed to get hold of Roubles. We have sold father's gold watch and thought that for two months we would be free of worry.

Then round about the 10th [January], in an enormous new price rise, everything went up two or three times and with it nearly all food disappeared. We would be doing well if our money lasts out till the end of January. On the

Black Market, for quite a while, the dollar had traded for 150 [Roubles] and now stands at 350. For five dollars one could and still can live for a month. Only one has to have them. We still have pieces of jewellery, from which we can live for about three months, but what then? All the time we have held on to the thought: stick it out till March, then everything <u>must</u> change, but the nearer March approaches, the more unlikely this becomes. For the last two or three weeks, all refugees, Jews included, have been gripped by a fever: go back home. And then, like a cold douche, the news spread, all Jews will be sent to … [the next few words have been crossed out]. I don't really believe that one would send people away in Walter's state of health, but even so one cannot know for certain.

If the family had indeed returned from Lwow back to their home in German-occupied Poland, such a move would have had fatal results. But instead, the family were still trapped in Lwow five months later.

The long delays and uncertainty with letters in both directions were an ongoing worry. In desperation my father approached Sir Michael Palairet. He had offered his help at the time of the Anschluss when my father was in prison, although by then he no longer had diplomatic status in Vienna. After my father's release, Sir Michael Palairet asked his old friend Sir Orme Sargent at the Foreign Office to get in touch with the Home Office to facilitate immigration procedures for my father.

By 1940, he had been promoted to the post of British ambassador in Athens. He suggested that my father should send him a letter that he would forward to the embassy in Moscow for onward delivery. This was an unusual, personal, unofficial offer. The ambassador in Moscow Sir John Le Rougetel was another old friend of Sir Michael Palairet, bound by the network of Eton, Cambrdge and postings in Vienna.

My father duly wrote to Mizzi on 16th April and took the letter to the Foreign Office in Whitehall. Sir Michael put it in the Athens bag the very next day, anxious to help my father without any delay. That was at a time when normal mail took weeks or months. The immediate attention which he gave to Paul's request has to be set against the background of his official duties. Nevertheless he found time to help a stateless refugee – whose daughter Eva was a fellow student at Oxford of his own daughter Ann – not normally the remit of His Majesty's government. What a truly humanitarian gesture!

Two ambassadors, two embassies, the Foreign Office in London and a member of another foreign legation in Moscow were all involved. My father's letter to Mizzi and her reply were conveyed in diplomatic bags, but only just in time.

On 27th June, the Moscow embassy reported that Paul's letter of 16th April had recently been delivered. Yet just two days later on Saturday 29th June Mizzi and her family were deported to the Urals.

How many days prior to that terrible event must she have received the news from her brother in London and handed over her reply, which she knew for certain would reach those she loved? No record of what Paul and Mizzi wrote to each other survives.

The report from Moscow reads:

BRITISH EMBASSY,
MOSCOW:
June 27th, 1940
(148/3/40)

Dear Sir Michael

I am sorry that I have not been able before this to give you any news about the relations, now at Lwow, of Dr Paul Neumann, whose letter dated April 16th you sent on to me in the letter of the 17th.

We took advantage of a recent visit to Lwow by a member of a foreign Legation here (such visits are quite exceptional nowadays) to ask him to do what he could to have Dr Neumann's message conveyed to the Unger family.

The person concerned was able to ensure the delivery of the message and to obtain a letter in reply, addressed by Madame Unger to Dr Paul Neumann, which we are sending to the Foreign Office to be forwarded to him.

Yours ever

John Russell

for J.H. le Rougetel

Sr M. Palairet, K.C.M.G., British Legation, ATHENS.

Sir Michael Palairet added a postscript when he sent this on to my father. The few hand-written lines reveal warmth and concern, and must have been a comfort to my father during these difficult times.

Athens
July 11. 1940

Dear Dr Neumann,

I have just received this letter. I hope the inc from Madame Unger reached you safely and that you are all well?

Yours sincerely
Michael Palairet (c/o Foreign Office S.W.1)

Mizzi wrote a detailed account of her deportation and of life in the camp, in a letter dated 19th July 1940, addressed to her brother Robert in New York. At the time, I was told that Mizzi had entrusted it to someone who was leaving Russia. She had avoided censorship. It must have passed through Lemberg (Lwow), as becomes clear in an explanatory note, which Lena added when she sent it to family and friends: (original in German)

Robert and Lotte (a family friend) write from New York where the letter from Lemberg arrived, that they have tried everything possible to help, without success. According to an official statement by the Russian Consul, they have become Russian citizens as a result of their allocation to this collective farm, and are therefore subject to Russian law, including the prohibition to emigrate. How terrible for them! For us there is only one way to help them, that is within Russia. But we must proceed with the greatest caution, especially never to mention their names. If anything in connection with the smuggled letter seeps out, they will certainly all be executed.

Lena was anxious to publicise her sister's fate to the widest possible audience. She sent it to the High Commissioner for Refugees, receiving the following reply:

February 14th 1941

Dear Madam,

I have to return to you the letter from Soviet Russia you gave me with my apologies for keeping it such a long time.

This letter is most revealing, and I would welcome your giving it if possible appropriate publicity. In reading it I could not but think of the many Jewish refugees I know who fled from Nazi territory into Soviet territory in the blind hope that their fate would be incomparably better.

I remain at your disposal should any further advice be necessary to help your relatives out of Soviet Russia.

Yours faithfully,
Dr Kullmann
Deputy High Commissioner

Lena must have replied immediately and also enclosed a translation, because Dr Kullmann wrote again:

February 26th 1941

Dear Miss Neumann,

Many thanks for your letter dated February 22nd 1941, and attached English translation of the letter of your sister.

I shall get into touch with a friend of mine on the editorial staff of the Manchester Guardian as regards appropriate publicity.

Yours faithfully
Dr Kullmann
Deputy High Commissioner

He acted promptly and the newspaper showed immediate interest. It was decided that it would be more effective if the necessary explanatory introduction were provided by an English correspondent and my father asked his great friend Vera Craig, the Secretary of the Parliamentary Committee on Refugees, to send it in.

Just three months later, as a result of the German invasion, Russia became a firm ally of the West. Thereafter, any criticism of Russian conditions would have been considered unpatriotic in the joint war effort, and the letter probably would not have been publishable.

The letter was published on the 5th March and appeared under the heading:

DEPORTEES IN URAL MOUNTAINS
Plight of Polish Nationals Taken from Lemberg
To the Editor of the Manchester Guardian

Then followed Vera Craig's own introduction:

Sir, - I enclose a letter which has come into my hands, written by a cultured Jewish woman to her brother in this country. She and her husband lived in Lemberg under Soviet occupation until June of last year, when they were deported with thousands of other Jewish refugees to the Ural Mountains.

Printed in the newspaper was a condensed and edited version of Mizzi's account. Her original correspondence is reproduced in its entirety here, in Lena's translation:

19th July, 1940

By now you will probably know what has happened to us, for at last on July 7th we were able to wire to Lwow and to instruct our nephew to let Ninon know at once, so that the news of our deportation must have reached you via Switzerland.

Since July 10th we are in hutments in a concentration camp in the middle of a wood in the Ural, and if it were not so ghastly it would be grotesque enough to make you laugh. From June 24th onwards there was terrible excitement among the refugees in Lwow, for every night thousands of people were arrested. But mainly single men, so that the general opinion was that they would be sent into the army or to labour camps. On Friday, June 28ᵗʰ, the day when the Russians invaded Bessarabia, a blackout rehearsal was ordered, and tens of thousands who had slept out for days, quietly went to their beds, thinking that they would be safe for one night. Then at 1.30 a.m. there was a great noise in our street. We looked out and saw two or three vehicles in front of each house. I forgot to say that on the previous night three men had come and asked for our passports and when they heard that we had registered for return to Cracow, they took their leave quite politely. My husband and I sat trembling for about an hour on the edge of our beds, then the doorbell pealed and two militiamen came in and ordered us to pack our belongings. In reply to our question as to where we were being sent, we were told: to Germany; but one of the men, in an evident access of pity, seeing that I was taking so little with me, advised me to pack everything, as we were to go to the centre of Russia. My husband had a heart-attack which lasted for many hours, and I literally dropped all I had in my hands, so that the packing was actually done by the children. You must know that on April 20ᵗʰ about 20,000 people had been sent from Lwow to the frontier of Mongolia and that they had written terrible letters from there, but whatever they wrote falls short of the truth. Our landlady behaved very decently at the end and gave us two pillows, a blanket (we possess two blankets ourselves), a water jug, a breadknife and a few other trifles — but few set out with so little luggage as we.

We drove with other people in a lorry to a suburban station, where an enormous train was standing, consisting of about 100 carriages. We saw a number of our acquaintances. Mr. I. was in the next carriage to ours and is now here with us. In each carriage to right and left at a height of about 5 feet, planks were fixed, making two tiers — but as by an unlucky chance there were 36 of us in our carriage (in the other carriages they numbered only 21) some of us had to lie below without any air. Up above on each side there was one small window, and it makes a terrible impression when you see faces appear at it — but this I only noticed on our arrival as later we were never allowed to leave the train. The door was closed from the outside all but a chink of about 3 inches and if the train escort happened to be annoyed about anything — for instance if we called out for a drink of water — or if the escort went away for their meals, the door was entirely closed. The door on one side of the carriage was always kept closed and there was a hole in the floor which had to serve as an outlet for everything. Imagine 36 persons in that plight, especially in the terrific heat which set in on our third day. All day long on that first day friends came to visit those who were to be deported. Those in charge tried to prevent them from approaching the train and drove them away with the butts of their rifles and with their revolvers – but in spite of that they returned bringing gifts of food. During the night our train was moved into the central station. There we saw a number of transports similar to ours, from Lwow and from provincial towns – but how many refugees were deported and whether this went on all night or longer, we cannot as yet ascertain. And yet it is of highest importance for us, for the world would take more notion of the fate of half a million people than of ten or fifteen thousand.

From the very first moment we were treated like the worst criminals. Only one man was allowed to go and fetch water for every carriage and that only under military escort. The population of the places where the train stopped hardly dared to come near the train and if you were lucky enough to persuade a little boy to post a card for you, some bigger fellow would immediately take it from him and tear it to pieces. We received the first food on the fourth day and then only had meals every second day, mostly during the night, in between we got only bread, but the shortage of water was the worst. We hardly had enough for drinking and there was rarely a chance of any for washing. Soon everyone looked indescribable and on several occasions I was near to fits of frenzy, especially when no water at all was to be had or when my husband, whose illness grew worse from day to day, was not allowed to leave the train even to relieve himself. The journey was so agonizing that I cannot describe it. Added to all, there was the anxiety as to whether we should be taken to the place where the other people from Lwow had been sent. Not until we proceeded northwards from Ufa, did we breathe again. Two or three times on the way we got newspapers – that too is a dreadful trial here that we don't know what is going on in the world. We get a newspaper only once a week.

On July 9th at 6 a.m. we got out of the train. It was already unbearably hot at 6 a.m. still we were thankful to see a river and a wood and a few fairly decent wooden houses. We were all put up somehow and were allowed to bathe in the river and to wash ourselves as much as we wanted and there was glorious

255

drinking water. You could not buy anything there and we were not allowed to telegraph, nevertheless we all felt fairly confident.

On the following day 96 of us were driven to the camp barracks, where we are staying now. That is to say only old people and children drove, the others had to walk. My husband lay for hours, clinging to the luggage, until the whole of his left side was so bruised and sore that he could bear it no longer and walked for more than two hours. The vehicles had no brakes and the road when uphill and downhill incessantly, shafts and wheels broke, human beings and horses sank into the mud, everything breakable in the luggage was smashed and literally "racked on the wheel" we arrive at 11 o'clock at night. It was still quite light. The climate here is the strangest you can imagine – on the one hand almost tropical heat with merciless burning sun, swamps, myriads of mosquitos, horseflies and other stinging and biting insects, on the other hand the short, light nights of the extreme north. Only between 12 and 2 a.m. does it become slightly darker, though we are in latitude 57. The nearest towns of any size are 50 and 75 miles respectively from here, but the station is 8 miles away and there is only that terrible road to reach it and besides we are not allowed to leave here.

We are in a clearing of the wood; there are two barnlike buildings into which tiny cubicles are built, then there is a sort of barrack-hut with the kitchen and the so-called store, an unused stable and an unusable lavatory – that is all. The barracks are alive with bugs, so that if any part of one's body has not been bitten by a mosquito in daytime, it gets a bite from a bug at night. We all look like lepers. Our cubicle is 9 feet square and about 7 feet high and contains three beds for the four of us, as there is no room for a fourth. The beds are iron stands covered with raw planks and thin straw mattresses. On two of the beds pushed together I sleep with the children, my husband on the third, but since June 28th there has been no question of any real sleep. Since three days we have got a small table and a bench which we induced a carpenter to make for us – the rest of the furniture consists of a few nails in the wall and two shelves which our boy fixed up. Nor would there be room for anything more. The window cannot be opened, but luckily one pane of glass is broken, which admits air but also gnats. The doors would not close, but Stefan has made a good lock to ours with the padlock from our laundry-bag. In other people's rooms goats come during the night and eat everything they can find. We get our meals from the above mentioned kitchen, which is equipped for 20–30 people and therefore not adequate for 130. Our food consists of soup, barley, sour uneatable bread and tea, morning, noon and night – the same thing every single day, so that, however hungry you are, you can hardly swallow it, and even for that you have often to queue up for more than an hour. I make some extra coffee every day out of tins and yesterday I cooked some beans; but that means a lot of trouble. We have built a few stoves near the river which is more than 200 yards away and have to run to and fro all the time. But this river is the only good thing here, for however tired one is after one's work, one is refreshed after a bathe in the river. You do your cooking on the riverside, you wash yourself and your belongings in the river and you drink its boiled water. It is most dreadful that there is no other drinking water, a thing that I miss quite specially. At first many people drank this river water unboiled, but they gave it up after several cases of fever. Some people are lucky enough to scrounge a little milk, but I have not been so fortunate yet. It is true that I am in a constant state of exhaustion through lack of sleep and food and through the hard labour we have to do.

Already on the third day we had to start work. The men cut down trees, the women drag the boughs away and saw the trunks to pieces. In the wood the temperature is still higher than in the camp and the plague of gnats absolutely unbearable. Stefan and Eva offered themselves for work voluntarily (compulsion only begins from 16 years on) and are both first-class labourers. I am less first-rate nor have any ambition in this direction, besides which I am invalided since yesterday. On the way to our place of work there is a bridge which I daily refuse to cross, because it is so weatherbeaten and high and without a railing. I would rather take off my shoes and stockings and wade through the water. Yesterday we went a different way and had to climb over a large trunk of a tree lying across the river. It did not look dangerous, but it had got terribly slippery through recent rains. Hardly had I put my foot on it when I fell into the water and injured the base of my spine and fainted. Somehow they dragged me back up the high steep bank and to consciousness. But for a long time I could not see properly and felt sick, my pulse was very quick – I think it was slight concussion. Today I can of course not move and am at home and you owe this long letter to that circumstance. At the almost daily meetings which go on till 11 or 11.30 p.m. (in spite of our having to get up at 5 a.m.) it is again and again impressed upon us that malingerers may be punished with imprisonment up to 6 months.

But I think that it will be at least a week before I can work again. Mothers with small children, people over 60 and those seriously ill are exempt from work. My husband was at first forced to work by these beasts, in spite of three medical certificates – that was terrible. He suffers most of us all, especially morally but also physically. He only takes a minimum quantity of his drugs in order to make them go further; for years already he has not been able to sit on a chair without a back and here he has only backless benches or the hard bed in which also he cannot rest. In addition to cleaning up while I am working he washes up the crockery and even that is too much for him. It is of course easier for the children and they take everything more lightly. But Stefan looks wretched and Eva suffers most of us all from bites. Equipment here is a difficult problem. We have all bought straw-slippers under which the natives wear footpads of thick jute. The authorities gave us some rags of old pillowcases which are entirely unfit for the purpose. Those working with an axe are supposed to have special gloves, but the gloves have not yet arrived. And then we all should have overalls to keep the gnats and horseflies as much as possible from our bodies – but what do we wear instead? At the beginning the women wore bathing suits or sleeveless dresses on account of the intense heat and the men had the upper part of their bodies bare. Now almost all wear pyjamas and tie the footpads like puttees round the bottom of their trousers. I worked for the first two days in one of my two silk dresses, now I wear a pale blue nightgown and a white apron over it. Eva wears a pair of Stefan's knickerbockers and a shirt with long sleeves. Each one would furnish a comic picture and I keep longing for a film operator to make a "cultural record" and a great poet like Werfel to write an epic about it. How do we return from work? Plastered over with dirt and clay, smeared with resin, streaming with sweat – indescribable. I have given up the attempt to get the dirt out of the children's trousers, luckily(!) Stefan fell into the river to-day so he is comparatively clean. The straw-slippers, stockings and footrags have to be washed every day and never dry over night. My husband had his head shaved by one of our fellow-travellers on the first day for fear of lice – as he cannot shave his beard daily he looks a sight. Our eyes, ears, lips are swollen with mosquito bites, everyone groans and moans and curses his fate – that is what we look like.

How long, oh God in Heaven must we endure all this, how long can we endure it? If only they had fetched us by day and given us a military escort to prevent flight and told us we might buy what we wanted and where we were

258

being sent and what we should require – that would at last have been humane and merciful. Each one would have had the medicines he wanted and something suitable to wear (as far as things were still obtainable in Lwow) enough pillows and blankets, wash basins and kitchen utensils. But as it is I have to borrow a basin each day, have no ink, no notepaper and nothing appropriate to put on. And if we, God forbid, should have to remain here over the winter when the temperature is 50 centigrade below zero and not, as we are supposed to be, moved to another camp with light and stoves, with nothing but our worn clothes, which already last year proved to be an absolutely inadequate protection from the cold, then God help us!

In the Manchester Guardian, Vera Craig concluded:

In reading this tale of human misery one cannot but pity the thousands of Jewish refugees who fled from Nazi-occupied territory to Soviet Poland in the vain hope that things would be better there-
Yours &c., C.

Vera Craig dated her letter March 1ˢᵗ and signed it just with the initial C. She left out her full name and address. She was, after all, a public figure writing in a personal capacity. She did not want to use her official, headed notepaper. She was anxious that the publicity which she was seeking for Mizzi and her family should not be thought to have been sanctioned by the Parliamentary Committee on Refugees. But even in a private capacity she was too well known. In view of the contents and the circumstances of her letter, the Editor granted her exceptional anonymity.

Lena sent a copy with a plea for advice to David Astor, newspaper publisher, editor of the *Observer*, philanthropist, and member of the prominent Astor family. As the son of Nancy Astor, the first woman to take her seat in the House of Commons, David was brought up in the aristocratic milieu of Cliveden, a gathering place for the political elite, but he had a lifelong compassion for the victims of oppression.

42 Belsize Square
London N.W.3
17th March 1941

Dear Mr. Astor,

I am not sure whether you remember me but I was very happy working for you for a short while in Lingfield last year. During that time I realised how much true sympathy you had with the suffering of people who were driven from their home through no fault of their own. I therefore confidently approach you with the story of the fate of my sister and her family.

When the Nazis invaded Poland they fled from their home, which was situated about 20 minutes from the German frontier to Lwow; and when the city was occupied by the Russians they as well as we over here hoped that the change would be for the better. For nine months they lived there under very difficult conditions; and one night in June 1940 they were packed into a train and sent to the Ural. How it happened and what befell them there my sister will be able to tell you much better than I could. I am enclosing translation of a letter which she succeeded in smuggling out of Russia. I just wish to mention that in the meantime my brother-in-law died and that my only wish is to get my sister and her children out of the hell as soon as possible. Relatives in Peru were able to obtain immigration visa for Peru for my sister and her children, but the difficulty is to get them out of Russia and I wonder whether you could possibly give me some advice on the matter.

Yours sincerely,

Lena Neumann

David Astor's reply was strikingly kind and generous:

23/3/41
As from 4 St. James' Square S.W.1

Dear Miss Neumann,

Your letter and the translation of your sister's letter have reached me today. I am deeply impressed and depressed by the latter. If you will please send me your sister's name and her address if you know it I could try to get the British Ambassador in Moscow to make enquiries about her.

I cannot think what I could do to assist her in getting to Peru. Please give me the particulars of your relatives in Peru. I don't think I could even send money to assist them as British subjects are not allowed to send money out of the country during the war. However I am enclosing a cheque for £20 to help defray the expenses you must incur in telegrams etc.

I hope you yourself are well and cheerful. Your sister shows in her letter such a marvellous courage and cheerfulness that I found reading it a real help and inspiration. I am sending it on to friends of mine to read as I think it a really fine example of human spirit and merit.

My best wishes to Billy [Lena's dog].

Yours David Astor

Lena's feelings when she received this sympathetic response can well be imagined:

42, Belsize Square,
London, N.W.3
26th March 1941

Dear Mr Astor,

It was extremely difficult for me to find the right words to express the deep appreciation and gratefulness I felt when I received your letter. Although I knew of course that you would sympathize with my sister's fate, the way you responded in complete and heartfelt understanding was far beyond anything I could have hoped for. I do not know whether to thank you more for your offer of active help or for the money you so generously sent.

I fully realise that nobody is able to get my sister out of Russia at the moment, but you may be able to get the necessary informations through the British Ambassador in Moscow..."

Of course Lena and my father Paul did everything they could to send money and food parcels to Mizzi, hoping that once Russia had become an ally of the West that the process would be easier. Lena immediately started her almost monthly consignments of clothes and food parcels, all carefully listed for their contents, nearly all stolen. Only very few food and clothing parcels via the Polish Red Cross arrived safely and it was not until after the war had ended that they were able to help substantially.

Lena, in her tireless but ultimately futile efforts to help her sister, approached the High Commission for Refugees set up internationally by the League of Nations.

> *High Commissioner for Refugees*
> *Under the protection of the League of Nations*
> *11D Regent Street, S.W.1*
> *October 2ⁿᵈ 1941*

Dear Miss Neumann,

Concerning Mrs. Fanny Unger and children, deported to Ural Forestry Camp.

At my request Monsieur M. Marlewski, the competent official in the Polish Foreign Office, has passed on the particulars about your sister and her family to the Polish Embassy in Moscow. In his reply he adds that the Polish authorities are already actively endeavouring to arrange for better living conditions for the number of Poles sharing Mrs. Unger's plight, but for the present he is obviously not in a position to give more precise details. However, he wishes me to be assured that everything possible will be done for Mrs. Unger.

As regards the sending of parcels to Polish citizens in Soviet Russia, it is suggested that you get in touch with the Polish Committee for Aid to War Victims, 89 Onslow Gardens, S.W.7. The parcel should not exceed five kilos in weight and should consist mainly of warm clothing.

Yours sincerely,

Dr. Kullmann

Deputy High Commissioner

Six months later Lena wrote another letter to the High Commission for Refugees, in which she set out again what had happened to Mizzi's family since the outbreak of the war:

42, Belsize Square,
London, N.W.3
Tel: Primrose 4250
April 13th, 1942

Dear Dr. Kullmann,

May I refer to our conversation today and enclose a letter to my sister – according to your advice I left the address blank.

Since you told me that your file concerning my sister has been destroyed you may welcome a brief summary of the case:

My brother-in-law, Engineer Walter Unger of Chorzow, was in a leading position in the State-owned chemical factory (P.F.Z.A.) Chorzow. When war broke out he, my sister, Mrs. Fanny Unger, and their two children, Stefan now aged 17 and Eva now aged 15½, managed somehow to reach Lwow in flight before the German Army. There they were allowed to stay until June 1940, when they were forcibly brought to a Forestry Camp in the Ural Mountains, the "Sverdlowskaja Oblast Ashtshytskij Rajon Afanasiewskij M.L.P., 59 Kwartel". The adventures of this journey are described in a letter which, as you may remember, was published by the Manchester Guardian and of which I enclose a copy. From June 1940 onward only very scarce news reached either us here or my brother in New York. My brother-in-law died in the Camp in October 1940, leaving my sister and the children apparently in a desperate condition. Of late the Camp seems to have been dissolved or else the people there put at liberty to go where they wanted. My sister's last postcard shows the address: "Sverdlovskaja Oblast Ashtshiskij Rajon Afanasiewskij Rozjezd". But since she wrote that card almost five months have passed and I am unable to say whether they are still staying there or not. The postcards invariably ask for parcels with warm clothing, food and medicines and for money.

Needless to say that I should be exceedingly grateful if you could – as you kindly offered me – hand over the enclosed letter for dispatch through the appropriate channels. It would also be of great assistance if you could advise me whether there is any possibility of transferring a small sum of money by cable.

Yours sincerely,

Lena Neumann

P.S. : - I also enclose copies of two of your letters to me

A week later, Dr. Kullmann wrote to Lena:

Dear Miss Neumann,

This is just a line to let you know that the particulars concerning your sister have been sent to the Polish Ambassador in Kuibishek with the repeated request to do his utmost to trace Mrs. Unger and her children. At the same time your letter to your sister has been forwarded to Ambassador Kot.

Should you wish to send money to your sister, it is suggested that you should apply to the Polish Minister of Finance, Stratton House, Stratton Street, W.I., who will make all the necessary arrangements for you. You might mention that Monsieur J. Marlewski, of the Polish Foreign Office, knows about the case through me. Parcels of clothing, food, etc. are despatched by the Polish Red Cross, 33 Belgrave Square, S.W.1.

Yours faithfully,

Dr. Kullmann

Deputy High Commissioner

Little did Lena know when she received this letter that in fact Mizzi and the children had already left the Ural camp ten days earlier, embarking on a six-week journey that would include a futile round trip of 3,500 km from north Kazakhstan to the south near the Chinese border and then back again to north Kazakhstan.

A couple of weeks after they arrived at last near Petropavlovsk, where they were destined to spend the next four years, Mizzi wrote to her sister in English:

10th June 1942

My dearest,

I shall try to write to you a long letter – don't be surprised if there will be a lot of mistakes and strange words in it. Besides that I have had no occasion to hear an English word or to read one besides your letters, my physical state is such a bad one, that I am sure that I would make mistakes in my own language too. You certainly would not recognize me. I have become an old, thin woman, without teeth in my mouth, a little foolish, always tired, always sad and if it would not be for Evi's sake, I am sure I would be dead since long. Steve doesn't need me, he is quite grown up.

The only real pleasure in my life is the mail and in the last days I have had several letters, cards and telegrams. Your cards from 23rd July 41, 6th Aug, 31st March, telegrams from April sent to me from our old address and a letter from the 13th April which I got through the Polish Embassy. You certainly cannot imagine, what they meant to us. That you, Robert and B.A. are sending parcels and money to us, is wonderful, only that we have not got anything. Not come the first parcels of whose existence I know since January. The Polish delegate at Petropavlosk, to where we now belong sent me word where they are, besides I got a telegram from the embassy that they have money for me – and here we are, in awful need for everything and cannot get them. I have been imploring people, going to town, to send you a cable with our new address, I don't know if it has been done and if you have got it.

We have left our old place on April 10th and have arrived here after 6 weeks of journey on Whitsuntide Sunday [24th May]. We were living in a wagon (80 men or 8 horses) all the time, but it was not as bad as I supposed it would be. If I would describe you all our adventures, it would fill a thick volume. We intended to go to a little place near Alma Ata not far from the Chinese frontier, but they did not want us there and sent us back north, not very far away from where we started. We made a trip from about 5,000 kilometres and are now in Lylin (sic), 40 kms west of Petropavlovsk. I awfully wanted to stay at Mamliutka, that is a little town at the railway, where the only people are whose acquaintances I made in these last years which I like but as we absolutely could not find there a room and as it is there very difficult to find a kolchos, where I am again alone, as I was all the winter in Rosjud – the children are working in the kolchos,

Steve is far away, that he comes home only on Thursdays, to wash and to take fresh linen. He is working on Sundays too. Now he is ill and since 10 days in Mamliutka living at our friends and going to the hospital for injections. He has for the 4th or 5th time since war began, a very bad furunculosis and is getting now injections with autovaccine. He is very bad looking, very tall and thin and ugly, with nothing but a nose in his face. Eve is bad looking too, but not so much, she is very much anaemic, has always to do with stomach and belly, and I have greatest sorrow with her.

I am the greatest Untam [clot] you have ever known, every little wound, for instance, grows with me to a very bad thing that does not want to get well (have perhaps diabetes), my right leg is like an elephant's, so thick and swollen. I have always something, that me very much hurts, the latest probably a broken rib.

That I am good for no physical work, you can imagine. I have grown a very dressmaker and in earning the milk we need with sewing. It is a kolchos, so that you get the products you earn, only in winter, where all the harvest is over – so later on, all it will be probably not so very bad with us, as we have also planted so very many potatoes; but for the present it is very bad, as we have no more things to sell. We are waiting for the parcels as for the messiah, because we need the things to wear them and to sell them. On the whole it is here much better than in the Ural, the land is much richer, everything is cheaper and you get things much easier than there. Only with 'flats' it is very bad. You have to live together with the inhabitants in one room and they are used to use their in-laws as servants.

We have left our first flat a week ago, because the woman was too bad and now that we are living with a better one and cleaner one (without lice and pumaises [bed bugs]) we must leave her again, because her sister wrote that she is coming to live with her. It is nearly impossible to get some decent corner in a room (without bed of course, we are sleeping on the floor) and I don't know what will be. 3 years of war, nearly, that is too much for me and my nerves.

Sometimes there are stars of hope, for instance in the last time, some people have left for Persia, but I don't know why they should happen to send us too, if we shall not be wanted for somebody outside.

If this letter reaches your hands and if you will have again the opportunity to send me a parcel, do send, please, soap, medicaments and sewing things (cotton, needles, scissors, buttons, thimble and so on) besides we need everything to wear and to eat. Do write, where all of are working, what you are learning of our friends, Ernst before all, Oskar, Henny and so on, of our relatives, Stefanie, Muzzo, and if you can, send me some books, Polish or English.

I'm thinking day and night of you and of the time, when we shall be united for good.

Kisses for all of you.

When Stefan was old enough, he joined the Polish National Army, the army of liberation, in Russia. He never returned. I asked Mizzi if she remembered the last time she saw him. She spoke about that day as if it had just happened, instead of a quarter of a century earlier. He had been ordered to report to the recruiting office for his call-up and was about to leave home. Her voice rose in anguish as she continued: "Ich wollte ihn noch rasch einen Laib Brot zu Mitnehmen kaufen, aber wie ich wieder nach Haus gekommen bin, war er schon weg" (I wanted to buy him quickly a loaf of bread to take, but when I eventually got home, he had already gone).

When war ended, Mizzi and her daughter Evi were still trapped in Kazakhstan. For months, Lena tried to enable her sister and niece, all that survived of this small family, to come to England. Despite having to deal with thousands of refugees, Dr Kullmann once again found time to reply in detail:

High Commissioner for Refugees
Under the protection of the League of Nations
19, Hill St., Berkely Square. W.1.
March 19th 1946

Miss Lena Neumann
42, Belsize Square
N.W.3

Dear Miss Neumann,

I have pleasure in replying herunder to the various questions raised in your letter of March 9th.

1. The repatriation of Polish civilians from Russia seems to have started and 120,000 to 170,000 Polish Jews are due to arrive in Poland from Russia in the spring. The Polish Government are said to have stated that steps have been taken to receive these Jews but that, in view of transport difficulties, the transfer would not be completed before the end of next summer

2. The Polish Government owing to shortage of man-power does not easily grant exit permits to Polish citizens, who are ethnically Poles but does not raise any objection to the departure of Polish Jews. In fact, up to 20,000 Jews have left Poland since V-Day, mostly for the Western Zone. Whilst I am unable to foresee what the situation will be next spring, I am inclined to believe that this exodus will continue and that the Polish Government will not obstruct it in any way.

3. Sisters are not at present included in the family reunion scheme announced by the Home Secretary on November 12th, 1945. For the time being, the authorities have declared that they are unable to consider any applications from individuals whose relationship to persons residing in Great Britain is not specifically covered by this scheme. Although this may be altered in the future, it would be inadvisable to count on such an alteration.

> *Yours sincerely,*
> *Dr. Kullmann*
> *Deputy High Commissioner*

It was arranged with Oswald Unger, Mizzi's brother-in-law in Warsaw, to notify a certain Beatrice Wellington, who was working there for the United Nations Relief and Rehabilitation Administration (UNRRA) of Mizzi's arrival. Bertha Bracey established a valuable contact which allowed communication to be conveyed by diplomatic bag at a time when mail took weeks.

Beatrice Wellington was only too willing to help. She was a Canadian schoolteacher who had previously acted as a representative of a Swiss Quaker group helping Jews escape from Czechoslovakia.

Bertha Bracey reported to Lena:

> *6 West Hilll Court*
> *Highgate N6*
> *1st April 1946*

Dear Leni Neumann,

Miss Wellington writes from Warsaw: "I have already cast my net in search of the family of Paul Neumann, and will let you have some word each week of progress. I think there is little doubt that have been returned to Poland from Russia".

268

That may not be much consolation, but at least it is something to have enquiries started so much nearer the place where they are likely to be.

Yours very cordially

    Bertha B

A letter from Mizzi dated 17th April 1946 from Mamliutka, north Kazakhstan, joyfully announcing her impending return, is mixed with the sad reflections of the loss of the men in her family. Walter had died aged 52 in the forestry camp near Swerdlowsk in the Urals in October 1940 and Stefan was killed aged 19 in October 1944 crossing the Vistula in the liberation of Warsaw.

Mizzi's letters from this time on were composed in English.

17ᵗʰ April 1946

My dearest sister,

At last our time has arrived and we are going home! It is not necessary to describe you our feelings. Since the end of February, we know, that in March our oblast will be repatriated, but in vain we waited all the month and the first days of April – only on the 9ᵗʰ we got passports and on the 14ᵗʰ we went to Mamliutka – they told, that the trains will be prepared for us, that is for the way on (about 1,000 persons) and in the evening we shall go away. In the meanwhile, the train was not yet prepared and it is quite uncertain, if we have still to wait one or two days or a week or more. We are now living in a Kino [cinema], perhaps 250 persons with lots of luggage, are sitting on our trunks and are waiting. Eve and I have no room to ly [sic] during the night and are already very tired. There is of course no possibility to cook and so we are living only from bread and are afraid that it will not be sufficient for the way. But everything is easily to be born [sic], as it is now already certain that we are on the way home to you!!! Oh, Lene, if we only could get very, very quickly visas! How impatient I am, you certainly cannot imagine. We have still to pass a hard time (I have for instance torn boots and here is, as the snow is melting, water and mud to the knees) the 3 or 4 weeks in the train will be very bad for us, as we have very little money and not very much food (we got here bread and flour, a little butter and sugar and conserves) and the first time at home, with nobody to await us, will be hard too, but the thought that we shall be reunited with you, lets me bear everything easily. Today is my wedding day, the fifth time without Walter. And 20½ months have already passed since Steve's death. But Eve is living, my only comfort.

I kiss you,

    Yours M.

Four weeks ago we got two food parcels sent away in January from Tehran.

Once on her journey back to Poland, Mizzi wrote again to her sister in London.

May 2nd 1946

My Dearest,

You certainly received my letter, written in Mamliutka, about 10 days ago. We waited in M. from Palm Sunday until Easter Sunday for the train to leave, living worse than herrings in the Cinema. It was a real relief when we boarded the train, although we are 52 persons in a 5 ton wagon. We left M. on April 25th and are moving very, very slowly, i.e. we are standing for eternities in every station, so that only yesterday we reached the Gorsklowskaja Oblast (Nishni Nowgorod) about 4-500 km distance from Moscow. And now we are going southward instead of westward, first to Penza, and there are rumours that from there we'll have to go via Charkow and Kiew – the southern route to Poland – much much longer, of course than if we went direct to the West, only God knows why. You can perhaps imagine how we are living, dirty, full of lice, with about twenty children who are screaming all day long and with several old ladies who are worse than the children. During the day it is terribly hot because we are cooking on a little iron stove, you can hardly breathe and during the night it is freezing cold – and in spite of all that we are in high spirits, because now it will be only a few days before we reach home. I am, of course, wondering whether they will give us the permission to go to Warsaw – as I now know that Oswald [Mizzi's brother-in-law, a judge] *and his family are there I think it would be the best thing for us to do to stay with them for the next future. It will certainly be easier to get passports, visa etc., in Warsaw than in Chorzow. The thought, that it is not altogether impossible that we shall see you in 6 or 8 weeks makes me mad with joy; only with you it will be possible for us to recover a little, to forget a little and to begin a new life.*

As I wrote you already from M. I received there in the very last days your postcards dated 26.I., 14.II., 17.II (together with Ernst) and 20.II., in which you wrote Oswald's and Jasiu's addresses — what a stroke of luck! You had certainly written before that Eva [Mizzi's niece, the daughter of Paul] *had got a little girl, but I did not get those letters. I wrote to Eva to Paul's address and hope that she has received my letter.*

If some magic worked and made us 29 years younger and Eva Auguste would be in the little bed instead of Thesesa Sybil and all our life would still be before us — would you like to live it all over again, again go through everything you have experienced? I often wonder how it would be to begin again in summer 1913 (after my matrick) but with all the experience I have now. I frequently think that everything is only a dream and only these thoughts helped me to bear all these years. I am dreaming of the past and the future day and night and I am trying to forget the present. In the first weeks after my illness, after I came back from hospital, I told Evi very much of our former life, very much about the Ferdinandstrasse and our journeys — how lovely were those memories! Do you remember the coconut in Munich? And the Nazi, who attacked us in the Gallery in Brunswick? And the shop where we bought hats in Schwerin? I also taught Evi all the songs I know. But now I have to end.

Yours truly, M.

Mizzi and her daughter finally arrived back in Poland, and she wrote to Lena.

Poznan 19.5.1946

Since last Sunday already we are in Poland, but only today I got a post-card. I wanted to send you a telegram, but it was too expensive. We did not go to Warsaw nor shall we go to our former home, because people get relief only at the last station and we need that relief badly; I am nearly barefoot, Eva has torn shoes and our clothes are in an awful state. We have to get 1,000 zloty each and some clothes or shoes. Everything is terribly expensive so that 1,000 zloty is now less than 10 before the war. We are going somewhere in the environs of Stettin. Please _do_ prepare some old things, clothes, linen, shoes (No 40) and send them at once when you get our address. And do write if it will be difficult or not to get Visa. I am today in such a bad state, I have such a heavy heart, after all I have seen and heard, as heavy as six years ago. If we only could come to you very quickly! People here are dressed wonderfully, how can they manage when prices are so high? Oh, Lene, if only I could see you very, very soon, I am at the very end of my strength.

Yours, Mizzi.

Oswald Unger's factual report hardly conceals the terrible journey and the chaos on arrival:

Engineer Oswald E, Unger   Translation   25th May 1946

Dear Miss Wellington,

I have the honour to advise you that Dr. Paul Neumann's sister Mrs. Fanny Unger and her daughter Eva are now in Poland, beginning from 17th May. I got this information from Mrs Unger's letter which she wrote to me immediately upon her arrival in Poland. I have been ever since looking for her. She arrived from Kazakstan by a transport No. 3123 through Lukow, Poznan and was discharged at Starogrod at Pomorze / Pomerania / Western Pomerania /. I got this information but to-day.

I have sent my employee asking him to find her and bring her to Warsaw.

When she will be in Warsaw or after I get further news, I will let you know immediately.

Eng. Oswald Unger.

Lena was in touch with Bertha Bracey and probably asked her to include letters to Mizzi in the Warsaw Bag. At the same time, she must have suggested that they call each other by their first names, which Bertha Bracey immediately modulated to Leni, in a gesture of friendly familiarity.

By mid-June, Mizzi and Ewa arrived in Warsaw.

My dear Leni,

Of course, I am only too happy to drop all formalities. I am so very glad that you at long long last have the comfort of knowing that your beloved sister is safe with someone who will look after her and her young daughter. I know it is only one stage, but it is surely the most painful which is over.

Things must begin to show upward climb to better conditions, easier communications and more general opportunities for a civilised and gentle life for all sorts of people.

When your sister has had time to rest a little and get some clothing she may very well with her languages be able to get a post so that she can earn a livelihood.

I'm sure Miss Wellington will do anything she can. I will write to her myself and make some suggestions.

You have still to help and strengthen her by your strong faith and confidence.

My love and blessings

> *Bertha*

Lena at once approached Beatrice Wellington, who replied to Lena promptly via the diplomatic bag:

> *29th June 1946*
> *United Nations Relief and Rehabilitation Administration*
> *Mission to Poland*
> *Warsaw*
> *(By Warsaw Bag)*

Dear Miss Neumann,

Thank you for your letter of 24th June. I had already written to Bertha Bracey describing Mrs Unger's condition and had asked her to pass information on to Prof. Neumann.

As long as I am here, no longer than the 10th July, you may certainly write to Mrs. Unger via me. But after 10th July I suggest you write c/o Mrs Jean Hadley UNRRA, using the same address for her as you have used for me to date. Miss Hadley is my secretary. She will remain in Poland for some months yet will be glad to forward letters to Mrs Unger whom she has met. However Miss Hadley may not be able to send Mrs Unger's letters out to you as frequently as I do, as there may be certain restrictions on this shortly. I hope Mrs Bracey has passed the news on to you and your brother.

Yours sincerely,

Beatrice Wellington

The following week, Lena did indeed receive the promised news of her sister from her friend Bertha Bracey:

6, West Hill Court, Highgate, N.6.
July 6th*, 1946*

Dear Leni,

You will be glad to have the following extracts from a long letter from Miss Wellington, who apologises for not having time to answer your and Paul's letters which she was very glad to have. I had suggested that Friends who are working in Poland might be recruiting local staff, and possibly could find a job for your sister.

"...As regards Mrs Unger, I am discussing this with the Quakers, and with other voluntary societies, but I think it is possible that her best chance will be in UNRRA, and I have therefore sent her qualifications to the Personnel Division here. With a bit of pushing she should be able to obtain a job here, and I shall let you know as soon as I have further word.

In the meantime I have seen Mrs Unger on various occasions. We, i.e. Phillip Zealey, Bill Egerton and myself invited her to tea one day when Maurice Webb and David Jenkins were still in Warsaw, and had an enjoyable conversation with her about her experiences in Russia.

Dr Paul Neumann wrote, asking for information about his sister's appearance, etc. ... would you tell him that when she arrived here from Russia with her daughter, they had little or no clothing; as they are of Jewish extraction I put them in touch with Mr Bein of the American Joint Distribution Committee, who immediately provided them with two of everything. Mrs Unger is now decently clothed and able to go to see her friends. As regards her health, she suffers from heart trouble which she says is the result of her experiences in

Russia. Her daughter is in rather a bad state of health, i.e. she has greatly increased in weight owing to an unbalanced diet, etc and she has a very unhealthy appearance.

Mrs Unger looks strong....Now Mrs Unger is staying with her brother in law, Judge Oswald Unger, who has a modest residence in Warsaw. He is able to provide shelter and some food, but is unable to help financially, or to provide the requirements of the two people. I think Mrs Unger is a very fine woman. In spite of all her vicissitudes she maintains a cheerful aspect and has evidently got the best out of her experiences in Russia.

You may be assured that I shall give her what personal financial help I can here from my own resources, and will do my best to get her a post either with UNRRA or with a voluntary society.

As soon as I see Mrs Unger again I will write you..."

Forgive more now. I have found the first few weeks in my new office quite exhausting, but now I am beginning to get really keen and to enjoy it very much indeed. I moved into my own small set of offices on Tuesday, and though they are not ideal, we are settling down very nicely and I think I am going to have a keen and friendly staff.

    Yours affectionately,
      Bertha

Around the same time came promising news from the UNRRA in Warsaw:

5ᵗʰ July 1946

Dear Mrs Neumann

Herewith a letter from Mrs Fanny Unger. I gave her the papers which had come. She has now gone to the British Consulate.

It is possible for Mrs. Unger to get a post in UNRRA, in work as an interpreter in the Save the Children Fund here. But no one can offer her a job when she is undecided as to whether she is going. This should be decided first.

    Yours sincerely
      Beatrice Wellington

However, within a week came a terrible setback in Lena and Paul's doomed efforts to get their sister out of Poland:

9th July 1946
UNRRA
11A Portland Place
London W1
(By Warsaw Bag)

Mrs Lena Neumann,

I understand from Mrs. Unger that she went to the British Consulate here and was told that she was not in one of the categories eligible for entry to England. I am afraid that in these circumstances there is nothing we can do here as the Consul takes his instruction from London. The only thing is to press the Home Office further.

In the meantime there is no reason why Mrs. Unger should not get a job here – with one of the relief organisations. In my view she should settle down and do this temporarily.

She is in need of money; I don't know to what extent her relatives here help; but it would be helpful if you or Prof Neumann (sic) could send her some money. If we can do this in a letter addressed to me I could ensure that it reaches her. A few pounds a week would make a great difference to her and her daughter.

I have put Mrs. Unger in touch with Mrs. M. Anderson, Save the Children Fund, who needs a woman like Mrs. Unger in her work.

Do let me know if there is any other way you wish my help. I am leaving Poland very shortly and therefore shall not write again probably.

With good wishes
    Sincerely
        Beatrice M. Wellington

About a year later Ken Holloway, my sister Eva's husband, a lieutenant in the army stationed in Berlin, managed to visit Warsaw for two days. He was the first member of the family from the West to see Mizzi.

Dear Paul,

...I would have recognised her quite easily in a crowd, for although she has her own characteristics, of course, the family likeness is very strong, and in talking to her I was continually, as it were, catching echoes of Lena and you, and even Hansi. As to how I found her (I mean how she is) it is hard to give a true picture when one takes into account the fact that I never knew her before the war. But as near as I can I must give you an honest picture, as no doubt you would wish: and no doubt you will take into consideration the briefness of my visit and my shortcomings as an on observer! There is no need for me to recount to you her sufferings of the last seven years, and I can only say that those sufferings are written on her face.

Tuesday afternoon we walked a little through the main streets of Warsaw, and Wednesday, as I said before, we had a car to take us around. As you will have heard and read enough about the destruction there, I don't need to say much about it. It's clearly far worse than Berlin, and you can see that the damage is mainly deliberate - it starts from the ground up, not as in Berlin from the top down. The ghetto, of course, was razed to the ground. It would so happen that just as we passed a plot of ground where there were some mass graves (victims of the 1944 rising), they were opening up one of the graves for relatives to identify the bodies (I suppose) and give them a proper burial: a horrid sight. Nearby was a Jewish Cemetery, which oddly enough the Germans haven't touched (the Krakow one, it seems, was ploughed in): but of course it had been entirely neglected, and a number of graves had been opened by thieves [looking for wedding rings]. *In one of the main squares a piece of ruined colonnade had been cleverly and sensitively made into a War Memorial. It has on it the names of all the places where Poles fought – in the West as well as the East – and Mitzi (sic) says she goes there often, because the name of the place where her son was drowned is on it.*

All the best
  Ken

My father died in 1948, without seeing his sister again. My mother and Lena received a great number of condolences, and Bertha Bracey's letter to Lena remembers a dear friend:

6 West Hill Court
Millfield Lane, N.6
20.4.1948

My dear Lena,

When I got back from a conference on the South Coast late on Monday evening, I found your letter written on the 16th with the unbelievable news of Paul's death. I am so grateful to you for writing to let me know, for I should indeed have been grieved to hear the sad news indirectly, or to have telephoned to ask to speak to him.

It was a great joy to me to have Paul's friendship, and he always had something interesting and stimulating to give. There was a beautiful sensitivity about him and his approach to people and events that I valued very highly...

...I hope this will not mean that Hansi's studies will be interrupted.

Had I been in London I would have come to Golders Green on Monday afternoon to share in the service of mourning for his loss, but also of thankfulness for his life and what he gave so generously and graciously to his friends.

Please let me know, if there is anything I can do for members of his family.

I hope you have good news of your sister in Poland, for I imagine this loss of your brother will make you think more still of her.

Once more, please accept my grateful thanks for sending me the sad news direct.

Yours in sincere friendship

Bertha L. Bracey

Mizzi and Eva did not continue their journey to England. Eva settled in Wroclaw, to join a friend, one of four sisters. She was accepted as one of the family. It was there that she finished her secondary schooling, in just two years. She had not gone to any school since 1941. Later, she took her Magister degree and finally her Doctorate in plant physiology. Mizzi decided to stay with her, to remain in Poland.

Mizzi came to London on several visits. I also saw them in Wroclaw in the late 1960s and early 1970s. I was in the country to visit the Polish State Music Company, to commission music engraving on behalf of American music publishing firms.

CHAPTER 16

Robert

On that Friday 11th March 1938, a few hours after Chancellor Schuschnigg's speech of resignation, Robert travelled to Paris where he was joined by his wife Nessy a few weeks later.

The following year he came to bid us farewell prior to their emigration to the United States and visited Eva and myself in Oxford. He took us out to lunch. Like Bernard Altmann, who also took my sister and myself out to lunch earlier that year before his emigration to the United States, Robert chose the Clarendon Hotel.

I can't of course remember the conversation, which may well have included questions about my violin playing and Eva's possible boyfriends. I can't remember what we ate except that I was usually hungry at boarding school.

But sometimes a tiny vignette of memory unaccountably remains firmly lodged, and so it is that I can recall the moment when Robert paid. The waiter came and presented the bill. Robert produced a crisp ten pound note, the equivalent of several weeks' wages. He must have changed his French francs for pound notes of high denominations! This was the first time I had seen a ten pound note. It seemed to have a special aura as it lay there on a plate, both of value but also because of its unusual eccentric appearance. It was black and white, not in colour. The text was old style, partly in italics, graceful and serifed, partly bold and upright.

In a small footnote, the signed declaration from the Governor of the Bank of England to pay the bearer the sum of £10 on demand gave the note the overall appearance of a handwritten 18th century promissory legal document.

The waiter brought back the change in notes and an array of coins, hoping for a large tip. Robert leafed through the notes. Then he picked up the coins slowly. He was unfamiliar with the appearance of the currency, compounded by the fact that it was outside the global decimal tradition, those half crowns, florins, shillings and sixpenny pieces. He must have noticed Eva's embarrassment. After the waiter had departed with a generous tip, Robert turned to her and asked: "hätt' ich das nicht zählen sollen?" (Should I not have counted it?)

In 1939 he emigrated from Paris to New York and like so many others started again. He set up his office as a consultant on investment policy and currency markets. With his previous Vienna experience on the board of the Kreditanstalt, he had that entrée of credibility and expertise. After the war, his European past was a great professional asset in the financial world of international markets and the growth of a global economy.

By the time I saw him in New York in the late 1960s and early 1970s, when visiting American publishers in connection with my music engraving business, he had a splendid office just off Wall Street. In true American fashion, he had to have two first names, and therefore added his father's name Wilhelm to his own, calling himself Robert W. Neumann. It was that proud nameplate on the door, so near to New York's stock exchange, that symbolised his success and greeted me in 1968 on my first visit. Robert had the aura of a great personality. It was diverse, his Viennese roots intermingled with the culture of the New World. I remember sitting in his office. The phone rang and he talked for half an hour long-distance. It was clear from his conversation that he was speaking to the other person for the first time. Then, near the end, he said, "call me Robert".

I can still hear his words. His transatlantic Viennese American reminded me of my father's so very different Viennese English. The accents were worlds apart, but were tinged with a familiar timbre: the Neumann voice, the sound of brothers.

He was blessed with a fabulous memory, a mental filing system on which he depended so much professionally for future reference.

He never retired. Already well over sixty, long past it on Wall Street, he became a father figure and regarded the young men who came to him as his 'children'.

I used to stay with Robert at his hotel, the Alamac west of Central Park. He had been a resident there for more than twenty years, ever since his separation from Nessy. There was nothing personal in his room. The only object still left from Vienna, was a portrait etching of Arnold Rosé playing the violin. I inherited the picture, which now hangs in our hall, and I am reminded of Robert as he stood in front of it, as he said that Rosé's right wrist seemed to be so very arched. "That's how they used to play," I said.

Arnold Rosé was the leader of the Vienna Philharmonic Orchestra for fifty-seven years, since he was 18. His string quartet occupied a prominent position in the musical life of the city.

Robert remembered the first time he heard them. It was a Christmas present, he said, for him and Lena. His mother Hermine was keen that he should hear good string playing and hoped that it would encourage him to practise. The age of the gramophone had not yet got underway, and concerts were eagerly anticipated.

It took place, as recorded in Lena's diary, on December 19th 1912. Lena was 22, taking her 14-year-old brother to hear four Beethoven Quartets. The programme included his last Quartet, Op. 135. Beethoven gave the second movement a metaphysical title: *Der schwer gefasste Entschluss* (the decision made with difficulty) and, in a heading, set to music, he asks a fateful question and gives a categoric answer: "Muss es sein? Es muss sein! Es muss sein!" (Must it be? It must be! It must be!).

The timeless universality of Beethoven's clarion call could so well be applied to the statesmen of Europe. Soon they would plunge the world into war, and the young Robert would join millions of others on the battlefield.

After the Anschluss, Arnold Rosé came to London and lived with an old friend of Lena. And thus it was, in 1941, when I was still at school, that he gave me a few violin lessons. Once, when I arrived, I saw the first violin part of *Götterdämmerung* on his music stand. He would be reliving bitter-sweet memories, which tied him to the Opera House. He was there during Gustav Mahler's directorship and witnessed his years of triumph. Typical of the fabric of *fin-de-siècle* Viennese Jewish society, there was also a personal connection which linked the two men. Arnold Rosé was married to Gustav Mahler's sister, Justine. His daughter, Alma, was named after Gustav Mahler's wife. She was a good violinist in her own right. Her father had taught her well. In 1932, aged 26, Alma Rosé founded the women's orchestra, *Die Wiener Walzermädeln* (the Waltzing Girls of Vienna). The ensemble undertook concert tours throughout Europe.

Once again, recollection and explanation reveal the dark side of the twentieth century. In 1947, the Vienna Philharmonic visited London for the first time after the war. Refugees besieged the artists' entrance at the Albert Hall and the stage door at the Royal Opera House, to see old faces, or to make new contacts.

Several times I met one of the violinists and we talked about Rosé, who had died the previous year. He described the scene at the first orchestral rehearsal after the Anschluss. Rosé, as Konzertmeister, took his usual seat at the first desk. And then he was tapped on the shoulder and told that he no longer led the orchestra. Soon he would leave Vienna and go into exile.

A tragic reunion with Rosé, or perhaps his refusal to see any of his former colleagues, did not have to be envisaged. He had died the previous August.

A delegation from the orchestra paid their posthumous homage at the crematorium. The visit is described in their published account 'Die Wiener Philharmoniker – ein Stück Weltgeschichte' (A Piece of World History) Edinburgh – London 1947. 'Einem Herzensbedürfnis pietätvollen Gedenkens galt unser Besuch und die Kranzniederlegung vor der Urne Arnold Rosés, dessen vorbildliche künstlerische Haltung uns unvergessen bleibt.' (A heartfelt desire of pious remembrance prompted our visit and the laying of a wreath at the urn of Arnold Rosé, whose exemplary artistic stature will for us remain unforgettable.)

How different are these words of contrition from those spoken nine years earlier, at the time of the Anschluss.

The evocative anonymous plural, unser Besuch (our visit) included Wolfgang Schneiderhahn, representing the orchestra as its leader. It was he who replaced Arnold Rosé. He was an old Nazi, still there after the war, like so many other musicians. I met one of the violinists, and we talked about Schneiderhahn's past. One day, he said, a high ranking Nazi official came and addressed the orchestra, and told them that they all had to join the S.S. It was a demand for total collective membership to enhance the cultural glory of the Reich. Nobody refused.

"Sie haben ihm einen Zettel hingehalten, und er hat halt unterschrieben. Wir haben bei S.S. Veranstaltungen gespielt. Es wurden Reden gehalten. Niemand hat zugehört." (They gave him a piece of paper to sign, and so he signed it. We played at S.S. functions. There were speeches. Nobody paid attention.)

Rosé's daughter Alma did not manage to escape and perished in Auschwitz. On January 27th 1945, the Russians liberated the camp, and the news of unimaginable genocide swept across the world. Alma, at one time, had been put in charge of the camp orchestra, *Das Mädchenorchester von Auschwitz,* which had to play twice a day at the main gate, as prisoners left and returned after a day's heavy labour. They had to provide music at S.S. functions and, according to some reports, played during the selections for the gas chambers.

A fortnight later, on the 10th February, Arnold Rosé alludes to his grief in a letter to Lena's lifelong friend Mathilde Hollitscher (Sigmund Freud's daughter). Mathilde's husband, Robert Hollitscher, was a violinist. From time to time, there was chamber music in the Freud home in Hampstead, and Mathilde had of course heard that I had become a pupil of Arnold Rosé. After Robert Hollitscher's death in 1959, she gave me the letter and told me to look after it. I put it into the framed Rosé portrait, into one corner where it would not obscure the image. As I walk past it I see him play with a silent gesture of musical eloquence. And then I see the small piece of paper with its message of unspoken grief:

10 febr. 45

Sehr geehrte, liebe gnädige Frau,

Mit besten Dank sende die mir geliehenen Bücher zurück. Sie haben mir über manche Stunden hinweg geholfen.

Sobald gutes Wetter eintritt will ich bei Ihnen vorsprechen und mal hören was mein ehemaliger College auf der Geige treibt! Mit herzlichen Grüssen an Sie Beide

Ihr sehr ergebener
    Arnold Rosé

(Dear Mrs Hollitscher,

With many thanks I am sending back the books which you lent me. They helped me to live through certain hours.

As soon as good weather arrives, I want to present myself to you and hear what my former colleague [Robert Hollitscher] *is up to on the violin! With warmest greetings to both of you.*

Yours very sincerely,
    Arnold Rosé)

In 1972 I was in New York when Robert had a heart attack and had to spend several weeks in an intensive care unit at the Mount Zion hospital on Fifth Avenue. Every day I went down to Beaver Street to collect his mail. He was strictly forbidden from doing any business, but he told the nurses that he would die without a telephone. At that time many of his 'children' sent personal messages of good wishes.

Robert passed away a couple of years later, his death marked in a newspaper announcement:

7th January 1974

ROBERT W. NEUMANN

Robert W. Neumann, a consultant on the foreign money-market, most recently to the Cummins Engine Company of Columbus, Ind., died yesterday in Mount Sinai Hospital. He was 76 years old and lived at 154 West 71st Street.

Mr. Neumann had been in banking in his native Vienna and in Paris before visiting here in 1939 to see the World's Fair. Hostilities broke out in Europe, and he remained, becoming a consultant on currency problems in international trade.

Surviving are his widow, Agnes of Kassel, West Germany, and two sisters.

The three eulogies at Robert's funeral on the 9th January 1974 so eloquently describe his composite persona, his profound excellence and his human qualities. They complement each other to build up a fuller portrait.

Rex A. Sebastian, Vice President, Dresser Industries, Inc., Dallas, Texas, spoke first.

When Libby asked me if I would make a few remarks about my dear and close friend, Robert Neumann, I said I would be honored to do so.

I know I speak not only for my family and myself but also on behalf of Robert's friends and associates all around the world.

As I reflected upon what I wished to say, a jumble of thoughts and memories entered into my mind. Therefore I found it extraordinarily difficult to organize my comments.

I decided, however, to speak from my own experiences with Robert, which were – thank God – both personal and business.

Robert and I were close friends from almost the first day we met in the early '60s. In saying this, I recognize that my friendship with Robert does not go back as far as his friendship with many of you here today – and this is my only regret.

Robert and I quickly established a relationship based upon mutual respect one for the other – and certainly on my part of admiration for him.

Although Robert and I were together often, unfortunately, as is too often the case between busy men, most of our conversations were by phone. However, even that provided a consistent highlight of any given day because his first words to me were always: "Hello, Rexy boy!".

This greeting was indicative of Robert – in that he looked upon me, and upon many others here today, almost as a son.

How would I describe Robert Neumann? First and foremost as a true friend – a friend who would do anything within his power for his friends.

Robert was a proud man and he had good reason to be. We all know of his professional excellence – he was certainly a foremost expert in the fields of foreign exchange and foreign finance. At the same time he had compassion and concern for others. Yet, he was often amazed at the honours and recognitions which were bestowed upon him.

Robert was a man I could count on for sound advice – and, afterwards, there was a continuous concern on his part until the situation that I had raised with him was properly resolved to his own satisfaction.

Robert was an entirely competent man. His original introduction to my own company was a situation involving several millions of dollars over which Robert was given complete discretion and control. He handled this situation extremely well – just as he did in many subsequent situations for us.

Robert was a man with real courage of his convictions. I referred earlier to the phone conversation ….

Rex Sebastian was followed by a Mr Schacht, who had known Robert much longer:

Robert was a man whom most of us have known most of our lives.

He was a man who led us unselfishly through the worlds he knew so well. He had two worlds – the world of international finance and the world of human beings – worlds which often, but not always, came together. He taught all much about both.

In the world of finance, he was unique. As a friend said — he was a true practising economist, but he would never admit to it. He helped to see the world through the disruption of the 20s, the tragedy of the 30s, the ruination and reconstruction of the 40s, the hope of the 50s, the sobriety of the soaring 60s, and the uncertainty of the 70s. Through all the turmoil and change, he never lost balance but continued to learn.

Currency was life blood to him — he had the wisdom and the insight to know what was happening and the courage to know that the unthinkable needed to be contemplated.

Some will say this treasure chest of knowledge has now passed. The most insightful people will realise that Robert's sole mission was to make his knowledge and judgement available to those who would listen.

For although Robert thought of himself as a "mere currency peddler", he taught us all much about business in general.

He taught persistency; those who sought his counsel had best listen. He taught insight — what does it mean and how does it affect us — there was never a we or they, only us. He taught about the world and how it operated and why we had better be interested in things like anchovies in Peru. The only mitigation in his passing is that he taught so much to so many — many others with the same experiences never realized the obligation of education that falls to those whose life-long experiences are unique.

Robert's other world was that of people. He taught us about loyalty and courage. He suffered through our disappointments with us and congratulated us on our successes. When loyalties conflicted, he had the wisdom to place his confidence in the individual. He taught us that emotions are to be cherished and shared — not hidden. He knew that friendships meant to accept as they were and not for what he wished them to were [sic] — he expected the same in return.

He was many things to many people. But he gave totally of himself, because he believed totally in his friends. He has led us all to many places — introduced to all he knew — proudly.

We always wish those we love the most would live forever: our joy is that we were given so long together.

The last speaker, whose identity is not recorded on the transcript, mentions Robert's office on Wall Street to which I myself went on several occasions. It ends with that tinge of panache and rhetoric so dear to Robert:

I am privileged to say a few words about Robert Neumann. I find it difficult to say solemn things about him on such a solemn occasion as this. Somehow it seems inappropriate to enumerate the usual catalogue of traditional virtues. Robert was never a champion of the restrained or the commonplace.

From his friends and business associates Robert received respect and admiration. But from his children – and there are many of us in this room today – he evoked all the emotions that children feel for their parent – a mixture of awe, respect, obedience, rebelliousness and sometimes even pique. But above all, we were bound to Robert by an unbreakable bond of love. No matter how far and how often it might be stretched, we were inexorably drawn back to him.

Like a good parent, Robert taught his children well. I often believe we learnt more at that battered and scarred old classroom on Beaver Street than at the famous universities from which we so innocently emerged: Yale, Stanford, Amherst, Princeton, Harvard and many more. Often it was slow going and Robert was not always a patient teacher. How many times have you heard him say,

"Children, what am I going to do with you?"

Now his children must do it for themselves, without him. But I have faith that because of him, his boys from places with strange sounding names like Indiana, Kentucky, Illinois, Texas and Ohio, will do his memory proud when they stand face to face at the ends of the earth with representatives of what Robert would have called an older and more sophisticated order.

Because what Robert finally taught us was toughness and self reliance. Above all, he was a fighter – no quarter asked, none given – no effort too great to be expended in protecting the interests of his beloved children and clients. Wrong sometimes, yes. Extravagent and difficult, yes. But a quitter – never! No man was ever a truer friend, a firmer support in need than Robert Neumann. He was a lion – noble, proud, fierce and strong. In this uncertain world, of one thing I am sure – that when Robert's heart stopped beating, as it did for that other Great Heart in the Pilgrim's Progress – "all the trumpets sounded on the other side".

Robert's funeral is so eloquently described to Lena in a letter of condolence. Dated 31ˢᵗ January, it is written by George Newlin, a business colleague and a close friend who must have heard a lot about Lena over the years and felt he had to write:

Dear Miss Neumann:

I have never enjoyed the privilege of meeting you, but since 1960 I have enjoyed the privilege of knowing your brother, Robert.

He has been so much a part of my life since then that, while I am not an overly sentimental person (my children think I'm a bit cold and overly intellectual), it is just now sinking home to me that never again will I hear his voice on the telephone; nor will I again hear him say "W. George Newlin, are you <u>sure</u> you did not have a Jewish grandmother?", when he wanted to praise some idea, comment, or question that I had stated.

To my mind, Robert's funeral was the greatest tribute I have ever seen paid to a man. People came from San Francisco, Dallas, Texas, Elkhart, Indiana – to say nothing of his friends who came to New York from our little town of Columbus and from New York where he lived.

All came out of love, affection, respect, and a great need to say "good-bye" to a wonderful and very warm human being.

For me, one of the most touching things was to see the reaction of my children who were closest to him. My daughter was terribly upset, and I know she wrote Libby Shub a very warm letter as well as one to her mother and me.

Earlier in my note, I quoted Robert saying, "W. George Newlin." Actually, as you will see by my signature, he had reversed my "given" names. I like to think that Robert sensed the fact that I preferred my second name to my first. He is the <u>only</u> person who ever reversed them.

I'd guess it is not likely that our paths will cross. But I wanted you to know what a place in the lives of others your brother had and how much he will be missed by "W. George Newlin" and his other friends in Columbus, Indiana.

Sincerely yours,

George Newlin

Fortunately for Robert, collective praise and recognition were not entirely posthumous. For his 75th birthday, on the 16th August 1973, Elizabeth Shub, a long-time friend, organised a surprise party. Robert describes it in a letter in German the following day to various members of the family.

August 17th 1973

Dear Lene and dear Anne,

Dear Schmunz [Mizzi] *and Eva* [Mizzi's daughter]

Dear Nessy

I thank you all from my heart for your dear and good wishes. Who should I thank especially? I don't really know. Nessy, because I received a sign of life from her? Schmunz and Eva and Hans, because they have not forgotten me? Anne for her very kind letter? Or – last but not least – Lene for her absolutely enchanting letter for which I immediately thanked her over the telephone. Anyway many many thanks.

…Yesterday was a great day. 18 Out-of-Towners conspired with Libby, I mean of course clients, and friends, came to New York, champagne, caviar and lots of gifts. Something else came in the last weeks, under the heading unpaid expertise, but which has given me much pleasure: five weeks ago I was invited to Chicago by the big bankers, by Price Waterhouse etc, to a luncheon in my honour, and I spoke for nearly two hours after luncheon.

And now I have been invited by Harvard University in Cambridge near Boston, to make a speech and subsequently hold a seminar.

And now to repeat, unpaid expertise but a lot of fun. All that should have happened to me 20 years ago.

Libby Shub sent us an audio cassette of Robert's talk at Harvard. It is wonderful for me to hear his voice, so familiar in its timbre to my father's, with its Viennese tonal substructure, now subsumed by American English. He treated his audience with anecdotal treasures and autobiographical vignettes.

One of my special memories of Robert took place in New York. He had just been to Rostand's Cyrano de Bergerac, which the Comédie Française had brought over from Paris. He was full of it, and quoted one of Cyrano's speeches. And now, as I think of the essential Robert, I borrow the last words of the play. Cyrano is dying. He reflects that later that day he will be in the presence of the Almighty. In spite of all earthly tribulations he will take with him one single thing. No one could have deprived him of that: *mon panache.*

CHAPTER 17

A conversion to Catholicism

On arrival in England my mother found that her old life was no more. She looked for a new religiosity which Judaism could no longer give her. She told me that earlier, in Vienna, she felt that the traditional social conventions of secular Judaism were gradually proving inadequate for her awaking life of the Spirit. For my mother, the trauma of being a refugee was fundamental. She sought her answers in conversion, by entry into the successor world of Catholicism, living in the Judeo-Christian tradition.

My mother's spiritual life was wonderfully balanced. For her there was no contradiction, only continuation. The Judaism of her childhood changed to token conformity, followed by uncertainty. Years later she told me that she felt ripe for conversion when her inner spiritual climate became troubled and full of turmoil. My mother throughout retained her belief in God and never considered becoming an unrepentant atheist like her older sister Bertha. She spoke of the shock of being uprooted, which made her question the fabric of her existence, the meaning of life, eternity, evil, redemption, salvation. She faced the sudden collapse of the old world, literally in a few minutes on the evening of the 11th March 1938. A few days later my father was imprisoned with the terrible possibility of his deportation to the Dachau concentration camp, at that time in 1938 the principal destination for Jews from Vienna. For nearly all of them it was to be their final station. We thought of my father all the time, hope cruelly interlaced with uncertainty, fear and despair. These weeks changed my mother forever.

I remember the day she told me that she had become a Catholic. The war had started. It was 1939 and I had come home for the Christmas holidays. I was at Magdalen College School, a boarding school in Oxford. We were alone in the drawing room. I was sitting in the large 19th century winged armchair, and she was closely opposite on a low Biedermeier settee. We had talked but suddenly we were silent. My mother looked at me, her face intense with the excitement of the impending revelation: "Ich bin katholisch geworden" (I have become a Catholic) she said. She leant forward and her hands took the hand on my lap and clasped it in a husk of protection and love, in the natural age-old gesture of blessing. And then she spoke of her great change, how she had received help and instruction from the Church and how deeply my father felt her inner life to be sacrosanct.

I asked her what she experienced at the moment of conversion. I was only fifteen but the love for my mother made me mature, anxious to understand the mystery of grace. She said that faith could not be willed. Belief was not the result of logical deduction. It was all about feeling the love of God and being able to pray, not demanding or rogatory but giving oneself. The moment came, she said, when she knew and recognised her ultimate certitude, for which she had longed, for which she had striven but which she could not bring about on her own. We embraced and kissed each other.

Her baptism took place on the 21st November 1938, only a few months after her arrival in England. On the certificate, made out five years later, the name of Max is entered under her father's name. My mother told me that she was too embarrassed to give the name of Mayer. "What sort of name is that?" is the question she wanted to avoid. The certificate has the timeless grace and eloquence of Latin used in official declarations:

Testimonium de Baptismo
Hisce praesentibus testificor, diligenti facta Investigatione, Teresiam Neumann natam die 18 mensis Augusti anni 1889 filiam Max et Clara

Braunthal (olim Gelles) in hac ecclesia Stae Mariae Assumptae apud Warwick St. London W1 baptizatam fuisse die 21 mensis Novembris anni 1938.

Datum die 10 mensis Decembris anni 1943

Petrus Harris

Min. Coadj.

This small piece of paper, with its perforated edge, torn out of a block book with numbered pages, this certificate No. 19, has printed Latin text, with dotted spaces for the entry of personal details. The document is used for either sex. Where the Latin requires masculine or feminine endings, the first part of the word is printed out, with the necessary modification to be added by hand. This Father Harris accomplished with a beautiful flourish of his steel pen and Indian ink. He highlighted more than two thousand years of Classical grammar. He wrote it. He spelt out the woman in it.

My mother had the most profound guidance throughout her Catholic life. She was introduced to the Dominicans and was helped by several remarkable fathers, eminent theologians and pastors. A few years after the war, my mother was admitted to the Third Order of St. Dominic. The Dominican priory is situated at Woodchester near Stroud, in Gloucestershire. It was there that my mother signed the vellum book of the Tertiary Order, it was there that she promised to fulfil her new obligations and it is there where she lies buried in the churchyard overlooking the beautiful Cotswold countryside. What a long journey, nearly ninety years, from her birth in the old ghetto of Vienna, in the Leopoldstadt, to her final resting place with the Dominicans in the heart of England!

Several Dominican Fathers played a special part in my mother's life. She attended Dominican retreats, days of prayer and meditation, of clarification and reflection. They were held in priories, convents and study houses in various parts of the country, were residential and usually lasted two days. A Father would officiate, he would pray, he would preach, he would lecture. For my mother, the retreats were a major part of her religious life. She regarded them as a withdrawal from the outer world into her inner sanctum. They were signposts on her quest for salvation. She made copious notes and I have selected some of her transcriptions for the period 1947 to 1949.

My mother told me on several occasions what a privilege it was for her to listen to the Fathers. The subject matter for her was deeply personal, the age-old mixture of intellect and faith, of philosophy and emotion. Her exercise books may look like college lecture notes, but they are passports to share her private thoughts, her intimate responses. Frequently she wrote important words in capital letters and often whole phrases, or small paragraphs were indented to highlight a heading. She followed the flow of the speaker and paragraphed her texts. She underlined words when they were spoken with emphasis. In fact her typographical and editorial interventions are remarkable. Many phrases are verbatim transcriptions.

Her handwriting, even and flowing, reminiscent of late nineteenth century calligraphic discipline, immediately reminds me of her in all her aspects. It is her exclusive seal, her unique graphic gesture.

Here was my mother, anxious to confirm her new faith, thirsty for the grace that would consummate her piety.

In November 1947, Father Richard Kehoe conducted a retreat at the Woodchester Priory. He spoke about 'Men of the Spirit', the history of the Judges, the great prophets, passages from Isaiah, Samuel and Ezekiel. The following day, marked Sunday in my mother's book, the theme was man's relationship to God, St. Augustine, the nature of temptation, the evil spirit, miracles as signs of God's work (the deaf hear, the blind see, the dead awaken). Father Kehoe dealt with the instinctive knowledge of God from within oneself. According to my mother, Father Richard Kehoe was charismatic, eloquent and had the gift of revelatory communication.

He ended the retreat with a clarion call. The heart is at the very centre of a human being, not just in an emotional sense. It can give permanent faith, constant hope and love of the Holy Spirit.

On the 15ᵗʰ November 1948, Father Conrad Pepler presided over a retreat at the Dominican Priory in Hampstead. He was the Prior at Blackfriars in St. Giles, Oxford, incidentally ecumenically situated next to Pusey House, the great High Church of England seminary and study house.

Father Pepler was a famous theologian and editor of *Blackfriar*, the Dominican periodical which published learned articles and book reviews, and to which my mother subscribed. My mother held Father Pepler in very great esteem. Her relationship to him, she explained, was deeply reverential, different from the spiritual intimacy which characterised her meetings with Father Kehoe. Father Pepler wrote articles in *Blackfriar*. She read and re-read them. His cogent prose was an illumination.

For his retreat, Father Pepler selected the mysticism of the mass, the sacrifice of Christ in the mass. He spoke of moral virtues, of outward sacrifice representing inner devotion, the very central part of religion. This led him to the meaning of prayer, not rogatory, but offering something to God, in the theological sense, an ascetic act. Fundamental is the real presence of Christ, the sacramental reality.

Father Pepler drew upon St. Thomas Aquinas, who believed that Christ's suffering was the outward sign of an inward grace, and that transubstantiation made one part of the sacrifice of the Eucharist.

My mother told me that the retreats were on a high theological level, but one could approach the main themes of the discourses at all stages of previous experience. One of the great gifts of the Dominican Fathers was their elucidation of fundamentals and the setting of detail in a universal context. Their exegis revealed text and dogma.

In January 1949, Father Mark's retreat concerned itself with St. Thomas Aquinas' *Summa Theologica*, the highest achievement of medieval theological systematisation and the accepted basis of modern Roman Catholic theology. St. Thomas Aquinas joined the Dominican Order in April 1244 and was held in great reverence by the Dominicans.

Father Mark described the Aristotelian and Thomist categories of virtue, intellectual, moral and theological. Hope was a theological virtue. The object of hope was God himself as the object of eternal happiness. This *beatitudo objectiva* removes any trace of self-seeking in one's approach to God. It shifts the emotional balance from loving the good, which we can see, to God himself. Hope is a prayer: Thy will be done, for Thine is the kingdom. Hope is not just *amor dei* but the imposition of God's will on oneself.

A few weeks later, on the 12th and 13th February 1949, my mother attended a retreat presided over by Father Ryan. The Thomist idea of existence was the main theme on that occasion. Father Ryan illustrated the profound Thomist legacy to philosophical thought by quoting from Maritain's *Court traité de l'existence* and Gilson's *L'être et l'essence*. He explained the Thomist definition of existence, and Aquinas' use of the Latin infinitive of the verb 'to be' the 'esse' elevated to noun status. Father Ryan elaborated on the distinction between the material and the immaterial and drew upon Aristotle's complementary principal of matter and form.

My father died in 1948. My parents had been happily married for thirty-one years. The day before the funeral my mother spoke to me with infinite sadness. For her, death was an end, but also a beginning. She would not exaggerate her mourning, nor make herself self-important with it. ("Ich werde meine Trauer nicht übertreiben, mich nicht damit wichtig machen".) She continued with her retreats, and as 1949 progressed they became more frequent.

On the 9th and 10th April, Father Gilby's theme was the natural and the supernatural. He discussed the Greek idea of growth, the Roman idea of order, the development of all the virtues, of intuition. Early Christians believed that man by nature wanted a free, equal share of everything in common. Father Gilby described the supernatural as a share in God's life. It was above the natural, superior, elevated, and specific.

Father Ryan's retreat in June 1949 had the title 'Mind and Imagination'. Thinking implied universality, imagining was confined to the moment of experience. He discussed intellectual consciousness, the contrast between mind and sense. Father Ryan brought in Plato's definition of truth as something beyond actual appearance. St. Thomas was quoted, from *Summa Theologica* book 1, question 84, dealing with the spiritual faculty and the material image. Father Ryan took Wordsworth's *Prelude* as an example where the imaginative faculty gives one an insight into the invisible usurpation of the soul. Wordsworth applied a religious vocabulary to nature (spirit, soul, prayer, faith, blessing, worshipper) and gave it divine sublimity.

On the 10th and 11th September the subject of Father Mark's retreat was sapientia (wisdom). He described St. Thomas' treatment of wisdom and dealt with his description of happiness. St. Thomas rejected the notion that happiness was buried within oneself and that it could be found by excavating, by exploring, by digging deeper and deeper into the make-up of human nature. He concluded that it is God who makes man happy because it is man's natural urge to be God-like. Father Mark praised Jacques Maritain's *Les Degrés du Savoir* (the degrees of knowledge), in which the author traverses the whole field of knowledge from science and metaphysics to the suprarational knowledge of the mystics, exemplified especially by St. Augustine. Father Mark considered Jacques Maritain one of the great modern exponents of Aquinas' doctrines, especially his commentaries on Aquinas' writings on metaphysics, and he gave Maritain's work a rather donnish subtitle to emphasise its all-embracing universality: "The misery and the grandeur of metaphysics".

Father Mark elucidated one of Aquinas' fundamental doctrines that man was not created to be God but to be the image of God. God could only be accepted by self denial. This is sapientia (wisdom) at its highest.

For this particular retreat, my mother wrote copious notes, sixteen closely written pages in her exercise book, about twice her usual amount. My mother's paragraph headings are stamped with the familiar vocabulary of Thomist theology: the neutral world prior to the Fall, the single human wisdom before the Fall, the choice after the Fall, the problem of sin, how sin even changed God, who created man which is a work of sin, the argument for the existence of God, either in the state of mortal sin where man is God, or in the state of grace in which man is accepting God, the crucifixion devoid of meaning without redemption, the wisdom of the Cross. Father Mark discussed faith, the Holy Ghost, patience, baptism, and spoke about St. Augustine's classification of sapienta as wisdom and, on a secondary level, scientia as knowledge. He described Aquinas' definition of true wisdom: the discovery of God within us, the reason for our existence, the basic relationship of God and man. Aquinas saw the Holy Ghost as the inner core, potentially God, leading to the Godhead, to the end, to the *finis*, the most important word in the *Summa Theologica*. He finished his retreat with an exhortation, transcribed verbatim by my mother: "It would be a mistake to turn away from the world and to think of wisdom as a psychological aid to attain grace. No, in the light of wisdom, judge the things of this world and direct your own lives. Wisdom will then be most active".

The subject headings indicate the range of theological elucidation, the constant themes of the retreats. I have often marvelled at the miracle of language. A small but essential vocabulary forms the fundamental building blocks for elaborate metaphysical edifices, for the construction of variable and adjustable theological universes. God can be discussed in an infinite number of ways. At that time I wondered if my mother ever got tired of listening to closely-related reiterative subject matter. She told me that even a slight change of emphasis often revealed hitherto unexpected facets and solved difficulties. And then she asked: "And how many times do you want to go to *The Marriage of Figaro?*"

On the 13th November, the heading for Father Pepler's retreat was contrition. Aquinas believed that contrition was part of penance, of confession, of communion. The bread and the wine at the altar were offered to God in reconciliation, and as a symbol of the acceptance of the will of God.

My mother obviously enjoyed the erudition and the romance of ecclesiastical Latin, and made sure that she wrote down much of Aquinas' patristic and scholastic vocabulary. In the context of accepting the will of God, of being broken down by it, ground down, crushed by it, Father Pepler quoted Aquinas' verb 'conterere', literally to grind down. Aquinas developed the idea of 'contritio' (contrition) as the agent for the destruction of self judgement, the necessary pre-requisite for the annihilation of self will. Obedience is needed to do God's will, which will form one's own will.

One of my special subjects for my history degree at Oxford has the title 'St. Augustine of Hippo'. In 1947 I attended a series of lectures given by Canon Jenkins of Christ Church, Oxford. He was a legendary figure, Regius Professor of Ecclesiastical History, a Doctor of Divinity, sometime Residentiary Canon of Canterbury and before that librarian and chaplain at Lambeth Palace. Prior to taking Holy Orders, he was closely associated with King's College London, first as lecturer in patristic texts and then succeeding to the college chair of Ecclesiastical History.

We felt the greatness of his presence. There were usually only about a dozen of us sitting closely round him. The lectures were held at Christ Church College, Oxford, in the large room, leading off from Cloisters, next to Hall. I see him now, a slender, sharp-featured small man aged seventy, his piercing eyes owl-like in their scrutiny. He would have come over from his rooms in Tom Quad, wrapped in his gown, his neck encircled by a thick scarf, irrespective of the weather. He would read his lectures, somehow oblivious of his surroundings, enjoying however his privilege to turn aside on some lengthy diversion, often obscured by humorous allusions or private jokes of great complexity. I remember his face looking for an appreciative smile from his over-awed audience.

On one occasion he told us that years earlier he had been asked to contribute an entry for a monumental project, the Encyclopedia of Christianity, a dictionary of the Church. The editorial board was too large, he thought, and consisted of eminent theologians of many persuasions, a veritable ecumenical dinosaur, as he called it. For the letter 'A' section he had promptly provided his article on Augustine.

And then he paused dramatically. His face was transfigured by the age-less mischievous smile of the school-boy. He looked over us, moving his head in semi-rotary surveillance. Were we all still listening? Would we all smile? He was the master now, not the boy. "They are still doing letter C," he said.

As we were leaving I stopped him. We stood in one of the most beautiful corners of Oxford, at the foot of the great staircase, leading to Christ Church Hall. The ceiling of the stairwell is ennobled by shallow vaulting, in the horizontal Late Perpendicular style. From the foot of the stairs, the slender central supporting pillar branches out at the top like the crown of a palm tree, in a circular form of delicate tracery.

The conversation could only have lasted a minute or less but the Tudor backcloth, so familiar and beloved, has heightened the reality of memory.

How do you spell Forstas I asked, and I then spelled out the name letter by letter: 'F' 'O' 'R' 'S' 'T' 'A' 'S'? Canon Jenkins had just spent some time, talking about Faustus of Milevis. In 383, Faustus had come to Carthage and spread the heretical doctrines of Manes, the founder of the third century Persian heresy. Augustine had become a follower, a Manichaean, some years earlier, and now hoped that Faustus would solve the many problems which had been puzzling him. But he became disillusioned and this eventually led to his acceptance of the Catholic faith three years later.

For Canon Jenkins, Augustine's contemporaries were very real. Faustus, the inadvertent agent of doubt, Faustus, the unintended prelude to conversion, Faustus the fraud, Faustus, the famous Manichaean propagandist, preacher of hotch-potch doctrine, and of course when discussing Augustine's polemic *Contra Faustum Manichaeum*, written about 400. From there, book 1, he probably quoted "Faustus, of African origin, born at Milevis, of a sweet discourse and clever wit", and from *Confessions*, book 5, "there had then come to Carthage a certain Bishop of the Manichees, Faustus by name, a great snare of the Devil, and many were entangled by him through that lure of his smooth language".

The name must have been uttered innumerable times but I could not recognise it in the sound. Canon Jenkins listened to my spoken seven letters. He looked at me with the split-second stillness of complete surprise. "Forstas, Forstas," he said, and suddenly in my anxiety I heard it. "Oh Faustus," I replied, giving the vowel sound the melodious Viennese diphthong of Goethe's *Faust*. Exactly what Claud Jenkins thought, as he walked back to the North side of Tom Quad, I mercifully do not know. I told my mother about it and we laughed.

My mother knew that I had a special interest in ecclesiastical history, doctrine and theology. Frequently she discussed her retreats.

And when she came back on 14th November 1949 we talked about the way Father Conrad Pepler had elucidated the Thomist doctrine of free will, the so-called 'voluntas'. It was then that I vividly remembered Canon Jenkins some two years earlier.

He had just finished a lecture on the way Augustine had written about the Fall, Original Sin and predestination and he quoted from the *Confessions* and the *Civitas Dei* in the original text. Naturally the word 'voluntas' occurred many times. But whilst Conrad Pepler had apparently pronounced the Latin in the accepted Continental manner, making the 'u' sound as in lunar, Claud Jenkins enunciated voluntas, with the central syllable exaggeratedly lengthened, the 'ant' in his word redolent of the old-fashioned public-school master.

I imitated Canon Jenkins' voice, repeating volantas, volantas, several times and we smiled, and shared our private world of Augustine and Aquinas.

Four days later, on the 18th November 1949, my mother was present at one more retreat, again with Father Conrad.

He defined contemplation. He described it as an act, a simple vision of truth, an intuition of God, a type of prayer beyond one's will, given by God. He spoke of the mind and the will "held by God". Contemplation was beyond imagination, beyond one's choice. It was a divine gift received passively because it was God who was active. One had to make oneself ready for the advent of God with prayer and meditation. Mysticism was a gift of God. It was a passive prayer beyond one's control, dispensed through the bond of charity.

Father Conrad Pepler explained the meaning of 'ordo', order, to live by the rule. It was not to be regarded as an end, but as an imposition from outside, leading one on to contemplation. There was one rule for life: love and unity in the presence of God.

As 1949 drew to a close, my mother longed for a deeper religious commitment. She must have sought Father Conrad's guidance, she must have told him that she felt ready for the noviciate, which would prepare her for admission to the Third Order of St. Dominic.

She wanted to become a Dominican Tertiary, the Holy Order reserved for the laity, with priests and nuns for the first two Orders.

On the 25ᵗʰ November 1949, soon after the second retreat, Father Conrad responded. He wrote to my mother:

BLACKFRIARS
OXFORD
Telephone 3607

Dear Mrs Neumann,

Father Francis says that it is perfectly all right for you to join the Woodchester Chapter if Fr Prior down there is willing.

I would suggest that you write to him and arrange to be received at your next visit. I hope you will be able to do this soon.

I was very glad to meet you at Grayshot.

> *Yours sincerely in S. Dominic,*
>> *Fr Conrad OP.*

There were difficulties and delays as is shown by Conrad Pepler's second letter of the 27ᵗʰ June 1950:

BLACKFRIARS PUBLICATIONS
(English Province of Order of Preachers)
Telephone: 47221
BLACKFRIARS
OXFORD

Dear Mrs Newmanm [sic],

Thank you very much for your letter. I hope I shall be able to see you at the weekend. I have not done anything about the Tertiaries because there has been considerable changing about, and now that Father Drostan is both Prior of London and director of the Tertiaries, I think we may be able to do something more successfully than we should have done...

> *God bless you*
> > *Yours sincerely in Dno.,*
> > > *Fr Conrad OP*

The letters speak with the venerable antiquity of the Monastic Age, its hierarchy, its diplomacy.

Father Richard Conran, the Chaplain and Director of the English Tertiaries, told me that the Priory at Woodchester was closed many years ago, and that the Tertiary register, which my mother had signed, was now stored in the Dominican archives.

Apart from my mother's signature, was there a document of admission, perhaps similar to a baptismal certificate? And as I asked the questions, I immediately felt that it was inappropriate. A Tertiary would hardly need written confirmation. I had imagined a few sentences in elegant ecclesiastical Latin. Instead, Father Richard described the service in which my mother, after a noviciate of about three years, would have been received into the Third Order. Father Prior and the Chapter would have celebrated a special service of admission. My mother had absolved her noviciate. She would have recited and affirmed her Tertiary vows, and Father Prior would have presented her with the monastic vestment of a Tertiary, the scapular. Now that she could wear the material symbol of her new religious identity, she was a Dominican Tertiary.

My mother showed me her vestment, her Dominican habit. Two pieces of white linen, smaller than postcards, were joined together by ribbons. They were placed over the head and worn under the clothes, hanging down in the front and in the back. The Latin 'scapulae' means 'shoulder blades', a natural symbolism for the Yoke of Christ, the *jugum Christi*. In Matthew, chapter 11, verse 29, Christ says: "Bend your necks to my yoke, and learn from me, for I am gentle and humble-hearted;

and your souls will find relief. For my yoke is good to bear, my load is slight."

The Tertiary scapular, for those who live in the real world, is a modification of the regular monastic habit of the monks, their two long panels practically touching the ground. At first my mother wore it continuously, a garment of obligation, of identity, but after some years I noticed that she wore it less frequently. Tertiaries observe a rule and recite a liturgical office. This is an obligatory vocal prayer of the Church, spoken by priests, nuns, clerics and Tertiaries upon whom this duty is imposed. It can take place at various times, in the morning, evening or night, at Lauds, Matins, Vespers or Compline.

How many times have I seen my mother reading her missal, the holy book containing the psalms, hymns, lessons and prayers? My mother's missal was a gift from the Dominican fathers. It is bound in black suede leather, and has the Dominican crest on the front and back, stamped into the leather. On the circular heraldic band is the motto: laudare, benedicere, praedicare (praising, blessing, teaching). In the format of a paperback, the book contains two hundred and fourteen pages of thin bible paper, with the traditional red ink for chapter headings, lesson numbers, for top-of-the-page calendar details, for psalm and hymn entries. Antiphonals and benedictions are similarly titled in red, as are the readings (lectiones) and the references to the Scriptures.

The missal, in its revised from, was published on the 14th September 1736 under the pontificate of Clemens XII, and my mother was presented with an early edition.

My mother talked to me about her Rosary. According to tradition, St. Dominic founded the devotion for the Rosary in the course of his missionary work and it was of special significance to the Holy Order. The chain of beads was kept in an ivory box, and with it was an old Rosary card. I remember it vividly. It was in the nature of a bookmark, thin coated cartridge paper, the text in ornate Old English type. It listed the fifteen mysteries of the Rosary, grouped in three sections or "chaplets", the Joyful, the Sorrowful, and the Glorious, all turning points in the lives of Christ and his mother. With the contemplation of each mystery, ten Hail Marys, so-called Decades, preceded by 'Our Father' had to be recited. It was customary, however, to choose one of the three chaplets, with its five Mysteries, requiring a rosary of five decades, separated by single beads for the 'Our Father'. The Rosary is the holy counting aid. My mother would have caressed the chain of prayer, holding the beads in place. With each 'Ave Maria' she would have released a bead to glide down and join those already used. And so she would have worked her way along until she had come round the full circle marked by a crucifix.

My mother was a good mixture of her parents. Her energy, her tenacity, her ambitions, all came from her mother.

Clara was poorly educated. Her German was not at all literate, as is shown in her letters. Her numeracy was basic. The few years at school in the Brody ghetto in the late 1860s and early 1870s hardly prepared her for marriage to a basically scholastic man, an autodidact, a quietist with messianic dreams, a true lover of music, a man without earthly ambitions, but whose life was enriched by German and French literature, which he read in the original. She made him a good wife and bore him six children. She loved him deeply and respected him. My mother told me that Clara had a pet name for Mayer, not Liebchen, Liebling or Schatz (dearest, darling or treasure) but simply Braunthal. Announcements apparently often began thus: "Braunthal, ich geh jetzt einkaufen" (Braunthal, I am now going shopping), "Braunthal, die Buben raufen" (Braunthal, the boys are fighting).

Clara lived for her children and made sure as far as possible that they should succeed. She was tremendously hard-working, supplementing my grandfather's meagre income as a book-keeper, when at the age of seventy, he was put on half-pay, by taking in washing or covering umbrellas, a thing she did when she was a girl.

My mother had Clara's single-mindedness and perseverance and added it to the natural religiosity and inquisitive mind which came from her father. She inherited his love of music and his intellectual personality, his searching curiosity. He was fundamentally religious, but in no way orthodox. He accepted his ethnic heritage and carried his religious luggage lightly. On Fridays candles were lit, and prayers said, or should I say on some Fridays. My mother never spoke of this as an automatic ritual. Her brother Julius relates that on the high feast day of the Passover, my grandfather would wrap himself in the ritual shawl, the "Talles" with the black hem, and wear the gold-embroidered cap.

I have Mayer's prayer book and very evocatively his Phylacteries. Sometime in the 1930s my grandmother must have entrusted these symbols of religiosity into my mother's care. She was the last one of Clara's children still left in Vienna.

The Phylacteries, the Tefilin, are small leather boxes, held in place by leather thongs. One box is strapped round the left arm, the other is tied over the forehead. Mayer wore them, I revere them. He took them out of their red raw-silk pouch by pulling the silk ribbon to open it. His hands touched the material with the intensity of the impending ritual. And now, as I hold the little bag more than a century later, I feel as if we were holding hands. My mother never mentioned them and probably Mayer put them on only on rare occasions. He may have bought them after his arrival in Vienna, or they might have come from his father in spite of the fact that the pouch has German as well as Hebrew printed on the outside. The little leather boxes contain words from the scriptures, written on parchment. They are intended to serve as a reminder of the constant presence of God and thus safeguard the wearer from committing a sin. They are not worn on the Sabbath or holy days since these days are in themselves a reminder of God. The word phylactery comes from the Greek. In my treasured Liddell and Scott's Greek-English Lexicon "phylake" means keeping watch or guard. On the fragile silk, the exquisite typography of the Hebrew liturgy and the traditional extra-bold German Gothic typeface unite the two languages in a decorative pattern of devotion. The miniature manuscripts written with the delicate skill of a medieval scribe are verses from Exodus 13. 1-10; 13. 11-16, Deuteronomy 6. 4-0, 11. 13-21, where the phylacteries are part of the text.

My mother passed on to me another religious article from the Braunthal household, a Mezuzah. On the small scroll, the opening verse of the Shema is inscribed in a miniature script and the parchment is housed in a small oblong wooden box which traditionally is nailed to the door post of a house. Shema is God's clarion call to His people, the fundamental prayer of Judaism, and proclaims God's eternal message to all those who enter.

She was leaving the world of Mayer's Hebrew prayer book, his Phylacteries, his Talles and the Mezuzah of her childhood. Her breviary, her scapular, her Rosary, would be her illumination.

CHAPTER 18

My mother in Italy

My mother made several journeys to Italy, and afterwards she often told me of the great personal impact the Italian Renaissance had made on her, how it contributed to her religiosity, and how with its imagery it consolidated adoration. Although she would enter a church or visit a museum and look at paintings or sculpture with secular appreciation and aesthetic enjoyment, and would bring to bear her art-historical experience and biblical knowledge, she could not entirely forget the foundations of her faith. The Catholic Church used its patronage to illustrate the Bible on altar pieces and frescoes, on pulpits and fonts, on ceilings and windows, on bronze doors and facades. She confessed to me that on one or two occasions the actual subject matter of a painting seemed to assume a separate identity, the certainty of belief.

One journey was particularly memorable. My mother decided to travel for a month in Italy and to stay in Assisi for a few days with the nuns in their convent, as their guest. Assisi, however, was only a staging-post in her itinerary, which was a real physical endurance test. But she was full of Braunthal energy and determination, imbued with cultural thoroughness and blessed with a robust constitution.

She wanted to travel as far as Sicily and bought a rail ticket that allowed her to interrupt her journey. She set off from Brussels, where her brother Alfred was living at the time, at 7.30 in the morning on Tuesday, 1st September 1964. She arrived in Milan thirteen hours later at 10.30 in the evening. She could not get a couchette and decided to travel during the day. For Wednesday, 2nd September her diary entry reads: "went at 7.30 to Florence, did not stop at Modena, was too tired.

It was good so because when I arrived in Florence at about midday the pensione where I wanted to stay had no single rooms ... Had a glorious afternoon, walked for five hours, saw the Duomo, the Baptistry, the Piazza della Signoria, walked and walked, the beautiful palaces, little courtyards, Ponte Vecchio!"

Thursday the 3rd September: "woke up very early, was on my way for 10 hours without eating or drinking, was 'berauscht' (intoxicated), the Uffizi, Santa Croce, San Marco. The Uffizi, what a beautiful museum, quite unique with its Italian collections. Was thrilled with the Botticelli, Bronzino portraits. Did miss the Barghello. Otherwise saw everything I wanted to see. Went to Mass at 6 o'clock in Santa Maria Novella. Was not tired, slept well."

I can so easily imagine my mother in the Uffizi Gallery, standing in front of Botticelli's Birth of Venus and his Primavera. More intriguing is her mentioning the Bronzino portraits. In Santa Croce she must have admired the Giotto frescoes, and the high relief of the Annunciation by Donatello. She wandered through the forty-four small monastic cells of San Marco adorned with beautiful frescoes by Fra Angelico, painted nearly five hundred years earlier.

And there she saw the Annunciation and the 'Noli me tangere', two iconic masterpieces of the Renaissance. In the small confined spaces of the two cells, the great confrontations speak with the additional eloquence of intimacy, the angel appearing to the Virgin Mary at her devotions, and Christ standing in front of Mary Magdalene. Mary holds a small prayer book, open to show that she has been praying. The Angel addresses her: 'Hail Mary, Ave Maria,' and she learns of the miracle for which she has been chosen.

Fra Angelico has invested the gestures with his genius. The Virgin, her arms folded, is bowing with reverential humility. By contrast, the arms of the angel are not crossed in supplication but placed across the waist, the right above the left, with the index finger pointing upwards to the face, the implied symbol of communication.

After the crucifixion, prior to his resurrection, Christ appears to Mary Magdalene who comes to find his tomb empty. He is disguised as a gardener and she does not recognise him. He reveals his identity and says "Touch me not" (Noli me tangere) for I am not yet ascended to my father". Once again, the hands illustrate the text and give reality to the unfolding drama.

Mary is kneeling in front of Christ in awe of his miraculous presence. Her arms reach out to him with open hands, curved outwards, in surprise and humility. The right arm of Christ points down to her, ending in a hand, full of command, as it signals distance and separation. The wrist is bent, the palm is made to face the ground between them, the stretched fingers and separated thumb illustrate the image of admonition.

My mother found the vocabulary of Italian Renaissance painting of enduring interest, and after her journeys we always discussed the highlights of her experiences. With the help of our art books and guide books we could go into great detail, and so it was that we could share our love for "the hand in art".

Of the many churches in Florence that my mother could have chosen for Evening Service she selected the Dominican church of Santa Maria Novella, of special significance to her as a Dominican Tertiary. She told me afterwards that the celebration of Vespers in such an impressive setting was a unique experience. And she described how the first sight of the marble façade, advancing towards her as she approached the large piazza, was like a beautiful drop curtain, a prelude to the mystery of the Mass which was about to be enacted. It is in a typical Tuscan Romanesque style, the upper part completed by Leon Battista Alberti in 1456-1470.

Santa Maria Novella is the most important Gothic church in Tuscany, and on her return she took me on a guided tour of the interior, her memory aided by our specialist library: frescoes by Cimabue, Filippino Lippi, Domenico Ghirlandaio, Nardo di Cione, altar-pieces and paintings by Vasari, Orcagna, Masaccio, statues and carvings by Nino Pisano, Ghiberti, Benedetto di Maiano, Giuliano Sangallo.

More Giottos were to follow because on the following day, on Friday the 4th, my mother travelled to Assisi.

The diary reads: "Went by the early train 7.30, but did not stop in Arezzo, was too keen to get to Assisi in time in case something would be wrong, but stopped all the same in Perugia, was thrilled by the charm of this medieval town. Had Mass in the beautiful duomo at 11 o'clock, was in Assisi already at 2.30, in the time I was expected and I liked this place from the first moment. Stayed there until the 14th".

My mother had planned a very energetic tour, both before and after her ten day rest in Assisi, as the entry for the 4th September clearly shows. She told me that in Perugia she went straight to the Fontana Maggiore, designed by Fra Bevignate in 1277, with bas reliefs by Nicola and Giovanni Pisano. Facing it is the façade of the Palazzo Priori, where she admired the bronze Perugian griffin and the Guelf lion, bearing chains, carried off from the gates of Sienna by the Perugians after a victory at Torrita in 1358. The latest suggestion about the figures is that the wings of the griffin were added before 1281 to an Etruscan body and the new lion made.

The hours that my mother had in Perugia were well spent. She arrived a little before 10 am, left her luggage at the station and then took a bus to the typical Tuscan hill town. She must have arrived at the top about half past ten, wandered through the streets, went to Mass at eleven, came out about three quarters of an hour later and explored the town, rather than go into the Sala dell'Udienza del Cambio, painted with frescoes by Perugino. There was so much to see, just walking through the town, church facades and noble gateways, along the Corso Vannucci through the centre of the old city, or along the Corso Garibaldi, an old medieval street with fine houses.

At about half past one, at the latest, she must have caught a bus back to the station for the 2 o'clock train to Assisi. What physical stamina! After all, in order to catch the 7.30 from Florence, she would have had to get up about 6 o'clock in the morning and leave the hotel well before 7 o'clock to get to the station in good time. Many people half her age would have been daunted by the prospect. She was seventy-five. Before her departure she said to me: "Ich möchte viel sehen. Vielleicht ist es zum letzten mal". (I want to see a lot. Perhaps it is for the last time.)

On the 5th September she recorded her time in Assisi: "Assisi. A wonderful place, had a wonderful time there: The nuns kind, the food too good, the room nice…went for a walk every day besides visiting the churches, met two very nice women from nearby Köln, went to Porziuncola, 3 times the Eremo delle Carceri, had altogether a lovely time, stayed from the 4th-14th."

The next ten days in her diary, her time in Assisi, are left blank. When she came back she told me that it was impossible to describe her practically daily visits to the Basilica of San Francesco. How happy I am, even now, because she had those leisurely days, staying in the town, being part of it, a feeling which you cannot get as a fleeting visitor. Assisi is the town of St. Francis, who stands next to St. Dominic in a complementary relationship. They were contemporaries, living their short lives in the last two decades of the twelfth and first two of the thirteenth century. They were the embodiment of the monastic age, each founding a Holy Order with the approval and formal sanction of Pope Innocent III.

For my mother, St. Dominic remained a distant figure, the austere Spaniard, a man of heroic sanctity, ever zealous to win souls from error by preaching pure doctrine. By contrast, the story of St. Francis is very human, full of colourful and dramatic incidents which decorate the walls of the Basilica of San Francesco. On the walls of the Upper Church are two great narrative cycles. The lower tier of frescoes illustrate famous scenes from the life of St. Francis, traditionally thought to be by Giotto, including the two iconic episodes, St. Francis preaching to the birds and St. Francis receiving the stigmata, the first saint known to have been thus marked by the reproduction of the wounds of the Passion of Christ in the human body. Above the fresco cycle by Giotto is another tier of thirty-four frescoes from Old and New Testament history by pupils of Cimabue. In the Lower Church my mother spent many hours admiring works by Simone Martini, Lorenzetti and Cimabue.

She went to the Eremo delle Carceri three times, probably walking the 5km to the forest hermitage of St. Francis. Here the saint and his followers would come at times and live in caves, and later St. Bernadine founded a convent there. My mother saw the cave of St. Francis with his bed hollowed out of the rock, and an ancient tree on which birds are supposed to have received his blessing.

But on the 14th September my mother said farewell to medieval and Renaissance Italy and travelled back in time, hundreds of years, to the art of Byzantium and another thousand years or more to the world of Ancient Greece. She went to Sicily.

On that day she wrote: "Left Assisi. 11.50 to Naples. Went straight on via Rome. Arrived Naples at 6.30. Arrived at port with excitement; had to queue for ticket etc. But boat was nice and crossing very nice. Did not mind having no couchette.

Tuesday 15th: Arrived at Palermo 8 o'clock in the morning. A lady I met on the boat was fetched by her husband. They brought me by car to the hotel they knew: Paradiso(!) but cheap. Was very tired but went out straight had some coffee in a bar and went out to make enquiries about trip round the island, ticket for Naples, etc. It was hot and nasty. So I went on a bus to Monreale. Stayed there until 5 o'clock."

My mother could not have had much sleep on the night boat and therefore sensibly chose to travel out to the cathedral of Monreale, up in the hills, some five miles outside Palermo, and spend a quiet day there away from the crowded city. But what a wonderful day! She told me how exciting it had been for her to be in that great Romanesque cathedral and to look at the mosaics that tell the story she had so recently seen in Assisi. They were made about five hundred years earlier, at the high point of Byzantine art in Sicily, and she was acutely aware of the artistic prelude to the Tuscan frescoes of Giotto and Cimabue. The mosaics with which the walls are entirely covered consist of scenes from the Old Testament, from the life of Christ, and from the lives of the Apostles.

After sitting up on board ship most of Monday night, and on Tuesday, sorting out her itinerary and tickets, prior to her excursion to Monreale, she nevertheless got up very early indeed on the following morning, to catch her train.

For Wednesday, the 16th she wrote: "Decided to make the whole tour round the island by train. So left Palermo at 7.35 for Segesta. Arrived there at 9.20. What a wonderful temple! Had a tough walk to it and to the theatre and back to catch the 12.30 train for Agrigento. But it was worth it, wonderful, beautiful, the temple so beautifully preserved! Had a long but most amusing journey through beautiful country. Arrived at 7.30, but I was lucky. Met at the station two very nice French young men who gave me the address of their pensione and all sorts of good information…"

She was only three hours in Segesta, and had to walk fairly briskly, first for about quarter of an hour or so, slightly uphill to the temple, and then very steeply to the top of Monte Barbaro to the theatre, a climb which must have taken about half an hour! But how amply was she rewarded! The temple is one of the best-preserved Doric temples in Sicily standing majestically in desolation, surrounded by lofty mountains, and the theatre commands a beautiful view.

In Agrigento, on Thursday 17th, my mother got up early as usual. She writes: "Went to the temples. Arrived there at 8 o'clock. It was beautiful. The temple of Concord wonderfully preserved. The cella and all the columns intact. The view from there to the town and the sea!"

Laid out for her was the world of the antique, the glory of Greece in Sicily. The temple of Concord, with its thirty-four columns and its architrave stands in a group of temples, their white stone set against an azure sea. And there, on the shore, below the old town of Agrigento is a memorial to the past from two and a half thousand years ago.

On Friday, the 18th September my mother wrote: "Got up early, packed and went for a coffee and to change money at the bank. Got the 9 o'clock train, arrived Syracuse at 3 o'clock… The town is beautiful and I like it here, will probably stay till Monday."

In the event, my mother left Syracuse on Sunday, arriving in Taormina at 5 o'clock. But even so, an afternoon, evening and whole day in Syracuse! She had done her homework, she saw a lot, and was too excited to write down details. On her return she told me of her precious hours, her visit to the Amphitheatre, a Roman structure of the period of Augustus and to the Greek Theatre, erected in the 5th century BC.

And then she walked to the famous quarries, the Latomia del Paradiso and the Latomia de Cappuccini, hewn in the rock to a depth of nearly 50 yards, and overgrown with the most luxuriant vegetation.

My mother stayed in Taormina until Friday the 25th. Her diary entries are enthusiastic. The entry for Monday, 21st September reads: "Taormina 'göttlich' (divine). A big room in a clean small hotel, bath and balcony with a view to sea and Etna… went to the Castello high up, a car stopped and two Italian young men invited me to get in, so it saved me a lot of climbing. On top only some ruins, but magnificent view. On way down I met them again."

For the next few days she walked down to the sea and up into the hills, and of course to the Greek theatre.

The inimitable language of the 1890 Baedeker edition of Italy, handbook for travellers, third part: Southern Italy and Sicily, describes the view from the hill on which the theatre stands as one of the most beautiful in Italy. It goes on to say: "The view is even more beautiful in the morning, when the sun rises above Calabria or from the sea, imparts a rosy hue to the snowy peak of Mount Etna, and then gilds the rocky heights beyond the theatre. Those who make a prolonged stay at Taormina will have the opportunity of observing some marvellous effects of light and shade."

For Friday, the 25th, my mother's entry reads: "missed the bus to get the train for Cefalu!! Have to take the train at 10 o'clock which goes direct to Palermo. Can't risk a later train because I have to take my ticket for the ship, get my bag from the hotel etc. Arrived an hour later (5 o'clock) went to Terreni to get my ticket, had just time to go to the Duomo, the Palace of the Normans, and to San Giovanni degli Eremitani (not the cloisters), rushed back to the hotel, fetched my bag, took a taxi to the station and port arrived in time, had a very nice cabin, slept very well."

What enthusiasm, what a rush! But my mother was driven by the certitude that this was her farewell to Sicily, a bitter sweet valediction.

She used her precious Palermo hours to visit the Palazzo Reale, the Palace of the Normans, as she calls it, because it contains the Cappella Palatina, perhaps the most beautiful palace-chapel in the world. As she entered the nave, she was enraptured by the wondrous magic of the general effect. She recalled the wooden roof with its Moorish cones, stalactites hanging from the ceiling in Eastern mystery. She admired the tall granite and cipollino columns, which support pointed Saracenic arches. Here, seven and a half centuries ago, King Roger II, the Norman ruler of Sicily, the builder of the Chapel, knelt and prayed. The walls are a beautiful postlude of what she had just seen in Monreale. They are entirely covered by mosaics on a golden ground, and radiant with oriental splendour. The Mosaics represent subjects from the Old Testament and the lives of Christ, St. Peter and St. Paul.

On Saturday , the 26th September, the intense itinerary continued. My mother was determined to fit in a brief visit to Pompeii, to walk once again through the city, destroyed by neighbouring Vesuvius in a violent eruption nearly 1,900 years ago.

She wrote: "Arrived at Naples at 6 o'clock, lovely morning, had coffee, went straight to Pompeii, had to wait there ½ hour for opening. Terrific, so much more had been done, but it was very hot and I was tired, and went back at 11.30, it took me 1½ hours. Arrived Rome 7 o'clock."

She told me how happy she was that she had managed the visit, to stand in Pompeii in the forum, elegant columns raising their accusing fingers up to a heaven that had opened up with a rain of fiery ash. And as a backcloth, sinister Vesuvius with thin smoke rising from the volcanic cone, a signal from the hot heart of the earth.

My mother stayed in Rome until the 1st October and was the guest of Dr Hans Coreth, the Austrian ambassador to the Holy See, and his wife Christl. In the early 1950s he had a posting in London as First Secretary, and it was at that time that my mother gave English lessons to his older son Clemens, who eventually would follow his father in a diplomatic career. The coaching was intense and in addition to practical conversation and translation had to include extensive grammar required by the Austrian syllabus which Clemens had to follow concurrently. But somehow in the stressed atmosphere of irregular verbs, idiosyncratic spelling, obscure vocabulary, indirect speech, in the welter of syntax, word and sentence analysis, précis, and the minefield of modal conjugation, my mother became part of the family. Clemens soon accepted her with affection and love and the parents became life-long friends.

What an opportunity to enjoy the hospitality of someone diplomatically accredited to the Vatican! And on Wednesday, the 30th September, one of my mother's unspoken wishes was fulfilled. She was invited to attend a Papal audience at St. Peter's. She writes: "Audience at 5 o'clock. Was in the Basilica of S.P. from 4 o'clock to 7 o'clock. But it was most impressive to sing the Credo with thousands. And the Pope's address was very deep and beautiful."

Hans Coreth had obtained for her a precious ticket of admission.

The previous Pope, Pope John XXIII, had introduced reforms in his Second Vatican Council, one of which was a greater interaction between the priest and his congregation. To make the religious service more immediate and accessible he constructed the two balconies along each side of the long nave giving a further good view of the altar than would have been possible at floor level. On the official photograph my mother is on one of the balconies, a few rows from the front, near the altar end, standing up in her excitement and looking down on Pope Paul VI as he is welcoming a procession of bishops and giving each his blessing.

The public audiences are secular in the sense that no mass is celebrated and therefore no liturgical vestments or mitres are worn.

On this occasion, the Holy Father stood underneath Michelangelo's dome in the heart of the basilica, the Vicar of Christ facing his faithful. The High Altar of St. Peter's, the central stage of the Catholic Church, frames him as he blesses.

My mother's last day in Rome ended with a flourish. In the evening, Christl Coreth drove her in a farewell journey through the city. My mother wrote: "Nachts. Rom bei Abendbeleuchtung: (At night, Rome flood-lit). Piazza MarcAurel! S. Maria in Trastevere!! Castello S. Angelo! Came home at 12 o'clock!"When my mother returned to London she described the grandeur and nobility of the equestrian statue of the emperor Marcus Aurelius, the gilded bronze of antiquity. It stood above the Forum, on the Capitol in the Piazza del Campidoglio, and is now housed for safer keeping in the Capitoline Museum. She was fortunate, still to see it lit up, under the Roman night sky, the ruler on his horse, imperious and eternal, in his right hand the short staff of command and pointing north to the Alps. He was bidding her farewell.

On Friday 2nd October, my mother, once again, got up early. She wrote: "Train at 7.40. Orvieto! Lovely weather, beautiful façade. Interior most beautiful romanische Kirche (Romanesque church). Frescoes, Fra Angelico!! Train at 12.45."

Right to the end she sustained her enthusiasm. She told me how memorable those few hours were. She was enraptured by the huge façade, covered by superb marble bas-reliefs from the 14th century. They depict the story of the Creation, the stories of Abraham and David, scenes from the Life of Christ, the Last Judgement, Hell and Paradise. There, in the Cappella della Madonna di San Brizio are the frescoes by Fran Angelico and Signorelli. In 1447 Fra Angelico with the help of Benozzo Gozzoli started the work which was finished by Luca Signorelli at the end of the 15th century.

Five hundred years ago, he produced one of the most remarkable fresco cycles of the Italian Renaissance, with beautiful nude figure studies.

And so, true to form, she fitted in one more masterpiece. She had travelled down and up the spine of Italy, and her diary would help her memory recall a unique month. There was one great omission. She did not make the detour to Venice. She was there with my father in 1936, the last time they were in Italy together.

CHAPTER 19

At the factory

On a brilliant summer's day in June 1948, I got up from my desk in the Examination Schools at Oxford with a sigh of relief. I had just sat for Final History Examinations, a memorable week of ten three-hour papers, for my Bachelor of Arts Degree.

As we were coming out, scores of undergraduates, well-wishers, friends, all cheered and shouted, "How was it?". And now, as I look back over my own life, I lengthen that question into an interrogative refrain, to cover the last sixty years or more of my own story.

Yes, indeed, how was it all?

I was acutely aware that my history studies would soon fade and that many details would sink into oblivion. What has remained, however, is the substance of the past, which formed the cultural framework of humanism in which music and art flourished.

How fortunate I am to have been presented with this precious luggage for life, enriched by the strict Latin and Greek, the classical world, then still taught in Vienna and at Magdalen College School, Oxford.

I started to look for work, and at the same time taught general subjects in various Inner London Education Authority Secondary Schools. In those days, one was allowed to teach just on the strength of an honours degree. The salary was calculated on a daily basis, no contract, no sick pay, no paid holidays. But it helped me to stabilise, to absorb memory of war.

I lived at home with my mother. My father had died in April 1948, at the age of 60, and my married sister Eva was living in South Wales.

My mother never pressurised me in my career search, but she must have shared the thought with thousands of other mothers: what will become of him?

My father had been prominent in the world of books. For half a century, my grandfather Wilhelm had been a respected and esteemed journalist. Uncle Julius had fought for his political ideals in the columns of the socialist press. It was this familiar background that made me seek out opportunities in publishing, not words, not books, not pictures, but music. I knew nothing about it, but it was precisely this mysterious speciality which made it so attractive.

There were at the time only about half a dozen or so firms with sizeable catalogues of classical music, as compared with the many book publishers which still existed as independent concerns. But I thought rather optimistically that I might find a niche somewhere in an editorial department, perhaps proof-reading or on the promotion or sales side. There was always possible work in the copyright departments or the hire libraries.

I went to see my father's former contacts, Victor Gollancz, the publisher, and Paul Zsolnay. I spoke to the music department of Oxford University Press, located in London, to Augener's, the famous music publishers, now no longer, and to many more.

And, in the spring of 1950, I was offered a job at Boosey & Hawkes, the music publishers. I was introduced to Ernst Roth, the managing director, through the good offices of Viktor Merz, the father of my close schoolfriends Joseph and Felix. The boys, together with their parents, arrived in Oxford in 1940, and for the last seventy years have been a permanent fixture of love and affection, which has earned them the appellation 'part of the family'. They had escaped from Brno, then in Czechoslovakia, where father Viktor had made a career as a composer. Ernst Roth was from Prague. The two men were old friends, bound by their heritage and their music. The friendship of their wives was even older, they had been together at primary school.

For ten years prior to the Anschluss, Ernst Roth had been head of publications at Universal Edition, Vienna. In 1938 he came to London with a wealth of musical publishing experience and was welcomed by Ralph Hawkes, the Managing Director, as his assistant.

Ralph Hawkes never pretended to be a profound musician, but he was rightly proud of his commercial acumen and of his outward-looking European vision of music publishing. As early as 1923, at a time when the majority of British music publishers were still rather insular, he travelled to Vienna and negotiated the sole agency for Universal Edition, with the copyrights of such major composers as Schoenberg, Berg, Bartok, Mahler, Webern and Kodaly.

Boosey & Co. and Hawkes & Sons merged in 1930, combining their catalogues: Hawkes with a long history of publishing military and brass band music and Boosey, an even older firm, famous for its vocal music, songs and opera editions.

By the time I joined the firm in 1950, Dr Roth had risen from a small office in the basement, where he had worked on the production of the Hawkes Pocket Scores (which had been his brainchild), to his office on the second floor as Managing Director. However, any title given to Ernst Roth would be misleading. He was so much more. He had studied philosophy and law, as well as music, in Prague and had pursued his studies in Vienna with Guido Adler; he was a good pianist; he loved painting and architecture; he had written several books, one of them a novel and another a philosophical work on the nature of music called *Vom Vergänglichen in der Musik* (the Transitoriness of Music).

I was fortunate at the time that there was no opening in the editorial department, nothing in their marketing, promotions, general sales, or copyright sections. They were fully staffed as far as their vast publishing programme was concerned: their symphonic music, their chamber music, their music for schools, their church and choral music, their song albums and song collections. No additional help was needed, certainly not for the prestigious military and brass band march cards, to be clipped onto trumpets, trombones and tubas. Nor did they need help for the catalogues, listing tens of thousands of titles: the vocal scores for operas, the pocket scores for symphonies and chamber music.

Instead, I was offered a position in production, and moreover the office where I was sent happened to be at the firm's printing presses and instrument making factory in Edgware, in North London, rather than in their London headquarters on Regent Street. That was a stroke of luck. It may have been a far cry from the dreaming spires of Oxford to the noisy printing works, from the dulcet sounds of many college belfries to the cacophony of brass instrument manufacture. But in Edgware, I watched and learnt. Elsewhere, I would not have gained the industrial experience, the ethos of manufacture that only a factory can give you.

On my first day, in April 1950, I was immediately plunged into the rough and tumble of industrial life. I was given a factory number and shown how to clock in. Hundreds of numbers in sections were printed on the periphery of a very large disk, which had a clock at its centre. A small plunger at the end of a long rotary arm had to be aligned, and then pressed into the correct numerical aperture. This was indeed clocking in. For the next two years I would punch the clock at 9 and at 6, Fridays at 5.30! The Personnel Officer told me that my annual holiday would be two weeks, lengthened to three weeks after fifteen years. A loud factory siren would signal the start and finish of a strictly one-hour lunch break. There were two official tea breaks.

The morning break happened to coincide with a popular light music programme, appropriately entitled *Music While You Work*. It was broadcast fortissimo over the factory radio. Soon I started to look forward to it. I expected it. I got used to it. There was always a slight variation in the duration of the musical content, which had to be fitted into the fixed overall length of the programme. This was done by lengthening or shortening the closing signature tune. I wrote out the signature tune, and for some weeks I listened out carefully for the very last shreds of faded sound. I pinpointed and dated the exact spot on the manuscript, until the density of my graphic cluster forced me to stop.

My office was right opposite the entrance to the canteen, and as soon as the long lunch siren started, I saw men sprint from all over the place to be the first in the queue. I soon found out that most people had their regular places.

Lunch was a culture shock, from the elevated table talk in College Hall, to the rough and ready chatter of the works canteen. After a while, I decided to take sandwiches, a thermos flask, and my violin. Soon the news spread that there was this chap who hid away during the lunch hour to play his violin. Not only did he do that every day, so the story went, but it always sounded the same. I was doing my scales.

At the end of the first week, I received my weekly wage. Electronic money transfers were a thing of the future. Hardly anyone could have afforded to wait to the end of each month, and the weekly wage was the general commercial custom. Apart from the payslip inside, the net amount was repeated on the outside. I suppose this must have speeded up the task of filling each paypacket. A man came round with a trolley and handed me my envelope. I was astonished at the lack of financial privacy, but he said he never looked at the figures.

I worked in the factory for two years and was responsible for the design and layout of the text that was added to all new publications. The engravers originated the actual pages of music. With their gravers and steel punches they cut and hammered the notation into soft pewter plates. From these they pulled single pages of high quality prints. The title pages, however, had to be separately typeset, and were then collated and printed together with the music in lithographic printing presses. It was here that I started to understand and appreciate typography.

There was of course a general house style which I inherited. The usual typeface was Monotype Bodoni, based on designs by Giambattista Bodoni around 1800. I liked it from the very beginning. It reminded me of the eighteenth century foliants which I had seen at Oxford. It is a classical typeface, timelessly aristocratic and noble, not too bold, with pronounced but delicate serifs.

The amount of text that I had to add varied considerably. Normally it would just be a single title page with the composer's name, the title of the composition, a descriptive subtitle and the firm's imprint. I drew the title pages with instructions to the typesetters concerning typeface and point size, and marked up the position of the words. First proofs came back, transformed from pencil to print, and that never lost its fascination. With symphonic works, I frequently had to provide the typesetters with an accurate list of the different instruments that were required for performance. Traditionally, this orchestration was printed on a separate page facing the music. Where music had been edited, there was sometimes an explanatory preface. I had to keep up-to-date all the advertisements that were usually printed on the back cover. Important new publications had to be added and out-of-print works, never to be reprinted, were taken out. That meant checking the stock and consulting the print history.

Jack, a kindly elderly gentleman, sat next to me in our small office. His full-time job was to record the date and the quantity of every single item that passed under the printing press rollers. With his neat small handwriting, he filled the index cards, many of which had been started decades earlier. Some titles were single items, for instance song albums or orchestral pocket scores. The number of pages to be reprinted was then a simple arithmetical task. But Military and Brass Band music, with nearly forty different instrumental parts, usually of varying length, posed a different problem of costing. The publisher's ongoing question - how much will it cost to print? - posed at regular production meetings, needed the print history of the cards which were carefully scrutinised.

The total stock was continually monitored. And for this a separate card index was kept in another department. The usual term stock room is of course humorously inappropriate. It was more like a large aircraft hangar, where thousands of carefully labelled stacks of music waited for despatch. With quiet efficiency, a certain Mrs Ryder ruled over her domain with the help of about a dozen assistants.

I remember Mrs Ryder collating the separate instrumental parts of reed and brass band. The music was sold in folders. The average length of each part was perhaps two to four pages, but there were so many of them, the flutes and piccolos, the clarinets, then all the different trumpets, horns, trombones and tubas, the percussion, the sidedrum, the bass drum!

Mrs Ryder sat at a very large electric turntable. Round the

periphery, the parts were stacked in their correct sequence. With two foot-pedals, she controlled the speed, and then she started to pick up each part as it passed in front of her and added it to the set which she was collating. After the turntable had revolved a full circle, she had completed the set which was now neatly in its separate folder.

New publications and reprints started to land on my desk. No proofreading or editorial intervention was expected. That had already been done. But perhaps something after all, had slipped through the net and could be marked up, in case of a reprint.

With metal engraving, spelling mistakes in the text of songs and operas occurred rarely because the words were carefully engraved letter by letter. No keyboard rapidity here, as the single letters were hammered into the soft pewter. There were special alphabet punches for this, and the quick selection and correct application of each letter punch was part of the engraver's skill.

Once or twice, I discovered mistakes which had the tinge of deliberate schoolboy humour. In the English version by Edward Dent of *Don Giovanni*, the engraver could not resist the temptation of changing a single letter. The Commendatore, in response to the Don's ribald laughter in the graveyard scene, is supposed to say: "Before tomorrow's dawn, your laughter's ended." How the engraver must himself have laughed as he hammered in the letter "d" instead of the "l" as he gave Don Giovanni a daughter!

Vocal scores, to help identification, have the titles of the composition engraved in small print at the bottom of each page. In William Wordsworth's *Intimations of Immortality*, a letter 't' was left out of the last word on two consecutive pages. The engraver rightly hoped that the double error would not be picked up in the proof-reading, as footnote titles are not always carefully scrutinised.

Wordsworth, the nature poet, is describing autumn melancholy that follows spring awakening. Finzi's music, set for tenor solo, mixed chorus and orchestra, has reached a passage of reflection: 'The Pansy at my feet Doth the same tale repeat: whither is fled the visionary gleam? Where is it now, the glory and the dream?' And just below this double-page spread of music are the two Immoralities.

The first performance was scheduled for the Three Choirs Festival at Gloucester Cathedral on September 5th 1950 and rehearsals were about to start, when the obviously deliberate mis-spellings were noticed by the cathedral music staff. The music was sent back. More or less overnight, about two hundred correction strips had to be stuck over the offending words. All this happened a few weeks after I started work. It was to be the first of many last-minute music production panics.

The engravers closed ranks. They could not exactly recall who had punched in the text on those pages. But I am sure they enjoyed a good collective joke.

At the factory I saw the lithographic rotary printing presses, still old-fashioned with manual machine minders, women who stood on pedestals and fed in each sheet of paper as the drums rotated.

The men making clarinets ensured that the holes which they were carving out of the instrument were in exactly the right place. They monitored their work by blowing their instrument and watching the result on an electric 'magic eye' box recorder. If the note was exactly right, the 'eye' would widen to its widest extent. No need here to listen carefully to make sure that every single note was correctly manufactured! That would in any case have been impossible in that industrial concert hall with dozens of simultaneous instrumentalists.

The noise in the brass instrument workshop, where trumpets, trombones, horns and tubas saw the light of day, was indescribable. Tubes were cut and hammered. Valves were drilled, cones were shaped on lasts. The manager told me with pride that he had a standing order of one bass tuba a week for the United States, to be shipped on the Queen Elizabeth or Queen Mary. Soldering, casting, smelting and coating were combined to meet the contradictory requirements of mass production and individual accuracy, without which the instruments would be technically unplayable.

But from the very first day, the symbolic heart of the factory became for me the engravers' workshop. About eight men sat at a long workbench, much of their work a division of labour. I was privileged to watch their ancient craft. I saw the hand presses, the flatbeds on which proofs were pulled, and the jars of specially thinned printers ink for use on Indian paper negative tissues. In the metaphorical beehive of the factory, the engravers were the queen bees, they were the linchpin on which the entire musical edifice rested. You had to have the music image to print it, you had to print it to play it, and you had to have musical instruments for performance.

That was sixty years ago, and even then, alternative methods of creating the musical image were used: cheaper, quicker but never better. It was not until computer software was perfected that the complex problems of music notation could be tackled on a computer keyboard.

CHAPTER 20

Men from Vienna

In 1952 I was promoted. I was put in charge of about two dozen freelance copyists. My production office was now situated in central London at 23 Berners Street. The locality had the allure of a musical enclave. In those days music publishers were near each other. Some have now combined, others have moved. Urban modernisation has taken its toll of eighteenth century town houses, including number 23.

It was a beautiful Georgian townhouse, and for nearly 100 years had been the premises of Rudall Carte, the flute manufacturers. Boosey & Hawkes had bought the firm at the beginning of the war. Mr. Foster, the director, filled the elegant bowed shop window with a range of instruments. Piccolos, concert flutes and bass flutes were there on display in wood, metal or silver. Gold flutes were in the safe.

I had to walk through his shop to get to my office, and we soon became friends.

Members of visiting Continental orchestras occasionally came in for last-minute adjustments to their instruments. I remember the First Flute of the Vienna Philharmonic Orchestra, asking me to act as an interpreter. He had just finished the final morning rehearsal for the evening concert. A key on his flute was insufficiently responsive. It was urgent. He had to have it. The programme included Beethoven's *Leonore Overture No. 3,* with its revelatory first flute run-up near the end. Those who knew the work listened out for it, he said. And it was difficult enough to play, even with a perfect instrument.

Hawkes & Sons had a long history of importing from France and Germany violins, violas and cellos, which were copies of seventeenth and eighteenth century Italian instruments made by famous makers. There were Hawkes Amati and Maggini violins, the Hawkes Professor violins, the Hawkes 'Tyrolese' violins. Double basses were not left out: the Hawkes Professor and then the probably more expensive Hawkes Exelsior.

On arrival at Berners Street, I soon noticed that a disproportionate number of double bass players were walking through to the workshop at the back. Mr. Branker, the manager, told me that ordinary luthiers would not touch double basses unless they were by Stradivarius or Guanerius. For them they were pieces of furniture! Over the years he sold me a quarter-size and a half-size violin. They became part of the violin-playing requirements of the extended family, one nephew, two daughters and so far one granddaughter.

Unforgettable was the moment, perhaps two years after I arrived, when the delivery man carried two beautiful giant elephant tusks straight past my office, to the repair shop at the back. Mr. Branker said they were for the bagpipes! The bags were made in Scotland, the descant recorders on which the tunes were played, and the loud drone pipes over the shoulders, were made in the instrument factory. But the pipes had to be decorated with traditional rings of ivory round the bell and shaft. They would be finished off at his workshop. They would be fitted with time-honoured skill. The instruments would then be assembled and tested.

For Mr. Branker it was a new venture. He had restored period instruments, with their baroque carved pegs and their inlaid tailpieces. This would be an industrial process applied to individual piecework. He told me that I could have the tips of the tusks. They were too small and could not be used and I said that I would like to collect enough for a chess set. I had a friend who had a lathe and could carve the thirty-two pieces. I would have to be patient, he said. It would take a while. In the event, it took much longer than he thought.

The testing of the pipes was very loud. Soon the patients in the nearby Middlesex Hospital started to complain. Could that terrible noise be stopped? Could the windows be shut?

A factory workshop with shut windows was impossible. Mr. Branker had to admit defeat and henceforth the pipes were tested in Edgware.

From the shop, I was faintly aware of flautists trying their instruments prior to purchase. I could hear Mr. Branker at the back perhaps, checking out a repair on a violin or cello. The basement was put to good use. There, a Mr. Kay ruled supreme over his small printing department. He had two offset litho presses on which very small runs of as few as fifty copies could be economically printed. It was a house dedicated to music.

Using pen and ink rather than metal engraving, my team had to produce the instrumental material for the contemporary music catalogue. I supervised the last decades of a manual process, the calligraphic copying of the two dozen or more separate orchestral parts of a symphony or an opera. The music was copied with a fine mapping pen using very opaque Indian ink and if necessary, had to be scratched out with a razor blade. Transparent sheets of music manuscript paper had staves printed on the obverse, to enable possible corrections to be made.

I particularly remember the months leading up to the premiere of Benjamin Britten's *Gloriana*, commissioned for the Queen's Coronation in June 1953. Britten was renowned for the speed at which he could compose, but eventually everything becomes urgent. I gave out the copying of the orchestral parts with the production slogan: "it's a panic", one grade more intense than: "it's a rush job". The cast and the chorus had to have their separate music much earlier than the orchestra, to study their parts. For that, separate vocal scores were being prepared. The music was transcribed, reduced so to speak, to be playable on the piano. Only then could soloists and chorus start to learn their roles and to rehearse. By the spring of 1953, Covent Garden was getting more and more anxious. Frequent telephone calls were made to the library, the department which would ultimately send over the music to the Opera House. At the height of the vocal score crisis, the library assistant rang me to say that David Webster, the General Administrator of the

Royal Opera House Covent Garden, had just phoned to say that they had to have the vocal scores at once. He also said that Madame Fifi was waiting. I laughed and then she asked, "is there really a Madame Fifi?" Poor Madame Fifi, how often has she been called upon to act out the role of a Prima Donna?

Dealing with a commercial product like music is bound to have its fair share of the bizarre and the disastrous and this was by no means the only episode.

The head office in Regent Street and my office in Berners Street were only about ten minutes walk apart. And frequently Dr Roth rang up and said, come over now. When I followed his command, on that spring day of 1956, he gave me nearly two hundred pages of very large folio sized original manuscript, which he had just received from Benjamin Britten. It was the full score of the first act of a ballet, *The Prince of the Pagodas*. The first performance had already been scheduled for the autumn, but Britten was still working on it. Dr. Roth told me to take it now, take it immediately, and organise the work. Everything else must be dropped. How ironically relevant that verb turned out to be. I took the score, which was lying on his desk as I came in. He had been looking through it. I scooped it up and thought I could save a few precious minutes and go back to my office by bus, instead of walking. It was at the end of the day, the rush hour had started, the responsibility for what I was carrying seemed to weigh me down. It was not only a metaphysical burden, but extremely heavy. Britten usually commissioned special manuscript paper on which to compose his large works. The pages had forty-eight generously spaced staves and were extra wide. They were single-sided, loose, not all held together, in sections of four, in fact a very large, heavy, floppy paper bundle.

As I stepped into the bus, it jerked forward on its onward journey, and the first few pages of the score slipped out of my gripping clutch. "There, you've got your pages" said a kindly lady as she gathered them from her lap.

In the event, Britten could not finish the composition by the agreed autumn deadline. In July, Dr. Roth called me over again. "It's all been postponed", he said, "till the end of the year" and lapsing into German, as he frequently did, he added: "jetzt stehen wir da, wie gewaschene Pudel" (now we are standing here like washed poodles). I remember the tremendous relief. No longer would I be on practically daily standby, giving out sections of the manuscript, organising a division of labour, seeing to the proof-reading and the corrections, and then the second reading to make sure that they had been done. I could after all go on my short two-week holiday. I still remember getting up with a smile and saying, "jetzt kann ich auf Urlaub fahren" (now I can go on holiday).

Operas are major production projects. I prepared the orchestral parts of Britten's *Gloriana*, the *Midsummer Night's Dream*, *Billy Budd* and other sizeable works like Prokoviev's *Fiery Angel* and Arthur Benjamin's *A Tale of Two Cities*.

There was not all that much time for the production of the vocal score and the orchestral parts of Igor Strawinsky's opera *The Rake's Progress*, the premiere of which took place in September 1951.

That was a dramatic event in its own right.

Originally, an agreement had been negotiated with La Scala, Milan, but Strawinsky changed the venue to the Fenice in Venice. He would now receive a substantial sum and conduct the first performance. Dr. Roth had to become a great diplomat, as at first La Scala insisted on their contract and wanted to take the matter further. The performance went well. Dr. Roth told me that Strawinsky had his head buried in the score as if he were seeing it for the first time. He never looked at the stage.

The Fenice organised a grand reception at the Palazzo Loredan the following day, and only then, afraid that there might be a last-minute hitch, they had stipulated that they would pay the fee. Strawinsky was led into the Great Hall of the Municipio by guards of honour and Venetian dignitaries. After speeches of praise and as he was leaving, he whispered to Dr. Roth: "Have you got the cheque?"

At about that time, Dr. Roth announced that Strawinsky was changing the spelling of his name to a central "v" rather than the Germanic "w", and this should take place in all future reprints. I was very amused when not long later, a memorandum from Dr. Roth was circulated in which we were informed that henceforth he would be known as Ernest rather than Ernst.

Songs and operas are often published with additional German or French translations, sometimes inappropriate ones. I was not at all surprised when the Hamburg Opera questioned the text in one of the audience songs in Benjamin Britten's *Let's Make An Opera*. The music sheets are given out beforehand for the audience to join in.

In one of the songs, children on stage are playing a ball game and are singing traditional words: "throw me high, throw me low, to the walls of Jericho". The German - which has now been corrected - read: "wirf mich hoch, wirf mich tief, wirf mich bis nach Tel Aviv". What must the German audience have thought about the long throw to modern Israel?

When Solti conducted about half a dozen performances of *Il Seraglio* at Covent Garden, he knew when to expect a slight audience titter, as they read the surtitles in English. The hero, Belmonte, arrives at the Barbary coast in search of his beloved Constanze, who has been abducted. Bassa Selim, the Turkish potentate, takes him on as an architect, and invites him in to his palace. As Belmonte leaves, he sings: "für Kost und Quartier dank' ich Dir", which was translated as: "for board and lodging I thank you". That sounds more like bed and breakfast at a boarding house on the seafront than a lavish residence.

During my weekly meetings with Ernst Roth to discuss production schedules, he would often talk about some of his favourite topics. "Music is neither a force for good nor evil. It is totally amoral," he would say. "Look, the Germans love Beethoven and Schubert, but it has not made them any better. They still kicked out the Jews." On another occasion he said to me: "music may be very beautiful, but that does not prove that it has a spiritual or metaphysical content. In any case, what is meant by spiritual?" His observations usually ended with a question.

He was always interested in what I had to say. Our off-duty conversations were often in German. His German was perfect, although he had not spoken it on a daily basis for more than a decade.

Dr. Roth was extraordinarily gifted as a translator, both into English and into German. Everything he did was finished in record time, for instance he translated Martinu's opera *The Marriage* from English into German in three days. He put into English, practically without hesitation, some of the most difficult German lyrics for the new edition of the Richard Strauss songs. It was during that time that he gave me the *Six Songs*, op. 68, which he was in the process of preparing. "We will both translate these six Brentano poems over the weekend, and then compare the results," he said. On Monday, he triumphantly produced his six translations. I had only managed to do the first poem by sitting up until the early hours. "That's because it's called *An die Nacht*" he said, and roared with laughter.

His sense of humour helped him to cope with the many trials and tribulations of music publishing. Proofs of title pages were sent to him after they had passed through various hands. Once, when the word fugue was spelt without the second 'u', he quipped: "in 36-point Bodoni Extra Bold Capitals, you can easily lose a letter". When the printer asked why, on the title-page of Strauss's *Four Last Songs*, 'September' was the only title "in English", while the other three were in German, he replied "September is September is September".

His Austro-Hungarian heritage was responsible for the many aphorisms with which he graced his conversation. I was wondering about my future prospects and he said that every employee had a general's baton in his knapsack. At Universal Edition in Vienna, he had started as a 'Volontär' (an apprentice with pocket-money). The owner, the famous Emil Hertzka, ruled the office with a rod of iron. Every day, all desktops had to be cleared and at irregular intervals, Hertzka went round and pulled open the drawers to make sure everything was neat and tidy, even if it was out of sight.

For a man with such a background, collective decision-making did not exist. At the height of his powers, Dr. Roth determined the salaries of his senior employees and could hire and fire people at will.

He told me on more than one occasion that the professional musician in his daily practice is engaged in a power struggle to conquer certain works. And he confessed that his ambition and his feelings of responsibility towards himself to do his very best were greatly developed by his serious piano playing early in life.

He knew that I played the violin and that I was married to a concert pianist, and always asked what I had played at various chamber music evenings. When I mentioned the *Trout Quintet*, he said, "das spielt sich von selbst" (that plays by itself). For his own *Trout Quintets* in the past, they used to have an elderly professional double bass player who was always keen to come. It wasn't just for the Schubert. That was not the only reason. He used to eat an enormous number of Ischler Krapfen, crudely translated as Viennese chocolate and almond cupcakes. Once Dr. Roth said that he would like to play Beethoven's *Spring Sonata* with me. He had kept up his practising. It went well. He was reliving his Vienna days and his Prague youth.

For our music-making, we went a floor higher to Erwin Stein's old office, which housed a good Steinway upright. Stein had retired as editor, and the instrument must have been a permanent temptation. Malcolm Williamson, the Australian composer who had recently joined the staff told me that he was playing one day when the phone rang from downstairs. It was Dr. Roth: "Since when is that Beethoven in the catalogue?" he asked, couching his reprimand in a husk of humour.

Occasionally, during stressful times, when major compositions had to be copied simultaneously at very great speed, I lightened the atmosphere during our production meetings by presenting him with relevant operatic quotations which I copied out on minute pieces of music manuscript paper.

He was amused when I gave him the opening bars of Leporello's aria from *Don Giovanni*. I deliberately left out Da Ponte's text which he knew so well: *Notte e giorno faticar, per chi nulla si gradir.* For the Boosey & Hawkes edition of the vocal score for which Ernst Roth had arranged the piano reduction, Edward Dent's English edition has an inevitable doggeral connotation: "That's the life a servant leads! Who cares when he sleeps or feeds?"

In Vienna before the war, Mozart was sung in German. How often must Ernst Roth have heard the following in the Rochlitz transation: "Keine Ruh' bei Tag und Nacht. Nichts, was mir Vergnügen macht", which could be translated as: "Ne'er a rest by day or night; All my pleasures turned to blight".

Music and humour seemed to go together. In the summer of 1950, about six months prior to the premiere of *Billy Budd* on the 1st December, Erwin Stein came to see the engravers at the factory. He was anxious that Britten's notational idioms should be strictly observed. "I don't know anything about halyards or weighing anchor, about gunnery or the mizzen" he said, and smiled at me with the conspiratorial provenance of shared Vienna.

The opera takes place on board the battleship *Indomitable*, a 74, during the Napoleonic wars. Midshipman Budd is mendaciously accused of mutiny and is hanged at the yard-arm. When Ernst Roth first heard that Britten was working on Herman Melville's story, he is reported to have said: "An opera without a single woman in the cast!" In the event, it was a great success.

Erwin Stein, like Roth, had been at Universal Edition as editor, and was closely connected to the Second Viennese School. He was one of Schoenberg's first pupils (from 1906-1910), and his assistant in the running the famous *Verein für musikalische Privataufführungen* (the Society for Private Music Performances) after the Great War. Schoenberg, Webern and especially Alban Berg, had been his friends for more than thirty years.

When I started at Boosey & Hawkes, Erwin Stein was curious to know what operas I might recently have seen. I suppose it was a mild cross-examination for my possible future help with regard to the editing and production of operatic vocal scores. We spoke mainly about *Tristan* at Covent Garden in 1949, the previous year, and I told him how wonderful it was for me to hear Kirsten Flagstad as Isolde. And that triggered off his own memories of *Tristan und Isolde* nearly fifty years earlier. He was there in June 1907, when Mahler conducted. Anna von

337

Mildenburg and Eric Schmedes sang the title roles. Alfred Roller's revolutionary production and decorative costumes, innovative stage-sets and selective lighting secured the performance a special place in theatre history.

A few months later, Mahler resigned his post as Intendant (music director) of the Vienna Opera after ten successful years. Behind the scenes there had been intrigues and scandals, casting, repertoire and funding difficulties, and in the forefront an ongoing anti-semitic section of the Press.

Erwin Stein did not forget that. In 1954 the Vienna Opera came to London for a short season at the Festival Hall, bringing *Don Giovanni* and *Figaro*. "I am not going", he said to me, "because of what they did to Mahler".

Opera is prone to mishap, and over the last eighty years I have seen quite a few. Singers have to remember not only music but also text, usually in a foreign language. The orchestra has to play the right notes at the right speed. The conductor has to synchronise the stage and the pit. Scenery can shift in full view of the audience, lighting modulates and the cast must remember their movements.

And so it was on the first night of *Figaro*. Before the curtain went up, the stage manager came out to apologise on behalf of Erich Kunz, who sang the title part. He had twisted his ankle during the rehearsal, his acting would be impaired, and he craved indulgence. The announcement was greeted with a sympathetic clap.

In the complicated plot of intrigue, Figaro has to pretend that he has fallen from a balcony and hurt his leg. "e travolto m'ho un nervo del pied" (and I twisted my foot in the fall, in Edward Dent's translation of Lorenzo da Ponte). During the two bars of orchestral Andante which follow, Kunz genuinely hobbled across the stage in a gait which ordinarily he would have acted, and there, in with Mozart's magic of music, was the sudden gasp of sympathy from the audience.

Ernst Roth regarded music as a commodity like anything else, and he told me that he would have been just as successful as a textile manufacturer.

His own greatest commercial coup occurred in January 1943. Boosey & Hawkes bought the copyright of Richard Strauss, contained in the Fürstner catalogue. It was characteristic of Dr. Roth's vision of post-war Europe. Opera would become very popular, especially Strauss, such as *Rosenkavalier*. And Dr. Roth correctly surmised that Strauss's political compromises would soon be forgotten. If he had any private misgivings about Strauss he never showed them. However, he would never go back to Vienna on principle, as he said.

By the spring of 1957, I felt ready for my big leap: I left Boosey & Hawkes to set up my own music production business.

I started to work for G. Schirmer Inc., the well established American music publisher. In the competitive world of freelance music copyists, I was given this precious opportunity by Hans Heinsheimer, the Vice President. He too had worked at Universal Edition in Vienna. As Head of the opera department there, he had supervised the publication, among many more ephemeral works, of Berg's *Wozzek* and *Lulu* (for which Stein prepared the vocal score), and Kurt Weill's *Aufstieg und Fall der Stadt Mahogonny* and *Dreigroschenoper*. Hans Heinsheimer emigrated to New York where he joined the new branch of Boosey & Hawkes, and then, after the war, left and went to G. Schirmer. In 1974 he retired as Vice President. He had devoted his energies there to many of the leading composers of his adopted country, notably Samuel Barber, Elliot Carter, Leonard Bernstein and Gian Carlo Menotti. He had the publisher's instinct to introduce some of this contemporary music to the 5,000 American High School wind bands, and asked me to engrave the parts, condensed scores and often extremely elaborate full scores of many of these arrangements.

I always felt that for those three men I was more than just another employee. Hans Heinsheimer told me that he gave me work because he too had been at Boosey & Hawkes. For Ernst Roth, I was a close friend of the Merz family. Erwin Stein seemed to regard me with avuncular kindness and occasionally shared his private thoughts.

A most poignant occasion occurred immediately after the premiere of *Gloriana*. Britten had composed the opera to commemorate the coronation of Queen Elizabeth, with a libretto that told the story of the first Queen Elizabeth and the Earl of Essex.

The gala audience was disappointed. The applause was polite and restrained. They may well have expected a triumphalist epic. Instead, the Tudor drama was laid out in a series of static tableaux. In the Third Act, Essex bursts into the Queen's bedchamber, unannounced, and sees her without her wig. I still remember the flesh-coloured skullcap perhaps deliberately meant to shock, but not appropriate in front of the young Queen on such a festive occasion. Stein was incensed when he read that Essex's agitation, which is mirrored in the very quick and difficult passage given to the trombones, reminded the critic of the noise inside a boiler factory. Stein wondered, more to himself, if the words were libellous and actionable.

I had already been forewarned of the exceptional difficulty facing the three brass players by John Arthur, the star copyist. As he handed me the copied parts, he said: "I bet you they'll muck up those bars! They are full of terrible slides and at that speed!"

He was right, there were one or two imprecisions, but they may well have been First Night nerves. At any rate, when I went a second time, they were not repeated.

Arthur was graphically very talented and a musical all-rounder. He was two or three years my senior, and had spent some of the war years in the drawing office of an armaments factory. That is where he perfected his graphic dexterity and accuracy. His real love was music, especially big bands, and he proudly told me that he played the trumpet and the oboe. After the war, he used his drawing-board experience and orchestral knowledge and became a music copyist.

He helped me considerably when I was first put in charge of the copyists at Boosey & Hawkes. Stein was worried in case the orchestral parts would be difficult to read and lacking in orientation cues to prevent players getting lost when they were not playing. Arthur told me to ignore the categoric request that cues should be inserted after no more than 20 bars rest, irrespective of the context, and explained to me the principles of preparatory warning. He usually ended his practical observations with the empirical statements: "it's all according". Yes, how right he was. Under his guidance, I learnt how best to arrange clusters of accidentals, when to use octave signs or change clefs if music otherwise spread too much above or below the stave. Increased legibility was the watchword.

I saw him at work, the way he measured out each stave, to make sure there would be no overcrowding at the end of the line, and how he used the ruler to draw the stems and leger lines. I marvelled at the curvature of his slurs, with their delicately tapered ends and the clear and even lettering of his text matter.

But I learnt more than transcription. He taught me by example. He was able to produce a large quantity of pages when it really came to it. And each time, when he finished a stave, he looked at it with satisfaction. He became my successor at Boosey & Hawkes. We remained friends. He gave me the proof-reading of new publications. I in turn provided him and other former colleagues with copying work. *Manus manum lavat,* as my father would have said.

Music publishers are proud of their merchandise, that mixture of commerce and culture. Their business is often decorated with anecdotal vignettes of composers, publishers, musicians, even premises. Doblinger, in Vienna, in their eighteenth century building, are over a warren of much older cellars, covering a wider area of the First District.

Robert, the manager of their antiquarian music, which is kept there, told me that during the Turkish siege of the city in 1683, cannonballs were stored in that subterranean labyrinth. When the firm bought the house in the 1870s, they cleaned out the basement.

"Did they find a corpse?" I asked. "No, but they found a dead dog."

Patricia and I spent many hours down two very long steep flights of stairs, searching through high stacks of waltzes, polkas, quadrilles and marches by the Johann Strauss family and other waltz kings. The beautiful nineteenth century frontispieces now decorate our house.

At Schotts in Mainz, the anecdote has to be about their most famous composer, Richard Wagner.

The city is on the river Rhine, and in the nineteenth century, there was a great deal of local marine traffic. Some time in the 1840s, the composer was crossing the river in a small boat, which was carrying a box of money for Schotts. It fell into the water. That was the first time, so the story goes, that Wagner thought of his scenario: gold and the river, *Rheingold*.

On one of my visits in the 1970s, Patricia accompanied me. We were ushered in to the elegant boardroom and were received by the director, Willy Strecker. With a courteous bow, he offered Patricia a splendid nineteenth century Biedermeier chair. After a profitable discussion about impending production schedules, it was time to say farewell. We got up and Strecker bowed. "You have sat in Wagner's chair," he said. "Where he used to sit, when he came to see us."

In the 1970s, I paid a visit to Breitkopf & Härtel in Wiesbaden, where I was asked to copy out the orchestral parts for Busoni's piano concerto. The firm had moved to West Germany from Leipzig at the end of the war.

I was excited to work for the longest established music publisher, as Bernhard Christoph Breitkopf started to publish in 1719, more than 250 years earlier. The firm gradually built up the most impressive catalogue. Their most important composer was Beethoven, for whom they produced 25 compositions between 1802 and 1812, including Symphonies numbers 5 and 6 and the Piano Concerto No. 5, the so-called Emperor. In an air raid on Leipzig in December 1943, the firm lost its entire stock of engraved printing plates. One single piece of pewter survived, and Mrs Charlotte Sievers, the owner and managing director, told me how that one page was for her emotionally so symbolic. She was, after all, related by marriage to the firm's founder. She was now a cultural custodian, principally supervising the sale of the Gesamtausgaben. The list of composers whose collective works were published is remarkable, including works by Bach, Haydn, Schubert, Schumann, Mendelssohn and Wagner.

At Schirmers, in New York, Hans Heinsheimer did not change his name like so many others. Once Hans always Hans, he said. I did not enlighten him about myself. In the 1970s, the firm celebrated its centenary. What a unique commercial achievement in the American music publishing world! To celebrate, the Board of Directors asked Hans Heinsheimer, to choose a motto to be printed as a letter-heading on the firm's notepaper. In the hard-boiled Midtown Manhattan world of music publishers, he must surely know Latin, they thought, as he was a Doctor and a European. The motto was from an Ode by Horace: Laborum dulce lenimen (the sweet solace of labour). Probably no one had ever read any Horace and the only Horace they might have heard about is from a schoolboy comic strip entitled *Tiger Tim*. The Schirmer motto was encircled by a green spreading oak tree. Oak for strength, green for growth, Hans Heinsheimer explained. I certainly did not agree with that quotation, as I sat up until the small hours, copying Leonard Bernstein's Symphonic Poem, appropriately called *The Age of Anxiety*.

Soon the firm would be sold to Macmillans, the book publishing giant on Third Avenue. Gone were the portraits of Gustav Schirmer I and Gustav Schirmer II, and gone was the beautiful samovar which stood in the place of honour in the boardroom overlooking Fifth Avenue. Nobody knew how it ever got there.

In 1956, the music world was celebrating the bicentenary of Mozart's birth. Baerenreiter, in Kassel, West Germany, was launching the publication of the Gesamtausgabe, which eventually would come out in over fifty volumes and take half a century.

When I saw the prospectus, I suggested to Karl Voetterle, the founder of the firm, that we should publish a Mozart wall calendar in English and German. There would be illustrations of Salzburg and Vienna, with Mozart connections, pictures of Mozart and his family and facsimiles of his manuscripts. The project was abandoned. But in 1973, a family contact changed all that. I paid a visit to Nessy in Kassel. After her separation from Robert in New York, she decided after the war to return to her hometown in Germany. An aunt and a publisher in Kassel gave my visits a double incentive.

Rainer Schuhmann was the production manager at Baerenreiter and for the next twenty or more years he supplied me with some of their production schedules. Mathias Pincher, Rudolf Kelterborn and Giselher Klebe were some of their prolific composers.

Rudolf Kelterborn, for instance, wrote two operas. The full score of *Der Kirschgarten* (Anton Chekhov's *The Cherry Orchard*), takes up 375 pages of large manuscript paper. For *Ein Engel kommt nach Babylon*, the score was even larger: 440 closely-written 45cm long pages!

Giselher Klebe was even more prolific. His opera *Gervaise Macquart*, based on Emil Zola's *L'Assommoir*, extends to 712 pages, a massive work, even considering his wide handwriting. Later he wrote *Die Fastnachtsbeichte,* this time 889 pages. The story is based on Carl Zuckmayer, the author of among other things *Der Hauptmann von Köpernick.* There was *Ein wahrer Held* in three acts based on Synge's *The Playboy of the Western World*, for which the 624 pages were particularly difficult. I remember taking considerably longer over the work because the full score was full of a multitude of second thoughts. After my retirement, the Bodleian Library in Oxford took my archive of 180 manuscript scores, ranging from Samuel Barber's *Toccata Festiva* to *Suite for Orchestra* by Bernd Alois Zimmermann.

Karl Voetterle started his career as a music publisher on a bicycle selling choral song sheets and ended with not only Gesamtausgabe of Mozart, but also of Berlioz and Schubert. Let him speak of how he chose the curious name of his firm. He did not want it to be named after him. Not for him Breitkopf, Schott or Schirmer. In his autobiography *Haus unterm Stern* (the House under the Star) he recalls the night he was out after a concert. He looked up at the night sky and saw the constellation of the Big Bear, Ursus Major. He thought proudly of himself riding on the animal and therefore named his firm Baerenreiter (bear-rider).

When I told my mother that I was about to visit somebody called Voetterle in Hessen, she said "Well, that was probably a Nazi". Under pressure from Berlin, Schuhmann told me that Voetterle published a songbook for SS functions. Once, when there was a big clear-out he found the booklet and its cover, he told me, was decorated with the SS runes.

How strange that after all those years I should be using my pre-war German for business. My trips across central Europe and beyond the Iron Curtain could sometimes bring the past into collision with the present. On one occasion, crossing into West Germany with my British passport full of border stamps, the German border guard, unaware that I would understand, made a sarcastic aside to his colleague that here was a much-travelled Jew. For this I obtained an official apology. I visited Poland regularly because of my work for Polish music publishers and used to visit my aunt Mizzi (Schmunz) and her daughter Evi. Travelling one day by train from Wroclaw to Hungary, I discovered once on board that I would be passing through Auschwitz railway station, the main town station that once connected to the branch line of the camp. I looked out of the carriage window at the deserted platform where Nazi camp officials used to disembark. In the distance I saw one small lone figure, a boy.

The firms which entrusted me with their manuscripts and relied on me to copy out the separate orchestral parts, often in a hurry, read like a roll-call of the world's major music publishers.

Book publishing provides text in dozens of different languages, but the language of music is global. And so it came about that a few great Continental publishers sufficed to provide the core of the classical repertoire, which they published in their editions of collected works. Bach, Beethoven, Mozart by Breitkopf und Härtel; Wagner by Schott; Verdi by Riccordi; and the general classical music catalogue by Peters Edition. In England, Boosey & Hawkes, Augeners and Novello had similarly offered a wide catalogue.

Alongside pen-and-ink copying, metal engraving was also still practised, although virtually at the end of nearly four hundred years of history. Oxford University Press wanted metal engraving for their two-volume edition of twelve hundred folk songs from the Cecil Sharp collection. Schirmers in New York asked me to engrave the vocal score of Rossini's *Italian Girl in Algiers* with a new English translation. Baerenreiter Verlag commissioned me to provide them with the music engraving for one of their volumes of their complete Schubert edition, their so-called Gesamtausgabe. The music was for piano duet, that is for one piano and two players.

With many works I remember the detailed instructions that went with the order. This was no exception. The house style for the series had to be strictly followed. There was a long list of typographical niceties. The editor was of course anxious that his input should easily be recognised and differentiated from Schubert's original manuscript. Some dynamics (p, f, mf, etc) had to be engraved upright, slightly bold, instead of in their usual italics. They were Schubert's originals. Editorial slurs and accents were in brackets and there was the additional differentiation of round and square brackets. But perhaps the most innovative feature was the fact that the music for the two players had to be engraved on the same page, one part above the other, rather than on facing pages. The page size would be like normal sheet music, rather than the special landscape format traditionally used for piano duets. This has great musical benefits, but it is more difficult to find page turnovers, always a problem of layout.

Computer software overtook my trade by the end of the century. But I left a lasting legacy: for years to come, orchestras worldwide will play from pages that I and my employees enscribed. And once in a while a musician may spot another of my legacies on the music-stand: hidden somewhere on the page, tiny enough to escape the proof-reader, dances a happy dog or rabbit.

Chapter 21

Bilingual

I can now look back on three quarters of a century living in a bilingual world. In Vienna, I had for a short time an English governess. I came to London with more than just the rudiments of the language. I had, with help, read Treasure Island, various Dr. Dolittle books and books about the Trojan war. I was old enough to have had a few years of secondary schooling and to have been introduced to the drama and poetry of Schiller and Goethe.

In 1938, when we first arrived, we spoke mainly German to each other. Then, when the war started, we naturally used English in public, although we of course continued to speak German at home. With my sister Eva, I usually spoke English. She went up to what is now called St. Annes College, Oxford University, in the autumn of 1937, six months prior to the Anschluss. In 1944, she married Kenneth Holloway, who had been at Merton College, Oxford. Although they overlapped by one year, they did not know each other as students. However, they later established that they had both attended *The Ascent of F6* by W. H. Auden and Christopher Isherwood at the Oxford Playhouse. They actually met for the first time in the personnel department of a large South Wales factory. He was the manager, about to be called up. She was directed there by the Ministry of Labour, as part of her civilian war service. After the war, they moved much nearer to London, to Hitchin in Hertfordshire, and I saw Eva more often.

With my aunt Lena, it was German at home, English in the street. With Branch (Anne Zweig) it was inevitably German.

As a boarder at Magdalen College School, in Oxford, I was immediately plunged into the assimilation machinery, the new language. It wasn't just English words that I had to speak, but also what I had to swallow. On my very first evening, I thought I was being offered black coffee, but as I raised the cup to my lips, I had a terrible shock. I asked a boy, what is this? Bovril, he said.

The assimilation was made even more effective by virtue of the fact that I had to translate my Latin and Greek prose into English via another language: the intermediate staging-post of familiar German. At school there were other refugee boys. Walter Jellinek from Vienna and the Merz brothers from Brünn kept my German alive.

Then there was my service as a Sergeant Interpreter with a Royal Air Force Disarmament Unit, taking part in the invasion of Germany. After the war, I used German on my business trips to Germany and Austria, visiting music publishers. I continued to speak German with family and friends, especially with my mother, who lived another half century.

My pre-war classical education in both Vienna and at Magdalen College School has recently been unexpectedly re-activated. In 2010, Patricia, as a mature student, achieved her Masters degree at the Open University, with a Distinction for her thesis on the Greek chorus. In an echo of my adolescence, I sometimes help Patricia with her translations for her Ancient Greek studies at the City Lit. Greek words suddenly re-surface in my memory after over seventy years.

I have lived with the duality of two languages, German and English. And I have lived with a geographical duality as well.

To return to Austria was a sudden, snap decision. It was in 1981, when I was a schoolmaster and was on the Easter holiday. Patricia and I had just started our two weeks in Cornwall. I was sitting on the cliff-tops near Lands End on my second day there. I vividly remembered the mountains around the lake of Altaussee, which I had looked at during so many pre-war summers. I wanted to see them again. So we packed our bags immediately and travelled by car over a thousand miles to the lake of my childhood. We had to stop on the way to insure our car and collect our passports. When we arrived in Altaussee, my friend from pre-war days, Hans Angerer (Hackl), was out. As he entered the house, his wife said that somebody had come, whom he had known years ago. He looked at me and said one word: "Neumann", and we embraced.

After that, I visited Altaussee regularly with my wife Patricia and sometimes with my two daughters on holidays, renewing pre-war friendships with local families in the village. Much has changed and there are of course no longer any Viennese Jewish families spending their summers there. In due course, over a dozen years, I would climb all of the surrounding mountains. In pre-war days I was not very keen to walk uphill! Patricia and I went for several years to the Salzburg Festival during the 1980s.

After some hesitation, I returned to Vienna itself. There, I was warmly received by my former school, where the staff showed a knowledge and understanding of the past and received me with great respect. I have revisited the altered places of my childhood: the Ferdinandstrasse, the Gersthoferstrasse. I have returned to the gates of the actor Thimig's house where my grandfather Wilhelm had been photographed before the war, and Patricia took a picture of me on the same spot. The houses where my parents were born have now been pulled down, as so much else in the Leopoldstadt, and redeveloped.

In 2013, the Österreichische Nationalbibliothek, Austria's national library, bought from me some of my archive of books, documents and letters. *The Neumann Collection* comprises more than 50 first editions, mostly published at Zsolnay, by authors including Franz Werfel, Oskar Jellinek, Robert Musil and Felix Salten, privately printed editions of Sigmund Freud's early letters, and signed limited editions of plays by Arthur Schnitzler, all of which would have been burned had they stayed in Austria.

At the same time, the Music Department of the Library bought twentieth century orchestral full scores by a range of European and

American composers, which I had in my possession because of my work in music publishing, including works by Stravinsky, Howard Ferguson, Martinu, Leonard Bernstein and Aaron Copland.

In March 2013, the Nationalbibliothek commemorated the 75th anniversary of the Anschluss with an exhibition of books and music written by Jewish authors and composers, some of whom were murdered in concentration camps. And now in my ninetieth year, I was invited as a guest of honour (Ehrengast) to the opening ceremony of this exhibition, entitled *Nacht Über Österreich, Der Anschluss 1938 – Flucht und Vertreibung* (Night over Austria, the Anschluss 1938 – Flight and Expulsion).

With my son Paul and daughter Helena, I attended the evening's events at the Hofburg Palace, which is home to the Library. First was a small private preview in the Library's magnificent Prunksaal, where the exhibition was displayed, followed by a concert and speeches in front of 800 invited guests in another part of the Hofburg. Director Dr. Johanna Rachinger mentioned me in her speech to the President of Austria and the guests:

…Und nun zu George Newman. Am 14. März 1938 stieg der damals 14 jährige Gymnasiast mit seiner Mutter am Wiener Westbahnhof in den Zug und floh über Zürich nach London. Sein Vater, der Rechtsanwalt Dr. Paul Neumann, blieb zurück, um seine Kanzlei aufzulösen. Er wurde eine Woche später verhaftet und war dann 3 Monate im Wiener Landesgericht inhaftiert, bevor er seiner Familie nach London folgen konnte. Paul Neumann war Gesellschafter des Zsolnay Verlages, bis 1933 einer der bedeutendsten deutschsprachigen Verlage, der den Nazis als Juden-Verlag galt und sich ab 1933 den Verhältnissen anpasste, um auf dem deutschen Markt überleben zu können.

Das Archiv des Zsolnay Verlags befindet sich heute in unserem Literaturarchiv. Die Übernahme von Büchern und Dokumenten aus der Sammlung Neumann durch die Österreichische Nationalbibliothek, ist jetzt, nach 75 Jahren, eine symbolische Rückkehr und außerdem freuen wir uns natürlich, dass George Newman leibhaftig da ist.

(…and now to George Newman. On 14th March 1938, the schoolboy, then 14 years old, boarded a train at the Vienna Westbahnhof with his mother, and escaped via Zurich to London. His father, the lawyer Dr. Paul Neumann, stayed behind in order to wind up his affairs. He was arrested a week later and was then imprisoned for three months in the Vienna Municipal Prison before he could follow his family to London. Paul Neumann was the Managing Director of Zsolnay Publishing, which until 1933 was one of the most significant German-language publishing houses, which the Nazis classified as a Jewish publisher and which from 1933 adapted itself to circumstances, in order to survive in the German market.

The archive of Zsolnay Publishing is today located in our literary archive. The transfer of books and documents from the Neumann Collection to the Austrian National Library, is now, after 75 years, a symbolic return and in addition we are of course happy that George Newman is with us today…)

These words were met with prolonged applause, before Johanna Rachinger could continue with her closing remarks.

Before the concert and speeches, there was a special reception for only a dozen or so guests in the Prunksaal, where the exhibition was on display. Here I was introduced to the President of Austria, Heinz Fischer. I had done my 'homework' in advance, because I knew that I would have the opportunity to meet him. Heinz Fischer became President in 2004 and was re-elected for a second term in 2010. On becoming president, he suspended his membership of the Social Democratic Party, as he considered the appointment to be non-partisan.

I asked him if he had read any of my uncle Julius Braunthal's books, for example *Die Geschichte der Internationale* (The History of the International). Yes, he said. "Alle drei Bände?" (all three volumes?) I asked. "Natürlich!" (of course), he replied with emphasis.

Later that evening at the concert, he came up to me where I was seated in the front row, and we spoke again and shook hands. Every seat in the hall was taken, with labelled places for VIPs at the front, except for one empty chair behind me. The Ambassador for the Federal Republic of Germany did not attend.

351

EPILOGUE

Patricia and I met at a concert at the Austrian Cultural Institute in London. The very first piece we ever played together was Bach's *B minor Violin Sonata*. I remember how she began her accompaniment before the violin entry with a contradiction of serenity, tranquillity and yet forward-looking anticipation. I was looking at her at the time. I still see her sitting there at the piano, for the very first time playing with me.

A few years ago, Patricia and I celebrated our Golden Wedding. Half a century of happiness and love were interlaced with music. I heard her Chopin *Etudes*, with which she began her musical days. And from me on the violin and then on the viola there was the more amateur response of Ševčík exercises and scales. Patricia had only just completed her studies at the Royal College of Music, where she won the Chappell Gold Medal, when she was asked to play Rachmaninov's *Second Piano Concerto* at the Festival Hall with the London Symphony Orchestra. At the opening night of the 1962 Promenade Concerts in the Albert Hall, she performed Grieg's *Piano Concerto* with the BBC Symphony Orchestra. I remember her cadenza in the first movement and the rapt silence of thousands of listeners.

She was on the keyboard Faculty of the Royal College of Music and was appointed a Fellow in 1997. Alongside her teaching, she broadcast her own special series of programmes on BBC Radio 4 and on the BBC World Service called *Piano Parlour* and *Piano Portraits*. She talked about nineteenth century piano virtuosos and played excerpts from their compositions. She researched and wrote her own script. Her style was wonderfully epigrammatic and anecdotal.

We share a love of opera, and over the past half century or so, we have attended hundreds of performances, spread out like a mantle of pleasure across England and Europe: Vienna, Venice, Milan, Pesaro, Rome, Verona, Bologna, Salzburg and further afield in New York. Like my aunt Lena, I too have kept an opera book detailing every opera with the cast list, as well as listing concerts we have attended.

Opera can be hazardous. The human voice is fallible. Will the star tenor or the prima donna sing on the night? Will a giant, seated in the row in front, obscure the view? Offstage dramas are also memorable. For the 1987 season, the Vienna Opera had just modernised the ticket office with computerised pre-booking facilities. When we picked up our tickets in the morning for the evening's performance of *Pagliacci*, starring Placido Domingo, we were told to arrive early and sit down in our seats, because the newly installed computers had failed and there had been some double-booking. As we hurried in, we saw extra gilded chairs standing ready for disappointed patrons.

For more than fifty years, Patricia and I have conversed in the wordless language of music. We played the Bach, Mozart, Beethoven and Brahms Violin and Piano Sonatas, and the beloved Schubert Sonatinas. Patricia was the star in our chamber music evenings, sitting at the keyboard for the Brahms, Dvořák and Schumann Piano Quintets and the Mozart Piano Quartets. Sometimes, a minute detail remains fixed in my memory. I remember rehearsing the third movement of Schubert's *Trout Quintet*, which has the theme of the song. As I played the upbeat to the theme, I saw that Patricia was smiling. Afterwards, I asked her why she smiled. She said, "It was so very Viennese, that lilt to your up-bow".

Two grand soirées were especially memorable: on the 29th January 1966, I gathered together an excellent group of professional musicians to join Patricia in Beethoven's early *Piano Concerto in E*ᵇ (1784). Exactly two years later, on the 29th January 1968, our chamber music included three *Brandenburg Concertos*, 3, 4 and 5, whilst our three little children were asleep upstairs. Sometimes music went on late. On the 31st December 1975, the music started at 7pm and was interrupted by supper at midnight. Thirty-nine people sat down to a New Year's Eve celebration. We played the *Brandenburg Concertos* and also Schubert's

Trout Quintet. After supper, the music continued at 1.30am with two Mozart String Quintets and finished at 3am.

Naturally with such a mother, it was to be expected that the three children Paul, Joanna and Helena would learn the piano. For Paul, his second instrument was the flute. I started Joanna and Helena on the violin, and they continued their studies with Yfrah Neaman.

Soon they joined the family music-making. On the 16th August 1975 for my mother's 86th birthday, Patricia arranged Johann Strauss's *Tales from the Vienna Woods* for piano, flute and three violins. And the children gradually brought their own friends. With two daughters able to play the chamber music repertoire, I became a viola player. The two Brahms Sextets and Schoenberg's *Verklärte Nacht* were added to our repertoire, and then the Mendelssohn Octet, scored for double string quartet. The last movement ends with a very loud section of triumphant runs, hammered out by eight players. Luckily, we have the room and live in a detached house!

Patricia taught our three children the comfort of the keyboard. She taught me how to listen and count, how to synchronise and to blend, from bold self-assurance to a transient whisper. It was a dialogue for life, with the cycle of the Mozart, Beethoven, Brahms and Bach Sonatas played again, and then again and again.